D0079265

THE CHINESE LAUNDRYMAN

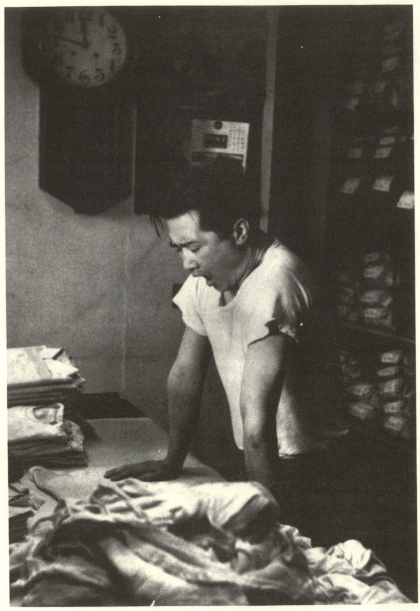

Credit: Leonard McCombe, *Life* magazine; © 1947 Time, Inc.

THE
CHINESE LAUNDRYMAN

A Study of Social Isolation

PAUL C. P. SIU

Edited by JOHN KUO WEI TCHEN

NEW YORK UNIVERSITY PRESS
New York *and* London

© 1987 by Paul C. P. Siu
Introduction and Foreword © 1987 by New York University
All rights reserved
Manufactured in the United States of America

Library of Congress Cataloging-in-Publication Data

Siu, Paul C. P. (Paul Chan Pang), 1906–1987
  The Chinese laundryman.

  Originally presented as the author's thesis (Ph.D.)—
University of Chicago, 1953.
  Includes bibliographies and index.
  1. Laundry workers—United States. 2. Chinese
Americans—Social conditions. I. Tchen, John Kuo Wei.
II. Title.
HD8039.L32U675 1987   331.6'2'51073   87–5609
ISBN 0–8147–7859–3
ISBN 0–8147–7874–7 (pbk.)

c 10 9 8 7 6 5 4 3 2
p 10 9 8 7 6 5 4 3 2

Book design by Laiying Chong.

To my teacher and friend,
Professor ERNEST W. BURGESS

PAUL C. P. SIU
Red Bank, N.J.
1986

To the memory of
HELEN HWEI LAN ONG SIU
and PAUL CHAN PANG SIU

JOHN KUO WEI TCHEN
Chinatown, New York
1987

CONTENTS

ILLUSTRATIONS

Frontispiece

MAPS

FIGURES

TABLES

FOREWORD

by DANIEL J. WALKOWITZ

The Chinese Laundryman: A Study of Social Isolation has had a long underground reputation among a select group of students of the Chinese experience in America. It has been more than thirty years since Dr. Paul C. P. Siu completed the manuscript of this book (1953) and fifteen years prior to that before he began work on it. Thus, taken all in all, this study is nearly a half-century old. More remarkable, then, is the contemporary quality of the research questions, the analysis, and the evidence. More than a decade after Siu completed his work, practitioners of what has come to be called the "new social history" began to focus on the lives of ordinary people, those whom Dostoevski called the "insulted and injured":[1] censuses, tracts, diaries, letters, and oral histories have been mined to uncover the attitudes, values, and behaviors of workingmen and women, much as Dr. Siu had done for the Chinese laundryman decades earlier. It took the scholarly community time to catch up to him.

Except for minor stylistic and typographical considerations, Dr. Siu's dissertation is published here untouched. Siu's conceptualization of the immigration experience (the "sojourner" thesis) and the range of his insights and information on the social world of Chinese laundry workers in America are remarkable. This work is itself a valuable primary document; it provides an extensive repository of letters and transcribed stories of laundrymen's lives. Historians of labor, of immigration, as well as of urban life, will no doubt benefit greatly from reading this work.

The dissertation is in fact a primary document in the sense that it reflects the strengths and weaknesses of the "Chicago School of Sociology," discussed by John Kuo Wei Tchen in the Introduction. The work, then, mirrors the generation in which it was produced, one that saw

publication of such classics of immigration history as Oscar Handlin's
The Uprooted (1951). Sympathetic to the hardships of the immigrant
experience, both Handlin and Siu emphasize what they describe as the
"social disorganization" of immigrant families uprooted from their homelands and, in the case of Chinese men, separated from their wives. Both
authors lament this "disorganization" as a threat to traditional family
roles, though Siu appreciates the cohesive role of laundry-worker kin
networks and the persistence of Chinese traditions. Historical sociology
of that era tended to overlay the notion of disorganization with the moral
baggage of the era, but for Siu the problem was exacerbated by his im-
mersion in the culture he was studying. For instance, the Chinese censured
those laundrymen who squandered money on prostitution or gambling,
jeopardizing their ability to meet their family obligations in China; Siu
finds them "maladjusted." Similarly, for Siu some women are "old maids"
(p. 251); some are "over-sexed" (p. 259)—both sexist terms that a contemporary editor would blue pencil. Such sociological jargon and sexual
stereotypes can temporarily blind the reader, but those who persist will
discover a progressive analysis and documentation that supports Siu's
main thesis. Before turning to that analysis, however, I would like to
discuss the book as a historical document, for that is rooted in Siu's
methodology and sources.

The first three chapters are fairly traditional methodological preambles
and provide a statistical background. They hardly prepare readers for the
wonders to follow. So, again, persist! What follows are among the most
interesting parts of this book—numerous long, quoted passages, anecdotes
of life among laundrymen. Some are several pages long. Siu makes use of
census materials and city directories to outline the growing decentralization of Chinese laundries in the city. However, he did the bulk of his
research as a participant observer: he lived with his kinsmen for two years
as an insider from the same cultural background, spoke the same dialect
as the laundrymen, and worked alongside them as a laundry supply agent.
In addition, Siu drew on his eight years of experience as a Boston social
worker.

Historians today would probably employ oral history in a comparable
study, taking some care to identify at least the salient characteristics of
individual testimonies. Participant observation, however, which has a long
tradition in sociological and anthropological research, generally does not
presume to record conversations word for word. Rather, such studies

reflect stories written down sometime after they were told to the inter-viewer-group member. For the most part no source is given, and we are provided only with the author's reflections on the typicality of the nar-rative. In the quality and character of his lengthy stories, however, Siu is in very distinguished company. The book shares a family resemblance to that of two other urban historical story tellers: Studs Terkel, the well-known Chicago oral historian, and Henry Mayhew, the nineteenth-cen-tury English social investigator whose articles detailing the lives of the London poor were published by the *Morning Chronicle,* a London daily. Although Siu's stories are sometimes used to make fairly limited points, they document with extraordinary detail his broader argument concerning the persistence of Old World traditions and mores among laundry work-ers. And the minimalist analysis hints at the quality of the stories as primary sources for urban immigrant culture.

One example is the story of T. M., a lonesome and "sex-hungry" laun-derer. Siu observes that, when Chinese men emigrated to America, they left their wives in China. Lonesome and alienated by a racist, hostile American culture, Chinese laundrymen like T. M. confined themselves to the isolation of their laundries and their "Chinatown." In response, Siu argues that some gambled and that, for example, some formed what he calls "bachelor marriages," and some sought out prostitutes and so on; and some resorted to both gambling and sexual "relationships." T. M. turned to what Siu called "promiscuity." He took a customer, a white woman, as a lover. After being warned by a Filipino customer (who claimed he had been the same woman's lover) that she was a married woman who "made a lot of trouble," T. M. decided to drop her. Unfor-tunately, the woman then informed him that she was pregnant with his child. Distraught, T. M. expressed traditional Chinese concerns about his reputation, anxieties produced by the fact that she had not accepted money from him and so could not be considered a prostitute:

> I was so upset after she left. I wondered if she could make any trouble. Can my name be spoiled? What I want now is not whether she can sue me, I want to get it over with so that nobody knows anything about it. She can't put the thing on me? She had been the mistress of the Filipino. What is more, she is a married woman. Now if she has a baby, how can she blame me? . . .
> The trouble was that she didn't take my money after I had relations with

her. If she had taken my money, why, then she was just a regular prostitute. . . .

I hope she will not come back again. Oh, yes, I told her I could not do
anything more with her because my wife didn't like it. She said, I might
have a wife in China, but not here. You see, she seems to know something
about our Chinese people here. (pp. 261–62).

T. M.'s solution belied the extent to which at least some Americanisms
had begun to penetrate his behavior: "From now on, 'C.O.D.' method is
the safest. Doing something like this with that girl is too troublesome"
(p. 262).

The stories often seem to run on; occasionally they take on a life and
meaning of their own. At times they resemble soap operas, at other times
these vignettes (the longer akin to short-short stories) appeal to the social
historian's instincts in that one is permitted to see into the private lives
of ordinary people. Siu and his laundry workers tell a wonderful story,
but Siu's ear for the nuances of social relations also makes the stories
significant historical records. Thus, the longest narrative (pp. 281–87),
an anecdote illustrating how intermarriage prevented a Chinese man from
returning to China—a point that could have been made with a substantially briefer excerpt—also reveals much about kin and clan relations, the
centrality of Chinatown in the launderer's social experience, gambling,
Sunday Schools, work alternatives for the Chinese male, and the family
economy of the Chinese in America.

The many anecdotes, documents, letters, interviews, and stories that
appear in this work not only make it an important source for the study
of Chinese laundrymen in America but also for gaining insight into family
economy, work, the immigrant experience, and the problem of the cultural
exchange between Old World and New World cultures. The manuscript
is eminently worthy of publication for these qualities alone. But, in fact,
the book has become a classic in the emerging field of Asian American
history for its analytic insights, too. In this regard, it makes a significant
contribution to labor and ethnic history as well.

Dr. Siu focuses on one city, one industry, and one ethnic group—
Chinese laundrymen in Chicago, a group about which we know very little.
The industry was a natural choice: according to the 1920 U.S. census, 30
percent of the Chinese employed in the country worked in laundries.[2] And
the pattern persisted in Chicago as late as 1950, when 430 of the 669
businesses operated by the Chinese there were found to be laundries.[3]

Indeed, the experience of the city per se looms large in this manuscript. But the focus on Chicago itself is the least important ingredient in Siu's story. For Siu, the laundrymen live in isolation inside their laundries, leaving only to visit Chinatown; they live and work only for return trips to China. Yet the city of Chicago does have a distinct importance: among American cities it remains a city with one of the longest histories of class and racial violence and urban machine politics in the nation—a history made famous by events like the 1886 Haymarket massacre, the 1919 race riot, and the emergence of the Daley machine. Siu mentions Chicago residential segregation, notes the launderer's employment of black women, and traces the dispersion of laundries throughout Chicago neighborhoods. But the larger social context of Chinese lives in Chicago remains unexamined. We learn nothing, for instance, of Chicago politics, its labor movement, or the city's racial policies between the two world wars.

In contrast, this work is particularly informative concerning the history of laundries and the Chinese in America. Neither is a field about which much is known, and in both regards Siu fills important gaps. Siu's work prefigures much of the best work in the "new labor history." He begins to answer recent calls for a history of social relations in America that is broad enough to include that of shopkeepers working and living at the interstices between the working class and entrepreneurship.

At the time Siu wrote, labor history focused almost exclusively on the trade-union movement. Labor historians writing since the mid-1960s have made the culture of the workplace, the labor process, and the life of the working-class family central to their story. But only recently have feminist labor historians turned their attention to those who fall between being petty producers and artisan-shopkeepers.[4] Not surprisingly, perhaps, most of this work has been concerned with the early stages of industrialization. Siu, however, describes an ethnic occupational group that continues to play an integral part in the modern urban economy, and for which we have no history. Comparable ethnic occupational concentrations in later periods of industrialization—groups such as Jewish tailors, Italian shoemakers, Irish saloonkeepers—variously make up little understood parts of ethnic communities. And for the Asian or Orthodox Jewish communities today in New York, histories of the Korean greengrocers or of jewelry-electronic retail stores would undoubtedly resonate with Siu's presentation of Chinese laundrymen communities in ways that we do not yet have much knowledge of.

There has been no comprehensive study of laundry workers as a whole. Female laundry workers have received some attention, primarily when they entered the factory system with the rise of the power laundries at the turn of the century.[5] The Chinese laundryman does not exist in this literature, and the family and hand laundries they operated, that as late as 1939 accounted for 39 percent of laundry work,[6] recede behind the history of the power laundry.

Again, Siu fills the gap. Separate chapters describe the Chinese laundry-work process, the workplace, employment patterns, the tradition of cousin partnerships, the division of profits, collective lending institutions (the *woi*), weekly labor routines, leisure activities, and not least, the values and attitudes that inform the laundryman's "purpose of life in America, namely, the support of the Chinese family and the accumulation of money for a return trip to China" (p. 27).

Excerpts from two interviews demonstrate Siu's ability to document the tensions inherent in doing laundry work and the contradictory responses it elicited from laundrymen who were always looking back to China.

> I don't know how to iron well enough yet. I am not allowed to iron shirts, as Shu-lung is afraid that I will spoil the shirt. If a shirt is spoiled, he has to pay for it. I can help to iron rough things such as underwear, towels, and shorts. Some people can iron eighteen shirts in an hour, but I don't think I can do even four. The iron is too hot. You might burn the shirt, if you don't know how to handle it. If it is too cold, well, of course, the shirt would not be burned, but you can't do a good job with a cold iron. You must have it just right and do it quick. Ironing is by no means an easy thing.
>
> One thing is good in this country, so long as you are willing to work hard, you don't have to worry about eating and clothing. But in China, you have nothing to do. (pp. 116–17)
>
> People think I am a happy person. I am not. I worry very much. First, I don't like this kind of life; it is not a human life. To be a laundryman is to be just a slave. I work because I have to. If I ever stop working, those at home stop eating.
>
> But I get used to it. After you are on it so many years, you have no more feeling but stay on with it. After all, you can't get rich but you don't have to worry about money as long as you can work. If my father had let me stay in school, I could have graduated from middle school; then I might

not have come. I could find something to do in China. It is better to be a
poor teacher in China. You could have been happier. (p. 130)

Although labor historians have largely ignored the history of Chinese
laundrymen, the Chinese in America generally are only somewhat better
served by their historians, though this broader area of study has at least
begun to receive serious scholarly attention. Again, however, the history
of the Chinese in America remains in its infancy and, at its best, draws
heavily upon Paul Siu's work and ideas.[7] Siu's treatment of the Chinese
immigrant, though, offers a model that can enrich more than the history
of the Chinese in America; it promises to enrich American ethnic and
immigrant history generally as well.

The currents sweeping through social history in the 1960s and 1970s
have revitalized the history of labor, the city, and the family, as well as
of blacks, women, and Native Americans. With some important exceptions—the work of John Bodnar being the foremost[8]—immigration history has been relatively underdeveloped. As Tchen notes, Siu's
"sojourner" thesis offers an alternative to the unilinear assimilationist
arguments that have dominated immigration historiography. As important, Siu succeeds in tracing the relationship between the Old World and
the New in ways that other historians have been pleading for. For example,
much is now known about the Irish, English, and Germans in America,
but precious little is known about the meaning and impact of their cultures
of origin. Siu suggests that the Chinese remained particularly attached to
their native villages, a conclusion that seems warranted by the evidence,
though comparable studies of other groups need to be done. What Siu
has richly documented, however, is how thoroughly and fundamentally
Chinese life continued to structure the concerns and social relations of
the Chinese launderer in America. In his words, "The Chinese became
laundrymen at first to escape labor agitation against them; the technique
[the job choice] is American, but the structure [the way they let their lives]
is Chinese" (p. 296). The distinction is crucial for Siu, and its elaboration
makes this book important, not merely for our understanding of the history of laundry work or the Chinese in America, but as a model for the
study and understanding of the American immigrant experience.

Daniel J. Walkowitz
New York City

NOTES

1. This Dostoevski reference is from Alfred Kazin, Memorial for Herbert G. Gutman, New School for Social Research, October 1985.

2. Betty Lee Sung, *Mountain of Gold: The Story of the Chinese in America* (New York, 1967), p. 188.

3. Rose Hum Lee, *The Chinese in the United States of America* (Hong Kong, 1960), p. 266.

4. See, for example, Christine Stansell, "The Origins of the Sweatshop: Women and Early Industrialization in New York City," in *Working-Class America: Essays on Labor, Community, and American Society,* ed. Michael H. Frisch and Daniel J. Walkowitz (Urbana, Ill., 1983): 78–103; Sean Wilentz, *Chants Democratic: New York City and the Rise of the American Working Class, 1790–1865* (New York, 1984); Paul Johnson, *A Shopkeepers' Millennium: Rochester, New York, 1820–1850* (New York, 1978).

5. See Sylvia Weissbrodt, *Women Workers in Power Laundries* (Washington, D.C., 1947); Lydia Ray Balderston, *Laundering Home—Institution* (Philadelphia, 1923); Agnes Jackman and B. Rodgers, *The Principles of Domestic and Institutional Laundrywork* (London, 1934); Ethel Best and Ethel Erickson, *A Survey of Laundries and Their Women Workers in 23 Cities* (U.S. Department of Labor, 1930); Fred DeArmond, *The Laundry Industry* (New York, 1950); and Rachel Bernstein, "Working Women in 19th Century America: A Case Study of Laundry Workers" (unpublished paper, Rutgers University, 1979).

6. DeArmond, *The Laundry Industry,* p. 17.

7. For example, see Sung, *Mountain of Gold* and Lee, *The Chinese in the United States of America.* The most sophisticated historical volume, Alexander P. Saxton's *The Indispensable Enemy: Labor and the Anti-Chinese Movement in California* (Berkeley, 1971), deals with the treatment of the Chinese in California at the end of the nineteenth century, not particularly with the Chinese experience.

8. John Bodnar, *Immigration and Industrialization: Ethnicity in an American Mill Town, 1870–1940* (Pittsburgh, 1977), and Bodnar, et al., *Lives of Their Own: Blacks, Italians, and Poles in Pittsburgh, 1900–1960* (Urbana, Ill., 1982).

EDITOR'S INTRODUCTION

by JOHN KUO WEI TCHEN

The immense importance of *The Chinese Laundryman: A Study of Social Isolation* is not evident at first glance. The title and its 1987 publication obscure as much as they reveal.

Dr. Siu's dissertation is the *only* investigation of what has been the major occupation of Chinese in the United States. I still find this fact amazing. After all, the Chinese laundry has been a seemingly ever present fixture of the urban streetscape. This everyday familiarity has been heightened by the pseudo-familiarity generated by Chinese "laundryman" caricatures in American mass culture.[1] The image of a pigtailed, "no tickee, no shirtee" "Charlie" jabbering away in nonsensical monosyllables was long set in the public's mind by melodramas, songs, pulp paperbacks, cartoons, and films. With the post-1960s decline of hand laundries, the portrayals have been less frequent. Now the occasional laundry worker is shown as a comical character revealing his "ancient Chinese secret" in cleaning clothes—a new, sudsier detergent.[2]

As with all racial and ethnic stereotypes, the cultural image brushes against the actual historical experience just enough to blur reality with fiction. This book begins to sort out this confusion. Indeed, once we as readers get past the laundry sign hanging from the storefront and enter the private world of work, rest, and desires, we discover a universe rich in human meaning and significance. In 1882, four years before the Statue of Liberty was inaugurated, the Chinese Exclusion Laws were enacted. The prohibition of immigration of all those of the laboring classes meant that those workers who were already in the United States—virtually all men—could not bring their wives and families to join them. Nor could any Chinese become a naturalized United States citizen. The imposed "social isolation" of that lone male world of the "Chinese laundryman" on Main Street was made a bit more bearable by the countercreation of sustaining relationships of "cousins" and community within Chinatown.

If the title lends itself to cultural misreading, the publication date is totally confusing. This volume marks the first publication of a 1953 doctoral dissertation written for the University of Chicago's Department of Sociology. The original field research for the dissertation was conducted in the late 1930s. But, most important, the memories captured herein stretch back to the 1850s—to the very beginnings of Chinese entrance into washing and ironing in America. Thus, Dr. Siu's dissertation bears witness to a collective memory dating back over 130 years. This work should have been published long ago. The reason it wasn't? The consequence of a subtle cultural discrimination process—but more on that later.

If the title and publication date reflect the ambiguities of Chinese image and experience in the United States, the jacket illustration, originally the frontispiece of the dissertation, is clear and explicit. Taken by Leonard McCombe for a 1947 issue of *Life* magazine, the yawning man is standing where he has spent years of his life. He is in front of the ironing bed shortly before midnight. Much laundry has been finished and are in neatly wrapped bundles on the shelves behind, yet piles of shirts still need to be done. A Chinese calendar marks the days, years, and decades from the nostalgic background image of a prosaic rural scene representing home. The intimacy of this moment is but a tantalizing prelude. Much more is to come.[3]

I first came upon Paul C. P. Siu's dissertation in 1980 while I was doing research for the New York Chinatown History Project's series of productions on Chinese laundry workers.[4] Like weary gold prospectors, we spent months digging through mounds of archival materials, getting nowhere fast. We found a gold fleck here, a photograph there, a quote somewhere else, but our gleanings were paltry indeed. I finally followed up a footnote citation of Siu's dissertation. Many other such leads had proved disappointing, so I was skeptical. The dissertation was on microfilm and terribly difficult to read, but as I spun through the reel I realized that this was a dazzling piece of work. During a time when I felt emerging Chinese/Asian American scholars were just inventing the wheel, this dissertation was a finely crafted watch. It surpassed the sophistication of most contemporary research in the field. Who was Paul C. P. Siu? Where had he been? Was he still alive? Why hadn't we known about him?

An anxious call to the American Sociological Association certified that he was active and in Michigan. The next call proved that he was real, healthy, and willing to advise us in doing our work. For the next several years we were in and out of touch but never able to meet. Finally a note from Dr. Siu arrived. He had moved to a nearby town in New Jersey.

During the past two years we have visited Paul and his wife, Hwei Lan, a number of times. I found Dr. Siu, a retired professor of sociology since 1972, a modest, soft-spoken man whose personal life paralleled much of what his dissertation described.[5]

Siu as Student

In 1906, Siu Chan Pang (Xiao Chenpeng) was born the oldest son in a village with 300 families of the Siu clan located in Taishan District by the coast of the South China Sea, southwest of Guangzhou (Canton). The area was a poor farming district with sandy soil and salty water. Nevertheless, his ancestors were "affluent farmers." His grandfather was a village scholar who wrote that the family "did not lift a plow for three generations." The family leased their land to local farmers. His father was the first in the village to defiantly cut off his queue (the braided pigtails imposed upon Han Chinese by Manchus) in 1911 when the Qing Dynasty was overthrown. But during his father's time the family wealth declined, as did China's. Following the footsteps of many Taishanese, his father journeyed to the "Golden Mountain," the common name for the United States, to find a means to support the family. Owing to a chain migration of related villagers, the majority of early Chinese in the United States hailed from this district smaller than the size of Rhode Island.[6] His father left when Chan Pang was a teenager, and since he wanted Chan Pang to have a better education, he sent his son to a Guangzhou missionary school. Here Siu Chan Pang attended the American-run Piu Ying School (middle school) and was given the Christian name Paul. He graduated and taught for a year.

Chan Pang's father may never have lifted a plow, but in America he washed people's dirty, smelly clothes. His modest St. Paul, Minnesota, hand laundry supported a family of eight back home. In 1927 he brought

Chan Pang, the eldest son, to the United States to further his studies.[7] He was admitted to Macalester College in St. Paul. The first night of sleeping in the laundry was a shock. The living and working conditions were austere at best. In the chill of the Minneapolis fall, there was no indoor heat. The only advancement a laundry could offer was to eventually own one's laundry shop or, possibly, run a restaurant. Unlike most Chinese immigrants, Chan Pang had a chance to study, but that was not without its own difficulties.

After a year in Minnesota, Chan Pang, now called Paul by non-Chinese, left for a bigger city with more opportunities. Chicago was bustling, growing—full of immigrants, diversity, promise, and problems. Like many other "self-financed" Chinese foreign students, he had no choice but to work during the day at "chop suey" houses and attend night school. Here he found many fellow Siu family clansmen including an uncle, a Peking University graduate turned "chop suey" house waiter. A few years later his father came to Chicago and established another laundry. Every Sunday they gathered socially in the Siu family clan association in Chicago's modest Chinatown.

Chan Pang's night-school studies were going slowly and badly. His interest waned. He was on the verge of quitting school. But, in the summer of 1932, an old Piu Ying classmate introduced him to Ernest Burgess, professor of sociology at the University of Chicago. Impressed by Siu's intelligence and looking for a Chinese student who could help extend his studies on families into the Chinatown community, Burgess offered him a scholarship.

With revived hopes, Siu entered the most prestigious school of sociology in the United States. Shaped by the vision of Robert Park, the sociology department sought to treat the city as a human laboratory. He, along with Ernest Burgess and others, inspired a generation of able students to investigate and explain life in Chicago. These faculty and students dominated this emerging social science through the 1930s. Chicago sociology came to define the very terms of modern sociology.

The emergence of this brilliant school was not due to the power of Park's charisma alone. The laboratory these sociologists chose to study was Chicago, and Chicago was in the midst of tremendous industrial transformation and social dislocation. Massive eastern and southern European immigration packed and then continuously burst the city's limits, forming new neighborhoods and filling newly expanding heavy industries.

As nativist, anti-immigrant feelings swelled, the federal government enacted the highly restrictive Immigration Act of 1924. The emerging industrial metropolis was outstripping its genteel WASP Victorianism. The
mansions of "robber barons" were being surrounded by poverty. This was
the Chicago of Jane Addams's pioneering settlement work at Hull House
and Upton Sinclair's exposé of the dehumanized working conditions of
the Chicago stockyards captured in *The Jungle* (1906). In 1919 a horrific
antiblack race riot, lasting nearly a week, tore Chicago apart. Thirty-eight
people died; 537 others were injured; and 1,000 lost their homes to fire.
Aggravating such volatile racial relations was the migration of many poor,
rural southern blacks to Chicago. They were actively recruited to fill the
unskilled factory jobs formerly offered to newly arriving European immigrants. The 1924 Immigration Act had halted that exploitable labor
reserve.

From the vantage point of nineteenth-century, upper-crust Victorian
WASPs, these dramatic changes were most visible in the city's streets.
Migration coincided with the unparalleled escalation of crime, drunken-
ness, idleness, prostitution, and other antisocial kinds of behavior. Could
these newcomers be assimilated into genteel culture? Many thought not.
Eugenics, advocating a predetermined hierarchy of human races, was their
faith. What could be done? *The Birth of a Nation* (1915), D. W. Griffith's
immensely popular glorification of the Ku Klux Klan, and "progressive"
President Woodrow Wilson's segregation of the federal bureaucracy were
emblematic of acceptable social solutions.[8]

Robert Park's urban research orientation pushed faculty and students
to step out of ivory tower Hyde Park and make sense of the apparently
chaotic city around them. Park's 1916 seminal essay, "The City: Sugges-
tions for the Investigation of Human Behavior in the Urban Environment,"
was both a paradigm for his student's work and an outline exhorting the
faith of social scientific analysis.[9] Not only would they study the city and
begin to comprehend it as a whole; they would also influence public
perception of Chicago and its problems. It was believed that their "objective" studies would reveal that urban poverty, disease, and behavior
troubles were the consequence of "social disorganization" rather than of
such immutable factors as the innate racial inferiority popularly ascribed
to impoverished ethnic and racial groups. According to Burgess, "The
social scientists at the University of Chicago did not share, for the most
part, the prejudices against these people that were commonly expressed.

Quite often they defended the foreign groups publicly and spoke out for tolerance, sympathy, and understanding."[10] Here Siu found some openness to the complexities of being a Chinese student in America.

Beginning with the Japanese invasion of the Chinese province of Manchuria in 1931, many Chinese students engaged in patriotic activities to aid in national resistance. In 1936–1937 as an activist of the Chinese Student Association of North America, Siu traveled to Boston, New York, and other cities throughout the East. Through the association's activities and magazine, students worked to alert the American public about Japanese imperialism. Perhaps more important were their efforts to unite overseas Chinese in pushing Generalissimo Chiang Kai-shek to fight the Japanese and not Chinese Communists. Siu's travels had an important side benefit. They provided him with an opportunity to visit and learn about Chinese communities in other parts of the United States.

Dissertation Context

By the time Siu arrived at the University of Chicago in 1932, the sociology department had developed beyond what Burgess later termed a "social work" orientation toward a more scholarly understanding of "the social and economic forces at work in the slums and their effect in influencing the social and personal organization of those who lived there."[11] The operative key words were "objective," "scientific," and "detached." Robert Park scolded students who expressed what he considered a sentimental, humanitarian attitude to those being studied. So deep was his faith that he was known to scream in class, driving some to anger or tears, "You're another one of those damn do-gooders."[12] Nevertheless, Burgess has since emphasized that "although the objective was 'scientific,' behind it lay a conviction that this analysis would help dispel prejudice and injustice and ultimately would lead to an improvement in the lot of slum dwellers."[13] This driving objectivity, defined as the denial of subjectivity, created different tendencies in the department.

Professors and students became actively engaged in studies with settlement houses and other social services. And when the federally sponsored Works Progress Administration (WPA) was instituted in 1935, many joint WPA–Department of Sociology projects were undertaken. Census-based spatial maps (such as those in Chapter 3 of Dr. Siu's study) were first

developed. Then a more qualitative approach emerged in what was re-
ferred to as seeking out the "personal document." This approach became
seen as a means of understanding social psychology. Borrowing from the
anthropologists' method of participant observation, sociologists placed
themselves throughout Chicago's poor neighborhoods.[14] Nels Anderson
arrived as a student at the department in 1921. He had lived as a hobo
for part of his life, and Burgess encouraged Anderson to write about the
experience. In 1923 *The Hobo* was published as Volume 1 of the University of Chicago Press Sociological Series. This work was soon joined by
other locally focused studies: Louis Wirth's study of Jews, *The Ghetto*
(1923); Clifford Shaw's case study of a young delinquent, *The Jack-Roller*
(1930); Pauline V. Young's empathetic *Pilgrims of Russian Town* (1932);
William F. Whyte's study of an Italian male adolescent gang life, *Street
Corner Society* (1944); and other sociological monographs. Their focus
was not simply descriptive; it was also analytical, focusing on the "behavior patterns and processes of adjustment and change as the immigrant
adapted to the new economic environment, and prospered."[15] The opti-
mistic ideal was to "scientifically" facilitate the adjustment and assimilation of immigrants in American society.

Given this sociological mission, the Chinese population in Chicago fascinated and puzzled the professors. In a retrospective comment, Burgess
wrote that Chinese were "one of the cultural groups most deviant from
the typical native American culture; [they] provided sharp contrasts which
clarified theoretical issues that otherwise might be vague." The Chinese
American experience was deemed "deviant." "Also," Burgess continued,
"the attendance of Chinese graduate students provided an opportunity
for insightful research that otherwise could not be done."[16] Here entered
Ching-Chao Wu, Rose Hum Lee, Paul C. P. Siu, and others.[17]

Besides promoting rigorous, systematic, "scientific" inquiry into any
group studied, the department did have a commitment to social justice—
viewed, however, in narrow terms. It was in the context of adjustment,
assimilation, and accommodation to the prevailing society. Even racial
groups were pushed through this theoretical sieve. Blacks who migrated
from southern plantations to northern cities were considered comparable
to European peasant immigrants.[18] Given pervasive violence against non-
whites and de jure segregation, this limited perspective made it especially
difficult for black, Asian, and other nonwhite scholars to embrace this
paradigm. Chinese laborers, as mentioned earlier, were excluded from

immigration and could not become naturalized citizens. Their sociological construct a priori defined Chinese in America as "deviant" from the American "norm," which was determined by the primarily white, Anglo-Saxon, Protestant, male experience. Indeed, all nonwhite groups proved "deviant" in this framework. Scientific inquiry was thwarted by racially claustrophobic categories.

When it came time to select a dissertation topic, Louis Wirth first encouraged Siu to explore why "modern" science did not develop in China. Wirth's suggestion reflected some of the school's Eurocentrism. British historian Joseph Needham has since abundantly illustrated that science flourished in China, but not along Western lines.[19] Siu worked on the subject for a year, writing a special study for Wirth. But no funds could be found to support this project. Wirth then suggested that Siu examine what he knew best. In the participant-observation tradition, he could explore some topic related to Chinatown. That meant either the "chop suey" houses, where Siu waited tables, or the Chinese laundries of his "cousins." He picked the latter. Wirth's own book, *The Ghetto,* a study of the Jewish ghetto and social isolation, provided a key comparative reference point.[20]

In 1941 Siu married a fellow student, Hwei Lan Ong. She was a Dutch Chinese born in Indonesia but raised in Shanghai who was completing a master's degree in social work. Two years later they had a daughter, Joanne. Suddenly Siu had a family and had to make a more substantial living than that of a scholarship student. By 1945 Siu had completed seventeen of his eighteen dissertation chapters. However, a job opened at the International Institute in Boston, a social service agency that specialized in immigration and naturalization problems with a special emphasis on the city's Chinatown. Professor Burgess encouraged Siu to take the job as a strategic means of learning more about the situation of Chinese immigrants.

The Siu family built a happy life in Boston amid the many Chinese intellectuals and community they helped and befriended. But, after eight years of community work, Siu decided to return to his dissertation before the university's completion deadline expired. Professor Burgess had already retired, and other faculty had moved elsewhere. Nevertheless, he finished it in 1953. The study embodied some twenty-five years of field-work and community engagement.

Special Insights

Before Paul Siu began to write "The Chinese Laundryman" he lived for a couple of years in a clansman's Evanston house. Nearby was a Moy's laundry, a Siu's laundry, and others. He visited them regularly, helped out by writing letters home, learned what they joked about, and observed how they interrelated as "cousins." Siu spoke the same dialect and was himself a "cousin" to them. Indeed, besides having a laundry-worker father, he had worked as a laundry supplier before starting his fieldwork investigation. His unique vantage point distinguished him as an "insider" in an era when most participant observation was done by "outsiders." As such, he was a part of the personal lives of laundry workers.

Siu has written an intimate "thick description" of the laundry experience.[21] His allegiance to Chinese laundry workers was clear and unambiguous. This close identification separated him from the assimilationist strain at the department. Indeed, Siu's role in explicating the laundry worker experience is closer to what black anthropologist John L. Gwaltney has defined as a "native anthropology." Writing in 1980, Gwaltney argued for an anti-Eurocentric, anticolonial fieldwork methodology that respects "perspectives, philosophies and systems of logic generated by populations which are usually expected to produce only unrefined data for the omniscient, powerful stranger to interpret."[22]

By carefully learning about the actual experiences of the laundry workers, Siu made two major theoretical breakthroughs. He developed the concepts of the "immigrant economy" and the "sojourner." Early on Siu had consulted with Professor Everett Hughes, who noted the "peculiar" pattern of immigrant groups clustering around specific occupations, like the Greek ice-cream parlor, the Italian vegetable stand, the Jewish clothing store, and the Chinese laundry. Siu coined the term "immigrant economy" to describe the means that immigrants developed to subsist in the highly competitive urban economy.[23] This concept insisted that academics recognize immigrants as having positive and separate identities from those "normative" mainstream occupational roles of American society. It discerned a certain fortitude and creativity within the immigrant's daily activity. Siu took immigrant urban phenomena seriously and analyzed them on their own terms.[24]

The term "sojourner" came from fellow student Clarence Glick, who used the term casually in referring to the Chinese migrants to Hawaii intent on making money and returning to China.[25] Siu gave the term a sociological dimension and weight. In an important essay, "The Sojourner," published in the *American Journal of Sociology* in 1952, Siu defined the sojourner as one who "clings to the culture of his own ethnic group as in contrast to the bicultural marginal man. Psychologically he is unwilling to organize himself as a permanent resident in the country of his sojourn. When he does, he becomes a marginal man." Here Siu broke with Robert Park's definition of the immigrant as a helpless marginal man—one who is caught between "two worlds in both of which he is more or less a stranger."[26] Park's concept assumed an inevitable pattern toward assimilation and an a priori desire of the immigrant to assimilate. The Chinese laundry worker simply did not fit this mode. Instead, Siu drew directly on German sociologist's Georg Simmel's seminal idea of the "stranger" on which Park had originally based his theory.[27]

This conceptual breakthrough acknowledged the variant experience of the nonassimilation of any given migrant group. Italians and Greeks, for example, had regularly been described as "birds of passage." During certain years, greater numbers of eastern and southern Europeans returned to their homelands than immigrated to the United States.[28] Given Siu's framework, there could be a variety of other sojourner types besides the Chinese laundry worker, who had considerably fewer options. In other terms, the WASP, Eurocentric immigration model of Professor Park and the Department of Sociology was placed in its proper context. The older European immigrant pattern, if indeed there was one, was just one version of Simmel's stranger—Park's marginal man. The Chinese laundry worker-sojourner was another. In this fundamental sense, Chinese were no longer a "deviant" type but simply a different type.[29] Chinese sojourners could also choose to become settlers. But they were sojourners first and foremost because of a complex racially exclusionary interactional process.

Siu wrote: "Under the [restrictive] race and ethnic situation [of the United States], the Chinese immigrants were driven to make a choice, and they founded the laundry as a form of accommodation to the situation. But, since its establishment [in the 1850s] the laundry has served to isolate the laundryman and, therefore, has created a type of personality which is directly contrary to the expectation of assimilation." In essence, "the Chinese laundry is an immigrant economy and the laundryman a sojourner."[30] The Chinese, restricted from free immigration, gaining citizenship,

and having families, created hand laundries. In turn, this institution protected—but also isolated—Chinese. The specific immigrant institution
and the particular sojourner attitude shaped and determined each other.
Like yin and yang, they were components of a dialectical historical process. Those Chinese workers who chose to stay resisted anti-Chinese rac-
ism by clawing out some turf for hand laundries, and this dynamic created
the socially isolated sojourner attitude. During a period of such racial
hostility, assimilation was virtually impossible, so most launderers simply
withdrew hopes for assimilation in American society. It did not matter
whether they intended to stay or not when they first arrived—they were
certainly not welcomed to settle in the United States. Home could not be
found in the "Golden Mountain." Perhaps more than ever, it was with
their families back in China. But that village home was one that many
never had the chance to return.[31]

Siu's dialectic anticipated the "interactional framework" proposed in
one of the cutting-edge studies of contemporary "new social history."
Bodnar, Simon, and Weber's 1982 book, *Lives of Their Own*, compares
black, Italian, and Polish workers in twentieth-century Pittsburgh. In many
key respects, Siu's work is comparable to their excellent and important
study, though his work preceded theirs by thirty years.[32]

Perhaps these significant contributions are not so surprising. Paul Siu,
the laundry man's son who became a scholar, was personally close to,
and deeply empathized with, those he studied. He did not use them as
"objects" for detached academic scrutiny. These values have made his
interpretation resonant and seminal. Indeed, it has been the very subjectivity that Park so harshly criticized his students for that informed Siu's
study with a deeper, more penetrating objectivity. "Only those with an
interest can be disinterested."[33] In this sense, Siu's ability to probe and
articulate the consciousness of Chinese laundry workers made him an
"organic" intellectual in the manner Antonio Gramsci defined it.[34] He
spoke for the class of Chinese laundry workers. But who was to listen?

Siu as Sojourner

After Siu's dissertation was finally approved, he and his wife hoped to
return to China with their daughter and apply their skills to help build a
new nation. But, with the outbreak of the Korean War, he found that

route blocked. He originally intended to study for seven years and then return to China. However, those seven years stretched out to seven times that. (He did not have a chance to visit China until 1976.) Suddenly he found himself a Ph.D. without work. Dr. Siu and his wife returned to the Midwest, and he eventually found a teaching position at a small college in Kansas. They moved from one small college to another. He rose up the ranks to a full professor by the end of the decade. As was the experience of many Chinese American professionals during this time, however, each step of the way he encountered much subtle and not-so-subtle discrimination.

In Chicago, Boston, and throughout the Midwest the Sius experienced racial intolerance. First they had problems with housing. A telephone inquiry would assure them that an apartment or house was available, but a face-to-face visit would tell them it had just been rented. Dr. Siu was considered exotic and inscrutable. Students complained that his English was too hard to understand. One student was amazed to see a wall full of English-language books in his office. After all, how could an "Oriental" absorb and teach whites about Western civilization?

By 1959 the Sius found a permanent academic base in the Detroit Institute of Technology. Here he found a more tolerant attitude. As a full professor, and later as chairman of the department, he worked with a mix of Canadian, black, white, and foreign students. "No one complained about my English in Detroit!"[35] Dr. Siu retired in 1972.

Working as an academic, Siu separated from the laundry workers he knew so well. He rose through the ranks but was neither able to have his dissertation published nor gain the recognition his scholarly contributions so richly deserved. The University of Chicago Press felt that his dissertation was not sufficiently "marketable" for publication.[36] As a Chinese professional in America, his career strongly suggests that he received less recognition for his talents than comparably educated and accomplished white colleagues. His intellectual interests and hopes soon shifted toward understanding the problems of "New China."

Given his experiences living in the United States for sixty of his eighty-one years, it may not be surprising to discover that Siu still thinks of himself as a sojourner. In this regard, his life parallels that of many Chinese laundry workers. He wrote in 1985: "I have finally settled down in Shadow Lake Village. The word 'village' makes me think of my native village in my home country. Although the reality of my life lies only in

New Jersey, I often reminisce about the native village where I grew up, my relatives in the old country, and my parents. All these memories now seem distant and irretrievable. They cause me to feel deeply the grief and loneliness of life."[37]

At long last, this dissertation is available for all to appreciate and build upon. The few remaining laundry workers that Dr. Siu lived among and represents herein are unlikely to read this learned, English-language volume. Nor is it likely that those Americans who had supported various forms of Chinese exclusion and discrimination will open this book. But one can hope that perhaps their respective children and their children's children will. Its publication is an act of reclamation, a reclamation of a collective memory long silenced in American society. Now the strong, clear voice of that memory is able to resonate freely.

My gratitude goes to the following individuals who have contributed insights, comments, and corrections to my understanding of Chinese laundry workers and what has been discussed in this introduction: Thomas Bender, Richard Bernstein, Patricia Bonomi, Fay Chiang, David Chin, William Chin, Gene Eng, Melanie Gustafson, Yuet-fung Ho, Jeanne Houck, Raymond Lou, Judith Wingsiu Luk, David Reimers, Pauline Toole, Daniel Walkowitz, and Rengiu Yu. I thank them all.

NOTES

1. I prefer to use the term "laundry man," "launderer," or "laundry worker" over the one word "laundryman." Dr. Siu uses the latter term in an era when a gender tag was appended to ethnic identifications, as in "Irishman" or "Chinaman," and blue collar trades, as in "postman" or "washerwoman." In the 1980s, I find "Chinese laundryman" too full of negative cultural connotations to be a very useful descriptive label.

2. "Charlie" was a generic name used by non-Chinese to address Chinese launderers. Their actual names, Chinese or English, were often ignored in preference for "Charlie" the "Chinaman." This usage was common before Earl Derr Bigger's detective character "Charlie Chan" (1925). For more on laundry stereotypes and stereotypes of Chinese, see Chapter 2 and Paul Chan Pang Siu, "Meizhou Huaqiao Xiyidian de Cangshang" ("Overseas Chinese Laundry Workers in America: Then and Now"), *Qishiniandai [The Seventies]* (Hong Kong, April 1977), pp. 42–45. Also, William Purviance Fenn, *Ah Sin and His Brethren in*

American Literature (Peking, 1933); Harold R. Isaacs, *Images of Asia: American Views of China and India* (New York, 1972); Dorothy B. Jones, *The Portrayal of China and India on the American Screen, 1896–1955* (Cambridge, Mass., 1955); Edward Said, *Orientalism* (New York, 1978); and William F. Wu, *The Yellow Peril: Chinese Americans in American Fiction, 1850–1940* (Hamden, Conn., 1982).

3. The dissertation is published herein as it was originally submitted to Dr. Siu's University of Chicago Department of Sociology dissertation committee in 1953. I fully concur with Professor Walkowitz's observations that some of the language in the dissertation lapses into dated sociological jargon. In addition, the moralistic tone of some sections, such as the chapter on prostitutes, reflects the moral values of the time. These values themselves deserve historical scrutiny.

4. The New York Chinatown History Project has produced two major bilingual productions, both entitled "The Eight Pound Livelihood: Chinese Laundry Workers in the United States." (The term "eight-pound livelihood" was used by New York launderers to refer to their life of using an eight-pound iron.) The productions are a major traveling exhibition produced in conjunction with the New York State Museum (1984) and a half-hour video-documentary coproduced with WNYC-TV (1984). Our six-year study will culminate in a third production, a book due for both English- and Chinese-language publication in 1987. Information about these productions can be obtained by writing: NYCHP, 70 Mulberry Street, New York, New York 10013.

5. All information about Dr. Siu has been gathered from a series of private interviews and correspondence, 1985–1986 (NYCHP Archives, Paul Siu Collection).

6. This labor migration/immigration process was tied to larger political-economic developments in the United States. See Lucie Cheng and Edna Bonacich, "Introduction: A Theoretical Orientation to International Labor Migration," in Bonacich and Cheng, ed., *Labor Immigration Under Capitalism: Asian Workers in the United States Before World War II* (Berkeley, 1984).

7. The 1882 Chinese Exclusion Act prohibited laborers from entering, whereas merchants, scholars, and students were exempt. Those laborers who were already in the United States could stay; however, their wives and families could not join them. The act was repealed in 1943 with a quota allowing 105 Chinese to enter the United States each year. However, Chinese American GIs were able to bring "war brides" from China to join them in the United States. Hence, they created the *first* generation of working-class Chinese families in America. The young Siu Chan Pang entered as a student, which was quite unusual for a laundry worker's son. For more background history see Victor G. and Brett de Bary Nee, *Longtime Californ': A Documentary Study of an American Chinatown* (New York, 1972).

8. Paul Boyer, *Urban Masses and Moral Order in America, 1820–1920* (Cambridge, Mass., 1978); Reginald Horsman, *Race and Manifest Destiny: The Origins of American Racial Anglo-Saxonism* (Cambridge, Mass., 1981); Lary May,

Screening Out the Past: The Birth of Mass Culture and the Motion Picture Industry (New York, 1980); and William Stanton, *The Leopard's Spots: Scientific Attitudes Towards Race in America, 1815–1859* (New York, 1960).

9. This essay appears in: Robert Park, Ernest Burgess, and Roderick McKenzie, *The City* (Chicago, 1967), pp. 1–62.

10. Ernest Burgess and Donald Bogue, ed. *Contributions to Urban Sociology* (Chicago, 1964), p. 5.

11. Ibid.

12. Robert E. L. Faris, *Chicago Sociology, 1920–1932* (Chicago, 1970), pp. 35, 57.

13. Burgess and Bogue, ed., *Contributions*, p. 5.

14. See Chapter 1 for comments on this methodology.

15. Burgess and Bogue, ed., *Contributions*, p. 325; see Faris, *Chicago Sociology*, pp. 65–87, for a broader interpretation of the department's breadth and depth.

16. Burgess and Bogue, ed., *Contributions*, p. 326.

17. An assessment of the many Chinese students studying sociology at the University of Chicago deserves its own study. Some of their dissertations and theses were: Wu Ching-Chao, "Chinatowns: A Study of Symbiosis and Assimilation," Ph.D. diss., 1928; Bingham Dai, "Opium Addiction in Chicago," Ph.D. diss., 1935; Rose Hum Lee, "The Chinese Communities in the Rocky Mountain Region," Ph.D. diss., 1947; Belulah Ong Kwoh, "American-born Chinese College Graduates," master's thesis, 1947; Ernest Ni, "Social Characteristics of the Chinese Population: A Study of the Population Structure and Urbanism of a Metropolitan Community," Ph.D. diss., 1948; Liang Yuan, "The Chinese Family in Chicago," master's thesis, 1951; and P. Y. Liao, "A Case Study of a Chinese Immigrant Community," master's thesis, 1951.

18. See Robert Park, "The Assimilation of Races," Park and Burgess, *Introduction to the Science of Sociology* (Chicago, 1969), pp. 756–62; Everett Hughes and Helen Hughes, *Where People Meet: Racial and Ethnic Frontiers* (Glencoe, Ill., 1952), p. 31. For a penetrating analysis of Park's views see John H. Stanfield, *Philanthropy and Jim Crow in American Social Science* (Westport, Conn., 1985), pp. 38–60.

19. Joseph Needham, *Science and Civilisation in China*, vol. II. "History of Scientific Thought" (Cambridge, England, 1969).

20. Robert Park had retired by the time Paul Siu entered the University of Chicago; however, Siu recalls meeting him at least once. In fact, Park suggested that Siu study the phenomenon of gambling in Chinatown. Siu went as far as drafting an outline entitled "The Gambler: A Sociological Study of Gambling in Chinatown, Chicago." Park's death soon afterward curtailed the project. Siu later wrote about the "chop suey" restaurant. See "Zasuiguan zai Meiguo" ("Chop Suey Restaurants in the United States"), *Qishiniandai [The Seventies]* (Hong Kong, December 1977), pp. 50–52. Also see Renqiu Yu, "'Chop Suey,' Chinese or American?" New York Chinatown History Project, *BU GAO BAN* (Winter 1986); Louis Wirth, *The Ghetto* (Chicago, 1956).

21. Clifford Geertz, "Thick Description: Towards an Interpretative Theory of Culture," in *The Interpretation of Cultures* (New York, 1973), Chapter 1.

22. John Gwaltney, *Drylongso: A Self-Portrait of Black America* (New York, 1980), pp. xxii–xxx.

23. See page 1. Also see Paul C. P. Siu, "The Isolation of the Chinese Laundryman," in Burgess and Bogue, ed., *Contributions*.

24. Siu saw his study as a direct extension of Wirth's "social isolation" theory as developed in *The Ghetto,* Park's classic essay "Human Migration and the Marginal Man," *American Journal of Sociology* (May 1928), and Everett Stonequist's elaboration of Park in *The Marginal Man: A Study in Personality and Culture Conflict* (New York, 1937).

25. Paul C. P. Siu, "The Sojourner," *American Journal of Sociology* (July 1952); Clarence Glick, "The Chinese Migrant in Hawaii," Ph.D. diss., University of Chicago, 1938.

26. Siu, "The Sojourner," p. 34. It is important to note that there have been at least two usages of the term "sojourner," that defined by Siu describing the Chinese laundry worker experience and that defined by such analysis as in Gunther Barth in *Bitter Strength: A History of the Chinese in the United States, 1850–1870* (Cambridge, Mass., 1964). Barth uses the term loosely to describe Chinese newcomers who would "make money to return to China with their savings for a life of ease. . . . Their goal kept them apart from the flood of other immigrants who came to America as permanent residents" (p. 1). Consequently, Barth argued that "the sojourner's pursuit of their limited goal influenced the reception of the Chinese in the United States who were, as a result, excluded from the privileges and obligations of other immigrants" (p. 1). This simplistic "blaming-the-victim" position ignores the fact that many white immigrants did not or did not intend to stay in California. This thesis has been persuasively refuted by Wu, *The Yellow Peril,* pp. 7–9, and by Sandy Lydon, *Chinese Gold: The Chinese in the Monterey Bay Region* (Capitola, Ca., 1985), pp. 22–23. Siu's definition is far more complex and historically specific. For a critique of Siu's sojourner concept see Raymond Lou, "Chinese American Historiography: The Dialectics of Invalidation," American Historical Association, Annual Meeting, 1985. Also see Peter S. Li, "Ethnic Businesses Among Chinese in the U.S.," *Journal of Ethnic Studies* (Fall 1976), p. 35.

27. Siu, "The Sojourner," p. 34; and Donald Levine, Ellwood Carter, and Eleanor Gorman, "Simmel's Influence on American Sociology" (part one), *American Journal of Sociology* (January 1976), p. 831.

28. Dr. Siu had not heard of the term "birds of passage" when he developed the definition of "sojourner" (first used by W. B. Taylor, "Birds of Passage," *American Journal of Sociology,* November, 1912); however, the experiences described are strikingly similar. For discussion about these variant sojourning experiences, see Thomas Kessner, "Repatriation in American History," in Select Commission on Immigration and Refugee Policy, *U.S. Immigration Policy and the National Interest,* Appendix A, Washington, D.C., 1981. For an incisive theoretical discussion, see Bonacich and Cheng, "Introduction," pp. 27–29.

29. Dr. Siu also uses the sociological term "deviant" as a way to describe the sojourner as a variant type of Simmel's "stranger" (see pp. 294, 299). However, in a more fundamental sense, he opened the way for a more differentiated view. (See Levine, "Simmel's Influence," p. 831)

30. Siu, "The Isolation of the Chinese Laundryman," p. 429.

31. See pp. 294–301.

32. John Bodnar, Roger Simon, and Michael Weber, *Lives of Their Own: Blacks, Italians, and Poles in Pittsburgh, 1900–1960* (Urbana, Ill., 1982), p. 6. Dr. Siu's emphasis on racial social isolation is extended in Benjamin Ringer's magnum opus on U.S. racial relations, *We the People and Others: Duality and America's Treatment of Racial Minorities* (New York, 1983).

33. Terry Eagleton, *The Function of Criticism* (London, 1984), p. 16.

34. Antonio Gramsci, *Prison Notebooks* (New York, 1971), pp. 3–14, and Carl Boggs, *Gramsci's Marxism* (London, 1976).

35. Dr. Siu taught at Kansas Wesleyan, Kansas; Park College, Missouri; Yankton College, South Dakota; and the Detroit Institute of Technology, Michigan. I would speculate that it is unlikely the same student would have been surprised that a professor from Germany or France had read so many English-language books. Asians in America, by virtue of perceived skin color distinctiveness, are usually thought of as "foreigners," not as Americans. Despite the fact that I was born in Wisconsin, non-Asian Americans are constantly surprised at how good my English is. This comment is the flip side of what Dr. Siu encountered. The problem relates to Western culture's "Orientalism" as described by Said (Said, *Orientalism*, pp. 1–6).

36. Dr. Siu was told by the University of Chicago Press that a book about Chinese launderers would not sell but that a book on "sojourners" might. This point relates to a double problem—that of the evaluative criteria of publishers and that of the "tastes" of the book-purchasing public. The great majority of books by or about Chinese Americans have been privately published or published by a small press after being rejected by major publishers. Rose Hum Lee, Siu's classmate at the University of Chicago, helped to finance the University of Hong Kong's publication of her book, *The Chinese in the United States of America* (Hong Kong, 1960). See Frank Chin, Jeffrey Paul Chan, Lawson Fusao Inada, and Shawn Hsu Wong, ed., *Aiiieeeee! An Anthology of Asian-American Writers* (Washington, D.C., 1974), and Elaine Kim, *Asian American Literature* (Philadelphia, 1984). Dr. Siu was told by Professor Burgess that Siu's dissertation came out too late to be published by the University of Chicago Press. The "golden age" was past, and Whyte's 1944 book (William F. Whyte, *Street Corner Society* [Chicago, 1944]) was the last of Park's sociology series.

37. Paul C. P. Siu, "A Sojourner's Monologue," New York Chinatown History Project, *BU GAO BAN* (Summer 1985), p. 7.

EDITOR'S NOTE

I wanted to keep the full flavor of Dr. Siu's original 1953 Ph.D. dissertation manuscript and therefore made a minimum of content and stylistic alterations. The primary changes made were as regards to the usage of Chinese terms. For example, Hongkong was made Hong Kong, li-chi-nuts standardized to li-chi nuts. Otherwise, Chinese transliterations have been kept as they appeared in Dr. Siu's dissertation with some editing for consistency and typos. The great majority of Chinese names and terms in original manuscript are transliterated from Taishan dialect, a rural district of Kwangtung [Guangdong] Province from which the great majority of pre-1965–68 Chinese immigrants in America came.

Names have been edited to follow a single format for the sake of consistency and to help distinguish family and given names. For example, Toy Shi Shan has been standardized to Toy Shi-shan. People with two-character names remain the same, such as Moy Tong.

Bracketed transliterations have been added for terms and phrases using the Hanzi Pinyin system (a transliteration system for Putonghua, or standard Chinese). Pronunciations are approximately the same as corresponding letters in the English alphabet with the following major distinctions: vowels = Italian or Spanish values; b = s*p*in; c = it*s*; d = s*t*em; g = s*k*y; q = *ch*urch; r = pleasure with a strong mixture of r; x = s*h*ingle; z = tha*t*'s all; zh = Italian *c*ielo.

An asterisk * denotes a colloquial Taishanese term not common to Putonghua, and therefore difficult to transliterate into Pinyin.

Dr. Siu was consulted on all Chinese names and terms in the manuscript. In the cases in which sayings have already been translated into English, the bracketed Pinyin transliteration has been provided. Renqui Yu was instrumental in making these transliterations possible.

I would like to thank Carl Prince of the New York University History Department and Colin Jones of New York University Press for making the publication of Dr. Siu's dissertation possible. My appreciation also goes to Despina P. Gimbel, managing editor of this project. As usual, I'm hopelessly in debt to Judy Susman for her personal support and shrewd editorial advice. But most of all, my deepest thanks go to Dr. Paul Chan Pang Siu and Helen Hwei Lan Ong-Siu for sharing with me their intelligence, memories, and fried chicken. With great sorrow, I must report that as this book was nearing completion, Helen Siu and then Dr. Paul Siu died.

CHAPTER I

INTRODUCTION

1. The Problem

AN INTERESTING PHENOMENON in a community's economic life is the occupational selection of its immigrant groups. The Greek ice-cream parlor, the Italian fruit stand, the Jewish clothing store, and the Chinese laundry, for example, are some of the characteristic specimens— interesting because of the fact that these were not the usual occupations of the owners in their homelands, but are new social inventions by these different ethnic groups in America as ways and means to struggle for existence in the symbiotic level of the community life. Other features, such as small capital investment, long working hours, relative or kinsman partnership, may be considered as similarities among them, and these features may serve as a basis for treating them as a type which may be called the "immigrant economy." Further, it is of interest and significance to focus our attention on the relationship between the personality of the individual and the type of occupation he takes, the cultural background and the urban environment that play into the situation. The problem, therefore, is essentially one of social adjustment in a particular situation under which attitudes and values can be observed and described.

A study of the Chinese laundryman is promising, for he represents a minority group which has been in extreme isolation and therefore may be in the slowest process of being assimilated. An understanding of his particular situation may offer a strategic means for securing increased knowledge of the types of personality which are the product of race and culture contacts and conflicts, and the relationship of the person to the social institution found under a given situation with reference to race and culture. To put it simply, we are interested in the man and his institutions and attempt to inquire into the situation as to how he becomes isolated and to analyze his behavior and conduct in the situation.

Almost all Chinese laundrymen in Chicago are first-generation immigrants. The laundry began to flourish with the labor agitation against Chinese cheap labor on the West Coast about three generations ago. Since then the Chinese have not been considered as competitors in the labor market. The occupation chosen, to be sure, is a form of accomodation, and since its founding, it has become institutionalized with a characteristic pattern of its own. At present the Chinese laundry can be found in every neighborhood in the urban community where the Chinese immigrant can make a living. It is reported that the Chinese in the United States are found mainly in five or six occupations, and that of the laundryman is seventy-four times as numerous as that of any other occupation.[1] The Chinese were not laundrymen until they arrived in this country to join their relatives and friends. They migrated to "Old Gold Mountain"[2] (America) as economic adventurers, like most minority groups in this country. They are known in China as *wah-chao* [*huaqiao*] (overseas Chinese), meaning temporary Chinese residents abroad. A peculiar feature of these temporary visitors is the fact that they stay on in this country, ten, twenty, thirty, forty years or more, yet cling to the cultural heritage of their homeland. Indeed each Chinese laundry is a Chinatown in every neighborhood, and communication between the laundryman and his relatives and friends in China is far closer than with his next-door neighbors in America. His social contacts with people other than his fellow Chinese in this country tend to be commercial and impersonal. This is a case of social isolation.

C. C. Wu, in his dissertation,[3] gives no substantial evidence of assimilation of the Chinese in this country, but presents instead, scanty information about the marital adjustment between Chinese students and their American wives. The Chinese students, in fact, do not represent the mass of Chinatown. The student, while he shares the common heritage with the mass of immigrants in Chinatown, is, at least, less isolated in the sense that he does not have as much language difficulty as the laundryman. The student tends to be modernized before his sojourn abroad. The students are from every province of China, while the immigrants in America are from a few districts in the vicinity of the city of Canton, Kwongtung Province [Guangzhou, Guangdong Province], in South China—the Chinese New Orleans. In contrast with the students, the majority of regular Chinese immigrants are from rural areas; they are the villagers. The Chinese laundrymen, especially, come from the area where the clan system flourishes strongly, and where villages are predominantly one-clan villages; everyone, every family within it, has a surname common to all.

The economic basis of these villages is agriculture. Ever since the invasion of Western manufacturing products, the farm economy in this region, as well as in other parts of China, has been virtually ruined. With the increase of population in this region, the farm became too small to accommodate all the sons of the families. Sons of the farmer felt that it was undesirable to subsist by plowing land, and were anxious for economic adventure abroad. Contacts were established in Hong Kong so that foreign vessels would take them to America and other parts of the world. The news of the "gold mountain" in California stimulated everybody's desire to undertake the adventure. And they have been coming ever since, by all sorts of ways and means, in spite of the legal exclusion and social discrimination that they have experienced in this country.

The natural history of the Chinese laundryman is a process of contact, conflict, accommodation, and isolation instead of assimilation. Socially he is a stranger. He closely approximates the ideal construction of symbiosis without communication. The life organization of the man as well as the structural pattern of the laundry as an institution have remained relatively static during the last three generations or more. In comparing it with the Jewish clothing store, for instance, the latter appears to make some progress in the course of the process.

The static character of the Chinese minority in this country is certainly not because they are culturally determined not to be assimilated. In a different situation, as shown by Glick in his study of the Chinese in Hawaii, a somewhat different picture is presented:

> Among the Chinese in Hawaii the main stages in this sequence have been a plantation period, with social isolation and residential and occupational segregation; a period of urbanization, with residential segregation but expanding occupational distribution; a third period, still in process, with residential dispersion within the city, continued infiltration into all parts of the occupational structure, and increased social contacts with other groups in the interracial society.[4]

In contrast with this picture, the Chinese in the continental United States still represent predominantly social isolation with residential and occupational segregation. Chinatown is still the social center except in the case of its decline and consequent failure to maintain its institutions, as shown by Lee.[5] The existence of the Chinese laundry with its established structure unchanged, as in large American cities, is in marked contrast with the Hawaii situation.

Having stated in this way our problem of inquiry, let us set forth a hypothesis as follows: The Chinese laundryman is not a marginal man as Park and Stonequist described him [ed. note: see p. xxxii]; he seems to be characteristically another type of stranger who represents a tendency toward isolation on the one hand and retardation of assimilation on the other hand. It is another type, or another deviant type, in the area of race and culture relations—"the sojourner." The sojourner clings to the cultural heritage of his own ethnic group in spite of many years of residence abroad. The Chinese laundryman seems to be a sojourner rather than a marginal man, particularly in the racial situation in continental United States. The concept "sojourner" is relevant to the case of the Chinese laundryman insofar as he is viewed under the existing situation. We recognize that the situation may change, and so the personality of the individual may likewise make a different response to the changing situation. We are content, at any rate, to point out that up to the present time the Chinese laundry remains a folk institution which is organized on the basis of the Old World heritage of kinship system and personal relations, and that the laundryman's life organization is oriented to social isolation and segregation, and that the laundry is an instrumentality to that effect.

2. Method of Research

Having set our problem, our method of investigation cannot be other than the typological method. Its techniques include ways and means of collecting and classifying information and material. Our principal technique, however, is interviewing of different kinds.

Participant Interview

The interviewer is regarded as one of the group. The interview always involves more than one person. It is carried on freely and naturally as ordinary conversation between friends and relatives, although the interviewer sometimes takes the liberty of guiding the subject matter of the conversation. The conversation would be written down as soon as the interviewer had time to do so. Sometimes it had to be written in Chinese to maintain the original meaning. When the material was to be used, it was then translated into English. The persons who took part in the conversation did not know that the interviewer was making a study or was gathering information.

Life-History Interview

The relationship between the interviewer and interviewee is again natural and free. The interviewer was interested in the interviewee personally, and the latter was made willing to tell the story in story-telling fashion. Sometimes it is about the interviewee himself, and sometimes it is about someone he knows well. The life-history interview may take several meetings, but some take only one. Like the other interviews, it cannot be recorded in front of the interviewee. It has to be remembered as fully as possible and be written down later.

Opinion Interview

This is conducted when the interviewer has only one specific question to ask. It is in the nature of information-seeking for a specific purpose, or to prove a specific point which needs additional factual evidence. This type of information is largely related to historical points of interest. Sometimes it is about figures and numbers. Sometimes it is about specific information on inter-personal relations.

Social Service Interview

The interviewee came with a personal problem which puts the interviewer and the interviewee into a client-worker relationship. This sort of information is largely found in Chapter 13, "Immigration Problems," and 17, "Out-Group Contacts and Deviant Types." The interviewees came to be helped, and sometimes the help was nothing but writing a letter in English and sometimes in Chinese, too. This sort of service gives the interviewer a chance to read personal letters and to keep a record of them.

The investigator lived with a group of his kinsmen for two years. During that period he was able to act as a participant observer and was able to take weekly and daily records of the life of the laundrymen in the neighborhood. The worker speaks the dialect spoken by most of the Chinese laundrymen. In fact, he was himself brought up in the same cultural heritage. He has friends and relatives among the laundrymen. He knows the cultural background well enough to comprehend the personal problems of the laundryman. This, however, may be an advantage or it may be a disadvantage. The disadvantage is bias and loss of sight of some of the significant points and interests from the cultural standpoint.

Besides this, the investigator used to serve as a laundry supply agent at the time when the study began in 1938. Actually, some of the materials used in this study were collected earlier.

The quantitative data used in the study are from different sources, the U.S. Census, reports from the Department of Justice, and personal data. The most important source of quantitative data were the Chicago city directories. Chapter 3, "Growth and Distribution of the Chinese Laundry in Chicago," depends very heavily on such data; otherwise it would be pretty unintelligible.

The investigator had eight years of social work experience which gave him contact with information and materials which he had no chance to obtain in Chicago. The materials were used to substantiate the hypothetical statement and to illustrate the findings in Chapter 13.

Professors Burgess and Blumer obtained materials for use in Chapter 2. These are largely recollections of Americans of earlier experiences with Chinese laundrymen. The materials are from a certain stratum of American society, namely, the college students. What do the common people as a whole think of the Chinese laundryman? Can it be the same as the students, or is it different? This is still an unanswered question.

There were about 2,000 to 2,500 Chinese laundrymen in the Greater Metropolitan Region in 1940. Our study covers one-fourth of them superficially, and about one-tenth of them extensively. There was, therefore, a matter of selection of cases. As a matter of fact, it may be considered as sampling in a qualitative way. But the investigator must confess that he could not pass over those individuals whom he knew best. There were about fifty of them.

The investigator had traveled very extensively over many cities in the Middle West and the East. He found the mode of life of the Chinese laundryman in other cities identical with the Chicago situation. The investigator also had studied the Chicago and the Boston situations in more detail and compared the two. Differences are found only in minor points.

Our methodological problem is one of classifying cases and developing new groups if some of them do not follow the general pattern. It is an attempt to build up an ideal type and treat every case as a deviant type from the ideal construction. The materials are used, therefore, in the light of our frame of reference as stated in our problem of research.

NOTES

1. Clarence E. Glick, "The Chinese Migrant in Hawaii" (Ph.D. diss., University of Chicago, 1938), pp. 143–46.
2. "Old Gold Mountain," United States of America; "New Gold Mountain," Australia; "Red Hair," Canada.
3. Ching-chao Wu, "Chinatowns: A Study of Symbiosis and Assimilation" (Ph.D. diss., University of Chicago, 1928).
4. Clarence E. Glick, "The Relation between Position and Status in the Assimilation of Chinese in Hawaii," *American Journal of Sociology* (March, 1942).
5. Rose Hum Lee, "The Decline of Chinatown in the United States," *American Journal of Sociology* LIV (March, 1949).

CHAPTER II

THE CHINESE LAUNDRYMAN IN THE EYES OF THE AMERICAN PUBLIC

THE CHINESE IMMIGRANT comes to America as an economic adventurer; his residence in the community is regarded as a mere sojourn, for he intends to return to China. The whole situation, however, is not merely what he does and thinks as a sojourner; it is also how the American general public reacts to his presence in the community. It seems, therefore, advisable to examine how the American public sees him in the neighborhood.

1. Stereotype of Conception

The American public feels superior to Chinese immigrants, particularly to the local laundryman residing in his quaint shop. He is often the butt of ridicule for failing to conform to the accepted behavior code of the community. Children chant that the Chinese eat dead rats and make a dollar out of fifteen cents.

> Chinkie, Chinkie, Chinaman,
> Sitting on the fence;
> Trying to make a dollar
> Out of fifteen cents.
>
> Chink, Chink, Chinaman
> Eats dead rats;
> Eats them up
> Like gingersnaps.

From the comic strips and from motion pictures, children visualize him as a "criminal" and even a potential "murderer." The origin of this fantastic stereotype is revealed in the following document:

> The first impression I had of the Chinese laundryman fixed in me the conception of the hard-working, docile Oriental, capable of sly, criminal behavior if given a chance. This impression came rather casually some dozen years ago when I watched some neighborhood rascals soaping the Chinaman's store window and calling such names as "dumb Chink" and "Ding Dong." The laundryman kept right on working, only occasionally looking at the window, but making no expression of disapproval, through gestures or otherwise. His very indifference seemed to indicate his timidity and docility. Yet, on the other hand his "criminal" appearance (which had been pretty thoroughly stereotyped for Chinese in general through movies and comic strips) seemed to convey the idea that he gladly would have slit a few of their throats.
>
> Practically all my knowledge of the Chinese laundryman has come to me through indirect experience from other than face-to-face customer relations. Consequently, what others told me about the Chinese laundryman has pretty well determined my earlier attitudes toward him. He has been pictured, and quite correctly, as a slavelike worker, fond of working long hours for very low pay, as one who would do this in sheer gratitude to get away from the perpetual rice-and-birds'-nest diet of China.

The stereotype version of the laundryman is predominant among children. They get it from the "Fu Manchu" type of movies and by hearsay from adults. Elders deliberately or involuntarily furnish the child a mysterious notion about the neighborhood laundryman. Thus the children develop a fear of him, imagining all sorts of evil things he might have done. Children, generally, keep away from him and his laundry shop. Only by personal contacts, perhaps, can one learn that he is just as human as anybody else.

> My first experience with a Chinese laundryman came when I was nine years old. My mother sent me to the laundry with some clothes to be washed and ironed and be ready that same day.
>
> Now I had heard all sorts of weird stories about "Chinamen" and was rather afraid. I had heard that they chased boys with a red hot iron and did all kinds of mysterious and sinister things in their back rooms. I also knew that they acted and talked "funny" and you couldn't know what to expect from them.
>
> However, when I actually went to the laundry office things seemed a bit

strange all right, but not at all sinister. There were shelves with bundles of laundry in there on both sides of the room. The laundryman was ironing with an old-fashioned iron and greeted me with a smile when I came in. He took my bundle and then took two pieces of paper out. He marked them with my name in Chinese and then gave one to me. He told me in broken English to bring the piece of paper back to claim my laundry. When I returned with the ticket he gave me the laundry and figured out what it cost on some kind of board with beads on it which he seemed to count rapidly.

After that I always had a liking for Chinese laundrymen. Today I have a difficult time understanding how people have any contempt or hatred for them, although I suppose they may have heard the same stories I have and never actually had any experience with them.

The observation, in the first case, that the laundryman was hard-working, was correct. His gesture of indifference to the mocking game of the neighborhood rascals could be related to his response to being conceived as having a criminal appearance. That the laundryman is "fond of working long hours" can be understood only from his point of view. It seems clear that misunderstanding and prejudice came from "weird stories" as in the preceding case. Fear developed through hearsay and weird stories. The fear, however, turned into curiosity. The laundryman, being away from his family, tends to be fond of children; and the gift of *li-chi* nuts [*lizhi*] is, perphaps, a fatherly gesture to the boy; it could be more than an "attempt to promote patronage" as it was interpreted. What conventional understanding there was between the laundryman and his young customer!

The laundryman has been an enigma to me from my earliest recollection until recently, for, as a child, I had been given the impression that he was the "kidnapper" of bad little boys, placing them in his bag and carrying them away to unknown places. Many were the times that I watched the bag intently from a distance, in order to see some "squirm" or move, or hear some muffled groan of his victim in his fat bag. If he glanced at me, I disappeared.

When I was a large boy, I began to take shirts and collars to the laundry. My fear began to diminish, but, behold, I began to look for evidence of the "dead rats," the delicacy of which they were fond; for we had, in our boyhood groups, discussed the Chinese and their love of "dead rats" just as we craved chicken, candy, sweet potatoes, et cetera. Sometimes, after getting our clean laundry, the Chinese, in his attempt to promote patronage and to be friendly, gave us lagniappe, a dried, soft-shell nut with a sweet center similar to a prune in appearance, that was like giving us poison at first. Try as hard as we might, however, we could not find anything "rattish" with the gift, which, after many misgivings and struggles of indecision in adherence to our code of scorning and fearing all that was Chinese, we gulped down in haste and went back for more on our next trip.

The change from fear to curiosity, as further illustrated in the following case, is not so much through direct contacts with the laundryman, but with other Chinese and through education. It seems, however, that the movies and comic strips have had too deep an influence on the man's early life and makes his curiosity naive.

My earliest recollection of meeting a Chinaman was when I was somewhere between the ages of six to nine. I walked several times past a store which had a horrible stink. This stink was a bad one but still an interesting one. One day I had to enter this store to get some collars. I was scared to go in though I did not know why. I took a deep breath as I entered the store. The men had such immobile faces, their teeth were funny, they wore dresses, had long hair, and seemed so strange. I thought I would be killed if I didn't get out quick. I remember the tingling feeling I had in my back as I left; I thought they would stab me or something. It took all my self-control not to run or to look back.

The only time I remember my parents saying something about them was when I walked past the store with them and said that the Chinaman's store was real spooky. One of my parents then said: "Look out or he will cut your head off." I did not believe it and said so; my parents did not insist further. I never wanted to go back to the store again.

When I was ten I saw a movie in which the Chinese were the spooky crooks or bad guys. They were always connected with night. They didn't say anything but they were always doing murders, stealing, importing or being smuggled across the border half dead, inside of crates full of straw. I never hated them because in real life I never met any. But I always knew that the Chinese in the movie was the bad guy. Sometimes he would be a jolly cook.

When I was sixteen my idea of the Chinese was that they did everything in a complicated way. This I got from going to the Field Museum, looking at the Chinese displays. My high school teacher said that they were the most civilized people in the world, and the most polite. They knew how to insult you in subtle, clever ways. When I chanced on one of the first sex books (something by Montegazza in German) I read the refinements in their sex life and the elaborate, complicated sex perversions they engaged in.

From seventeen on my attitude toward Chinese was that it was a liberal way of regarding them if I thought of them in a cosmopolitan manner. If I could only get hold of one I'd ask him a lot of questions. Liberalism has always been associated with tolerance, in my way of thinking.

I would like to meet an educated Chinese on campus. I think they are quite reserved and hard to approach. I asked a Chinese here how it was that his brother had an interest in our music, since ours was so different. How did his brother get to learn about our classical music? I was bending over backward trying to acquire a taste for Chinese music. The Chinese called me stupid and all around insulted me. What I learned from this experience is that it is hard to get rapport with a Chinese on short notice. Perhaps you really have to know them before you can attempt an interview. When I was sixteen I told myself that I'd get to know a Chinese when I was in college. Nine years later I cannot say that I have succeeded, although I would like to have a Chinese friend. I suppose the attitude I have is that it would be quite a catch for me if I had a Chinese friend. I would get quite a bit of attention, if not notoriety, which I would not mind having occasionally.

To compare the preceding case with the following, they are essentially the same, and show that it is hard to be free from the stereotype. What is meant by a liberal attitude toward the Chinese as shown in the above case is not clear. Perhaps it implies sophistication by recognizing that the Chinese do have a culture and are "law abiding" after all, as stated in the following case:

R. S., a rather impressionable Negro, lived with her grandmother in a large southern Illinois town. There she had no contact with Chinese laundrymen, or with any other Chinese, and her opinion of them was formed entirely from the vivid motion pictures she saw involving Chinamen in villainous roles.

At the time R. S. traveled to Chicago to join her mother, she had a preconceived notion of Chinese as violent, mysterious people with an unwholesome habit of snatching their enemies from obscure alleys into still darker back rooms through sliding panels, and there disposing of them efficiently and silently by thrusting knives into their backs.

When R. S. had occasion to pass a Chinese laundry, she walked hurriedly by or crossed the street to avoid coming within snatching distance of these small shops.

Because of having formed adverse impressions in childhood which were not pleasantly counteracted by later experiences, and because those early impressions were vivid, and hence not easily lost through disuse, R. S. was extremely surprised upon entering high school and making the acquaintance of a young Chinaman to find that the Chinese are as law-abiding as other American citizens.

How the stereotype originated is quite clear; it involves all Chinese in this country. One of them is bad, all of them are bad, and all Chinese in America are laundrymen if they are not of a violent and murderous nature. It shows what an important role the movies and comics play in shaping mass behavior.

Even the few people who take a friendly attitude and attempt to see the Chinese laundryman as a fellow human being soon find out how wide are the barriers between the East and West. They find it difficult to meet; or if they become acquainted, to converse freely. At best, with very rare individual exceptions, they learn to know them only on the surface and in highly formal relations.

2. The Chinese Laundryman as a Thing

The presence of the Chinese laundryman in the neighborhood is, therefore, taken for granted. Nobody knows anything about him. The contacts he has are commercial and impersonal. In fact, the word laundryman has the same meaning as the word "laundry" to most of his customers. When the American thinks of the laundryman, he usually thinks of the laundry shop where he takes his white shirts. The person and the institution are the same thing. "He serves a purpose as a laundryman and then the people of the community forgets about him."

> The Chinaman is more or less welcome in the neighborhood as a laundryman, but he is not recognized as a social constituent of the community. He works in his little, steaming shop all day and far into the night, but he is never seen in any other place in the community. He serves a purpose as a laundryman and then people forget about him. They know little about his life, his family, what he does in his leisure time, the hours of his work, the way he thinks, et cetera. They know that he does an excellent job of starching their shirts, and this seems to be sufficient for them. They eagerly turn away from the fact that they should be trying to satisfy the other needs of the Chinese laundryman, as well as his financial needs.
>
> The individual values the laundry as a functional part of his everyday or every-week life. It is a convenient place to have his shirts and collars cleaned, cheaper perhaps than the regular wetwash. The wife or mother is relieved of the tiring job of ironing and that is probably the only thing the women think about the laundryman, besides the cost of the bill. In general, the

neighbors and patrons of the Chinese laundry accept it as part of the community and think about it no further.

Human relations on the symbiotic level are likely to be impersonal and commercial. Not only the Chinese laundryman, the druggist, the grocer, the barber, and the tailor as well, are no exceptions. Personal relationships can be established only on the social level. Common interests and sentiments can prevail only through primary contacts. The neighborhood grocer may have primary-group contacts, but not the Chinese laundryman. The difficulties which the laundryman has which are different from most of the people in these other services is the fact that his cultural heritage is so vastly divergent from the dominant group. This, together with his language handicap, racial visibility, and, perhaps, his un-American standard of living, makes him an undesirable individual for anyone to have as a personal friend. So people either treat him as merely a "laundry machine" or with an indifferent emotional reaction as something unpleasant or "creepy."

> I asked one man what he thought of Chinese laundrymen and he said he never used them. Queries to other people elicited either this reply or a reply much like, "I always send my shirts there." It would seem that the adult community defines Chinese laundrymen as washing machines, not really persons. . . . The first reaction of every person I have encountered was that the Chinese laundryman was a service institution which one did or did not use. Only upon being pressed did they even become aware of the Chinaman's human possibility. He is a laundry, not a person. . . .
> Some persons do have an idle curiosity about the Chinese laundryman which they do little to satisfy. And strangely enough, some persons fear him just a little. After a remark about using him or not using him that most people made when he was introduced into the conversation, many persons I spoke to made a further remark like, "They're sort of creepy," or, "I don't know, but every time I see one I feel uncomfortable."

Using the Chinese laundryman as a subject of discussion, a group of college girls concluded that he is a sort of public utility. It is another term; like the wash-machine conception used previously, the laundryman is simply a thing.

> They agreed that Chinese laundrymen run small hand laundries, that they own and operate their own establishments, that they are willing to work

hard and for long hours, and that they are definitely considered "foreign" and "different" in the neighborhoods in which they live. Beyond this, opinion was divided. Most of the girls were under the impression that they do not speak English well enough to talk easily with their customers. Some who had not patronized them said they believed that they reputedly did fine work very cheaply; more experienced girls denied this, saying that their work was not cheaper and no better than any other laundry and, moreover, they were undependable. None of them knew anything about the social and cultural side of the lives of Chinese laundrymen. They admitted that the community usually takes them for granted and does not attempt to become acquainted with them. The only concrete impressions were those which defined them as an economic utility like bank tellers or the man who reads gas meters—though more mysterious because less familiar.

3. Antipathy and Sympathy

Naturally not all Chinese laundrymen in the city are of the same type of personality, same temperament, and attitude toward their customers and the persons they come into contact with. Some of them make a good impression on people; others do not. As a result, we have two sides to the picture, or variety of opinion of the general public about the Chinese laundryman.

The materials obtained may not give a full picture, but we believe they represent fairly well the attitudes of the general public. To average Americans, the Chinese laundryman is either a stereotype or something useful as a tool. Now we should like to consider the question as to what extent do various individuals think of the Chinese laundryman differently. Under what conditions are the variations of opinion formed? Evidently the differences are related to the personal experiences, social background, and personality of the observers themselves; some are indifferent, some are skeptical, and some are trying to be friendly. The following narratives represent the impressionistic attitudes. The observations are based on impersonal and casual acquaintance.

Although I have never had any dealing with Chinese laundrymen, I have formed a somewhat vague, indifferent picture of them, based on the very few times I have gone into their shops with friends. For one thing, I could never make out what they were saying; they were rather difficult to understand. The stores I have been in were very poorly and scantily furnished and the smell was starchy, I always thought of rice. The man appeared a humble servant, trying his hardest to please the customer. Although I really knew nothing about how good his business was, I always had the impression that it was fair and that the profits were meager—anyhow by the time they were divided among the owners and helpers. He also seemed like a foreigner, an inferior foreigner who was all right as long as he stayed in his place; and it also seemed that he wasn't trying or anxious to get out of his social group or position in society.

I have never had occasion to use the service of a Chinese laundryman, and therefore my impressions are confined to those acquired while idly looking in their windows as I passed.

They seemed to me to be very small, very expressionless of countenance, and either very hard working or very indifferent to the ordinary pleasures, comforts and interests of life, since they seemed always to be in their shop ironing when other shops were closed and their proprietors elsewhere.

As a child I used to be fascinated by the calendars hanging in their shops. It seemed so odd that the "pretty girls" were Chinese and not American. Their shops appear always very neat and clean. The workers appear always to be working and never chatting with each other.

I took a batch of laundry to a Chinese laundryman once in Philadelphia. The Chinese laundryman, short, tubby, somewhat greasy, perhaps it was sweat from his steamy work room . . . steam pipes along the low ceiling . . . works late . . . careful . . . honest, always precise though slow, methodical, calm, doesn't worry if something should go wrong. Probably has a lot of money stored up somewhere, though he leads a humble life, desires little, face expressionless except slight smile infrequently, restrained in conversation . . . still says, "No ticky, no washy; come again Fliday," holds hands together in front of stomach and bows slightly as he says this, smiling slightly . . . usually a tubby wife hovering in the back work room behind the partition . . . with some kids running around . . . whole family lives in the tiny shop . . . she cooks in it, too, in the back, inside room. Usually has a son who is well dressed, a white collar worker in the city . . . comes home frequently . . . all in one family . . . keep in close touch . . . see each other whenever possible . . . lots of other Chinese (probably family) constantly dropping into the shop to talk a little or just sit and smoke.

The impressionistic person tends to interpret the Chinese laundryman's mode of living from his own standard of living by more or less an ethnocentric point of view. The ethnocentric individual has never tried to understand others different from himself with scientific objectiveness.

Consequently anything different from himself would be inferior, funny, or queer.

The following statement, although still an impressionistic point of view, yet seems to have sympathetic understanding of the laundryman's hard work, and does not think of him as a mysterious person. This point of view, perhaps, may be regarded as the point of view of the laundryman's regular customers. The customer has constantly come into contact with the laundryman, observing his activities which may gain impersonal appreciation to a certain extent.

> The Chinese laundryman seems to me a small, quiet, and conscientious man. I would trust him to do good work and give honest service. He seems hardly a part of the American community. I have often wondered what he does with his spare time—of which he doesn't seem to have much. I don't visualize him as being a mysterious person.

The Chinese laundryman has friends; he makes friends with persons of good will, persons with some special interest, and, perhaps, with persons who are just as lonely as he is. Why the grandfather in the next narrative befriended the old "Chinaman" is not known. However, it shows that a personal relation seems to be established.

> However, not all Chinamen, nor all white men, are averse to being friends. Take the case of my grandfather. Taking a walk every evening he would see an old Chinaman bent over a hot ironing board. He would buy ice cream and take it in to him, or have it sent in on hot summer evenings. When grandfather's birthday came along, he received special Chinese delicacies from his friend, the Chinese laundryman. Later, when the Chinaman decided to go back to China to be with his wife and children, and to die there, he left his address with grandfather. When my uncle traveled around the world, he visited the Chinese family, and was royally entertained by the son of the old Chinese laundryman.

Obviously, some people in the community are more or less open-minded because of religious, humanitarian, and cultural interest. These people may not treat the Chinese as their equals and associate with them, but they do not approve of the prejudicial attitude of others toward the Chinese laundryman. They may be depended upon to defend the Chinese laundryman in case of injustice and falsehood against him.

The reaction of our family to the Chinese laundryman was undoubtedly very different from that of most people. My people were missionaries, ministers, and church deacons. The Chinaman was a poor benighted heathen to be converted and then patronized in order to encourage his clinging to the faith. An old gentleman had been a personal friend of my grandfather and we still have a beautiful teapot he gave our family.

As I grew older, and met people outside of my own immediate circle, I found others did not have the same attitude as my family. To some people the Chinaman is a symbol of Eastern vice and disease. He is someone to be avoided and dreaded. When I was in high school the perennial story about the person who got leprosy from binding an open wound with a handkerchief washed at a Chinese laundry was being circulated, and grew to such proportions that a newspaper article was printed to deny the rumor and to show the falsity and absurdity of it. But undoubtedly the Chinese laundryman had a miserable time because of it. Credibility was lent this tale because of the old habit of the laundryman of spitting water through a tube held in the mouth in order to sprinkle the shirts they were ironing. This has always been a matter of great curiosity to me. I imagine they did this because it sprinkles lightly and evenly, making the shirt easier to iron.

The only Chinese laundryman I knew in my youth was an old man with a wife one rarely saw and a handsome son who was the reason for my taking the laundry over and calling for it so cheerfully. Now I notice most of the laundries seem to be cooperative affairs, with from one to ten Chinese working in them. My family also gave considerable praise to these workers for their unflagging industry.

Despite families such as mine who did not actively disapprove of the Chinese laundryman, his social position was and is a desperately lonely one. We did not associate with him, we merely kept from criticizing him. Also, his social status is such that he is way below the other Chinese in the community who are scholars and antique dealers and restaurant owners. Then, because the West looks down on the East, he is classed far below any white man, no matter in how menial a position the white finds himself. However, it should be remembered that, personally, the Chinaman looks down on Western civilization as crude and uncultured and backward, which must give even the laundryman a mental feeling of superiority.

Church people, especially those who conduct Sunday School classes for Chinese, tend to have closer contact with some Chinese laundrymen. Those who attend Sunday School are young men with a different outlook from the older Chinese. They find it a means of getting acquainted with Americans, especially women. Sunday School attendants are very self-conscious. Some try very hard to please their teachers. Through Sunday School contacts, the teacher and pupil may become friends.

After having inquired from several people about Chinese laundrymen I came to the conclusion that they were trying very ambitiously to adapt themselves to our American way of living. They seem to be a rather conservative group of men, satisfied with the work they are doing and spending long hours at their work, always aiming to do their best. They are anxious to better their understanding of the English language. They can read and write English but they are not satisfied to stop at that. They are loyal to their own country as well as being good citizens of the United States. They are well posted on the wars, both the European and the Chinese wars.

One woman I spoke to said, "You'd be surprised, they're smart." Their leisure time is spent quite wholesomely—going to church on Sunday and visiting their relatives in Chinatown. They also go to the movies. They are well-behaved and dress very well when they go out. This woman also remarked that they buy the best brands of foods. I don't know how characteristic this would be of all Chinese laundrymen. She also said that when they go out they take a cab. I certainly take an attitude of tolerance towards them as they are doing their part to make the United States an American nation and not one in which each nationality is trying to retain all of its customs and traditions.

On the contrary, preoccupied with the conventional stereotype, some people in certain lower social strata may ridicule the Chinese laundryman. A good example of this type of people may be taken from a conversation between a clerk in a low-class hotel and an alcoholic roomer.

HOTEL CLERK: "I don't use their laundries, no more, after they tore up a couple of shirts on me. You can't argue with the bastards; they don't talk English. They know what money is; they can count better than Americans. They save every cent. They eat nothing but rice. If I done that, I'd be a millionaire. Over in China, they fight among themselves, a civil war, and they've always been fighting the Russians. But they aren't civilized, that's why they can't fight. A good modern army could clean out the whole country. I was reading in the paper, where the people over there consider a dog the best kind of meat. Ha, ha, not hot dogs either. I guess they cook it with rice— I'm glad I'm in this country."

ROOMER (JIM S., NICKNAMED DEMENTIA PRAECOX): "Ha, ha, I had a bottle on me and asked the Chink in the laundry if he wanted a drink—he's crazy, he just laughed like hell, said, 'Me no drinkee.' So I said, 'You want the pipe, you know, smoke the pipe like this [demonstrating].' He was too dumb to understand me. They are dopey as hell. They don't know what country they are in. I hear the white hustlers go for them, because they pay off. I know a hustler around the Grove that takes them. A guy told me, and he believed it, that Chinese run sideways, ha, ha. I don't tell them from Japs; they all look alike to me."

The merit of the documents just presented is that they represent the difference of opinion among types of people in America. None of them can be taken as true or false. Some laundrymen are progressive, and some are conservative. The impressions that people have of them obviously would be on a purely personal basis. A statement by a student of sociology reflects, however, a consensus of opinion about the Chinese laundryman.

> The Chinese behavior, on the whole, is very much like ours. Non-association would be the better word to use in this case. The Chinese simply do not associate with major groups, mostly because the set of prejudices and traditions of the white people keep them apart. Americans are inclined to think them inferior, as they think any alien is inferior who has a low standard of living. The Chinaman is the same as any immigrant that comes over, the difference being that the Italian immigrant is given the chance to assimilate where the Chinaman is not, being of Mongoloid stock. Hence, we find a clannishness among the Chinese and any case of intermarriage is very rare.

4. The Place of the Chinese Laundryman

What people generally think of the Chinese laundryman presents a clear picture: he has not much of a chance in this country. As he is not treated fairly, the causes of his isolation and nonassimilation are obviously not entirely his own choice. It will be shown in later chapters that Chinese take up laundry work as a means of survival in a strange land—a job they care to do only temporarily. Like any other human being they, too, have desires not merely to get rich but to enjoy a social status that commands respect and dignity. Naturally if the Chinese laundryman does not see any chance of getting such satisfaction in this country, he would tie this hope to his native land, and become a sojourner.

The humanitarian conscience of some Americans may be troubled, for sooner or later the high ideals of this democracy have to be lived up to.

But the present temper of the majority seems not quite ready to give the Chinaman a "break." According to the following statements, he should stay in his place or there would be trouble:

> If he didn't live in the back of his shop, it is certain that he didn't live in the neighborhood. . . .
>
> It has been interesting, to me at least, to speculate as to what response he would have met had he chosen to enter some other field of endeavor in that neighborhood. He might successfully have operated a catering service (Chinese food, of course), a curio shop, but what if he had chosen to operate a dress shop or a drug store? My guess is that the establishment would have folded up within a few months, if not sooner. His white customers were prepared to patronize him as a laundryman because as such his status was low and constituted no real competitive threat. If you stop to think about it, there's a very real difference between the person who washes your soiled clothing and the one who fills your prescription. As a laundryman he occupied a status which was in accordance with the social definition of the place in the economic hierarchy suitable for a member of an "inferior race." As a druggist, the situation would have been something else again. Furthermore, what would have happened had he, through his occupation, become wealthy? In a country that has long had the tradition of the possibility that any one of us may achieve financial success, the situation might have been accepted. Certain it is that the public conception of him was one of hard work and frugal living, and it was generally believed that had money hoarded away in an old sock or a tin can. But if his presumed wealth had taken an ostentatious turn, the reaction of the whites would hardly have been pleasant.
>
> As to his religion, the neighborhood was not at all concerned. . . . Whether he burned incense before a figure of Buddha or a candle before an icon made little difference. But if he had married a white woman, to say that scandal would have ensued would be an over-simplification of the fact.

As long as the Chinese laundryman is satisfied to accept his inferior position, trouble can be averted as illustrated by the following comments:

> My opinion of him is quite natural as long as he remains only a laundryman. . . .

> The attitude seems to be, in my group, that he is all right as long as he stays in his place and does not try to do too much. . . .

> One thing I like about them is that they keep their place and don't try to mix with the white people.

One very common rationalization on his place is the following:

> The Chinks are all right if they remain in their place. I don't mind their
> working in the laundry business, but they should not go any higher than
> that. After all, there aren't even enough jobs for us whites, without them
> butting in. Besides, we could never compete with them. They naturally work
> harder than us, and for much less pay.

The worry that the Chinese laundryman would work for a higher social
status in the American community is not real; the actual situation is that
there is no such possibility. In general, his capacity for social and economic advancement is limited. Only occasionally did some younger and
more ambitious person leave the laundry and take a "better" job. The
laundry as an economic institution which has a century-old history will
be described in full detail later. But the Chinese laundryman, in his present
mentality, seems to realize that his chance for a livelihood is with the
laundry.

CHAPTER III

GROWTH AND DISTRIBUTION
OF THE
CHINESE LAUNDRY IN CHICAGO

THE CHINESE LAUNDRYMAN, as Americans see him, is not a person, but a thing. He, however, definitely performs an economic function in the urban way of life, and people are "glad to have him, so long as he stays a laundryman." It is not a recognition of the person, but the need of the individual who does a job which occupies a place in the symbiotic level of community life. The laundryman and the laundry seem to be identical.

The symbiotic function of the Chinese laundry in Chicago may clearly be seen in its relationship to the general patterns of the growth of the city. This ecological aspect of the Chinese laundry throws some light on the role the laundryman has played in the growth of Metropolitan Chicago.

1. The First and the Pioneer Chinese Laundry

In 1872, one year after the Great Chicago Fire, when the city grew from a commercial town to an industrial center in the Middle West, the first Chinese laundry to open its door for business was located at the rear of 167 West Madison Street.[1] It had no name. As it was probably the only Chinese laundry in town, perhaps no other name could have been more appropriate than just "Chinese Laundry." But the "Chinese Laundry" disappeared in 1873. Was it omitted from the record, or had the Chinese laundryman failed to make his enterprise successful? No one knows. A year thereafter, in 1874, there were eighteen Chinese laundries in Chicago.

This sudden reappearance of the Chinese laundry marked the beginning of the pioneer period. From 1874 to 1879, the next five-year interval, the growth of the Chinese laundry was slow, and there was no distinguishing change in its spatial distribution. This period, therefore, may be considered as a pioneer period. The largest concentration of laundries was along Madison, Clark, State, and Randolph Streets. At that time, the business center was not on State Street, but on Lake Street. The distribution of the Chinese laundries was then really at the periphery of the Loop at that time. This pattern is exactly the position it takes in any "satellite city" and suburban town. In fact, this is the typical pattern of its growth in the city.

But its high concentration around the business center in this period was something amazing and unusual. It means the city as a whole was undergoing some tremendous changes. Analyzing carefully the name and address of each of these laundries during the pioneer period, we find they tended to segregate along only a few of the streets in the present Loop, as shown in Table 3.1.

The concentration of the Chinese laundry in this period was around the location where we now have the high skyscrapers and busiest business thoroughfares. Nearly all of the Chinese laundries were located in the present Loop, especially South Clark Street where the first Chinatown was soon to appear. The few scattered outside of the Loop were found not farther away than Kinzie Street on the north, Halsted Street on the west, and Twenty-second Street on the south. Distribution by community is shown in Table 3.2.

If we look at the numbers and spatial distribution of the Chinese laundry in this period, it had not changed much; but if we inquire into the situation, by checking each individual laundry, and seeing how many of them remained, how many of them failed, and how many of them were newly established during each of the fiscal years, we then have a picture of tremendous movement and change. For example, we have 18 laundries for the fiscal year 1874–1875, and for 1875–1876, one year later, the number increased to 27, 11 of which remained from the previous year. Sixteen new ones had been established, and 7 of the old ones had failed. This pattern of mobility was especially noticeable in this period and for one or two decades following it, because the city at that time became sort of a boom town after the Great Fire. On the whole, however, those which survived were of higher percentage than those which failed,[2] and the num-

TABLE 3.1
Distribution of Chinese Laundries in Chicago
(1874–1880)

Street	1874–75	1875–76	1876–77	1877–78	1878–79	1879–80
Madison	3	6	5	6	3	7
Clark	3	5	10	10	6	12
State	3	3	4	5	7	4
Randolph	2	4	2	4	0	3
Washington	1	1	0	0	0	1
Wabash	1	1	0	0	0	1
Adams	1	0	0	0	0	0
Harrison	1	0	0	0	1	0
Desplaines	1	0	0	0	0	0
Halsted	1	1	1	2	1	1
22nd	1	2	2	2	1	1
Lake	0	1	1	1	2	2
12th	0	1	0	0	0	0
Cottage Grove	0	1	1	1	1	1
Kinzie	0	1	1	0	1	1
Wells (5th Ave.)	0	0	1	1	1	1
Canal	0	0	0	0	1	1
Van Buren	0	0	0	0	0	0
Milwaukee	0	0	0	0	0	1
TOTAL	18	27	28	32	25	37

TABLE 3.2
Distribution of Chinese Laundries by Communities
in the Pioneer Period
(1874–1879)

Community	1874	1875	1876	1877	1878	1879
Loop	15	21	23	28	21	31
Near South	1	3	3	3	2	2
Near West	2	2	1	1	1	3
Near North	0	1	1	0	1	1
TOTAL	18	27	28	32	25	37

ber of new laundries was highest. The comparative average is 13.6, 12.6, and 16.4, as shown in Table 3.3.

It is clear that on the average nearly half of the Chinese laundries failed each year, while more than that many new ones were founded at the same time. This means a slow but steady increase in spite of the high pressure of competition among themselves and probably with laundries operated by Americans also.

TABLE 3.3
Comparison of Success and Failure of
Chinese Laundries
(1874–1880)

Year	Total Number of Laundries	Number of Previous Year's Laundries Remaining	Number of Previous Year's Laundries Which Failed	Number of New Laundries in the Fiscal Year
1874–75	18	—	—	—
1875–76	27	11	7	16
1876–77	28	18	9	10
1877–78	32	19	10	13
1878–79	25	7	25	18
1879–80	37	13	12	25
Average	27.8	13.6	12.6	16.4

It was at this time that the fellow countryman of the Chinese laundry-man came in increasing numbers, and most of them sought to make a living in the same occupation. And while the city was expanding, so was the Chinese laundry enterprise.

2. The Chinese Laundry in the Process of Expansion

The expansion began in 1880. During the fiscal year of 1880–1881, the number of Chinese laundries in Chicago was 67; the next year it increased to 97; and a year afterward it was 165. This remarkable increase marks the beginning of an era of expansion. The pattern of the movement seems to be a stretching out from the center of the city toward its periphery. This tendency is shown distinctly by comparing Map. 3.1 with Map. 3.2. There we see the tremendous increase in the number of Chinese laundries in the center of the city, as indicated on Map 3.2, while increases are also found in different communities surrounding the Loop. In 1883, the total number of Chinese laundries was 199. Chinese laundries could be found in almost every neighborhood. So, besides a high concentration in the present Loop community, Chinese laundries were found along Milwaukee and Grand avenues to the north, along Halsted Street and Blue Island Avenue to the west, and along Archer Avenue to the south. The majority of them, however, were still segregated around Clark, State, and Madison streets in the present Loop. Halsted Street on the West Side was getting ahead of Randolph Street downtown.

During the next decade, from 1883 to 1893, Chicago emerged as an industrial city, to become a metropolis. The Chinese laundry also entered upon a new phase of life. Its numerical increase was from 199 in 1883 to 313 in 1893. The most spectacular change in distribution is that the number of laundries which formerly were located in the present Loop was greatly reduced, while those in the communities immediately around the Loop tended to increase. The direction of expansion in this period, generally speaking, was like that of the last decade, the increase was most marked on the West and North sides. On the South Side, although the increase was not so great, yet the movement had stretched much farther south and extended as far as Englewood and other South Chicago communities. To the north, the Chinese laundry had already invaded the Uptown community, and to the west, it was found as far as Austin.

Disregarding the expansion of Chinese laundries into new neighborhoods, and their increase in numbers in the period from 1883 to 1893, the general distribution had only slightly changed. The main streets where Chinese laundries were segregated were still Clark, State, Madison, and so on, as shown in Table 3.4.

Clark Street was still in the lead in number of Chinese laundries, in spite of its decline from 12.6 in 1883 to 6.8 percent in 1893. On State Street, they had increased in number but declined in percentage for the same period. On Madison and Randolph Streets, there was a decrease in both numbers and percentages. These were the four main streets along which the Chinese laundry first originated in its pioneer period, and grew into great concentration during the next decade; and in spite of the outward movement, the center of the Chinese laundry enterprise was recognizably maintained along these streets. New streets in the present downtown area which the Chinese laundry invaded were Van Buren, Wells, Lake, and Wabash. On the West Side, on Canal, Blue Island, Desplaines, and Ashland, there were new developments. Those laundries previously on Canal and Blue Island disappeared in 1893; while Desplaines and Ashland, on which there had been no laundries, each now had five. Of course, the most significant development on the West Side was Halsted Street. In the vicinity around Halsted and Madison Streets, there was a segregation of Chinese laundries. It was probably the time when this area first developed into some sort of "satellite city." On the Northwest Side,

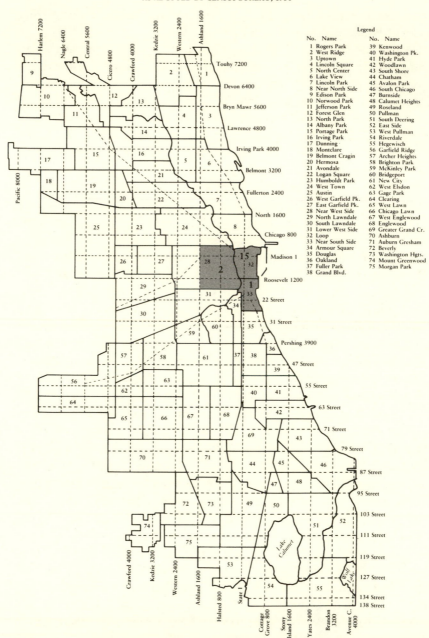

COMMUNITY AREAS OF CHICAGO
AS ADOPTED BY CENSUS BUREAU, 1930

Legend

No.	Name	No.	Name
1	Rogers Park	39	Kenwood
2	West Ridge	40	Washington Pk.
3	Uptown	41	Hyde Park
4	Lincoln Square	42	Woodlawn
5	North Center	43	South Shore
6	Lake View	44	Chatham
7	Lincoln Park	45	Avalon Park
8	Near North Side	46	South Chicago
9	Edison Park	47	Burnside
10	Norwood Park	48	Calumet Heights
11	Jefferson Park	49	Roseland
12	Forest Glen	50	Pullman
13	North Park	51	South Deering
14	Albany Park	52	East Side
15	Portage Park	53	West Pullman
16	Irving Park	54	Riverdale
17	Dunning	55	Hegewisch
18	Montclare	56	Garfield Ridge
19	Belmont Cragin	57	Archer Heights
20	Hermosa	58	Brighton Park
21	Avondale	59	McKinley Park
22	Logan Square	60	Bridgeport
23	Humboldt Park	61	New City
24	West Town	62	West Elsdon
25	Austin	63	Gage Park
26	West Garfield Pk.	64	Clearing
27	East Garfield Pk.	65	West Lawn
28	Near West Side	66	Chicago Lawn
29	North Lawndale	67	West Englewood
30	South Lawndale	68	Englewood
31	Lower West Side	69	Greater Grand Cr.
32	Loop	70	Ashburn
33	Near South Side	71	Auburn Gresham
34	Armour Square	72	Beverly
35	Douglas	73	Washington Hgts.
36	Oakland	74	Mount Greenwood
37	Fuller Park	75	Morgan Park
38	Grand Blvd.		

MAP 3.1   Distribution of Chinese laundries in 1874.

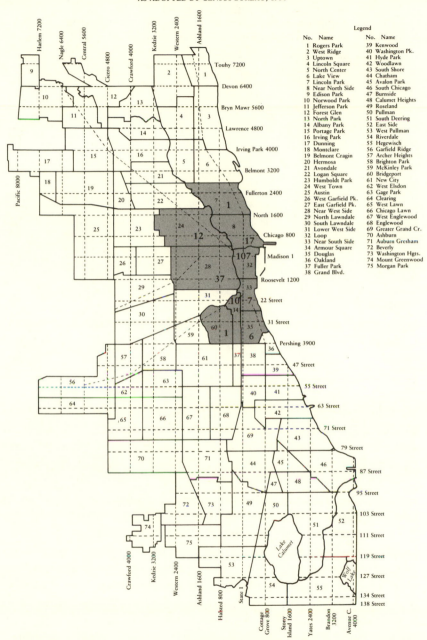

COMMUNITY AREAS OF CHICAGO
AS ADOPTED BY CENSUS BUREAU, 1930

Harlem 7200
Nagle 6400
Central 5600
Cicero 4800
Crawford 4000
Kedzie 3200
Western 2400
Ashland 1600

Touhy 7200
Devon 6400
Bryn Mawr 5600
Lawrence 4800
Irving Park 4000
Belmont 3200
Fullerton 2400
North 1600
Chicago 800
Madison 1
Roosevelt 1200
22 Street
31 Street
Pershing 3900
47 Street
55 Street
63 Street
71 Street
79 Street
87 Street
95 Street
103 Street
111 Street
119 Street
127 Street
134 Street
138 Street

Pacific 8000

Lake Calumet
Wolf Lake

Crawford 4000
Kedzie 3200
Western 2400
Ashland 1600
Halsted 800
State 1
Cottage Grove 800
Stony Island 1600
Yates 2400
Brandon 3200
Avenue C. 4000

Legend

No.	Name	No.	Name
1	Rogers Park	39	Kenwood
2	West Ridge	40	Washington Pk.
3	Uptown	41	Hyde Park
4	Lincoln Square	42	Woodlawn
5	North Center	43	South Shore
6	Lake View	44	Chatham
7	Lincoln Park	45	Avalon Park
8	Near North Side	46	South Chicago
9	Edison Park	47	Burnside
10	Norwood Park	48	Calumet Heights
11	Jefferson Park	49	Roseland
12	Forest Glen	50	Pullman
13	North Park	51	South Deering
14	Albany Park	52	East Side
15	Portage Park	53	West Pullman
16	Irving Park	54	Riverdale
17	Dunning	55	Hegewisch
18	Montclare	56	Garfield Ridge
19	Belmont Cragin	57	Archer Heights
20	Hermosa	58	Brighton Park
21	Avondale	59	McKinley Park
22	Logan Square	60	Bridgeport
23	Humboldt Park	61	New City
24	West Town	62	West Elsdon
25	Austin	63	Gage Park
26	West Garfield Pk.	64	Clearing
27	East Garfield Pk.	65	West Lawn
28	Near West Side	66	Chicago Lawn
29	North Lawndale	67	West Englewood
30	South Lawndale	68	Englewood
31	Lower West Side	69	Greater Grand Cr.
32	Loop	70	Ashburn
33	Near South Side	71	Auburn Gresham
34	Armour Square	72	Beverly
35	Douglas	73	Washington Hgts.
36	Oakland	74	Mount Greenwood
37	Fuller Park	75	Morgan Park
38	Grand Blvd.		

MAP 3.2   Distribution of Chinese laundries in 1883.

TABLE 3.4
Comparison of Main Streets Where Four or More
Chinese Laundries Were Located
(1883–1893)

Street	1883		1893	
	Number	*Per cent*	*Number*	*Per cent*
Clark	25	12.6	22	6.8
State	22	11.1	27	8.4
Madison	19	9.6	15	4.6
Halsted	13	6.5	20	6.2
Randolph	12	6.0	6	1.8
Milwaukee	12	6.0	16	5.0
Van Buren	10	5.0	11	3.4
Wells	8	4.0	7	2.1
Archer	6	3.0	14	4.3
Canal	6	3.0	—	—
Blue Island	5	2.5	—	—
Lake	5	2.5	7	2.1
Grand	4	2.0	—	—
Chicago	—	—	11	3.4
Cottage Grove	—	—	7	2.1
Division	—	—	7	2.1
Wabash	—	—	6	1.8
Desplaines	—	—	5	1.5
Ashland	—	—	5	1.5
Wentworth	—	—	4	1.2

Milwaukee Avenue, like Halsted Street, was quite a spot for the segregation of Chinese laundries. Four laundries which formerly appeared along Grand Avenue were no longer in existence by 1893, while along Chicago Avenue and Division Street the Chinese laundries gained new favor. On the South Side, there was an increase both in numbers and in percentage in favor of Archer Avenue, while new places were found along Cottage Grove and Wentworth avenues in 1893.

The outward expanding movement continued; by 1903 only 16 Chinese laundries remained in the Loop, while the total number dropped from 313 in 1893 to 209 in 1903. Numerically it was about a 35 percent decrease. But the interesting change in this decade is the greater expansion toward the periphery of the city, especially a marked southward movement as indicated on Map 3.4 in comparison with Map 3.3.

The Chinese laundry during this period was in the process of change from centralization to decentralization. Such a phenomenon, of course, reflects a new era in the economic and social life of the city as a whole. It was probably the time of new developments on the near South Side, especially along the lake front. The number of laundries increased along Sixty-third Street and Cottage Grove Avenue, and along Halsted Street and Wentworth Avenue. They also appeared in Englewood and its neighboring communities.

Chicago was not a full-grown metropolis until a decade later. In 1913 one spectacular change was the disappearance of Chinese laundries entirely from the Loop. Another marked showing was that they seemed to be most evenly expanded and distributed in every direction, west and north as well as south. In 1912 there were only 300 Chinese laundries in Chicago, but in the very next year, 1913, the number increased to 368, and the next year to 416. This increase marked the beginning of new developments on the far North Side. Chinese laundries then appeared along Broadway in the Uptown and Rogers Park regions. Parallel to Broadway, Chinese laundries stretched farther north into the same areas. There was 1 laundry in Uptown in 1903, but in 1913 the number had increased to 8. There was no laundry in the Rogers Park community in 1903, but in 1913, 3 are listed. There was only 1 laundry in Lake View community in 1903, but in 1913 there were 10.

Another interesting development in 1913 was found in the far west regions, such as South Lawndale, North Lawndale, East Garfield Park, West Garfield Park, and Humboldt Park. In the last decade only 4 laundries were found in this vicinity, but in 1913 there were 41. Farther west in Austin, there were 2 laundries in 1893, 4 in 1903, but the number had increased to 11 in 1913.

On the South Side of the city, the most interesting spot was Englewood: 13 Chinese laundries were there in 1893, 15 in 1903, and 37 in 1913. Other new areas which developed were the Woodlawn and South Shore communities: in 1903 there were no Chinese laundries in Woodlawn and only one in South Shore, but in 1913 their numbers were 18 and 9, in the Woodlawn and South Shore communities, respectively. There was no increase nor decrease in the Washington Park and Hyde Park communities. Both of them had 7 laundries in the last decade, and the number was the same in this decade. Douglas and Oakland showed a tendency to decrease rather than to increase.

Within the next decade, from 1913 to 1923, numerically the Chinese laundries rose to a new height, from 368 in 1913 to 523 in 1918; but

COMMUNITY AREAS OF CHICAGO
AS ADOPTED BY CENSUS BUREAU, 1930

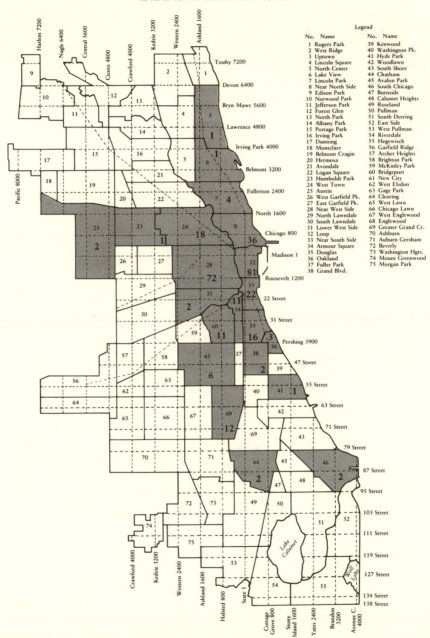

Legend

No.	Name	No.	Name
1	Rogers Park	39	Kenwood
2	West Ridge	40	Washington Pk.
3	Uptown	41	Hyde Park
4	Lincoln Square	42	Woodlawn
5	North Center	43	South Shore
6	Lake View	44	Chatham
7	Lincoln Park	45	Avalon Park
8	Near North Side	46	South Chicago
9	Edison Park	47	Burnside
10	Norwood Park	48	Calumet Heights
11	Jefferson Park	49	Roseland
12	Forest Glen	50	Pullman
13	North Park	51	South Deering
14	Albany Park	52	East Side
15	Portage Park	53	West Pullman
16	Irving Park	54	Riverdale
17	Dunning	55	Hegewisch
18	Montclare	56	Garfield Ridge
19	Belmont Cragin	57	Archer Heights
20	Hermosa	58	Brighton Park
21	Avondale	59	McKinley Park
22	Logan Square	60	Bridgeport
23	Humboldt Park	61	New City
24	West Town	62	West Elsdon
25	Austin	63	Gage Park
26	West Garfield Pk.	64	Clearing
27	East Garfield Pk.	65	West Lawn
28	Near West Side	66	Chicago Lawn
29	North Lawndale	67	West Englewood
30	South Lawndale	68	Englewood
31	Lower West Side	69	Greater Grand Cr.
32	Loop	70	Ashburn
33	Near South Side	71	Auburn Gresham
34	Armour Square	72	Beverly
35	Douglas	73	Washington Hgts.
36	Oakland	74	Mount Greenwood
37	Fuller Park	75	Morgan Park
38	Grand Blvd.		

MAP 3.3 Distribution of Chinese laundries in 1893.

COMMUNITY AREAS OF CHICAGO

AS ADOPTED BY CENSUS BUREAU, 1930

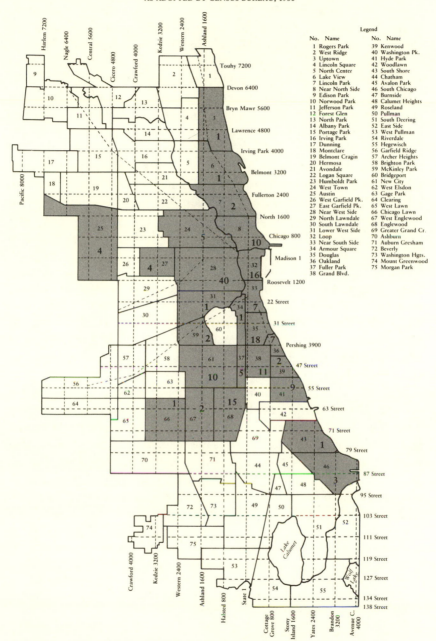

Legend

No.	Name	No.	Name
1	Rogers Park	39	Kenwood
2	West Ridge	40	Washington Pk.
3	Uptown	41	Hyde Park
4	Lincoln Square	42	Woodlawn
5	North Center	43	South Shore
6	Lake View	44	Chatham
7	Lincoln Park	45	Avalon Park
8	Near North Side	46	South Chicago
9	Edison Park	47	Burnside
10	Norwood Park	48	Calumet Heights
11	Jefferson Park	49	Roseland
12	Forest Glen	50	Pullman
13	North Park	51	South Deering
14	Albany Park	52	East Side
15	Portage Park	53	West Pullman
16	Irving Park	54	Riverdale
17	Dunning	55	Hegewisch
18	Montclare	56	Garfield Ridge
19	Belmont Cragin	57	Archer Heights
20	Hermosa	58	Brighton Park
21	Avondale	59	McKinley Park
22	Logan Square	60	Bridgeport
23	Humboldt Park	61	New City
24	West Town	62	West Elsdon
25	Austin	63	Gage Park
26	West Garfield Pk.	64	Clearing
27	East Garfield Pk.	65	West Lawn
28	Near West Side	66	Chicago Lawn
29	North Lawndale	67	West Englewood
30	South Lawndale	68	Englewood
31	Lower West Side	69	Greater Grand Cr.
32	Loop	70	Ashburn
33	Near South Side	71	Auburn Gresham
34	Armour Square	72	Beverly
35	Douglas	73	Washington Hgts.
36	Oakland	74	Mount Greenwood
37	Fuller Park	75	Morgan Park
38	Grand Blvd.		

MAP 3.4   Distribution of Chinese laundries in 1903.

they dropped back to 397 in 1923. Despite the discrepancy in numbers at the middle of the decade, the general pattern of distribution of the Chinese laundry, as Map 3.6 indicates, in 1923 seems to have maintained the trends apparent in the previous decade. The northward and westward expansion, which started in the last decade, was still in its significant increase, while the southward expansion had almost stopped and in some areas symptoms of decline could be observed.

The greatest increase was found in the Uptown community on the far North Side; there were 8 Chinese laundries in 1913, and in 1923 the number had increased to 20. There was only a slight increase in the far west communities. South Lawndale had 5 in comparison with 4 in the last decade. North Lawndale had 19 in comparison with 12. East Garfield had 12 in the last decade, but 10 remained in 1923. West Garfield had 4 in 1913, and 2 more in 1923. Humboldt Park had 6, and now 9. Austin had 11, and now 15.

On the South Side of the city, the spotlight should be once again focused on the Englewood community. It was the most significant area in expansion, having 12 laundries in 1883, 15 in 1903, and 37 in 1923; but now the number decreased to 18. Meanwhile, there were decreases also in Woodlawn and South Shore communities—from 18 to 12 in the case of Woodlawn, and from 9 to 5 in the case of South Shore. There were no other marked changes in other South Side communities.

A decade after the First World War, the numerical increase of the Chinese laundry reached the highest peak in its history; in 1928 there were 704 Chinese laundries in the city of Chicago as compared to 421 non-Chinese laundries found in the same year. See Figure 3.1. Since that period, it dropped to 476 in 1935. The numerical growth of the Chinese laundry in the past seventy years may be best illustrated in a graphic presentation such as the following:

Of its ecological growth, the process of expansion of the Chinese laundry seems to follow closely the concentric zone theory.

The typical processes of the expansion of the city can best be illustrated, perhaps, by a series of concentric circles, which may be numbered to designate both the successive zones of urban extension and the types of areas differentiated in the process of expansion.

This chart represents an ideal construction of the tendencies of any town or city to expand radially from its central business district—on the map "The Loop" (I) [Siu has defined Zone I in Map 3.1]. Encircling the down-

COMMUNITY AREAS OF CHICAGO
AS ADOPTED BY CENSUS BUREAU, 1930

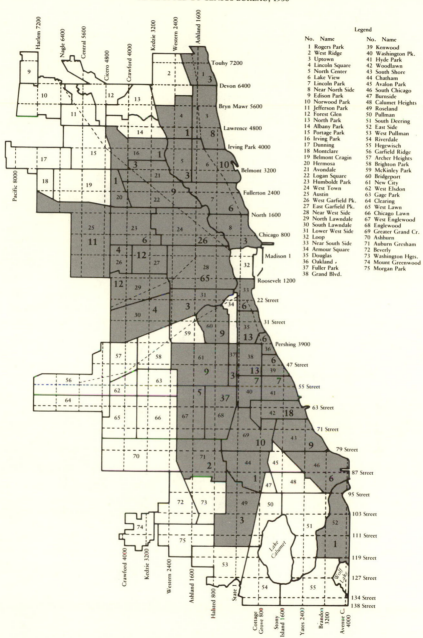

Legend

No.	Name	No.	Name
1	Rogers Park	39	Kenwood
2	West Ridge	40	Washington Pk.
3	Uptown	41	Hyde Park
4	Lincoln Square	42	Woodlawn
5	North Center	43	South Shore
6	Lake View	44	Chatham
7	Lincoln Park	45	Avalon Park
8	Near North Side	46	South Chicago
9	Edison Park	47	Burnside
10	Norwood Park	48	Calumet Heights
11	Jefferson Park	49	Roseland
12	Forest Glen	50	Pullman
13	North Park	51	South Deering
14	Albany Park	52	East Side
15	Portage Park	53	West Pullman
16	Irving Park	54	Riverdale
17	Dunning	55	Hegewisch
18	Montclare	56	Garfield Ridge
19	Belmont Cragin	57	Archer Heights
20	Hermosa	58	Brighton Park
21	Avondale	59	McKinley Park
22	Logan Square	60	Bridgeport
23	Humboldt Park	61	New City
24	West Town	62	West Elsdon
25	Austin	63	Gage Park
26	West Garfield Pk.	64	Clearing
27	East Garfield Pk.	65	West Lawn
28	Near West Side	66	Chicago Lawn
29	North Lawndale	67	West Englewood
30	South Lawndale	68	Englewood
31	Lower West Side	69	Greater Grand Cr.
32	Loop	70	Ashburn
33	Near South Side	71	Auburn Gresham
34	Armour Square	72	Beverly
35	Douglas	73	Washington Hgts.
36	Oakland	74	Mount Greenwood
37	Fuller Park	75	Morgan Park
38	Grand Blvd.		

MAP 3.5   Distribution of Chinese laundries in 1913.

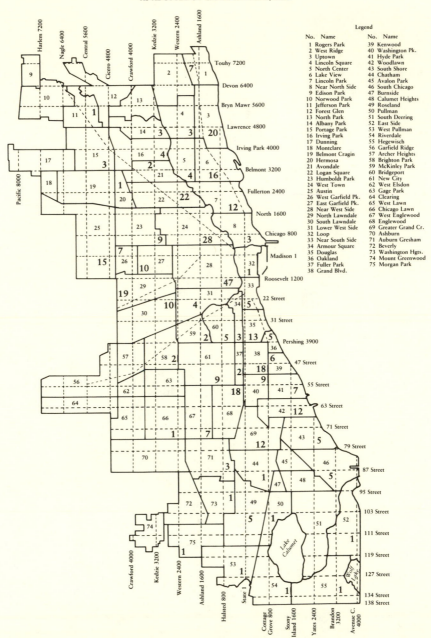

COMMUNITY AREAS OF CHICAGO
AS ADOPTED BY CENSUS BUREAU, 1930

Legend

No.	Name	No.	Name
1	Rogers Park	39	Kenwood
2	West Ridge	40	Washington Pk.
3	Uptown	41	Hyde Park
4	Lincoln Square	42	Woodlawn
5	North Center	43	South Shore
6	Lake View	44	Chatham
7	Lincoln Park	45	Avalon Park
8	Near North Side	46	South Chicago
9	Edison Park	47	Burnside
10	Norwood Park	48	Calumet Heights
11	Jefferson Park	49	Roseland
12	Forest Glen	50	Pullman
13	North Park	51	South Deering
14	Albany Park	52	East Side
15	Portage Park	53	West Pullman
16	Irving Park	54	Riverdale
17	Dunning	55	Hegewisch
18	Montclare	56	Garfield Ridge
19	Belmont Cragin	57	Archer Heights
20	Hermosa	58	Brighton Park
21	Avondale	59	McKinley Park
22	Logan Square	60	Bridgeport
23	Humboldt Park	61	New City
24	West Town	62	West Elsdon
25	Austin	63	Gage Park
26	West Garfield Pk.	64	Clearing
27	East Garfield Pk.	65	West Lawn
28	Near West Side	66	Chicago Lawn
29	North Lawndale	67	West Englewood
30	South Lawndale	68	Englewood
31	Lower West Side	69	Greater Grand Cr.
32	Loop	70	Ashburn
33	Near South Side	71	Auburn Gresham
34	Armour Square	72	Beverly
35	Douglas	73	Washington Hgts.
36	Oakland	74	Mount Greenwood
37	Fuller Park	75	Morgan Park
38	Grand Blvd.		

MAP 3.6   Distribution of Chinese laundries in 1923.

FIGURE 3.1 Number of Chinese laundries in Chicago at five–year intervals (1873–1938).

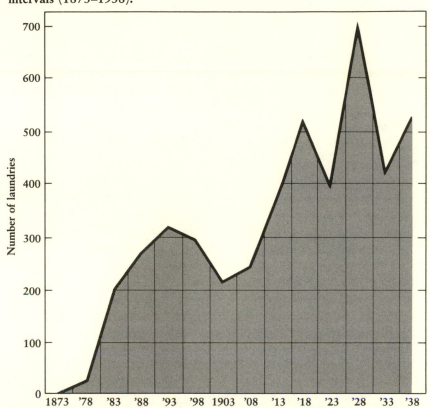

SOURCE: From 1878 to 1918, data compiled from the Lakeside City Directory of Chicago; for 1923 and 1928, from Polk's Chicago City Directory; for 1933 and 1938, estimated by the author based [ed. note: both directories were standard sources of information during this period] on data obtained from Chung Wah Association for 1935 and 1940.

town area there is normally an area in transition, which is being invaded by business and light manufacture (II) [corresponds to Map 3.2]. A third area (III) [see Siu's Map 3.3] is inhabited by the workers in industries who have escaped from the area of deterioration (II) [see Map 3.2], but who desire to live within easy access of their work. Beyond this zone is the "residential area" (IV) [Siu's Map 3.4] of high-class apartment buildings or of exclu: .e "restricted" districts of single family dwellings. Still farther, out beyond the city limits, is the commuters' zone—suburban areas, or satellite cities—within a thirty- to sixty-minute ride of the central business district.

If this chart is applied to Chicago, all four of these zones were in its early history included in the circumference of the inner zone, the present business district. The present boundaries of the area of deterioration were not many years ago those of the zone now inhabited by independent wage-earners, and within the memories of thousands of Chicagoans contained the residences of the "best families."[3]

The Chinese laundry started in the present Loop area in the latter part of the seventies, and it grew during the next decade into an enormous concentration within that same area; meanwhile it began to invade Zone II (see Table 3.5). About 1893, the center of its concentration shifted from Zone I to Zone II, while a number of Chinese laundries began to appear in Zones III and IV. During the first decade of the 'eighties, as shown in Map 3.5, while Zone I had no more Chinese laundries, Zone II was still maintaining its concentrated position, Zones III and IV, nevertheless, were already invaded by Chinese laundries in large numbers.

Chicago was a full-grown metropolis at the early part of the nineteenth century. In 1913, there were no more Chinese laundries in the downtown area, the Loop (Zone I), while the percentages of distribution were 34.1, 29.0, 32.3, and 4.6 in Zones II, III, IV, and V, respectively. It is obvious that the city in itself was expanding toward its periphery, creating some sort of vacancy within the inner zone of the city. "Better people" [more affluent] sought better residential areas in the outer zones. Responding to such a condition, the Chinese laundry expanded farther outward. In 1923,

TABLE 3.5
Expansion of Chinese Laundries between 1874 and 1935

Year	Zone I		Zone II		Zone III		Zone IV		Zone V	
	Number	Per cent	Number	Per cent	Number	Per cent	Number	Per cent	Number	Per cent
1874	15	83.3	3	6.7	—	—	—	—	—	—
1883	107	54.6	88	44.8	1	0.5	—	—	—	—
1893	81	26.4	192	63.0	13	4.2	20	6.5	—	—
1903	16	8.0	87	43.7	42	21.1	45	22.6	9	4.5
1913	—	—	126	34.1	107	29.0	118	32.3	17	4.6
1923	1	0.3	112	28.2	137	34.5	126	31.7	21	5.3
1935	—	—	89	18.3	172	35.6	201	41.4	23	4.7

NOTE: Data for the first five years are compiled from Lakeside City Directory of Chicago; for 1923, from Polk's Chicago City Directory; for 1935, from names and addresses obtained from Chung Wah Association [ed. note: better known as the Chinese Consolidated Benevolent Association, or C.C.B.A.], Chinatown, Chicago. With the exceptions of 1874, 1923, and 1935, numbers and percentages given are not compiled from the actual number of laundries of the year, on account of the change of names of some of the old streets. Year and number of the unplotted laundries are as follows: 1883, real total, 199, 3 unplotted; 1893, 313, 8 unplotted; 1903, 209, 10 unplotted; 1913, 396, 28 unplotted.

Zones III and IV had higher percentages of Chinese laundries than Zone II; the ratio is 28.2, 34.5, and 31.7; the radial distribution is getting higher toward the outer zones. Expanding radially as such is clearer in the figures given for 1935—only 18.3 percent of the Chinese laundries are found in Zone II while 35.6 percent are in Zone III and 41.4 percent in Zone IV. The concentration was then greater and greater toward the outer zones. Of course, numbers for Zone V, the commuters' zone, could not be high because here again it is a sort of transition between the metropolis and its suburbs. The Chinese laundry then tends to cross the city boundaries and invade the suburban areas. In fact, the municipal boundaries of the city are quite unimportant, as is shown in the case of the expansion of the Chinese laundry. In many instances, the laundries stretched out as if unaware of the city boundaries (see Map. 3.6). In Oak Park, Cicero, Berwyn, and Evanston, many Chinese laundries are obviously cases of such a character. On the far South Side of the city where some of the heavy industries are located, there is a typical commuter zone within which only a few Chinese laundries can maintain themselves.

3. Present Distribution of Chinese Laundries

Since the city itself has ceased to grow with its former impetus, the distribution of the Chinese laundry today is not very much different from one or two decades ago; there are now 591 (1942) Chinese laundries in Chicago, besides those in the suburbs (see Map 3.7). From 1935 to 1940, the numerical increase was about 19 percent. The distribution of Chinese laundries in the city's suburbs is given in Table 3.6.

Like other business enterprises, whether the Chinese laundry can maintain its sustenance is closely related to changes in the social and economic conditions of the city as a whole. After the First World War, the intense competition of increasing numbers of non-Chinese laundries and the growth of the steam laundry began to make itself felt in the Chinese laundry's struggle for existence. As a result, the Chinese laundry adopted modern machinery. At the present time one can hardly find a Chinese laundry without a steam boiler, a mangle, a water swing, and a wash machine. Most of them give mending service free of charge, and some run a call-and-deliver service with an automobile. The price charged by the

COMMUNITY AREAS OF CHICAGO

AS ADOPTED BY CENSUS BUREAU, 1930

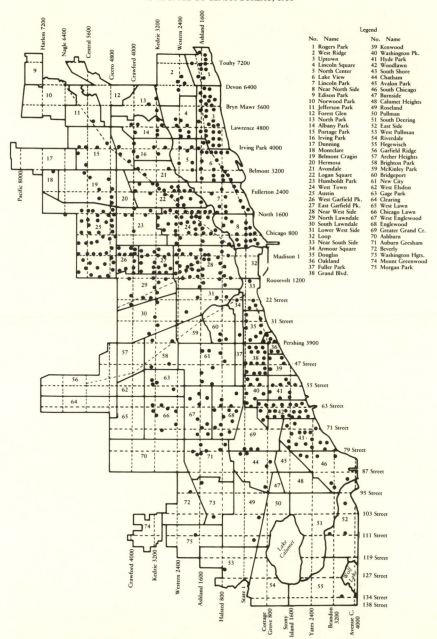

Legend

No.	Name	No.	Name
1	Rogers Park	39	Kenwood
2	West Ridge	40	Washington Pk.
3	Uptown	41	Hyde Park
4	Lincoln Square	42	Woodlawn
5	North Center	43	South Shore
6	Lake View	44	Chatham
7	Lincoln Park	45	Avalon Park
8	Near North Side	46	South Chicago
9	Edison Park	47	Burnside
10	Norwood Park	48	Calumet Heights
11	Jefferson Park	49	Roseland
12	Forest Glen	50	Pullman
13	North Park	51	South Deering
14	Albany Park	52	East Side
15	Portage Park	53	West Pullman
16	Irving Park	54	Riverdale
17	Dunning	55	Hegewisch
18	Montclare	56	Garfield Ridge
19	Belmont Cragin	57	Archer Heights
20	Hermosa	58	Brighton Park
21	Avondale	59	McKinley Park
22	Logan Square	60	Bridgeport
23	Humboldt Park	61	New City
24	West Town	62	West Elsdon
25	Austin	63	Gage Park
26	West Garfield Pk.	64	Clearing
27	East Garfield Pk.	65	West Lawn
28	Near West Side	66	Chicago Lawn
29	North Lawndale	67	West Englewood
30	South Lawndale	68	Englewood
31	Lower West Side	69	Greater Grand Cr.
32	Loop	70	Ashburn
33	Near South Side	71	Auburn Gresham
34	Armour Square	72	Beverly
35	Douglas	73	Washington Hgts.
36	Oakland	74	Mount Greenwood
37	Fuller Park	75	Morgan Park
38	Grand Blvd.		

MAP 3.7   Distribution of Chinese laundries in 1940.

TABLE 3.6

Oak Park	19
Evanston	13
Gary	13
Hammond	7
Maywood	5
Wilmette	4
Cicero	3
Blue Island	3
East Chicago	3
Berwyn	3
Forest Park	2
Melrose Park	2
Chicago Heights	1
La Grange	1
Glen Ellyn	1
Park Ridge	1

Chinese laundryman is usually one or two cents cheaper in comparison with the same work done by the non-Chinese laundry.

In order to make a living, the Chinese laundryman has to operate his place in a good location. The patronage is obtained not from where people work, but from where people live. Furthermore, its patronage is mostly certain kinds of people among the city's population, and in certain particular areas. In the process of its expansion, the Chinese laundry seems to move along with these kinds of people, and the dominant feature of its present distribution is exactly so. The largest concentration of Chinese laundries is in the area of apartment houses where the inhabitants are young married couples, "white-collar" office workers of the salaried class, where in many cases both husband and wife are working. The other area that draws a high concentration of Chinese laundries is the rooming-house area where people are highly mobile, with single men and women who are detached from family ties. The single-family neighborhood draws less, and the immigrant and industrial areas draw still fewer. Such a general phenomenon is clearly shown in Map 3.7. In the apartment house areas such as Rogers Park (#1), Uptown (#2), and Lake View (#6) along the North Shore; Hyde Park (#41), Woodlawn (#42), and South Shore (#43) along the South Shore; and West Garfield Park (#26), and East Garfield Park (#27) along Jackson and Washington Boulevards, we see the densest location of Chinese laundries. In the rooming-house areas such as the near North Side and near West Side, we have also a large concentration of Chinese laundries, especially along North Clark Street and West Van Buren Street.

In contrast with the apartment house areas and rooming-house areas, there are only a few Chinese laundries in the immigrant settlement communities such as Lower West Side (#31), South Lawndale (#30), Armour Square (#34), Near West Side (part of #28), and West Town (#24), and in the region which one author described as the "slum."

The characteristic location of the Chinese laundries, viewed from another angle, is largely on lines of transportation, especially along some of the principal street car lines, or around the "satellite loops" and business districts. We can be sure of the presence of a number of Chinese laundries at Wilson and Broadway, Crawford and Madison, Halsted and Sixty-third. They are, however, usually not on the main street if the rental is too high. Most of the Chinese laundries in the vicinity of bright-light centers are located on side streets where the rental is moderate, and closer to the dwellings of its patrons. In smaller business districts, we generally find Chinese laundries located along the main streets as well as on the side streets.

Like the drug store, the grocery store, and the barber shop, the Chinese laundry appears in almost every neighborhood, in spite of its selective tendency to expand out to more promising areas, as described in the last section. In fact, some of the laundries remain in the slum, some find sustenance in the "Black Belt," and some venture out to the commuters' neighborhoods and to the suburbs. In this way, the distribution of the Chinese laundries creates a phenomenon not of numbers but of kind of laundry as located in different areas within the city. Each of these types is characteristically adapted to the nature of the local neighborhood and consequently symbolizes the character of the community life. In the areas of deterioration and poorer neighborhoods, the Chinese laundry usually tends to be a one-man laundry or operated by an old man. In such an area, a laundry sometimes is operated not as a business proposition but as "just a place to stay." As long as there is enough business to keep the man alive, he stays on. The physical feature of the Chinese laundry in such an area is likely to be one of the fenced-counter type—the counter is locked all the time and a fence is built atop of it, looking like a jail from without.[4] A doorbell is usually attached to the door as a signal of the arrival of a visitor. A visitor to a Chinese laundry of this type describes:

As one approaches a Chinese laundry he notices the lettering on the window of the shop which appears to be the work of an inexperienced printer, probably the Chinese himself. . . . As we open the door a tinkling bell informs the men in the rear of the shop that customers are present. As we gaze about the shop, we notice how dark and dismal it is. The air is heavy with moisture and rather musty, making us feel uncomfortable in a very short while. A counter which appears to have been constructed of planks and crude boards confronts us and behind the counter are several shelves with package upon package of laundry neatly stacked. Behind the shelves appears to be some lattice work to which is tacked some black cloth—the only separation between the shop and the laundry and sleeping quarters.[5]

This type of laundry sometimes appears in other areas, but the slum and the "Black Belt" seem to be its usual habitat.

In contrast to this general feature we find in the apartment house and residential areas a different type of Chinese laundry. It generally is operated by three or four men who are of younger age. There are no fenced counters within. The window is decorated by a neon sign. Some of them do not lock their counters, and the doorbell is also unnecessary. Practically no laundry of this type can be found in the slum.

NOTES

1. It is listed among eighteen other laundries of that year in Edwards's 1872 Directory of the City of Chicago [ed. note: a standard directory of that time]. It is printed in special letters: **Chinese Laundry**. Evidently its proprietor had paid the publisher to have his place advertised.

2. Except during the fiscal year 1878–1879, more than two-thirds of the old laundries failed; the number dropped from 32 to 25. No authentic reason can be given for such an unusual change except the "rebuilding boom" in the center of the city during that time. It is quite possible that some of the buildings on Madison, Clark, and Randolph Streets had to be torn down, and therefore some of the Chinese laundrymen were temporarily forced out of business.

3. E. W. Burgess, "The Growth of the City," in *The City*, ed. Robert E. Park and E. W. Burgess (Chicago: University of Chicago Press, 1925), pp. 50–51.

4. A more detailed description of the physical features of the Chinese laundry appears *infra*, Chapter 5.

5. Private survey document.

CHAPTER IV

ORIGIN OF THE CHINESE LAUNDRY

THE FIRST CHINESE LAUNDRY in Chicago was founded in 1872, but it was not, to be sure, the first in the United States. The Chinese immigrant did not become a laundryman until after his arrival in this country. How did he become a laundryman? What was the situation in which the Chinese laundry originated?

1. The Frontier—Open Labor Market

Around the middle of the last century the Pacific Coast region was the great Western frontier. Explorers and adventurers from other parts of the continent thronged there for new opportunities to become rich, principally by gold mining. Later the frontiersmen and other settlers increased in number. The community also developed some industries which were greatly in need of labor. Because the East and South were not much closer to California than the western shore of the Pacific Ocean, and because the Rocky Mountain Range constituted a barrier before the construction of the trans-continental railroad, the Chinese laborers were imported in large numbers to the West Coast by clipper ships. The only port of embarkation on the other shore was Hong Kong, and the only adventurers were Cantonese who made the initial contact with the sea captain of a clipper.

The first immigrants from China to modern California were two Chinese men and one woman, who arrived by the clipper, "Bard Eagle," in 1848. The men went to the mines and the woman remained as a servant in the family of Charles V. Gillespie, who came hither from Hong Kong. In February 1848, the number of Chinese men in California had increased to 54; and in January, 1850, to 787 men and 2 women; and in January, 1852, to

7,512 men and 8 women. By May they had increased to 11,787, of whom only 7 were women.[1]

They came to fill the need in the labor market.

> They performed the more arduous and less stimulating tasks connected with mining and farming, while the masses of the native population were speculating in gold and land. Under these conditions of mutualism the invading Chinese were not only unopposed, but were actually welcomed in the country. Their primary group traits of honesty, loyalty, and industry were extolled by the press as being distinct assets in the Pacific Coast development.[2]

This tolerance and appreciation caused the migration of Chinese laborers to increase rapidly. In San Francisco a reception was held in 1850 for the "China boys" by the leading citizens of the community. Like most social events between races, certain elements of formality and social distance were maintained. But the reception at least revealed the public opinion of the time.

> In the summer of 1850 there were about one hundred Chinese in San Francisco. The first public recognition of their presence in our city was made an occasion of general interest. . . . Arrangements were accordingly made by a committee consisting of Mr. Woodworth, Major Geary, and myself. In the afternoon of the 25th of August, 1850, their entire number assembled, and were conducted in procession, two by two, to a large platform on Portsmouth Square. In their rich national costume, not omitting the costly fan to shelter them from the sun, they were objects of marked observation. In turn, they were addressed through Ah Sing, the interpreter, by Mr. Woodworth.[3]

As labor was still an open market, Chinese immigrants were probably employed in most of the industries on the Pacific Coast. The majority of them, it seems, were in gold mining, domestic service, farming, and other personal services. On the frontier, as always, there was an unequal sex ratio of a high percentage of males to females. The lack of women in the community created the great demand for household and personal services such as laundry work, cooking, hotel and restaurant keeping. The first Chinese laundry was probably established about the middle of the last century but exactly where and when it has been impossible to authenticate as there no longer exists any record of it. There is Jones's story[4] that the first Chinese laundry was established in San Francisco. Early in the spring of 1851 one Wah Lee hung a sign over his door at Grant Avenue and Washington Street. It read: "Wash'ng and Iron'ng." Wah Lee, as it was told, was an unsuccessful gold miner turned laundryman. Where did Wah Lee learn the trade? No one knows. If he had been in a mining community, he might have had some experience with "wash'ng and iron'ng" before his return to San Francisco. It seems, however, that the Chinese laundry did not formally come into existence until the bubble of gold speculation had burst or begun to burst.

As Wah Lee was an unsuccessful gold miner, he might have been one of those ejected by the white miners. Losing his livelihood, he might have gone to San Francisco where he founded the first Chinese laundry at the heart of present-day Chinatown of that city. This evidently was his way and means of survival in facing the ill-feeling against Chinese competition in the mining towns.[5] The social and economic condition of the times in San Francisco provided an opening for this kind of personal service.

The San Francisco of the 1850s was a city where all the gold seekers from around the world congregated. There were white men and black, yellow men and brown. They swarmed into the port, tarried long enough to get themselves outfitted and stocked with provisions, and then headed as fast as they could to the gold mines and to the virgin hills where gold could be found. San Francisco had a transient population turnover of thousands every week, but no permanent settlers, or practically none.

But those that were here—the merchants, potential bankers, financiers, and gamblers—managed to have some kind of community life. Not only that, the men of San Francisco made a reputation for being the most elegant and best dressed males in these parts. In winning this social crown they were led by one John C. Calhoun, statesman and fashion arbiter of the period. The hard shirt front and the rigid collar, in pure and resplendent white, was the symbol of good taste and respectability. If the stiff shirts felt uncomfortable to some wearers at times, and the collars took on the effect of a hangman's noose, the men always sought consolation in the fact that their attire exacted the town's admiration and respect.

But it cost money for the San Franciscans to achieve such stylishness and respectability, for the laundry bills were terrific. In order to have their linen washed, starched and ironed to the right degree of whiteness and rigidity cost them eight dollars per dozen, sometimes even more. The men didn't mind paying from three to five dollars for an order of ham and eggs or a steak, but eight dollars just to scrub and iron some pieces of shirt was an excessive price. So there were grumblings aplenty. And not only that, there was also the annoyance of waiting from six to eight weeks for one's laundry to come back each time one sent it off, for mostly they were shipped to the Hawaiian Islands to be washed. And then the shirts might return with buttons missing or collars separated.

But complaint was useless. If one wants to have his linen washed in the city he could give them to the Mexican girls who toiled at the lagoon. This method, however, was sometimes disastrous, for these washerwomen bang the shirts on cobblestones, and after a few hangings there is very little shirt left.[6]

As some Chinese in that period were employed in household work, it was quite possible for them to pick up "wash'ng and iron'ng" as part of the domestic duty. Wah Lee might be the pioneer or one of the few who first started the trade simultaneously in the same region. The pioneer, however, could not monopolize it very long. In 1855, J. P. Anthony, who searched for novelties in a Chinese section in San Francisco, said that he was amused at the sign of "King Lee," which at first glance you might take for "King Lear," announcing washing at so much per dozen.[7] It is reported that Wah Lee's employees learned the technique and soon they set up their own laundry shops. Judging from the present-day pattern, the Chinese laundryman tends to hire and to join partnership with his own clansmen, so both Wah Lee and King Lee might have been members of the Lee clan.

Indeed, from Wah Lee's lone enterprise there soon sprung up a dozen other Chinese laundries throughout the city. Then fifty, then a hundred. The number of Chinese laundries, now an institution in California, increased with the growth of San Francisco as the metropolis of the West. In the next twenty-five years, over five hundred laundries dotted the city alone, not counting the hundreds that were all over California, in every town and mining and lumber camp, from Yreka to San Diego. In San Francisco alone the number of Chinese who earned their rice over the washtub and the ironing board in the 'eighties was well over 7,500. Next to chop suey, the laundry was the second greatest contribution of the Chinese to California civilization.[8]

Before 1870, the principal occupations of the Chinese immigrants were not, however, laundry and chop suey, as they are today. According to the U.S. Census Report, the Chinese were distributed in 138 occupations.[9] About 1861, after Wah Lee presumably founded his laundry enterprise, more than 50 percent of the Chinese were engaged in mining, about

20,000 out of 34,933 persons. But in 1870 the census discloses that the number of Chinese laborers in mining decreased to less than 30 percent, 17,069 out of 63,199.[10] The other occupation in which the Chinese immigrants were employed in large numbers was railroad building.

> On July 1, 1862, President Lincoln signed a bill providing for the building of two roads, one from the Missouri River westward, the Union Pacific, and one from the Pacific Coast eastward, the Central Pacific, the two to be continued till they met and formed one long line. The Central Pacific Company was organized one year before, with Charles Crocker as one of the directors. He took charge of the building of the road, and, in order to accomplish the task as soon as possible, he resorted to Chinese laborers. "They were arranged in companies moving at the word of command like drilled troops—the 'Crocker's battalion' they were called." As the demand for Chinese labor for railroad work was very great, sometimes as many as 10,000 of them were employed, and the contractors could not get enough of them in California. Consequently, they imported them directly from China.[11]

But soon the road building was completed, the Chinese laborers were dismissed, and the problem of employment arose. Still the Chinese railroad laborers did not take to laundry as their main occupation *en masse*. They turned to farming. They were, as a matter of fact, largely farmers in their native China before their adventurous trip across the ocean. Naturally hundreds returned to their homeland after their dismissal from railroad building, but those who remained found work in farming and in agricultural labor. One author reported that at one time, of the 25,000 mechanics and laborers employed by the Central Pacific Railroad Company, 15,000 were Chinese. In the 1870s and 1880s many turned to the land for a living. In 1870, 90 percent of the agricultural labor in California was Chinese; in 1880, 75 percent.[12] According to McWilliams, the Chinese had gone into the celery-growing and citrus industries in Southern California.[13] Not only railroad workers turned farmers but also the miners.

> With the increase of population, mining ceased to absorb general attention, and people turned to agriculture. Certain keen business men realized that by reclaiming the marsh land, they might reap a great profit. The work of reclamation consisted in building dikes, gates, and ditches, preventing overflow of rivers. The land that was first selected for reclamation was the

delta formed by the Sacramento and San Joaquin Rivers. White laborers could not be employed on account of malaria. At length the task was turned over to the Chinese.[14]

In San Francisco, Chinese labor was ready to do any kind of work. Some of them were employed by woolen goods manufacturers.

> The California woolen goods were then the best made in the United States, but financially it was a failure. Louis McLane, one of the most sagacious businessmen on the Coast, was induced to make a searching examination into the affair. He reported to the stockholders: "Dear labor is the obstacle to your success. Stop paying American workmen three dollars a day and substitute Chinamen at a dollar and a quarter, and then you will make money." This suggestion was quickly applied, and in 1870, out of 395 employed in the manufacture of woolens in San Francisco, 253 were Chinese.[15]

McWilliams wrote that

> Among the great cultural contributions of the Chinese in Southern California was their development of the fishing industry. For, with the exception of the Indians, they were the first fishermen in the state. During the period of 1860 to 1880, Chinese fishing villages dotted the Coast from Monterey to San Diego. Large Chinese fishing junks could be seen in the waters off the Southern California coast, with the Chinese chattering and grabbing at the fish as they bounce and dance on the deck.[16]

They developed an immense industry, and in 1870, the Chinese were exporting $1,000,000 worth of abalone annually, and a decade later their annual shipments of dried shrimp to China were valued at $3,000,000, according to McWilliams.[17]

2. Labor Agitation Against Chinese

The labor situation on the Pacific Coast, beginning with 1868, was chaotic. After the completion of the railroad, thousands of white as well as Chinese laborers were out of jobs, while a mass migration of new settlers came from the East, and in the same year the United States and China signed the Burlingame Treaty, which gave Chinese immigration a new impetus. The struggle for existence became grim and acute. White labor complained about Chinese competition. Gradually the situation provoked vehement outbreaks of antagonism. There were serious riots against Chinese in many sections of the Pacific area. Harlow wrote:

> In 1871 there was a serious riot in Los Angeles, when fifteen Chinese were hung and six shot to death. Hard times and the labor troubles of 1877 brought anti-Chinese feeling to the fore again in San Francisco, where it was fomented by the Kearneyites, and in July, 1877, several laundries in San Francisco were wrecked and a number of Chinese killed. Upon the publication of the Morey Letter a mob attacked the Chinese quarter in Denver, October 31, 1880, and did much damage before it was dispersed with fire hose.[18]

On October 24, 1871, one of the worst race riots in American history took place in the City of Los Angeles, for on that day a mob of one thousand Angelenos, armed with pistols, knives, and ropes, descended on Chinatown. "Trembling, moaning, wounded Chinese," reported the *San Francisco Bulletin*, "were hauled from their hiding places, ropes quickly encircled their necks; they were dragged to the nearest improvised gallows. A large wagon close by had four victims hanging from their sides . . . three others dangled from an awning . . . five more were taken to the gateway and lynched. . . . Looting every nook, corner, chest, trunk, and drawer in Chinatown, the mob even robbed the victims it executed . . . $7,000 was extracted from a box in a Chinese store." Stealing $40,000 in cash, the mob lynched nineteen Chinese. On the night of October 25 the heroes of the raid paraded the streets of the town, displayed their booty, and were acclaimed by the mob. As a result of a subsequent grand jury investigation, one hundred fifty men were indicted for this murderous assault, but, of these, only six were sentenced and they were soon released.[19]

"California became transformed into a battleground for determination of the issue whether the immigrant from the Orient or from the Occident should perform the manual work of the Pacific Coast," says Schlesinger. "In this connection it is suggestive that the notorious Dennis [*sic*] Kearney, arch-agitator of the sand lots against the Chinese immigrant, was himself a native of County Cork. The victory ultimately fell to the European immigrant and his American offspring."[20]

This resulted in a great change in Chinese occupational selection and distribution. They attempted to escape from persecution and exploitation, seeking refuge in the area where the population was less antagonistic, and adopting occupations which white labor did not want. The Chinese then turned laundrymen. But before the agitation calmed down, even Chinese laundrymen in the Pacific area suffered from race riots, and all sorts of devices were instituted to limit their activities.

> In 1870 a local ordinance was passed that no basket could be carried hung on poles, as this was an obstruction to traffic. This was, of course, aimed at the Chinese laundrymen who delivered their linen in the traditional manner by the use of the baying pole. Later a special tax of $15.00 per quarter year was levied upon every person employed in a Chinese laundry. A third law which indirectly also hampered the Chinese laundryman in the pursuit of his livelihood was a fine of $35.00 imposed upon every person found sleeping in a room containing less than 500 cubic feet of space for each person.[21]

Considering the terrific congestion in which the Chinese were forced to live in those days, this law, as one historian has put it, "made the slumbers of practically every Chinaman in San Francisco illegal." The old-time Chinese had the habit of sticking nickels and dimes in their ears for convenience' sake. And although this was never prohibited by law, the local Board of Supervisors actually debated making it an offense to use one's ear as a purse.

> And not only did the law make things hard for the Chinese laundryman. Physical persecution was also part of his lot, for the hoodlums of old San Francisco delighted in making a diversion of persecuting him. They would stone him from afar, or upset his laundry baskets. In the first wave of anti-Chinese riots in San Francisco in July, 1877, the first Chinese property to be attacked was their laundries. Life never lacked excitement for John the Chinese washerman in those days.[22]

Over-population and persecution made the Chinatown go to the East and Middle West; the Chinese migration followed the railroad which they helped to build. According to Dr. Wu, in 1870, 73 percent of the Chinese gainfully employed were in California, but in 1920 only 43.4 percent were there.[23] Evidently the agitation against the Chinese in the Pacific area calmed down after the Chinese moved eastward and were spread in wider areas, gradually taking up their laundry and chop suey enterprises. So, in 1872, someone had alrady come to Chicago and established a laundry shop at the location near Clark and Madison Streets.

3. The Laundryman's Own Story

How did Chinese immigrants learn the trade? How did the eastward movement take place? So far it is still an unsolved puzzle. Perhaps the Chinese laundry was really founded by Wah Lee in San Francisco about 1850, but it has been next to impossible to authenticate this fact. Here is what the laundryman thinks is the origin of the Chinese laundry:

> The laundry business began in a small town near San Francisco and Portland. Some goodhearted ladies of the church saw some of our countrymen were without a place to live and things to eat. They offered the boys something to do, helping them on wash days. These men learned how to wash and iron then. We Chinese villagers never learned how to do washing and ironing in China.
>
> I don't know how the laundry became a Chinese enterprise in this country. But I think they just learned it from each other. After all, laundry work is not difficult; it requires no high skill. All one has to do is watch how others do it. It would not take long either.
>
> In the old days, some of those follows were really ignorant though. They did not know even how to write down numbers. When a bundle of laundry was done, he had to put down the amount charged for the work. Being so illiterate, he could not write the numbers. He had a way though and what a way! See, he would draw a circle as big as half dollar coin to represent a half dollar, and a circle as big as a dime for a dime, and so on. When the customers came in to call for their laundry, they would catch on to the meaning of the circles and pay accordingly. It is indeed laughable.[24]

This is the story of how the Chinese learned the trade from household duty in those days. Another story told by another laundryman in Chicago was that some of the laundry work was offered to the Chinese by the miners of the gold-mining towns and camps. The frontier life again was the source of the origin of the laundry. There was a demand because of the lack of women and the mobility of population.

> At that time people came over here and went to building railroads. I was

in railroad building too, the first time I arrived, but the job did not last long. Then I found another job in a fishery. It was only seasonal work. I worked only several months in the year. When I was broke, I could ask some of the white men in the camp to lend me several dollars. They trusted me. The next season I found work again and paid them back the money.

Well, when we were doing nothing most of the time, some white men came and said, "John, you wash my clothes and I'll pay you." So some of our countrymen took the offer and they found odd jobs like that. Some made pretty good. I didn't make so good.

There were very few women in the camp. Like our Chinese countrymen, the whites did not bring their women folks. Then who would wash their soiled clothes? They did it themselves, some of them. Most of them were too lazy to do it. That was how Chinese learned to make a few dollars by doing the laundry work for them.

At that time my younger brother and my nephew were already in Chicago. Later they wrote and asked me to come here to join them. Finally I decided to come. Soon after my arrival, I began to work in their place, learning how to iron. Later I opened this place. I have been here almost forty years.[25]

This narrative tells of the situation under which the Chinese became laundrymen and also how this new type of work spread across the country. The pattern of folk relationship is disclosed in which the first laundrymen urged others to join them in a given locality as soon as the pioneers could find sustenance locally. The following document reveals the actual conditions of hardship under which the Chinese carried on their struggle for existence as they brought the Chinese laundry eastward:

With the completion of the railroad, the Chinese who had been building it lost their jobs. Those who did not save for a rainy day starved to death. Some began to travel toward the East. They usually traveled in small bands of several persons. They bought a hundred pound sack of rice, divided it into small sacks and each one of them carried one. On their way they cooked whenever they found wood and water. On their way they stopped to buy a pound of fat for cooking. If they had money, they could buy some meat, but if they had no money, they might take off their shoes, roll up their sleeves, and catch some fish for dinner in the pond. Then they made an earthen stove, took out the fat and began to fry the fish.

Some of them finally reached Chicago. At Lake and Clark Streets they first found their lodging place. Later a store was established.[26]

We may assume that the Chinese laundry originated as a gradual step of accommodation to a new situation under the impact of labor agitation on the one hand, and the economic condition of the frontier life on the other hand. How it actually came about does not matter too much to the sociologist anyway. The interesting thing is its development into some sort of formally established pattern of the laundry which is carried on as a common symbol of understanding. In other words, it is institutionalized in a character of its own. It is a product of a cultural heritage under the impact of a race situation in America. The Chinese took it as a means of survival and as a temporary job, and it became a prelude to his social isolation which created a situation of personal adjustment for the individual.

NOTES

1. H. H. Bancroft, *History of California* (San Francisco: History Company, 1884–90), VII, 336.

2. R. D. McKenzie, "The Oriental Invasion," *Journal of Applied Sociology*, X (October, 1925), 120–30.

3. Albert Williams, *A Pioneer Pastorate and Times* (San Francisco: Bacon and Company, 1882), pp. 224–25.

4. I. Jones, "Cathay on the Coast," *American Mercury*, VIII (1926), 454–55.

5. Alvin F. Harlow, "Chinese Riots," *Dictionary of American History*, ed. James T. Adams (New York: Charles Scribner's Sons, 1940), I, 367.

6. William Hoy, "Tales of the California Chinese" (unpublished radio talk, San Francisco, September 16, 1940).

7. J. P. Anthony, "Our Streets," *Pioneer* (May, 1855), p. 76.

8. Hoy, *op. cit.*

9. U.S. Census: 1870, I, 704–15.

10. *Ibid.*

11. Helen E. Bandini, *History of California* (New York: American Book Company, 1908), pp. 197–99.

12. Luther Gulick, "Chinese Exclusion Acts," *Dictionary of American History*, I, 365–66.

13. Carey McWilliams, "Cathay in Southern California," *Common Ground* (Autumn, 1945), pp. 34–35.

14. Ching-chao Wu, "Chinatowns: A Study of Symbiosis and Assimilation" (Ph.D. diss., University of Chicago, 1928), p. 26.

15. *Ibid.*

16. McWilliams, *op. cit.*, pp.32–33.

17. *Ibid.*, pp. 33–34.

18. Harlow, *op cit.*, p. 367.

19. McWilliams, *op. cit.*, pp. 35–36.

20. Arthur M. Schlesinger, "The Significance of Immigration in American History," *American Journal of Sociology,* XXVII (1921), 71–85.
21. Wu, *op. cit.,* pp. 84–85.
22. Hoy, *op. cit.*
23. Wu, *op cit.,* pp. 84–85.
24. Private interview document.
25. Private interview document.
26. Private interview document.

CHAPTER V

PHYSICAL STRUCTURE OF
THE CHINESE LAUNDRY

THE CHINESE LAUNDRY in America has a century-old history, the history of a minority group struggling for existence on a cultural frontier. It became institutionalized, having both a physical and social structure, and both of these aspects bear the imprint of the ethnic background. Its physical structure is the interior arrangement and the exterior appearance which are symbolized by the red sign, the ironing "bed," that is, board, the counter, the abacus, the mouth sprayer, the laundry ticket, and so on. To the American, these features are quaint. The use of tools and implements, facilities and utilities, no doubt has changed from time to time with the introduction of new inventions and business competition. The adoption of machinery, for instance, is a necessary step to cope with the highly efficient modern steam laundry. In spite of the use of modern tools, some patterns of its physical structure bear the unique features of the Chinese laundry, and these seem to be rather persistent and resistant to change.

1. Exterior Appearance

Within walking distance from apartment houses, rooming houses, and single-family dwellings, the Chinese hand-laundry shop tends to be at a convenient location for its customers. It is easy to spot it if one looks for the red sign with white lettering—a plain wooden sign (sometimes a metal one) painted on a red ground with white letters: "Wah Lee Hand Laundry" (or similar name of Chinese phonetics). It is hanging above the doorway. The same type of lettering may also be seen across the front window of the shop.

If one looks into the window, there is not much decoration, but one or two billboards stand within—the advertisement of the laundryman, announcing the price of work, collars turned, and mending free. There is a low screen which is put up from the floor across the window, making the office within semi-private from the pedestrian's observation. But one could not fail to identify the laundryman's Oriental look and the decoration of the shop at a glance. The window may hold a few plants, perhaps of the Chinese evergreen variety, or other art objects. In general, the laundry shop window is seldom as attractively decorated as a business house should be. Sometimes it even appears to be dirty, desolate, or in bad taste. To explain the reason for this condition, one might say that the Chinese laundryman works too long hours; he is tired after a day of hard work. He can clean his house on Sunday but it is his only time for recreation and relaxation. To a tired worker, housecleaning is worse than working, one can realize. The Chinese laundryman may not actually care whether his shop window is clean and good looking or not as long as he has enough patronage.

The Red Sign

It seems that the selection of the color red for his sign is by no means a mere accident; it has a cultural meaning. Red, according to the Chinese traditional meaning, symbolizes good luck and prosperity. The greatest festival in Chinese society, the New Year holiday, is symbolized by using red on practically everything which has a cultural meaning. The pioneer Chinese laundryman perhaps wanted prosperity and good luck; he was too superstitious to use any other color. I was told that in bygone days, the sign-maker tended to be a person the laundryman knew personally. If one man started making a sign for one Chinese laundryman, he would make it for all of them in the city. In some instances, the sign-maker was Chinese. If it was made by a non-Chinese, the man had to know the Chinese psychology or he would not have their business. Once the symbol was adopted, the others followed suit. Unless under special circumstances, the sign of the Chinese laundry tends to be red. In the better areas nowadays, it is made of metal, or some of them even have a neon sign in the window.

2. Interior Arrangement

The interior arrangements are of two parts: first, the interior setting; second, the representation of cultural symbols. When we consider the interior setting, we are describing it in typical terms, and if it varies, the construction of different buildings is responsible for the differences.

The Interior Setting

The shop of the Chinese laundryman is not merely his place of work, but is also a place for sleeping and cooking. The typical interior setting of the Chinese laundry falls into four parts. First is the front section, which usually occupies one-third of the space of the house, constituting the office-workshop of the laundryman. Here he does all his ironing, receives his customers, and has other secondary social contacts. In this front section one sees his quaint ways of doing things: the ironing "bed," the abacus, the laundry shelves, the lock-counter, and secret cash drawer. Second, immediately behind the curtained doorway at the center of the house, usually between the laundry shelves, are the living quarters, or just sleeping space. In this space behind the laundry shelves are the laundryman's bed and that of his partners and employees. The bed is usually a narrow couch or army cot. Third, the drying room takes a large space within the laundry shop; it is generally located in the center or rear part of the house. The drying room is a construction of tin plates built along a wall, half-way up to the ceiling. Overhead, within the drying room, about a dozen strong iron wires are strung across in parallel lines, just as high as the laundryman can conveniently reach them, to put up the wet laundry for drying. In the center of this drying room there is the old-fashioned coal stove. A strong fire has to be built in the stove when drying is needed. Fourth, there is the rear section, where almost all the laundryman's machines are located, and indeed all his other important facilities, including the cooking stove and washing machine, washing sink, lavatory, and steam boiler. A diagram may give a better picture (see Fig. 5.1).

It would be trite to go into a detailed description of every item in the interior arrangement of the laundryman's shop. A few things, however, must be explained before we take up the more interesting feature—the representation of cultural symbols. Some of the machinery in the diagram

FIGURE 5.1 View of the interior of a typical Chinese laundry.

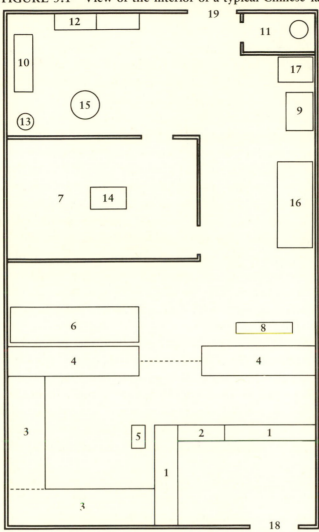

Legend

1. Counter	11. Lavatory
2. Entrance under counter	12. Sinks (wooden)
3. Ironing beds	13. Steam boiler
4. Laundry shelves	14. Coal stove
5. Sewing machine	15. Wringing machine
6. Sleeping bed	16. Dining table
7. Drying room	17. Icebox
8. Mangle machine	18. Front door
9. Cooking stove	19. Back door
10. Washing machine	

may be considered optional, depending upon the prosperity of the laundry business. The wringing machine, the mangle, or even the sewing machine is not absolutely necessary unless it is a large laundry and as a means of competition. Some laundries even have installed shirt-ironing machines, but most Chinese laundries are still hand laundries.

It must be made clear that the laundry shop is not only the place where the laundryman works but it is also his home. He lives there, and so do his partners and employees. The Chinese laundry is seldom a large one. The average number of persons to a laundry is about two or three. In the diagram, we see only one space for sleeping. Suppose there are two persons in partnership in the business, where can the other man sleep? If this were the case, the space for the mangle machine would accommodate another bed, or some other arrangement. If this same laundry picked up some business, and another worker were employed, where would the third man sleep? In such a case, the employee might have to use an army cot and find a space somewhere—he might move the table, for instance. In some instances, employees may choose to live outside, as in the case of some of the larger laundries.

The washing machine, the steam boiler, and the drying room are regarded as essentials. The cooking stove in the laundryman's shop is usually a simple two-burner stove. The icebox is sometimes a very expensive electric refrigerator. In some laundries, on the other hand, there is not even an icebox. But the Chinese laundryman is never interested in a modern electric or gas stove in his shop; the modern stove is not good for cooking Chinese food and it simply occupies too much space in his small shop.

Immediately after one enters the laundry shop, one faces a counter of usual height. Shelves are built underneath the counter; usually some supplies and all sorts of miscellaneous items are stored on these shelves. Generally, one cannot get into the laundryman's office-workshop because the counter is built around it. The entrance to the inner chamber is through a low swinging door attached to the counter. It is locked from within. In order to get in, the loose section of the counter has to be lifted up and the hook underneath unlocked.

Why is the counter built this way? It seems the counter in the Chinese laundry serves two purposes: It is a customary facility for business trading, and it is also some sort of protective measure. As the Chinese laundry was founded under conditions of extreme conflict of racial riots and labor agitation against it, it could be the aftermath of the feeling of insecurity—some protection would be better than none. Even today, local hoodlums, robbers, racketeers, and prostitutes take advantage of the Chinese laundryman from time to time. With only a few exceptions, most Chinese laundries have counters built for protection as well as for business. In some of the worst areas in the city, the laundryman needs more protection. He builds the cage-like fence from the top of the counter up midway toward the ceiling. A hole about one foot square is opened for taking laundry bundles in and out. Such protection becomes a necessity, particularly after the laundryman is robbed.

> Recently some Chinese laundries in town have been robbed. An incident even occurs in daytime! On Sunday, Feb. 16 [1940] this month, Soo Ying Laundry at 146 Leland Street was shoplifted by two Americans at 12:30 p.m., while the workers were eating their lunch. They heard the door open and one of the workers rose to welcome the supposed customers. Suddenly one robber dashed into the inner chamber and drew a pistol, threatening to shoot the workers, who were then forced to go to the toilet. The other robber searched the house and took about twenty dollars. They then fled hastily.[1]

> Charles Moy has a laundry at 31 East 57th Street. In the evening of November 21 [1940], five men came to his shop with intent to rob. One of them put his hand into the pocket of his trousers, and it seemed that he was going to fire. They threatened Moy to give them money. Moy took it calmly. But suddenly Moy took a red-hot iron and thrust it at the robber's chest and burned him immediately. It hurt so bad that the robber cried and swiftly ran out of the house.
> This same group of robbers had been in another laundry of Lum Hin at Indiana Avenue just a few hours before they went to Mr. Moy's. They tied up Lum Hin with a bed sheet, and took about twenty-five dollars and six bundles of laundry.[2]

Another interesting item, perhaps also for protection, is the cash-drawer. It is an old-fashioned wooden structure, usually installed either underneath the counter or under one of the laundry shelves. A little bell is attached to it and every time it is opened it produces a tinkling sound. A stranger not familiar with the mechanism cannot open the cash-drawer and it wouldn't make a sound unless it was opened. In this cash-drawer, the laundryman keeps just enough small change for the day's use. A shoplifter seldom gets all the laundryman's money when he is robbed.

Representation of Cultural Symbols

One thing that stands out as distinctly quaint to an observer in the Chinese laundry is the appearance of the ironing board which the Chinese call an "ironing bed." It is a structure of planks and crude boards, always built along the wall, about two feet and three inches in width, four and one-half feet long, and two and one-half feet in height. If there is sufficient space in the house, two or three of these structures are built, usually one alongside of the other. After the wooden structure is built, it will be covered with heavy felt on top to almost the full length and width of the whole board. Atop of the felt pad a good strong piece of muslin cloth is hammered down with tacks. It is then ready to be tested. After it is used for the day, the ironing board is covered by a piece of oil cloth to protect it from dust and dirt.

The front side of this structure is surrounded by a piece of cloth, hanging down from the edge atop at almost the same height. Behind this screen, underneath the ironing bed, all sorts of things are tucked in: trunks, suitcases, baskets, and laundry supplies of all kinds. It serves as a closet. When not in use, a few things may be put on top of it, especially the abacus.

How does the Chinese laundryman find it expedient, and keep on using this ironing bed instead of the type used in the American laundry? To answer this question with authentic proof is almost like the proof of the origin of the Chinese laundry itself; the available evidence is next to nothing. An interesting point is that the laundryman calls it *hong-choong* [*tangchuang*] (ironing bed) instead of *hong-boan* [*tangban*] (ironing board). As the whole structure looks so much like the wooden bed commonly used for sleeping by the Chinese peasants in China, we might speculate that the pioneer laundryman could have converted his own sleeping bed into the ironing board. Imagine how he might do a laundry job when it was first offered to him in the mining town! He could wash the laundry in the stream, but where could he do the ironing? Under such a condition he might have tried to iron shirts on his own bed and found it practical. Later he could have constructed a separate ironing bed, with a little modification. He might also have gotten the idea of constructing his ironing board from the wooden bed he used to sleep in when he was in his native village in China. I was surprised to find that in some of the lodging houses in Chinatown, even today, the same kind of wooden beds are still in use in exactly the same way as they are used in China. Asking the men why they construct the ironing board that way, the answer generally is that they have always been so constructed and they find it very convenient and practical. They seem never to think of adopting the American-made ironing board. "That," one Chinese laundryman responded, referring to the American ironing board, "we Chinese would not use; it is impractical."

The Chinese laundryman has developed some techniques of ironing seemingly related to the use of his own kind of ironing board. The way he handles the shirt while ironing seems to need a lot of space. Among the Chinese laundrymen they talk about their technique and how to do it quicker and better. A quick worker is appreciated. They discuss how to handle a hot iron skillfully by spreading the shirt to be ironed in the proper way. The Chinese laundryman does not think he can practice his technique with an American type of ironing board. I have, however, seen the use of the American type in some Chinese laundries. I understand it is used because of space problems in the house when business is improving and there are not enough ironing beds. Some work could be done on an American type of ironing board, and so one worker is assigned to this job; he is the only one to use the non-Chinese board.

The Laundry Ticket

Perhaps the most amusing feature is the Chinese laundry ticket. Chinese characters are written on it. In pioneer days, as described in the last chapter, some laundrymen were so illiterate they did not know how to mark down the amount charged for the laundry service. Instead, they made circles to represent the sizes of different coins. Today, the American customers of the Chinese laundry can understand only the amount charged on the ticket. There are variations from place to place, due to local circumstances and individual attitudes. At present, two or three ways of numbering the ticket are seen in Chicago. Generally the ticket bears a serial number and a ticket number. One system is to adopt the "Eighty Characters"[3] as a series and begin with the Chinese word *tin* [*tien*], and so on until the series of eighty characters is exhausted. Recently laundry tickets have been printed in Chinatown in 100-sheet pads, about 5 × 3½ inches square, and in different colors. Some of these recent printings, however, do not use the Chinese eighty characters, *A, B, C, D*, et cetera, having been adopted as serial numbers instead. Whether it is in Chinese characters or in *A, B, C, D*'s, each pad is numbered from 1 to 100. Sometimes, the serial word as well as the number is duplicated on the ticket so that when it is used, it can be torn in two, each part bearing the same serial symbol, and number. Sometimes only the number is duplicated, but the serial word can be torn in two. Another way of marking the laundry is for the customer to write down his name and address on a piece of paper. He needs no receipt. When he calls for his clean laundry, he may be asked to write his name and address again, but in due time he becomes an old patron and the laundryman would not even bother to have him write his name and address.

A customer who prefers not to write his name and address is given a ticket which is torn in two, or a stub of a ticket. He calls for his clean laundry by presenting the stub which corresponds to the serial and number of the other half attached to the laundry bundle.

In all cases, on the laundry ticket attached to the bundle, one can see hand-written Chinese characters. This is a system the laundryman devel-

FIGURE 5.2   An example of a Chinese laundry ticket.

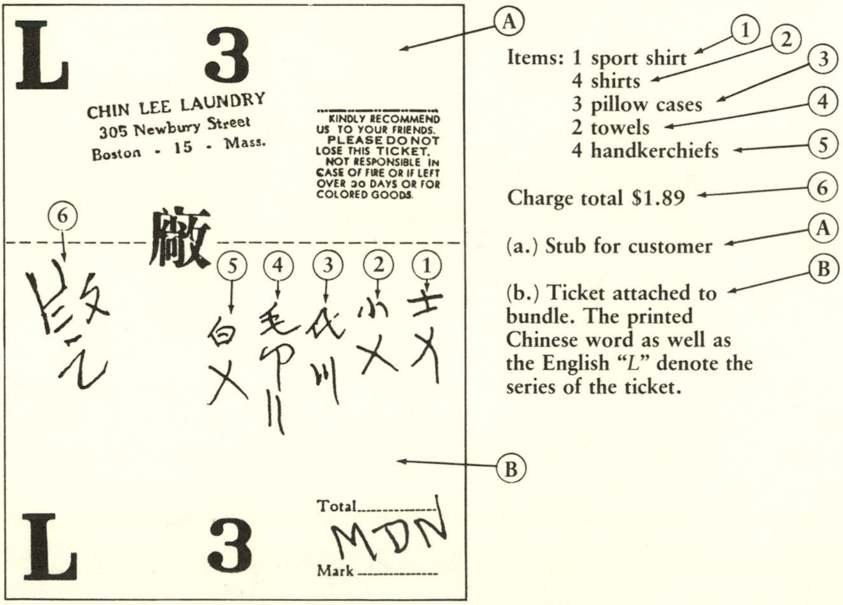

Items: 1 sport shirt ① ②③
       4 shirts
       3 pillow cases ④
       2 towels
       4 handkerchiefs ⑤

Charge total $1.89 ⑥

(a.) Stub for customer Ⓐ

(b.) Ticket attached to Ⓑ
bundle. The printed
Chinese word as well as
the English "*L*" denote the
series of the ticket.

oped to itemize the bundle. Usually the laundryman removes it as the customer pays and sticks it together with the stub the customer has just presented. He keeps it for reference. The customer probably has very little chance of studying the Chinese characters on the ticket; maybe he does not care so long as his clean shirts are nicely done. Sometimes the amount charged is in Chinese characters; the customer does not know how much he has to pay until the laundryman tells him.

The interesting point about the Chinese laundry ticket is the fact that American objects are given Chinese names by the laundryman when he writes the laundry ticket. For example, a pair of pajamas looks somewhat similar to a Chinese suit of clothes and so the Chinese laundryman puts it as *tong-sham-foo* [*tangshanku*]; herds-boys in China wear short pants and so American shorts become *ngoh-foo* [*niuku*]. Shirts are called "little sweat coat" and dress shirts, "big sweat coat"—*siu-hoon-sham* [*xiao hanshan*] and *dai-hoon-sham* [*ta hanshan*]. All the other laundry articles are abbreviated with Chinese characters which sometimes defy the most learned sinologist.

At the present time, almost all Chinese laundries in the city use two systems: (1) to let those customers who want to, sign their name, (2) to employ a serial ticket. The size, color, and serial are not all standardized. Whether handmade or printed tickets are used, the system of itemizing is universally adopted, though other things may vary. I have seen some Chinese laundries use the American type of laundry bill, but Chinese generally consider it impractical. In fact, many Chinese laundrymen cannot even read the items listed, and the cost of printing is much higher. I understand that the adoption of the American type of laundry bill was more or less demanded by the customers in certain areas in the city, and the laundryman had to accommodate himself to it. So a laundry may have itemized bills ready for only those customers who demand it.

The Abacus[4]

Perhaps the most unique cultural trait exhibited in the Chinese laundry is the abacus. I suppose no laundry can get along without one. A laundry without an abacus would be like a business office without a typewriter. The fact is that the Chinese prefer to use the abacus rather than a pencil and paper, and they are proud of it.

In spite of this pride, some Chinese have not learned how to use the abacus, and unless he is in partnership with one who knows how to use it, he has to look for a substitute. But it is not hard to learn, so most people learn its use before establishing a business.

Use of the Sprayer

The method of sprinkling the laundry for ironing has been one of the sources of the laundryman's misfortune. From time to time perennial rumors have circulated about him that diseases of all kinds originated from his work because he spit water through a tube held in his mouth (see Chapter 2, p. 18). Within the last two decades the use of the sprayer in the Chinese laundry has progressed rapidly from the mouth-blower to the gas atomizer. Now the mouth-blower, imported from China, is almost non-existent. Some Chinese laundrymen state that the mouth-blower meant hard work and that they enjoy the easy and superior results of the modern sprayer.

Three ways of sprinkling seem to have been used in the Chinese laundry. Presumably ever since the Chinese laundry was founded the mouth-blower had been used. It is made of brass, with a shape like any ordinary American-made insect sprayer except a tube is built on it instead of the little air pump. To make the water sprinkle out, one blows at the opening of the tube. I have also seen men dip a straw brush into a pail of water and then sprinkle the laundry by shaking water from the brush. This method, however, is applied to only certain processes of laundry work. In bygone days, Chinese laundrymen have used both ways. About ten years ago, I also saw American-made sprayers of all shapes and styles used in the Chinese laundry. More recently the modern finger-touch atomizer type of sprayer is very extensively used in different laundries in the city.

Use of the Iron

The Chinese laundryman has gone modern, too, with the use of the iron— modern electric irons of all makes are seen today in many Chinese laundries. Its adoption seems to be related closely to business competition, high-pressure salesmanship by the laundry supply agent, and, of course, the personal comfort and convenience of the laundryman himself, as in the case of the sprayer.

However, the old-fashioned solid iron piece type is still being used in many places. The persistence of its existence seems to be related to the technique of ironing developed among Chinese laundrymen. When in use, this type of iron has to be burned red hot on a gas stove. The laundryman picks it up with a strong hooked iron stick, dips it into a pail of water, then catches it with a specially made pad on his right hand, and quickly spreads the shirt and irons swiftly. Some of the young and able-bodied men prefer this old-fashioned iron; presumably it goes more easily and more smoothly over the shirt, correlated with the skill he has acquired.

The Curtained Doorway

The curtained doorway appears at the center of the laundry shop, usually between two laundry shelves, separating the front and rear parts. In China, bedroom doors are customarily decorated with a curtain, *foong leem [fenglian]*, as it is called. We understand the Chinese laundryman lives in his shop. Following the Old World pattern, he erected a curtain at the central aisle so as to create some privacy for himself.

We shall analyze his social environment in full detail in later chapters in relation to the question of why he lives in his shop instead of in a home somewhere else, as other business people do. At this point, however, one can see the problem from the preceding chapters, the history of the Chinese laundry, and the attitudes expressed by the general public toward the laundryman. Suppose he were to venture out to look for an apartment or a room in the neighborhood! He would surely have a hard time being accepted. His isolation in his laundry shop has been set since the founding of the Chinese laundry approximately one hundred years ago. And so the quaint ironing board, the protective function of the locked counter, the symbolic meaning of the red sign, the peculiar scheme of the laundry ticket, and the unique feature of the abacus and the curtained doorway become the characteristic structure of the Chinese laundry.

The modern features of machinery and other tools he employs show that progress has been made but slowly.

NOTES

1. *San Ming Morning News,* February 18, 1940 (a Chicago Chinese daily).
Translated from the Chinese.

2. *Ibid.,* November 23, 1940.

3. "The Eighty Characters," an old poem that every woman and child in
China can recite. Each sentence consists of four words; it begins with *Tin-deh
yuen huang* [*Tiendi xuanhuang*] (The beginning of heaven and earth was remote
and ancient). The meaning of some of the words and sentences is too mystical to
translate. It has long been used for playing lottery.

4. In Chinese it is called *hsoon poon* [*suanpan*], made of hardwood, looking
very much like a long narrow tray. In the tray a dozen or so metal sticks are
installed vertically, parallel with one another, and each goes through seven beads.
The tray is divided by another piece of wood horizontally across the upper side
of the tray, making two sections. On each column two beads appear in the upper
section, and five beads appear in the lower section. Each bead in the upper section
represents five points, and each bead in the lower section represents one point.
The bead on the left is always ten times the bead on the right.

CHAPTER VI

SOCIAL STRUCTURE OF
THE CHINESE LAUNDRY

S OCIAL STRUCTURE in the Chinese laundry is likewise established on the basis of cultural heritage and urban circumstances. What is the nature of the social relationship between the laundryman and his partner and employee? How is the laundry operated in the light of the cultural background? In another chapter the question of its relation to the urban environment will be considered.

The laundryman brings with him from China a set of Old World sentiments and economic traditions on which the Chinese laundry is established. It is essentially a folk institution which, of course, has been modified by the urban ways of living in America.

1. Division of Labor

The Chinese laundry is a small workshop. Some laundries are operated by one lone man, and some have five or more workers, but the majority are two- or three-man enterprises. There cannot be any division of labor in a one-man laundry, and the difference between a three-man and a six-man shop is a matter of volume of business. The question of division of labor seems to be very simple as the work is primarily routine with no claim to specialization.

In the case of the lone laundryman, he obviously has to manage to do all the necessary work according to his own routine, a matter of which thing to do first. Generally Sunday is the day of rest, but the laundryman may not be able to get out of the shop until one o'clock in the afternoon. Early Sunday morning, he may have to clean the house and after that he may like to sort the laundry bundles accumulated to be washed Monday morning. The sorting work is called *mai-funn.** It is simply a routine of marking the clothes, writing down the items on the laundry ticket, figuring the amount charged, and sorting the soiled clothes in the order to be washed. If it is a three-man laundry, for instance, one man can do the house cleaning, one the sorting, and one the cooking. Lunch should be ready as soon as the other work is done. A one-man laundry would take a much shorter time to sort, whereas a four-man laundry would take two men a much longer time. The laundrymen usually eat lunch before they take Sunday afternoon off. For this, the most happy time of the week, they share their profit before leaving.

The Profit and How It Is Shared

The Chinese laundryman and his partner and employee are generally relatives and friends. If two men are partners, they share the weekly profit equally. As soon as they have Sunday lunch, one man, who is usually the bookkeeper, calls the other man to count the money in their cash-drawer to see if the total is correct while he checks the figures, using the abacus. When the total is indicated, the money spent for food, laundry supplies, and other miscellaneous expenses incurred during the week are subtracted. Then the two partners agree to leave a certain amount in coins and small bills for change to use the following week; then each partner takes an equal share as his net profit for the week. The weekly income would not be too different from week to week within a period unless an accumulated laundry supply bill had been paid during the week and so the profit for the week might be a much smaller amount. Naturally, in the summer months, the profit is supposed to be better than during the other seasons of the year; likewise the summer is always the time when the laundryman needs extra help.

The procedure of profit-sharing would be the same if the partnership involved more than two persons. In an employer-employee relationship where two partners have hired a worker or workers, there are three ways of adjusting the employee's wages: (1) equal sharing of net profit like partners; (2) sharing according to the weekly profit, the employer reserving the right to have a larger share; (3) fixing the wages on a weekly, daily, or hourly basis. It seems the second is the most popular way. The first is practiced among very close relatives and friends, as between an uncle and nephew, brothers, close cousins, in-laws, and bosom friends. With the fixed wages, at the other extreme, the employee tends to be an "outsider," a non-Chinese, or a Negro woman, who is employed as a temporary helper. A Negro, who works three days a week—usually Tuesday, Wednesday, and Friday—may have her wages fixed on an hourly basis or by some other agreement between her and the laundryman. The Chinese employee, however, is seldom employed by hour or day, except in a special emergency.

In still another situation, the laundryman sometimes accommodates retired old men or young school-age boys. These people help on part-time or assigned odd jobs in the laundry shop. They receive compensation according to individual merit and the employer's conscience. An old man helps with the "rough work" in exchange for meals and a place to sleep in the laundry shop and may also have a "few dollars for carfare." A boy who helps do some ironing after school may earn enough to be independent, financially. The laundryman may not need a part-time helper; this is often an accommodation to the helper's need. The helper tends to be a close relative and friend. The helper fills the gap in the system of division of labor in the Chinese laundry, sometimes not so much in helping to get the work done as in keeping the laundryman company, particularly in those lone-man laundries. In the lone-man laundry, the laundryman has to do everything; there is no division of labor for him, except that he may have to hire a part-time worker.

Whether in a laundry of one man or in a laundry of more than one man, the routine of the work generally starts on Monday as a washing day. A week is divided into washing days and ironing days; Monday, Wednesday, and Friday are washing days, and Tuesday, Thursday, and Saturday are ironing days. Actually, therefore, there are routines established for each of the two; jobs each is supposed to do during each washing day and during each ironing day.

The Working Days

On Sunday morning the soiled laundry is sorted. The routine may vary in different laundries according to whether or not the particular laundry sets Sunday morning for sorting work: some of them do, and some of them do not. In some cases, soiled laundry is brought in by customers

Monday morning. Generally the laundryman cannot wash it unless it is brought in before a certain hour in the morning. Too, some laundries conduct a call-and-delivery service. Until a certain hour, one of the men would be out collecting soiled clothes from different families in the neighborhood. While he is out, the other men would do the sorting, washing, and drying work in the laundry shop. It becomes a process of established routine.

The routine for the three washing days as well as for the three ironing days may be considered the same, except that the volume of work may not be evenly distributed. The customers or patrons of the laundry actually control the work in this respect; it is determined by whether more patrons bring in laundry at the beginning of the week, the middle of the week, or at the end of the week. Under these conditions, on one of the washing days the laundryman may start to work as early as six o'clock and he may not finish his work until midnight. On other washing days he may be able to finish soon after supper, by eight or nine o'clock in the evening. Generally the Chinese laundryman works ten to sixteen hours a day, depending upon the volume of business. The question why he works so long and hard will be taken up later. At this point our focus of attention is directed to the daily routine of the washing day. What is its general pattern in the light of the division of labor?

The Sam Moy Laundry, located in a middle-class neighborhood in Evanston, a suburb of Metropolitan Chicago, consists of four workers. Moy Tong, forty-five; Moy Hong, fifty; Moy Wah, and Moy Ming, both about forty, are clansmen; the former two men are proprietors of the laundry, the latter two are employees. In this laundry the proprietors seem to play more responsible roles than the employees. Moy Tong, the oldest member in the business, and being one of the proprietors, keeps the book of accounting (in the Chinese way), and conducts the call-and-delivery service. Moy Hong, the partner, who joined Moy Tong last year, is largely responsible for shopping for food, ordering supplies, and cooking most of the meals. The work starts on Monday as illustrated in the following record:

Monday, June 10, 1940:—"Tong was first up this morning," said Wah. "It must have been half past five. I don't know why the devil he has to get up so early. *Del-ka-ma* [*diao tama*] (fuck his mother)! As soon as he got up, he made a noise so loud with washing basin that it woke me up. (Wah slept near the washing basin.) I was up about six then. Then the other fellows got up too.

"Oh, we had our breakfast long ago—not later than seven. This morning was earlier than ever. Had to start early on a hot day." At eight, Tong was going out to collect laundry. Hong and Wah were working inside. The steam boiler was working and the wash tub was moving. Ming was alone in the office where he sorted and marked the laundry customers had just brought in.

The house was too noisy when the washing machine was moving; people had to shout to each other to converse. As soon as the washing machine stopped, you knew the first tub of laundry was done and it was ready to be rinsed, wrung, and dried in a steady process. There are steps to wash one kind of clothing article first and the other kind later. This laundry does all white things first and then the colored things.

About 8:30 Tong came back with his load in a wooden trunk attached to the tricycle. As soon as Tong put down the bundles, he left again, saying he had to make another trip. Ming came to open the bundles and began his sorting and marking work again. Hong and Wah were still inside, each busily at work, rinsing and wringing, and soon they put all clean laundry in the drying room.

Soon Tong came back with his second load. He then joined Ming who was still sorting and marking. Having finished his job inside, Wah came out to pick up the pile on the floor and prepare for the second washing.

About 10:00 o'clock the wheel of the washing machine turned again. Customers came to leave their laundry or to call for clean laundry. Tong and Ming were the ones who took care of the customers; these two spoke English better. Everybody was active. At this time the mangle machine was started by Tong and he began to work with sheets, towels, and other so-called rough work.

From the washing machine to the wash tub and to the wringing machine and the drying room takes about one hour and a half. Soon after the washing was done Hong began to cook for their lunch. Hong said sometimes he had no time to cook. He could cook today because they started earlier and the work was not so heavy. In case it was too busy, they would make some coffee and get some cold meat and cakes for lunch and they probably would not eat again until late at night.

The afternoon work constituted three main activities: starching, damping, and ironing of flat-work. Hong did most of the starching work, with the help of Ming. Wah and Tong did the damping and ironing. Most of the flat work was done by the mangle.

The ironing was done by old-fashioned irons burning on a gas stove. About three o'clock in the afternoon Tong finished his work with the mangle and came to join the others in regular ironing. Hong had about finished his starching and began to set collars and cuffs on a machine which was

called *dai-goi* [*taji*] (big machine). Since every stiff collar and cuff had to
go through his hands, it would take him the whole afternoon and deep into
the night.

They did not eat their supper until 11:30 at night. Ming was the cook
because Hong had not quite finished his work, while Ming already had a
little time for smoking.

After supper, they all sat out in the yard to cool off before they went to
bed. But they did not sleep until 1:00 A.M. It was a heavy meal, a big bowl
of soup and large dishes of meat and vegetables. The shopping was done in
Chinatown Sunday afternoon.

It is obvious, therefore, that the principle of division of labor in the
Chinese laundry is sharing the work fairly and cooperatively by all its
members. The employers, in this case, are taking a little more responsibility; this, however, may or may not be true in other laundries. Sometimes
the responsibility may be defined by the personal asset of the individual.
Ming, in this case, is a person who can speak English better than the rest,
and so he is a spokesman for the laundry. He irons at the ironing board
near the counter and he receives the customers who come in. Of course,
in a smaller or a bigger laundry, sharing of responsibility would be modified by the individual condition of the particular laundry.

The same laundry was visited two days later, on an ironing day.

Thursday, June 20, 1940—at 5:30 P.M., when observer visited the laundry,
all of the men were still busy.

"We won't be through till eight o'clock," one responded to the observer's
inquiry, "may be still later in the evening. See, how much there is to be
ironed yet." He pointed to the huge basket of unfinished shirts, nearly half
full.

The observer learned that they got up early as usual with the intention
of finishing the work earlier. They did not eat their regular Chinese lunch;
instead, they ate sandwiches and cakes around 1:00 o'clock.

Everybody was ironing shirts and dresses.

On the ironing day, they can talk and joke with each other. As soon as
they see the observer, they usually ask for the news. The news then becomes
the subject of interest and discussion.

While the observer was telling them the news of the day, the traveling
Chinese food shop man, Yuen, who was nicknamed "Old Indian," came
in.

"Ah! Here comes my future father-in-law," joked Tong with the man.
"Didn't I tell you to bring my sweet-little-bride-to-be, too?" "Old Indian"
was trying to ignore Tong. The others laughed.

"Del-ka-ma!" "Old Indian" finally retorted, good humoredly, "I am going to bring you an old Negro woman, like it?"

"What is that? . . . So, you changed your mind!" responded Tong. "All right, don't forget to bring my bride-to-be next time. *Del-nea-ma* [*diao nima*] (fuck your mother). . . ."

Again "Old Indian" was trying to ignore Tong. He turned to Hong and asked, "What is the order, Brother Hong?"

Ming did not give the order right away and they continued to joke about Yuen's daughter. Finally Hong interrupted, "That's enough! Let's give him the order and let the man go. . . ."

"Speak, what do you have?" Ming said, urging the "Old Indian" who recited what he had in his wagon—meat, fishes, and vegetables from Chinatown. Then Hong gave the order after asking the preference of his fellow workers.

Then the goods were brought in, but Tong still wanted more fun. "Del-ka-ma! I told you I want to see your daughter and you think I am fooling," he continued. "Am I a good son-in-law to you? Am I not handsome? Am I not rich? . . ."

"Del-ka-ma! Look like a monkey! He is handsome. . . ." responded "Old Indian." "Two dollar and ninety-seven cents, please. . . ." He turned to Hong.

"Charge it. All right?"

"Come on! I have other places to go yet." "Old Indian" insisted upon his pay.

"Get it next time. . . ."

"Del-ka-ma! Next time . . . next week. . . ." "Old Indian" opened the door, pretending he was about to leave.

"Stop! Stop! Come back," called Tong. "The account has to be cleared every week, *ka-ma-kar-bei* [*tama ge bi*] (his mother's vagina)! Here you are. . . ." The traveling grocer was paid.

It was after six, but nobody was free to cook yet. The work would take a couple more hours and they did not feel hungry. Might as well finish it first.

About 8:00 o'clock the observer was there again; they were just finishing but had to *poun-funn** yet. [*Poun-funn* is a term the laundryman uses for the work of separating, distributing, and wrapping up the clean laundry.]

Hong told Wah to begin to cook and Ming was smoking. (He was the only smoker in the house.) Hong and Tong began the work of *poun-funn* soon after they had a drink, and Ming joined them as soon as he had a smoke. They lined up the clean laundry into tens of small piles and checked the marks with the laundry tickets which were previously marked. If the numbers and the variety were correct, then the bundle was wrapped in brown paper and the ticket was inserted into the twine which was used to wrap the bundle.

One by one they did it quickly, and soon the bundles were put up on the shelves.

Tong wanted to deliver a few bundles before it was too dark. The dinner was not ready anyway.

Underneath the counter there was a huge pile of soiled laundry the customers had brought in that day and the day before. Ming asked Tong whether they should start to sort and mark the pile tonight or tomorrow morning.

"That is not much," Tong said. "Take a rest and see how the others feel after supper." Then Tong went out to make the delivery.

Customers came in and went out. There was little conversation except greetings of the "Hello!" and "How are you?" variety.

Tong was gone about half an hour. They had dinner together inside of the workshop—roast duck, fish, and vegetable soup, and a large pot of rice. The observer was invited but he had had his supper.

After supper, they decided to take it easy—not to bother *mai-funn* (sorting and marking) until tomorrow morning.

After supper Tong went over to the chop suey house in the neighborhood to visit. The other men read papers and talked.

The difference between a washing day and an ironing day, as described, is merely in the procedure of the working pattern. At the end of an ironing day, there may be a few hours of rest, particularly Saturday afternoon and evening. In some cases people are willing to work harder on Friday so that they may be able to have free time on Saturday as early as possible. Saturday free time is possible only if the business is not so good or the partners are willing to make less money by employing an extra helper.

During free time, however, not all may leave the laundry; someone has to stay in "to watch the shop" (*muom poo*) [*wangpu*]. Except receiving the customers who may come to leave or to pick up their laundry, one is free to do as he pleases, within the house. In order to have free time out, members of the house have to take turns. At least one person stays until the shop closes about nine o'clock in the evening. The hour of closing depends upon the convenience of the customers. The laundry shop is for the convenience of the customers.

The essential characteristic of the type of division of labor in the Chinese laundry is that work be evenly assigned, for the profit is equally shared among its members. In the Chinese laundry, actually no one is a specialist; a particular man does a particular job, often just because he has gotten used to it or he has long been doing it. Cooking, for instance, is a very good example. Everybody in the Chinese laundry seems to be able to cook, but one among them may enjoy cooking or may be a better cook, and soon he prefers to do most of the cooking.

Naturally there are persons of higher capability, and yet they share the profit equally with the other less capable persons. To understand the situation more clearly, we now consider the nature of the partnership in the Chinese laundry.

2. Partnership and Ownership

The majority of Chinese laundries in the city are what may be called "cousin partnerships." Men of the same clan under the same surname tend to join one another as partners. To what extent is this true? The following data on Chinese laundries in five selected communities in Chicago illustrate the extent of cousin partnership.

We found three types of ownership among Chinese laundries in Hyde Park, Woodlawn, South Shore, Rogers Park, and Evanston. They are classified as cousin partnership, non-cousin partnership, and single-man ownership. The total number of laundries found in these communities is sixty-seven, with about 60 percent cousin partnership, about 28 percent single-man ownership, and about 10 percent non-cousin partnership. As long as two or more persons in a laundry are proprietors and belong to the same clan or have the same surname, it is considered a cousin partnership. In case a laundry has an employee, he is likely also to be a clansman. In a laundry in which an employee is a clansman, it is classified as single-man ownership. The single-man ownership has three alternative features: (1) a single man may work alone with no employee; (2) a proprietor may have

TABLE 6.1
Types of Ownership of the Chinese Laundry

Community	Cousin Partner	Non-cousin Partner	Single Man
Hyde Park	9	1	2
Woodlawn	9	3	8
Rogers Park	6	2	2
South Shore	8	0	5
Evanston	9	1	2
Total	41	7	19

NOTE: Data were obtained in 1940. Numbers indicate the number of units of individual laundries.

one or two Chinese employees who may or may not be "cousins"; (3) a proprietor may have a part-time Negro woman worker. In the non-cousin partnership group, the partners tend to be either kinsmen or friends and neighbors of the native district. In all three types, two or more clansmen may work together in a laundry. In the latter two groups, only one of the clansmen is the proprietor, or both are employees. Occasionally one will find a laundry which cannot be included under any of the categories given; it is a combination of ownership between clansmen and kinsmen—for instance, two brothers and a brother-in-law. But in a case like this, it seems almost like a cousin partnership. However, kinsmen such as brothers-in-law, father-in-law and son-in-law, and so on, with few exceptions seldom form a partnership.

The most significant feature of the partnership system of the Chinese laundry is essentially the Chinese clan transplanted. It is organized on the basis of clan sentiments and primary-group relationships. In fact, in some laundry shops a young boy lives with his father. The Chinese laundryman trying to create some sort of family life in his laundry shop, tends to bring young boys to America. Boys of adolescent age are seen everywhere in Chinese laundries. They have come to join father, brother, uncle, or grandfather. The boy lives in the laundry shop with his father and spends part of his time in school and part of his time helping with the laundry work. In most such cases, the boy turns out to be a laundryman eventually.

I first came to this country in the tenth year of the Republic [1921], when I was 25 years old. My father was here for some time before I came to join him. I came as the son of an American citizen. At that time my father had a laundry shop on this street; it was situated right next to the bank. I worked with him for three years, then he took me back to China with him. After a few months of visiting and reunion in the native village, I came back here again. . . . My father returned to the native village. . . .

I have four sons. The oldest one is a graduate from the National Academy of Aviation. He is now working for the Government. My oldest son is not very bright but industrious. . . . My third son is a much brighter boy. He is now studying in P School. . . . I must support him through college. My second son is different. He doesn't like to go to school. He prefers to work for his uncle [mother's brother] as a collector. My fourth son is coming over here soon. I plan to make him work instead of going to school. He should work, helping me to support his third brother to go to college. He will be here in a month or two.

Several months later when I visited this same laundry shop again, I saw a young boy in there. I was introduced to the fourth son who had arrived from China recently.

> "He is going to school now," said the father, "and when he comes back from school, he helps me a great deal. He knows how to iron now. I taught him for almost half a year. Although he doesn't work steadily, yet, after all, laundry is manual labor. It is not hard to learn.
>
> "If financially possible, I should like to let him stay in school. But business is not so good now . . . [May 27, 1939]."

> "Ah Chung [the boy's name] is not going to school anymore. He must work full time now. As we have two places, we need manpower to keep them going. . . .
>
> "He goes to Sunday School on Sunday. . . .
>
> "Yes, he can speak English a little better . . . even better than I . . . [August 19, 1941]."

Among the Chinese laundries, cases like this are popular. One may send for his son and his son sends for his grandson, from one generation to another. Two brothers and an uncle often work together in one laundry. The majority of them are so-called "cousins"; to a Chinese, everyone under the same surname is a cousin who may be closely related in the American sense, or may be just a clansman who belongs to the same village or the same native district.

Chinese immigrants, like other alien groups in America, always find their friends and relatives the closest ones with whom to be associated. No one would think of coming to America without having someone here such as his father, uncle, brother, cousin, clansman, kinsman, or friend. Customarily the laundryman would not think of taking a new acquaintance or *bei-shing* [*biexing*] (people of another clan) as his partner. When one looks for a partner, one usually selects a member of his own clan. The situation can be illustrated by two letters from a third cousin in Minneapolis to a newcomer in Chicago.

> Second Older Brother: Your letter reached me last week, saying that you and Cousin Teh-wu arrived in Chicago safely. How glad am I, your Younger Brother. I thought you were coming here this Tuesday or Wednesday but I waited until today and you didn't show up. I wonder what may have happened.

If you, Older Brother, want to take Cousin Teh-gun's laundry, you had better start to come here immediately. Come to my place first and then from here you can go to Cousin Teh-gun's place.

Best luck with your trip.

> Younger Brother,
> Teh-him
> July 28, 1921

Second Older Brother Teh-seng: Two days ago, I heard that a laundry in the same neighborhood was closed and so Uncle Kai's business turned out to be double as good. He, therefore, needs your help. As I received your letter, you said the same thing. I presume you are now working for Uncle Kai.

I, your Younger Brother, thought that there might not be any suitable place in Chicago and since Cousin Teh-gun's place is pretty reliable, I, therefore, decided to persuade you to come. Now, according to what you have said in your last letter, it impresses me that you prefer to stay in Chicago. I agree with you, prefectly. Because I know Uncle Kai's business is very good all the time. Now you work for him and when he goes back to China, you can buy the place from him. Isn't this a good plan? Secondly, some of our brethren in Chicago are financially well-to-do and our clan house has a *woi* [*hui*] (loan fund). Funds can be obtained much easier, in case you need money to purchase a business.

Cousin Teh-kung and Uncle Lu would like to buy Cousin Teh-gun's place very much. Cousin Teh-gun's partner, however, doesn't like Cousin Teh-kung. What is more, Cousin Teh-kung does not know how to do laundry work; he may not have the intention to keep it too long. That is why Cousin Teh-gun has not given Uncle Lu any definite answer. He is waiting to hear from you instead.

According to what you said in your letter, I presume you had better stay in Chicago. When one goes abroad, all he wants is to make money, and if he has a good place to work, with fair wages, Older Brother, he had better take it. When you have saved a little, you can then search for another way to follow. Later you can join Uncle Kai as his partner or buy his business from him.

I, your Younger Brother, and you, Older Brother, have been separated for a decade, how I long to see you again and chat. But, because of the economic condition, you, my Older Brother, better not think of it just now. We brothers, since we think for each other, we shall be seeing each other sooner or later. You can now only write me how you get across the border and how much it costs you and whatever you want to tell me. Please put it on with pen and ink and send it to me.

I am sending you ten dollars. Please accept it with a smile. It is just for car fare.

It is not all I want to say. I shall write again soon. Hoping you are well.

Younger Brother,
Teh-him
July 28, 1921

The sentiment of brotherhood, of care and concern, can be no better represented than in this case. One finds in his clansmen's place always room to accommodate him, and all sorts of aid and prospects are figured out for him. To join the partnership with one of the clansmen is sometimes taken for granted. It becomes a sort of conventional understanding. Partnerships with other people are only occasional, and so a man is free to take a partnership with friends and other relatives, but in case of any trouble the clansmen have something to say:

H. F.'s partner, T. F., wants to go back to China. H. F. bought over T. F.'s share himself and works alone. The business at that time was not good enough for two persons. It was in the midst of the depression.

Later H. F. hired a Negro girl as a part-time helper. He was getting along well this way until the business would get better. Then he thought of getting a man to work for him. Instead of hiring a clansman, H. F. had a man from the neighboring village.

Soon the business was getting still better. H. F. was so fond of his employee, he offered the man a partnership. It was accepted and the two became partners. After P. became a partner, they bought some new machines and they also managed to buy an automobile, and redecorate their shop. They did these things on installments.

Later H. F. was ill with an unknown malady and he could not work. His partner Pang had one of his friends to help or to work on H. F.'s behalf. This helper was paid full wages, thus it left very little for H. F. to live on. H. F., however, could still stay in the laundry shop, helping here and there. At last H. F. was getting weaker and he wanted to sell his share. Pang's friend, the employee, was interested in it, but he could pay very little. Finally H. F. accepted $300.00; the shop was formerly worth about $1,500.00.

H. F. is now sick and penniless, living in their clan house. This was the way some of his clansmen blamed him one Sunday afternoon:

"I am sorry for you, but you deserve it," began one of the elderly men. "When you wanted to sell your business, why didn't you let us cousins know? You are just a damn fool, letting some outsiders kick you out just like that."

"I did tell Cousin A. about it, but he thought the place was indebted too much. No one of us had any interest in it. . . ."

"Then sell the whole thing!" interrupted another man. "You might get much more than three hundred. Three hundred dollars! They gave you and you took it. Isn't that stupid!"

"Ah, scold me, Uncle. I have made a mistake, that's all, what more can I say. . . ."

"Cousin F.," another man took part and said, "When I heard you wanted to sell it, didn't I tell you to wait? I thought I might send for Cousin T. K. from St. Louis. But you wanted to throw it away right away!"

"But I couldn't wait. . . . I was so sick. I needed money for seeing the doctor. . . ."

"You are not dead yet! You are still sitting here. If you held firm, who would dare to sell it for you? If they dare to do that, do you think we cousins can just stand by and watch?"

Old World sentiments are clearly shown in this short conversation among the clansmen. One's personal affair is never strictly his own, but the affair of the group as well. According to the usual procedure, in case one wants to sell his business, he should announce his intention first to his clansmen. If there is no one among the clansmen who wants to buy it, then it may be sold to any one who offers a good price. The motto is: "even if one is being cheated, it should be done by a clansman rather than an outsider" [*feishui bu liu waijen tien*].

3. Employment—Who Is the Employee?

In looking for a worker, as in choosing a partner, the laundryman tends to hire from his own in-group, namely his clan. This factor needs fuller analysis, for there are complications in the situation of employment.

In the laundry shop, as it is known, both employer and employee have to work, eat, and sleep in the same place. This intimate social contact, perhaps, makes him very unwilling to think of taking a stranger. The problem of employment is never a purely business matter, but a personal affair as well. I have heard complaints of some laundry shop proprietors that they lack manpower and so they could not do this and that. This so-called "manpower," it must be understood, is in the limited sense. It only means that among his immediate circle, particularly sons, nephews, and close cousins, or clansmen, there are not enough men to help. If hired men are not available among their own clan, it becomes a problem to get a reliable person from outsiders.

H. C. and T. C., partners, talked about their need of a man to work for them.

"It is hard to get a man at this time of the year [summer]."

"What are you talking about? Do you have money? If you are willing to offer twenty-five dollars a week, you can get a dozen men right away. Many of them in Chinatown."

"Who doesn't know that! But if you hire an outsider. . . . I don't know. . . . I don't care for an outsider. Del-ka-ma! I can't even make twenty-five dollars a week myself. How can I pay so much for a worker?"

"Well, get whoever you like. I don't care. I know it is better to hire one of our men but none of them is free."

"I am going down there and ask H. [a neighbor and friend] to see if he can work."

"All right, but if he can't work fast, don't blame this and that."

The employment of an outsider is usually on a temporary basis, especially during the summer months, when the volume of business is increased and the demand for labor is greater. Often the outsider is not necessarily a stranger. He may be a man from the native district or a new acquaintance. A non-clansman employed in a Chinese laundry may get along famously with the boss and even become his partner as indicated in the case before last. In such a case, evidently some sort of friendship developed through close personal contact. The point in such an instance is association of personality rather than kinship sentiments. According to the formally established pattern of behavior in the Chinese laundry, the employment of clansmen becomes some sort of folkway. In some cases, in order to make room for a clansman, the proprietor may dismiss the outsider. Sometimes the outsider volunteers his dismissal so that the clansman may take over his job. Recognizing the clan sentiment, the outsider may have no hard feelings even if he is told to go.

It seems that most of the Chinese laundries which employ non-clansmen are those owned by people of small clans, or someone who is more or less detached from his clan affiliation. This type of isolated personality tends to make contacts with outsiders, and they may become friends.

When I was doing nothing in Chinatown, I used to be around Ho Toy Restaurant. There I met this fellow. Later I fixed up this place, I took him along. He has been with me ever since, two years ago.

All my clansmen are in New York—about one hundred of them. I am here in Chicago alone. I have very little to do with my cousins in New York though.

Yes, there are two Leis in Chicago besides me. I heard about them but I have never met them. They did not come from my native district.

Most of my friends are from Chungshan [*Zhongshan*] (a district in
Guangdong Province) and I am from Toyshan [*Taishan,* another district in
Guangdong Province].

I have a nephew in New York, but have not heard from him for a long
time. Since he has never written me, I, too, seldom bother to write him. I
don't know what has become of him and how he gets along.

This estrangement between relatives, to be sure, is not unusual. It is
simply an aspect of social disorganization of immigrant society. The remark about the lack of communication with his nephew in New York
seems to be a negative reaction of clan sentiment and concern about each
other. In his mind, perhaps, his nephew is still somebody.

Chinese employees are very reluctant to take a part-time job. A part-
time helper is likely to be obtained from clansmen, for they are usually
old men who have retired, living in Chinatown. But these old men are
not capable of giving much help in many instances. As an alternative, the
employment of Negro women has begun to take place in recent years.

During the depression, some Chinese laundries in certain areas of the
city were greatly afflicted. Those which formerly consisted of three or four
partners decreased to one or two, and many two-man laundries had only
enough work for one man. In some places, however, the dilemma confronting the laundryman was whether to hire an extra helper or to toil
through a job which is more than one man can finish but easy for two.
After paying high wages to a full-time helper, the proprietor can earn
scarcely anything. Under such circumstances, the laundryman prefers to
have just enough business so that he can manage himself; he does not
care if some customers, particularly some of those hard to please, stop
bringing in their work.

Generally the employer prefers a Chinese man if he can afford to pay
higher wages. Negro women, it is said, are not reliable. Some laundrymen
complain that if the day is too hot and there is too much work to do,
their Negro helpers do not show up as expected. In some places, however,
Negroes are steady workers. In one laundry, at least a Negro woman can
even mark the laundry ticket, writing Chinese characters on it.

The Negro helper works three days a week in the Chinese laundry;
usually on the ironing days—Tuesday, Thursday, and Saturday. Her
wages, although not without exception, are paid on an hourly basis, in
contrast with Chinese workers who are generally paid on a weekly basis.

Besides her wages, she may eat with the laundryman. Otherwise, the laundryman pays for her lunch outside. Some receive carfare from their employer.

4. Business Transactions

The Chinese laundryman tends not only to participate with, and to employ, but also to buy from, and to sell to, his own clansmen. When one wants to sell his laundry business, he usually goes to his close cousin or anyone else in his clan and says: "Brother, I must sell my business, for I am planning to make a return trip to our homeland. How would you like to take over my place? If you care to buy it, as you and I are brothers [clansmen], I shall take whatever you give me. If you don't take, I will have to offer it to someone else." Then he may approach another clansmen and say: "Cousin, it is my duty to inform you that I am going to sell my business. From an outsider I would ask three thousand dollars, but for you, as we are cousins, you can have it for two thousand and eight hundred dollars."

If none of his clansmen, for one reason or another, is interested in it, he then sells it to the one who offers the highest price. He can obtain a buyer by advertising in the immigrant press or by private connection through his friends and relatives. Almost all business transactions are conducted by the seller announcing his price and conditions to his friends and relatives, then the friends and relatives spread the news to their friends and relatives and so on. Soon someone comes in to see the place. The visitor is supposedly a man well acquainted with laundry work. He would observe the number of bundles on the laundry shelves, the machinery, the location, and the neighborhood. In case the visitor is interested in it, he begins to ask for the price or attempts to bargain about it, to learn more about its condition, and to see how the payments would be made. He is also interested in the rent, the lease, and whether the machinery has any unpaid installments. If the visitor is an old hand, these factors generally would help him to estimate whether the price asked is fair or not. In case it is considered satisfactory, the buyer-to-be may finally pay the proprietor an amount of money as a deposit. The formal business transaction can be made in any place agreeable to both parties.

Generally, among clansmen, it can be done in the clan house, before witnesses of other clansmen. The inspection of the laundry shop as just described may not be necessary also. Sometimes the business transaction may take place in the laundry shop, depending on personal trust and confidence. Between non-clansmen, it may take place at the National Association (usually known as Chung Wah Hui Kuon or Chung Wah King Saw [C.C.B.A.]) where business transactions of the National are registered and a small fee is charged. Occasional announcements are seen from time to time in the immigrant press.

> Business Transaction: Laundry—The laundry business located at 3607 Cottage Grove Ave., Chicago, Ill., owned by Moy Chung-shui, will be purchased by me. I have arranged and raised enough money to buy it. The business includes the whole facilities, the lease, and the machinery. The transaction will take place, before the public, in Chung Wah King Saw [C.C.B.A.] at 12:00 p.m., Friday, Aug. 15. If there is any person who may have business deals with Mr. Moy, such as loan, debt, and so on, which may be related to the laundry business, please be present at the time set so that it can be cleared between you and Mr. Moy. After the business transaction, I, as its new owner, would not be responsible whatsoever for any business account of its former owner. Hereby I solemnly declare.
>
> Wong Chi
> August 8, 27th Year of the Chinese Republic [1939].[1]

This type of announcement in the immigrant press may also appear on the bulletin board in Chinatown managed by the National Association. Usually it appears about one week ahead of the date set for the transaction. Its objective is clear—to let be known publicly the change of ownership of the business so that the right and privilege of its new owner is recognized and to avoid unnecessary responsibility and indebtedness. Notice that the lease is especially mentioned in the announcement. To the new owner it is important to be assured that the lease signed between the old owner and landlord must be valid even after the transaction. It is interesting to notice also that it fails to mention the business license, the gas and electric deposits; these items are included in the "whole facilities" mentioned in the announcement, all of which are transferable.

Change of hand from old to new owners is, however, only one kind of business transaction. There are transactions between partners and between employers and employees within the Chinese laundry. Suppose two men are in partnership and after a number of years of working together one of them, for one reason or another, wishes to drop out. Under such circumstances, one of the following ways can be arranged and settled if both of the partners agree: (1) a total sell-out of the business, (2) the one who wants to remain buys the share of the one who wants to drop out, (3) he gets a new partner to join in with him.

Total selling out of a business cannot be done unless the man who wants to remain agrees. It becomes his responsibility, however, to make the settlement either by buying the other share himself, or by choosing his own new partner among relatives and friends. He then may put a little advertisement in the immigrant press.

> Business Transaction: Laundry Shop Share—The laundry which is located at 4707 N. Damen Street, Chicago, is formally owned in partnership by Lau Yu-fon and Lau Him-chang. Because of ill-health, elder Yu-fon cannot work any longer and his share in the laundry, including total facilities, the lease, and the tools will be purchased over by me. The date of transaction will be held at Chung Way Association (C.C.B.A.), on March 2, at 2 p.m. In case elder Yu-fon owes anybody money in loan or in debt which may have something to do with this laundry, please be present at the date and place given. After the business transaction, no matter what sort of account exists between you and elder Yu-fon, it shall not have anything to do with the laundry. I solemnly declare hereby,
>
> Lau Him-chang
> February 24, the 30th Year of the Chinese Republic[2]

The procedure is almost the same in case a new man is taken in to join the partnership. The new man, if he thinks it advisable, likewise advertises a similar type of announcement in the immigrant press. The same may occur, although less likely, when a man is offered a partnership to join in a laundry business when he has been an employee in the place.

> Announcement of Taking Partnership: The laundry located at 108 W. Goethe Street, Chicago, is originally established and owned by Toy Shi-shan. Because of his indebtedness to an American loan bank, and in order to have money to pay his installments, he has offered me a partnership. From now on, all rights and privileges of the laundry belong equally and jointly to me and Shi-shan; he and I have become partners. Before the public, in the National Association [C.C.B.A.], the partnership will be registered at 2:00 p.m., Sunday, Jan. 14th. Hereby I may resume my right and declare.
>
> Toy Shi-kai
> January 9, 29th Year of the Chinese Republic [1940].[3]

It is clear from our discussion of the division of labor, partnership and ownership, employment practices, and business transactions, that the social structure of the Chinese laundry is constructed on the pattern of the sentiments and economic traditions of the homeland. They seem to be influenced little if at all by American models. The entry of the date of a business transaction in terms of the year of the Chinese Republic symbolizes the essential point that ideologically the laundryman is living in China even if his laundry is physically located in the United States.

NOTES

1. *San Ming Morning News,* August 8, 1939.
2. *Ibid.,* February 26, 1941.
3. *Ibid.,* January 9, 1941.

CHAPTER VII

THE LAUNDRY AND
ITS AGENCIES

IN HIS OPERATION, the Chinese laundryman comes into contact with some agencies which, in one sense, his laundry depends on, and which, in another sense, confine him to the laundry. These agencies supply necessary services, but at the same time constitute a barrier which stands between the Chinese laundryman and the general public.

1. Financial Resources

A Chinese laundryman can obtain money in three ways to join partnership in a laundry business or to establish a new one. He can get it by personal borrowing from relatives and friends, by obtaining a grant of *woi* [*hui*] (Chinese guild loan conducted among themselves), and by making a loan from a bank through a Chinese agent. At the time money is needed for a business purpose, one often has to raise enough in either one or more of these ways, depending upon the size of the amount needed and the personal connection of the individual.

Personal Borrowing

The laundryman comes to relatives and friends in America. He has his apprenticeship with them and, after he has learned the trade, he can either join a partnership with someone or establish a new business for himself. In some cases, the laundryman works as an employee. At length, he may save at least part of the money he needs. In case he has not enough, he usually confers with one or more of his clansmen and kinsmen whom he

considers as prospects for financial assistance. Table 7.1, taken in part
from a personal account of a laundryman, shows that he borrowed the
sum of two hundred and forty dollars from four different clansmen
December 2, 1927, for the purpose of opening a new laundry shop.

Personal borrowing from relatives and friends usually can never be of
large amount. The largest sum one individual can borrow from another
seldom exceeds two or three hundred dollars. In case one needs a sum as
large as a thousand dollars, he may have to raise it by more than one
means.

Borrowing is usually by personal appeal, through private mediation,
and by letter writing, depending upon the individual situation of confidence and trust. In face-to-face conference with a prospective lender, the
borrower must be trustworthy, for the lender usually asks for neither
interest nor a written "I owe you" statement. Borrowing is often done by
correspondence. One may write to his relatives and friends if a personal
conference is impossible. In case an obligation exists, the latter may think
of some way to raise the money even if he does not have it.

Among the Chinese immigrants, personal borrowing sometimes has to
be done through the mediation of a third person. The mediator usually
is an older man of the clan. His prestige is a sort of witness and guarantee
between the lender and the borrower, for borrowing is purely a matter of
trust and confidence. Usually there is no written agreement. The lender
sometimes prefers a third person to be a witness; sometimes he does it
to honor the mediator. The role of the mediator, therefore, is purely sen-

TABLE 7.1
Statement from a Personal Account

Name of Lender	Date Borrowed	Amount	Purpose
Brother T. F.	May, 1925	$ 20	—
Uncle C. H.*	Oct., 1925	100	—
Uncle C. H.*	Oct., 1925	40	—
Uncle S. K.	Feb. 2, 1926	40	—
C. S. Moy†	Mar. 25, 1926	30	—
Cousin T. H.	Dec. 2, 1927	100	New shop
Uncle H. K.	Dec. 2, 1927	100	New shop
Uncle S. K.	Dec. 2., 1927	20	New shop
Cousin W. T.	Dec. 2, 1927	20	New shop
Uncle S. L.	Feb. 2, 1928	10	Pay rent

* = a kinsman; † = a friend; others are clansmen.

timental and a moral support for the deal. Often, on account of personal dislike of one toward the other, the lender may be reluctant to give help to the borrower. Then an older man of the clan intervenes, trying to mediate the deal on the basis of Old World sentiments and customs. The one who has money will be ashamed if he refuses to help his poor cousin even though there is personal dislike between them. It is a matter of moral obligation, especially with close cousins.

One can get ahead easily with a well-to-do close relative backing him financially. A close cousin is obligated to help a newcomer with continual loans of as much as several thousand dollars in some cases. In the statement presented in Table 7.2, for example, a man by the name of Wai-pon borrowed a total of seven hundred and forty dollars from his cousin in

TABLE 7.2
Statement from a Laundryman's Personal Account

In the 9th year of the Republic		
[1920], Wai-pon borrowed:		
Once	$300.00	
Once	30.00	
Once	150.00	
Once	60.00	
Once	200.00	
Total	$740.00	
In the 15th year of the Republic		
[1926], Wai-pon borrowed:		
Once	$380.00	(for passport)
Once	200.00	(railroad ticket)
Once	50.00	
Once	70.00	
Once	1,862.50	(laundry share)
Total	$2,562.50	
Grand Total		$3,302.50
Wai-pon paid me back the		
following amounts:		
Once	$ 600.00	(from a woi grant)
Once	100.00	(in person)
Once	520.00	(in care of Lo-hom)
Total	$1,220.00	
Balance he still		
owes me		$2,082.50

NOTE: The statement was made to two elder men of the clan in America after the lender went back to China. The elder men who received a letter together with the statement may serve as mediators, advising the borrower to make good on his promises.

1920, when he was in Mexico. Six years later, when Wai-pon was coming to the United States, he again borrowed from the same man three hundred and eighty dollars for arranging his trip and two hundred dollars for traveling expenses, according to the statement of the bookkeeping. After he reached Chicago, he was evidently still very poor and he had to borrow again from the same relative, once fifty dollars, and once seventy dollars. It seemed that Wai-pon was first employed by this relative, or provided an opportunity to learn the trade as an apprentice. At length, when Wai-pon learned the trade, the relative offered Wai-pon a partnership. After he had paid back one thousand two hundred and twenty dollars, he still owed the relative two thousand and eighty-two dollars and fifty cents, when the relative made a summary of the account after Wai-pon returned to China.

This item is very interesting because it represents a special arrangement in the character of personal borrowing. It means the newcomer can take a partnership in a laundry without paying all at once to its former proprietor if the understanding between them is mutual. It is a special form of personal borrowing. It is more or less a personal favor extended to a relative.

Personal borrowing should be distinguished from personal loans. The former is purely a personal favor, with no formally signed agreement, including rate of interest and time limitation for repayment. The practice of personal loan, on the other hand, is likely to include a written agreement of the time repayment should be made and the rate of interest. Personal loans, however, seldom occur among immediate friends and relatives. Personal loans are made outside of the primary group circle. The lender usually is a business man in Chinatown.

A Grant of Woi[1]

The woi [*hui*], an immigrant institution, literally translated means "get together," or "put together," and is a sort of collective loan fund administered by a small group of persons usually affiliated with the clan or with a store in Chinatown. It is one of the ways, if not the main way, by which Chinese laundrymen obtain their financial resources to operate their laundry enterprise. One can secure a grant of woi either by his own right or by the right of a relative. In order to secure a grant, either one or both of them must be members of the woi.

The woi has two functions: One is to provide its members the opportunity of securing a sizable sum of money to establish a laundry shop, and the other is to make profit for its members in a business proposition. Each individual puts an equal amount of money into a pool, and makes it available for the one who is in need of funds for business. The prospective loan-maker signs a petition for the sum. He may receive it provided he offers the highest interest among the competitors.

The administration of the loan starts at the first month of the lunar calendar, after the joyous New Year celebration, and it is carried through each month until the end of the year. A new woi may be started again from year to year. The membership is usually from fifteen to thirty persons. The monthly investment is fixed for the first month, but the amount from the first month on may be varied according to the rate of interest offered each month. One woi may start with the fixed amount of fifty dollars, while the other may be fixed at forty to start. Supposing the basic amount set is fifty dollars for each member, and its membership contains fifteen persons, the total amount available would be seven hundred and fifty dollars to start.

As soon as the monthly dues are all collected from its members, the loan is then available for the needy member. It is usually administered on the last Sunday of each month. The winning applicant may secure the loan through a competitive bid. One wishing a loan may either be present in person or be represented by a trusted individual. Each competitor, before the administrators read and announce the ballots, secretly writes down the amount of interest he is willing to pay on a piece of paper, folds it, and hands it to the administrator. At last the administrator asks if there is any other applicant. At this moment, one can offer to pay the amount of interest orally. Immediately the competitors who have already put down an amount of interest on their ballots may be allowed to raise it. Finally, when there is no more bidding, the administrator opens the ballots one by one. In case two ballots are tied, the one opened first wins. As for the victor, he is the one who pays the highest interest; his name and amount of interest offered is entered upon a slip of paper and it is posted on the wall.

The same procedure is repeated every month. Except for the first month, the loan-maker would receive his in full, four weeks after the draw.

At the time the money is handed over to the loan-maker by the administrator, the loan-maker must sign his name on the book, and he must have a guarantor to sign also. In case the loan-maker fails to pay his monthly installment before the end of the year, it is the guarantor's responsibility; he must get the loan-maker to make good or he has to pay the back installments on the loan-maker's behalf.

The interest offered by the woi loan-maker is sometimes as high as 20 percent, in case of urgent need. Ordinarily, the interest is about 5 percent. The higher the interest offered, the less the amount the members of the woi invest per month. Supposing the interest offered is nine dollars and twenty-five cents, and the fixed monthly basic amount is fifty dollars; but, actually, all members, except the loan-maker, pay only forty dollars and seventy-five cents. It is the amount of nine dollars and twenty-five cents subtracted from fifty dollars. So, instead of receiving the full basic amount, the loan-maker receives only the subtracted total.

The following statement is written by a woi administrator to the loan-maker of the month who offers nine dollars and twenty-five cents interest in the eighth month of the circle of twenty members. Notice that seven pay fifty dollars for the month while twelve pay forty dollars and seventy-five cents. The former are members who have been granted loans; the latter are members who have not or who do not wish a loan. The man who receives the loan does not have to pay for that month. The next month, he pays fifty dollars and continues to do so until the retirement of the loan at the end of the twentieth month.

To Cousin Hin-wing:

This monthly woi loan entitled *tin** is granted to you, that you agree to pay an interest of $9.25.

by Teh-chow

December 26, 1928

*A series number in Chinese character. Tin [*tien*] means heaven.

The basic amount is constant while the subtracted amount varies from month to month. According to the above table, the current amount after subtracting interest is forty dollars and seventy-five cents. The loan-maker gets the grand total of the sum of both the basic and net amounts; as in the table, it is eight hundred thirty-nine dollars. After he received the loan, he had to pay fifty dollars each month for the next twenty months.

TABLE 7.3
Statement of the Month

Name of Members Granted Loans	Basic Amount	Name of Members Loan Not Granted	Amount Less Subtracted
Hong-yuen	$ 50.00	Sai-soong	$ 40.75
Wah-ching	50.00	Mau-hong	40.75
Wu-shui	50.00	King-on	40.75
Bin-soon	50.00	Lon-pin	40.75
King-jin	50.00	Hin-wah	40.75
King-won	50.00	Hin-ming	40.75
Sing-pon	50.00	Ling-ching	40.75
		King-pin	40.75
Total	$350.00	Yang-moy	40.75
		Hau-on	40.75
		Hau-on	40.75
		Sun-sam	40.75
			$489.00
Grand Total		$839.00	

It is clear that the joining of the woi is an investment. In case one does not need the money at all and he keeps on postponing his application until the last month, the final loan is automatically his. In this way he makes a profit from the interest paid by other members from month to month and at the same time he saves money.

Woi is of two kinds: One is administered by managers of different stores in Chinatown; the other is organized by different clans. The former takes membership from all clan affiliations, providing they also have connections with the store or have a personal relation with the manager. The latter takes only members of its clan. There are usually two administrators in the woi, the treasurer and the bookkeeper. The administrators are not paid for the work; their appointment, however, signifies prestige and confidence. The woi in the store, on the other hand, is administered by the proprietor; his property in the store gives him security and trust to control it himself, or he may appoint another person to administer it.

The laundryman who is working can easily manage to join the woi. In this way he may gain a fund large enough to establish his own business or to join a partnership with a clansman. A newcomer, however, may not be a member of the woi. In such a case, a close cousin who is a member of the woi, instead of lending his money directly, secures a woi loan on the newcomer's behalf. The newcomer then becomes an indirect member of the woi, for, from the month after he receives the fund, he would be responsible for paying the remainder of the monthly installments. Each month he has to hand over the payment to his benefactor who, in turn, pays the administrator. Of course, the benefited man can pay for it directly in the name of the benefactor, under certain circumstances. But if he fails to make good, the payment of the loan becomes the benefactor's responsibility.

Security Loan

Another alternative way to raise money is to make a loan from the bank. But how? Language difficulties and personal strangeness prevent the Chinese laundryman from approaching the banker directly. There are exceptions, of course, but the majority need help from someone who can interpret for them. The interpreter makes a commission on the deal. In some cases, the loan-maker does not even have to appear in the bank in person. The agent, competing for business, tries to make the deal as easy as possible, manages to be a go-between, and has the necessary paper signed and properly executed. The installments are paid either to the bank directly or through the agent.

The person best fitted for this job, of course, is a Chinese who can speak both Chinese and English. There are three individuals who advertise in the local Chinese newspaper that they can give the best service in security loans. The following is one of them:

> Attention whoever needs money urgently.
> I am an agent for a security loan—lowest interest,
> long terms to repay.
> Need some money right away?
> Please call me and
> I shall be glad to do the best I can for you.
>
> > BENNY GOON
> > 239 W 22nd Place
> > Chicago, Ill.
> > Phone VIC. 8520[2]

Through the Chinese agency, a laundryman can make a loan with only personal property as security. In the case of a newcomer, he may not have any personal property. The so-called personal property that the laundryman has, of course, is his laundry shop. It includes the facilities and the machinery within the laundry shop. In case the loan to be made is a sizable sum, there can be a guarantor requirement with the deal. Guarantors must be friends and relatives who can produce security.

The interest charged in such a security loan is very high. The agent has to make his commission and the bank has to make its profit. It is sometimes as high as 25 percent. The rate is lower, provided one can manage to repay the loan in a shorter period.

In case the laundryman fails to make good on his payments, unless special arrangements are made with the bank, such as paying only the interest, the latter may take legal action against the former. The laundry shop may be foreclosed. But cases of this seldom occur.

Another type of loan somewhat similar to the preceding one is what may be called a personal loan from a money-lender among the Chinese. The Chinese money-lender may be a storekeeper, a gambling house boss, or a laundryman of means. Differing from personal borrowing, a personal loan is a business proposition and an impersonal matter. The money-lender sometimes charges just as high interest as the bank, and the agreement also has to be signed. Such business, no doubt, is very profitable but not without risk. The loan-maker may fail to pay or may run away. The urban community in America is different from the village in China; one can easily move out of town and disappear. Since the agreement is signed in the Chinese traditional manner, it is more or less based on moral law rather than on legal terms in the American way. Legal action appears unlikely. If the man runs away without paying his debt, the money-lender can look for the guarantor or elder man of the loan-maker's clan or his immediate relatives, trying to get moral support if not actual repayment. Sometimes a greedy way of making interest in lending money can hardly receive moral support; a greedy way of making loan interest (*fong-chi-hoh-lee* [*fangzhi huoli*]) is spoken of as bad business, and it is against the mores.

In recent years, the personal loan seems to be losing popularity, while the security loan, through a Chinese agent, from American loan banks is gaining popularity. Of course, personal borrowing and woi loan-making are still popular. The other source of obtaining financial aid is from the laundry supply agent who makes loans to laundrymen as a way to keep their patronage as well as a good business proposition. Since it is connected with, and is in the nature of, business competition among laundry supply agents, we will take up this matter in the following section.

2. The Laundry Supply Agency

Another type of agency which seems to take away the laundryman's chance of making direct contacts with the general public is the different laundry supply agents who do most of their business with Chinese laundrymen. The agent, being an old acquaintance of the Chinese, usually can speak a few Chinese words to be sociable. Sometimes he just utters a word or two to make fun. The business relationship is impersonal, yet each is trying to gain the other's trust and confidence. Other conveniences are provided as ways of competition and accommodation on the part of the supplier to promote business relationships with the Chinese laundryman.

Three laundry supply companies, Central, Allegan, and Reliable, and one laundry machinery company, Keel, are the main suppliers for Chinese laundry shops in Chicago (see Figure 7.1). Central Company, the oldest of the three, has been doing business with the Chinese laundrymen for a long time. It changed hands several years ago, but, to the Chinese laundrymen, it is still *Gen-Ming-Ham* (Cunningham). Allegan, who used to work for the old Cunningham, started his own business on a small scale but now he has a big storehouse in Chinatown. He became a keen competitor of Central, and some laundrymen think that Allegan is now doing more business than Central. Reliable, the newest of the three, unlike the others, has its office on the far South Side of the city instead of right in Chinatown, and is the only company now (1942) advertising in the local immigrant press, *San Ming Morning News*. The Chinese characters in the advertisement translated read:

> ATTENTION, FRIENDS IN THE CHINESE LAUNDRY: We have large quantities of laundry supplies such as paper boxes, paper boards, twines, soap flakes, and all other things complete. We welcome the patronage of Chinese friends from far and near.
> Everything is price ceiling during war time. Better be careful with your

purchasing. If you want a bargain, please call us. We know the line of business best and will be honest with you and do our best to serve you.

If you are not sure about our price, the best way is to inquire of us. If you please either write or call (either Chinese or English) us and we will be happy to help you.

The Keel Company, which is also located outside of Chinatown, likewise advertises in the Chinese newspaper for a new type of gas drying room which only a few Chinese laundries have adopted. Keel Company has sold most machines to the Chinese laundries. The advertisement in English is:

> You Should Use Gas Drying Room. It is cleaner and easier to dry and to keep cool.
> We have new type of gas stoves. Its operation is easy and economical.
> The price is reasonable. Chinese friends of the laundry business, please try it.

All the laundry suppliers, interestingly enough, have to employ a Chinese clerk who answers the phone and takes the order. If there is no such person available, the non-Chinese clerk must be an experienced "old China hand" who is used to the half Chinese-English. The advertisement of Reliable Company states that Chinese may be used in both phone calls and writing letters. In the Allegan store, a Chinese is also employed.

The laundry suppliers for the Chinese laundry, furthermore, have learned the Chinese psychology. The laundryman likes to be trusted. He prefers to buy on credit and by charge account. Others pay C.O.D., but the price must be lower. In case he finds out any cheating on the part of the supplier, a resolution for boycott may take effective action. In some cases, however, the laundryman owes the supplier quite a bit of money and the latter may take the liberty of charging everything higher. The laundryman notices it and does not like it so much, but he cannot quit the supplier. If he does, he has to pay the debt immediately. So every supplier is willing to sell by charge account and carry the customers. The laundry supplier usually carries a complete list of laundry needs, including machinery and stoves. In case the supplier does not carry a particular commodity, he can be an agent, getting it on the laundryman's behalf. The supplier, sometimes, in order to keep the customer, has to do some sort of favor for the laundryman. One laundry supplier, it is known, even

FIGURE 7.1   Chinese laundry supply agency advertising.

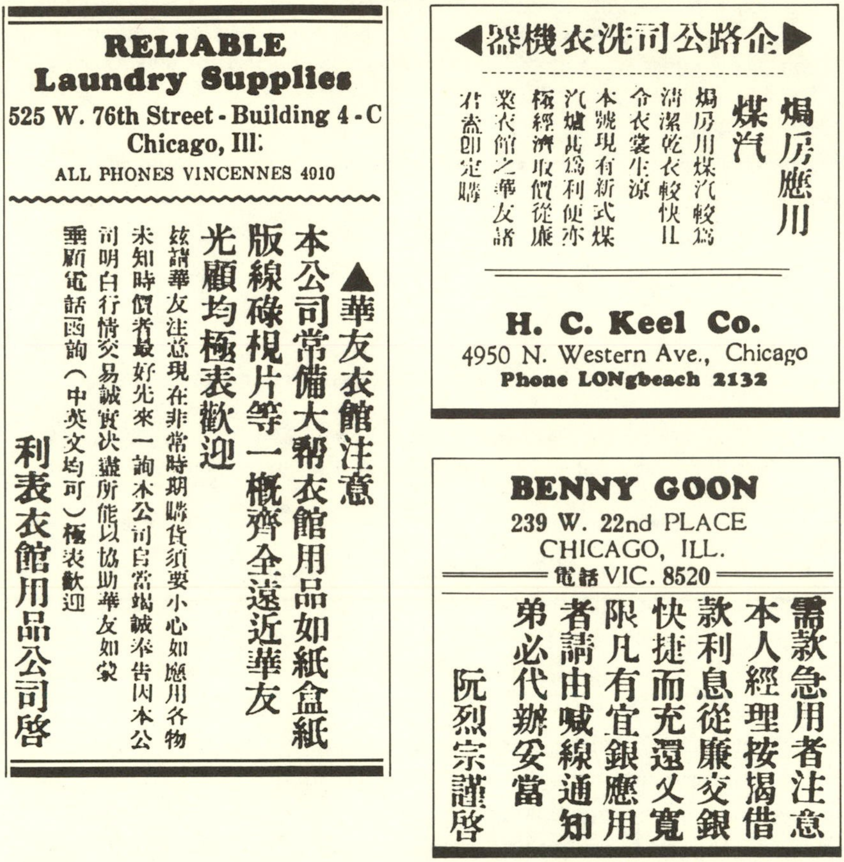

RELIABLE
Laundry Supplies
525 W. 76th Street - Building 4 - C
Chicago, Ill.
ALL PHONES VINCENNES 4010

本公司常備大幫衣館用品如紙盒紙
▲華友衣館注意
版線碌梘片等一概齊全遠近華友
光顧均極表歡迎
茲請華友注意現在非常時期購貨須要小心如應用各物
未知時價者最好先來一詢本公司自當竭誠奉告凡本公
司明白行情交易誠實决遠所能以協助華友如衆
奉顧電話函詢（中英文均可）極表歡迎
利表衣館用品公司啟

◀器機衣洗司公路企▶

焗房應川
煤汽

焗房川煤汽較為
清潔乾衣較快以
令衣裳生涼
本號現有新式煤
汽爐甚為利使亦
極經濟取價從廉
粟衣館之華友請
若益創定購

H. C. Keel Co.
4950 N. Western Ave., Chicago
Phone LONgbeach 2132

BENNY GOON
239 W. 22nd PLACE
CHICAGO, ILL.
電話 VIC. 8520

需款急用者注意
本人經理按揭借
款利息從廉交銀
快捷而充還义寬
限凡有宜銀應用
者請由喊線通知
弟必代辦妥當
阮烈宗謹啟

lends money to the laundryman in time of need. The charges of interest on the loan are at the lender's discretion, whether higher or lower, depending on the loan-maker's potentiality as a customer. No information is reported that the laundry supplier actually finances the establishment of the Chinese laundry. Most of the loans made from the supplier seem to be small sums. The laundryman, for instance, loses his battle at the gambling table in a Chinatown gambling house. He usually makes a loan of a small amount, enough to pay the rent or gas and electric bills. Another may need part of a larger sum being raised for a special purpose. The loans from the supplier seem to be easier to get than loans from the bank, for generally there is no formal signing of an agreement on the deal.

The suppliers have to watch the Chinese newspaper or the bulletin board for any announcement of business transactions in the Chinese laundry. The new hand usually advertises in the local immigrant press or puts on the bulletin board of the National Association an announcement, declaring the change of management taking place in the laundry, and only the old hand is responsible for whatever debt he may owe in connection with the laundry. The supplier has to depend upon his Chinese clerk to read these announcements. In case the laundryman selling out his laundry still owes the supplier something on an old account, the latter can collect it before it is too late. Such, of course, is the occasional case. On the whole, Chinese laundrymen are conscientious and honest. They are conscious of "having face" not for the sake of oneself, but for the sake of their own ethnic group.

A question may be raised here: "Why don't Chinese people operate a laundry supply business?" I am informed that one tried in the past but failed. One explanation is that the Chinese cannot compete with the non-Chinese who has already firmly established the business and who has ways and connections to get his commodities at wholesale, quicker and cheaper. Today, the laundry supply companies sell not only soap flakes, which the laundryman needs for his trade, but rice, which is the daily diet of the laundryman.

It is true some of the Chinese agencies supply the laundrymen with some necessities, but not the complete lines of supplies. This type of agency we will describe as the traveling Chinese store in the following section.

3. The Traveling Grocery Store

There are about twenty-five trucks, carrying meats, vegetables, imported and homemade foodstuffs, laundry and household miscellanies—something of a combination meat market, poultry farm, grocery store, delicatessen shop, and fish market, operated by stores in Chinatown or by private individuals, making daily visits to laundries and chop suey houses all over the metropolis, selling whatever goods they have. The traveling store does not stop at every Chinese laundry. It stops only at the places of friends and relatives. Each truck has only a limited number of places to go. If a keeper belongs to a bigger clan or is more influential, he probably covers more ground and does more business. Efforts to make new customers sometimes prove to be disappointing. Each truck covers a route in one day, usually on one side of the city. The keepers of moving stores who usually know each other and share the same group of customers, should avoid time conflict. They should not visit the same places on the same day.

The laundryman, on the other hand, expects the coming of certain moving stores on a certain day. He usually refuses to buy from a stranger, unless he does not expect any of his friends and relatives. Sometimes he purposely waits for the coming of certain things. Purchasing becomes a sentimental gesture rather than a commercial exchange: that is to say, he sometimes buys things he really does not need.

Traveling stores sell mostly fresh chickens and ducks, fish, Chinese delicatessen foods, and various kinds of Chinese vegetables. These things constitute the main part of their merchandise. Some of the traveling grocers sell only these commodities. The others, especially those representing a store in Chinatown, may carry a relatively complete line of merchandise, including laundry supplies such as shirt bands, shirt boards, bluing, buttons, twine, and what not. In all cases, however, foodstuffs are the main thing; anything else is a sideline.

The founding of the moving store is rather recent, not earlier than the end of the last world war. Its numbers have been increasing until the present maximum. What is interesting is the demand for such a luxurious type of personal service. The laundryman goes to Chinatown only on Sunday. That is the only time he does his shopping. He brings back to his laundry shop on Sunday evening, some dry goods which may last a whole week or more. But the fresh meat and vegetables cannot be kept more than two or three days. By the middle of the week, he is likely to be out of fresh foods. Of course, he can buy them in the neighborhood grocery store. They do patronize the neighborhood stores for some foodstuffs. But he prefers those prepared in Chinese ways. He likes Chinese vegetables. He does not mind if the price is a little higher. Some of the Chinese feel that they gain little out of life by working day and night, and so they can at least compensate themselves with good food. "Eat! Get something good to eat! Life is too dull and work is so hard" is the general notion. Under such psychological inclination, fresh meat and vegetables from Chinatown during the week are in demand. One man started it and found it profitable; the others followed suit. Pretty soon the laundryman has at least one traveling grocer stopping at his door every day. But he cannot buy from every man who stops. So he may excuse himself by saying politely or bluntly that he has already purchased enough from a "cousin" of his just an hour ago. The stranger may try again the next time and the next. His persistence may establish a business relationship or may result even in a friendship. But a non-relative can seldom beat a "cousin" or other relatives in the traveling store business.

In a four-man laundry on Chicago's far North Side, a train of seven traveling grocers stops for business one after the other during the week. Three of them are operated by relatives, including one cousin and two distant kinsmen. The rest of the four are operated by non-relatives, including one neighbor, one acquaintance, and two strangers. Their business with the laundry is shown in Figure 7.2.

FIGURE 7.2 Comparison of the amounts spent by a laundry in purchasing food from seven traveling stores (1936–1938).

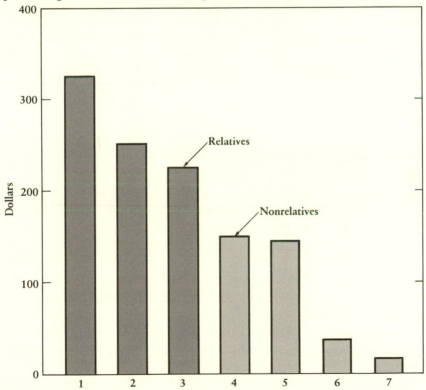

SOURCE: Compiled by the author from the account books of a laundry; this is not an actual food budget.

It is clear that the laundry buys more from relatives than from non-relatives. Columns 6 and 7 represent two traveling stores operated by strangers who tried but failed to make a steady customer. They either pass the laundry without stopping or visit it casually from time to time. In this particular case, Column 2 should run highest, for the man is a close cousin of the laundrymen. His volume of business with the laundry is in second place because during the three-year interval his business was suspended for a period of several months. Column 1 represents a traveling store operated by a distant relative and is in the first place because it comes every Saturday. Saturday is the laundryman's feast day. By Saturday evening, the work is probably all done, the laundryman would like to prepare a better meal; he has time to cook chicken, fish, and other favorite delicacies. The grocery which happened to come on Saturday usually meets a liberal customer. The bill is easily two or three dollars.

There are, of course, some who do not have friends and relatives in the traveling store business. If such is the case, one is then free to buy from anyone. Or a laundryman may be indifferent to his clansmen grocer and prefer to patronize an "outsider." Still others, either due to geographical distance or economic reasons, are seldom visited by the traveling grocers; they have to be content with meat and vegetables purchased from the neighborhood market.

4. Clothing and Jewelry Agents

Another service that keeps the laundryman in his laundry is offered by clothing and jewelry agents. The Chinese laundryman seldom buys his clothing in the clothing store like the general American public. When he needs a suit of clothes, he waits until a clothing agent visits him and it is ordered, tailor-made.

There are several Jewish tailors in Chicago who have the laundryman's business. The tailors, some of whom have been in business for years, like laundry suppliers, know Chinese psychology. A clothing agent has to hire an English-speaking Chinese to accompany him in a house-to-house visit. If the laundryman is finally convinced, the tailor takes the measurements and then plans for payment are made. The laundryman usually pays on the installment plan. He immediately pays five dollars as a deposit, and after the clothing is delivered, he pays two dollars a month.

In a similar way the jewelry agent deals with the laundryman. The most common things he sells are watches and diamond rings. Some laundrymen buy watches not only for themselves but for their sons and daughters who are back home in China. The agents are usually Jewish. One agent, for example, works in different sections of the metropolis. Once he demonstrated watches and diamond rings in a laundry near the university campus. On another occasion he was seen taking orders for a tailor shop.

But not all jewelry and clothing agents are Jews. Chinese are trying to make a living at it, too. One Chinese has been in such a business for many years. Like the Jewish agents, he carries not only diamond rings, but also shirts and underwear.

To what extent does the laundryman patronize the agents? My impression is that if a laundryman has any intention of buying a watch at all, he would be likely to buy it from an agent who comes to his shop. Wearing a watch is popular among immigrants. Some even wear diamond rings. The laundryman does not care much about the furniture in his shop, but he is fond of jewelry which he can wear and carry on his person. His living expenses for food and shelter are so little, he can afford, or rather inclines to get satisfaction from, possessing ornamental things. When he goes back to China the gold watch and diamond ring he wears will be the symbols of his wealth. It is so easy to buy on the installment plan, he can hardly resist the salesman's talk. So almost every laundryman has a gold watch, if not a diamond ring. For some, one is not enough; he wants to have a wristwatch and a pocket watch. If his son or nephew in China needs a watch, he sends one of them back to the home country. Soon he does not like the old one so much, and he buys a new one. Money does not matter; a man has to have satisfaction.

The same psychology applies to his purchase of coats from the tailor. He probably had not the time and the courage to visit a downtown clothing store. He does not feel at ease, walking into a store when the salesman tries to make a sale. He cannot really tell what he wants, but in his own laundry he feels at home. He can look at samples. He can bargain. His main concern is the material, and the style concerns him very little.

The tailor-made suit of clothes for the Chinese laundryman appears to have a particular pattern. It seldom follows the current fashion. In the vest, two extra pockets are made on the inside. In the coat, the owner's initials are sewed on the edge of the inner pocket. The workmanship as well as the material used is rather inferior, but the price is generally high.

The agent comes around once every month, collecting his payments. The laundryman may be willing to pay in full, if the tailor gives him a discount.

Sometimes a laundryman orders a suit of clothes in one laundry. The next time the agent comes to collect, he finds the man is working in another laundry.

In conclusion, with all these different agencies operating around the Chinese laundryman, it seems obvious that he is very well provided with essentials without much effort on his part, by outside contacts which seek him in the neighborhood. For other personal needs, he occasionally shops in the neighborhood for fruits and other foodstuffs. He may also patronize the neighborhood drug store, but he is rather inclined to go to the Chinatown barber. In case of sickness, the neighborhood doctor may be called in an emergency, but the laundryman often prefers an herb doctor, or to avoid language difficulties, he would rather see the American-trained Chinese doctor whose office is in Chinatown.

These things among others may be considered devices unwittingly instituted to keep the laundryman apart from the general public.

NOTES

1. Among the Japanese immigrants, the similar type of money pool is called *tanomoshi*; see S. Frank Miyamoto, *Social Solidarity among the Japanese in Seattle* (Seattle: University of Washington Press, 1939), p. 75.

2. The advertisement appeared daily in *San Ming Morning News* in 1943.

CHAPTER VIII

THE NEWCOMER AND THE
GOLDEN MOUNTAIN

ALMOST ALL Chinese laundrymen in Chicago are villagers from the Four Counties [or Districts] known separately as Toyshan, Hoiping [Haiping], Yenping [Enping], and Shunhwai [Xinhui] in the Southwest, a few hundred miles from the city of Canton, China. Toyshan County, especially, is the birthplace of the majority of laundrymen in America. These men were not laundrymen in China, and their usual occupation in China had nothing in common with laundry work. The majority of them were farmers and farm hands. Others were young village boys, village storekeepers, small Hong Kong merchants and office clerks, politicians, school teachers, students, seamen, playboys, and loafers. They were not the manual laborers in the Chinese cities known to the Western world as "coolies."

The immigrant term for newcomer is *shun-hsueng-lei* [*xing xiangli*] (new fellow villager). Perhaps it is of some significance to describe the attitude with which the shun-hsueng-lei takes laundry as his new occupation. The Chinese laundrymen, through generations of exclusion and subordination, have built a social and economic world of their own. The newcomer, before and after his arrival in America, is seldom an individual, but rather a member of the immigrant group. After some months in this country, the newcomer shares the attitudes and values of the group and becomes a member of "Main Street."

What are the newcomer's hopes and dreams before coming to America? How does he behave as a new member of the immigrant group, and how does he accommodate himself to the situation?

1. The Dream of the Golden Mountain

America, to the Chinese villagers, is a golden mountain. Tales of the
California gold rush spread around the Chinese villages in the old days.
There were stories of pioneer overseas Chinese from America returning
home with bushels of gold sand. Now, the immigrant brings home no
more gold sand. But his economic success in the United States has greatly
affected the social life of his native land; therefore, coming to America is
a dream for many. Although the Chinese Exclusion Act bars the entry of
Chinese labor, some can still come as merchants, merchant's sons, citizens
and citizens' sons or grandsons. Others can be smuggled in with the aid
of steamship and railroad agencies. The newcomer, in the expression of
the immigrants themselves, arrives with nothing but "a pair of bare
hands." The day he comes he finds a social organization all ready for
him. He will soon find a place in it.

It becomes a role to play, for those who are here to think of giving
their poor brother a chance to come. The immigrant laws may deprive
them of the right of a legal passport, but there are always other ways and
means of obtaining an entry. The illegal entry is always much more expensive. Sometimes it takes as much as three or four thousand dollars. If
one wants to get his nephew over, for example, he must have economic
means to do so.

All laundrymen have relatives in China, but only those who have money
and have good connections are able to have them come. It becomes a
matter of personal pride for one who can do so. His brother who has the
chance should be grateful. The poor brothers and nephews in China,
seeing others have the chance to become prosperous, write to their elders
in America, begging for assistance. For many, it becomes a dream—a
dream of going to the "Golden Mountain."

> Next Summer I shall be graduated. The graduation doesn't mean that I
> have the ability to make a living. I confess I have no special ability at all.
> If I find a job here in Canton, my earning would be hardly enough for me
> to live on myself, so how could I have enough to support my parents? When
> I think of this I am worried and sad. What is more, I am growing up. Being
> the only son, the duty of parental support will be on my shoulders alone.
> I, your Nephew, have thought of all sorts of possible ways of making a
> living, but every way seems to be of no avail. There is only one way which
> I consider best of all. It is a chance of going abroad. It is now merely a

dream. Whether this dream comes true, I can only depend on you, my Venerable Uncle, that you are kind enough to assist me. I now write you, hoping you can get me a citizenship passport. After graduating from middle school, I am expecting to have a chance to go to America. If you can be so kind to me, I promise I shall be a good and worthy nephew for you. Please answer me and give me encouragement.

This is a part of the letter written by a high school student in Canton to his uncle, a laundryman, in Chicago. The young man's father, younger brother of the latter, was an unsuccessful politician. An uncle, within Chinese mores, often plays the role of the father under certain conditions. A son would write a similar letter to a father.

Most of the middle school graduates nowadays in China become grade school teachers, and they may also get into politics and business. But it is interesting to see the psychology of those who regard coming to America as the best choice for their social and economic security. In the next letter, the same young man wrote again a year later.

Ever since I, your Nephew, graduated, two seasons have passed by. Observing the barren picture of the livelihood of our family, I am ever ready to fight for a better future. I am sorry to say, however, that I, your Nephew, as one who has no special skill, cannot be expected to accomplish anything great. In this wretched world, if one wants to do something, it is necessary to have a great deal of money. I wish I could get a position in one of the governmental bureaus. But in order to get it, I would have to play politics. Unless one can play *gin-chien-chu-i* [*jinqian chuyi*] (dollarism), he might as well give up the idea. I, your Nephew, belong to a poor family. I have no money to play dollarism and politics. I don't know how to play it. Of course, I can find a little something to do, but with a little job what I earn is not enough to support my parents. Oh! Poor family, old parents, and myself, I am growing up. How can I stay home all day, letting Father support me instead? As I think of my difficulties, I am so down-hearted. I am ambitious and I need your help. I have written you requesting you to be kind enough to arrange way so that I can go to America. I have not heard from you yet, Uncle. Please give me a definite answer so that I may have an idea what my future can be.

When Big Uncle was the treasurer of the Village Public Fund he was insulted by the villagers, insinuating that he was guilty of embezzlement. After he was removed from the position, he was humiliated by rude and disrespectful words. Ha! Can we, the offspring of the venerable *Sai-Po* (the grandfather), be insulted like that? If we do have a chance, how dare the villagers insult us again? When I think of it, I just don't know what to say.

I feel bad about it. All I hope is that in case I can get over to America, I shall be industrious and I shall see that our humiliation shall be washed away. I shall, secondly, pay you back for your kindness and promotion, uncle.

Although I, your Nephew, know very little, my ambition is big. I don't want to stand behind anymore. I know what to do when I have a chance. I hope heaven has eyes on me, gives me blessing. I hope you will help me, Uncle.

Whether the young man has the chance to come or not depends upon his uncle's financial condition and other personal matters. The significant point in such a case, however, is that of the right to ask for help on the part of the nephew. Furthermore, the state of mind of the writer seems to throw some light on the economic condition of the Chinese communal life. Coming to America is regarded as a "life line." Individuals who project a hope of coming to the "Golden Mountain" have all sorts of day-dreams and anxiety. This young man, perhaps, may be considered as a case typical of those who have moved from the village to the city, who have received some modern education, and who now face the big problem of choosing an occupation. They are, on the one hand, not trained to hold a position in any professional field, and on the other hand, are un-willing to lose their social status by taking a job as a common laborer. But teaching school will provide too little remuneration. To get a govern-ment position involves politics. Under such conditions there are hundreds of young men of high school and college ages, sons, nephews, brothers, cousins, and in-laws of all kinds, of the Chinese in America, who want to come to this country, the "Golden Mountain." Some of them are out of school but have had a hard time finding a suitable job. Others may be occupied but earn so little that they are supported partly by their elders in this country. Few may find their way to occupations of professional level, but, in comparison to an opportunity of coming to America, nothing in China seems to be of any value. In the following case, for instance, a young man who is an apprentice in a Western tailor shop in Hong Kong writes to his older brother, requesting the latter to arrange a visa so that he can come to America.

My own Big Brother:
    It has been a long time since I wrote you. The one hundred dollars you sent me is still in the bank. I am saving it for a special purpose.

I wish I could describe how I feel about bad conditions here in Hong Kong. Too many people here crowding to make a living. I would feel insecure even if I should learn how to handle my job. I am beginning to feel that I would like to go over to your place. Yes, I wish you could fix me up and get me over to America.

I know if I keep on with this trade, I might make a living with it. But the uncertainty makes me feel that my idea might deceive me. There are so many Western tailors in this city, and many of them with big capital. If I don't have the money to compete with them, I will be a lost cause. I thought if I want to learn the trade, why should I not go over to America to learn it. I shall have prestige as a tailor from America.

Anyway, my own Big Brother, I do want to go over to your place now. I want to go over to America to smell the new air. Will you let your Little Brother have that chance? I hope sincerely that you will think about such a proposition for me. I shall be waiting here for good news from you.

Our army chiefs are talking about recapturing our city of Canton. According to the newspapers, our army is only twenty miles from the city. Whether there is any good news we have to wait for it in the coming days.

I wish I were a soldier so I, too, could face the Japs and fight. I feel sick to see the Japs run all over our country and I as a man do nothing about it.

I think, if I cannot have the chance to go over to America, I might as well join the army. With the army I shall fight for my country.

Please advise me what to do, my own Big Brother, and help me out of this time of distress.

I am closing this letter with my wish that you are very well in America.

Your Younger Brother,
Chi-shee
28/5/41. [May 28, 1941]

The chance of coming to America is not merely the matter of a better economic outlook, but also a way of gaining higher social status. It is the "bigger prestige" and "new air" as he puts it. In China, the tailor does not rank high in the occupational hierarchy. To get his brother's quick approval, he threatens to join the army rather than to continue his apprenticeship in the tailor shop.

In the village, more and more young men want to do something other than farming. This is significant because it may mean the disintegration of the rural economy. Livelihood in the village becomes poorer and poorer. Everybody wants to go over to the "Golden Mountain." Everybody is anxious to have his or her loved one here. The next letter by a woman is written to her brother in America on behalf of her son.

Yen-hip [her son's name] wrote me several days ago, saying that you had written him and mentioned an opportunity for him to go to America. You suggested that Yen-hip confer with Brother-in-law Kong-fai [a returned immigrant from Chicago who is now an overseas agent in Hong Kong]. I thank you, my Brother, very much for your good heart.

I also talked to Brother-in-law about it and he said a way may be arranged but the expenses would be too much. I think, at any rate, if you have the intention, you must be able to do it. Please talk to Second Brother also. You both can help Yen-hip more easily.

If Yen-hip can only reach America, my Brother, you as his uncle, must look after him and make him work. You must take a portion of his wages to pay back the expenses for his trip. Please be kind to him and make him work.

Yen-hip is now grown up to young manhood. I wish we can arrange to get him married before he goes to America first. If he is a good son, he will work hard and save his money. After three or four years, he can come home and get married.

I, your poor Sister, do the farming at home. I just make enough to get along. We have no better outlook or hope. Several years ago I sent Hey-hip to work in Big Brother's store. He worked there about four years and since then he learned something. In case you need a helper in your business in America, I think Yen-hip is a good one. He will be able to take care of your business while you are away. In case you choose to come back home and let him take care of your business, he can do it, too.

Mother is so old. She certainly desires very much to see you. How very happy it would make us all, if we could only see you come home. Your family and mine are well. Please don't worry about us. All we hope is that you are well in America.

The desire of getting her son to this country is stimulated by the suggestion of a relative who merely expresses his willingness to consider the possibility. Often brothers in America may really plan to help their poor sisters by getting the sons over to America. In doing so, as a matter of fact, one is also helping himself, for the more members of his family group he can bring over here, the larger and stronger the social and economic influence he can exert both in America and in China. Often in a family of three or four brothers, they come one after the other; one helps the other until all of them are here. "They have four pairs of hands here," one would say. "How dare you belittle them?" To bring more members of one's family group to America becomes a way of fighting for social status. So the father's ambition is to get his son over, and so a proud uncle would boast that he has been able to arrange for a visa for a nephew of his to enter this country.

On the contrary, some laundrymen are so dissatisfied with their mode of life that they try to discourage the coming of their relatives.

> My brother asks me to get him over here. I have done my best to convince him that it is not so bright here as he thinks. But he doesn't believe me. He insists upon coming. He wrote lately that he is like "a man in a wrong occupation or a woman married to a wrong man." He thinks tailoring is a wrong occupation for him and that coming over to this country is the right one.
>
> See, I am in an awkward position. If I don't arrange the visa for him, he would say that I, as his older brother, do nothing to help him. See, when my father was living, he got me over here. As my father is now dead, it is my duty to help my brother. It must be my mother's idea. She urges him to ask me. I am willing to give him five thousand dollars in Hong Kong money. He can use the amount in whatever kind of business he pleases. But he must come over. In spite of it, he still wants to come over.
>
> Well, I had nothing more to say but promised him to do what I could.
>
> The trouble is that it takes two or three thousand dollars to arrange a passport. I have not enough money now. Ling [partner] can let me have some but he is going back to China in no time. If he goes back, where can I have the money to repay him? In fact, I don't know what to do just now. I'll wait and see. Perhaps a citizen's grandson's passport can be made cheaper. Probably it will cost about fifteen hundred dollars. But I don't know where to find one just now.

He does not want his brother to come because he seems to think that his brother can be successful in his present occupation. But with or without an occupation, it is hard to tell a "Golden Mountain" dreamer that there is not much gold in it.

2. Apprenticeship

The newcomer has very little idea about his future career before he arrives in America. The Chinese laundry, as it is called among the Chinese immigrant group, is *yee-shing-kuon* [*yisheng guan*]. The laundry is taken for granted as a "clothing store." In China, with the financial support of his father, the newcomer has received a modern education and has become accustomed to city life. Being of school class, the newcomer enjoyed a social status higher than that of the poor city folks of the "coolie" and manual labor classes. For some, life had been rather easy. He may have married early and his wife and children have been living with his mother in China, depending on his father's support. After arriving in America and working in the laundry, he is soon conscious of the fact that he has become a common laborer. He is disappointed, especially in the mode of living. He must now make new adjustments. The following cases illustrate the general reaction of the newcomer to his new environment.

(1) A practitioner of Chinese herb medicine.

Sun-ming, a young man twenty-two years old, arrived in Chicago from China two weeks ago. He graduated from a missionary junior high school and then took apprenticeship with a famous master of herb medicine in Hong Kong. After he finished his course, he set up his own practice in Hong Kong for three years, making about fifty dollars a month.

A few months ago, his second older uncle died in Chicago. His father was then left alone in the laundry. Planning to get Sun-ming over here to join them, P. W., one of the sons of his oldest uncle, made a woi loan of the clan house in order to assist his trip expenses.

Finally Sun-ming arrived. Immediately when he left the train, he was taken to his father's laundry where he began to help his father. The interviewer first met him on February 5, 1939, shortly after his arrival in Chinatown.

He said, "I had no idea that we Chinese people have to work like this in this country. The very first day, I had to begin to work. What is hard for me is to get up so early—five o'clock in the morning! I have not been accustomed to that in China. In China, life has been easy for me. I usually slept until nine or ten o'clock as I pleased. In case a patient came to see me, I took it easily and slowly. I had only a few cases a day. I had plenty of time for recreation. In the evening, I went to a show or to a teahouse with friends. What a comfortable life it was!

"Now, it is so different. I have to work all day long.

"That is right. If I had known beforehand that this is the way I would have to toil, I would never come here. I would rather have stayed with the family and be poor.

"Oh! I don't know. When I heard about a chance to go to America, the hardship just didn't occur to me. All I got excited about was to take the chance—going to America!

"Now I am here. I begin to feel America is work, work, work. It is nothing to get excited about.

"I have learned how to iron now. I am doing three or four shirts an hour. That is very slow, as I am told. But I will soon do better. After all, ironing is difficult work. It is only manual labor."

Sun-ming tried to get away from the laundry and practiced medicine in

Chinatown for a while, but he failed. Later he was employed in a chop suey house for about a year. Now, his cousin P. W. and a clansman have bought a laundry on North Clark Street. Sun-ming accepted an invitation to work there.

(2) A former playboy and business man.

What I want is to catch one thousand dollars on the lottery. Del-ka-ma! I am going back to Hong Kong and open a drug store. Why should I stay here and work so hard. Things make me so mad that I wish to go back now. . . .

The work in the laundry is too hard. I have to get up at five o'clock. That is terrible! When I was in China, I had two girls sleeping with me and I slept at least until nine o'clock. Del-ka-ma! I was almost falling asleep while I ironed the other day. Had not enough sleep!

. . . Immediately upon arriving, they brought me to their place [laundry of brother-in-law] and I had to begin to work. You should let a man rest for a few days. Why should they be so hasty to start me working right away? I ought to get a hotel room and have a couple of good night's sleep. When I took the train from San Francisco, I did not take [a] sleeping car. I was wrong to listen to an old man who was with me. I was sleepy and tired when I started work the first day.

Del-ka-ma! Now I begin to see what sort of life you fellows have had here. I thought it was easy to make money in America. That was why I spent so freely when I was in China. I thought I could spend all and make it back when I came over myself. If I had only realized the real conditions, I wouldn't have come, and I wouldn't have spent so freely.

See! I made about three to four hundred dollars [Hong Kong currency] a month and I did not save a cent of it. I spent my money right and left— on everything that made me happy. I had two places to keep mistresses. I smoked opium. Oh! I spent more than I made, as a matter of fact.

I was in the trucking business. I bought six trucks in Hong Kong and used them to transport stones and other materials for builders. I hired men to drive the trucks. I had connections with different builders. I made about three hundred dollars a month on the average. The business was good. Later I was not interested in the business. I didn't even go to see how the men were getting along. Finally I began to lose money on it. Then one or two of the trucks broke down. As my mind was not on business, I gave the last of the trucks to a friend of mine. He said he was going to pay me for that but I didn't care.

In this way I threw away about twenty thousand dollars.

What is the matter with me? Well, you don't have to ask. I had too much opium and too many women. I spent over five thousand dollars upon the first prostitute within two months. The second one, I lived with her for about two years. I don't know how much I spent upon her. It might be over ten to fifteen thousand dollars. I smoked opium with the second woman . . .

"Del-ka-ma! I'm not afraid of spending," I said to myself, "I shall go over to America and make back all I have spent." I never thought that life would be so hard here. . . .

He [his father] told me that life would be very hard in America. I thought he was just fooling me. Now I see that he told the truth.

The preceding cases may be considered as extreme types because of the marked ease and comfort of their life before they came to America. They were not entirely dependent on their elders, financially. Their decision to come to America may be largely due to their dissatisfaction or failure in their former occupation, and they took America too much for granted as a "Golden Mountain." This type has the hardest time in making an adjustment to the laundryman's mode of living, for they suffer not only physical hardship but also psychological disturbances. They have lost status. The third young man represents another type who is more of a village lad, but, on account of his elder's financial support, he could go back and forth between the city and the village. He is not trained for any profession and is not willing to take a lowly laborer's job. In fact, he is a sort of loafer. He, too, took the "Golden Mountain" too much for granted, and after he arrived he was disappointed also. But he may not feel that he has lost his status by working with his brother in the laundry.

(3) An unemployed young man, Moy Fo.

May 20, 1939.—Moy Fo, a young man twenty-four years old, arrived in Chicago to join his brother, Moy Ying, who is in partnership with a cousin, Moy Wing. Because of personal conflict, Moy Ying can hardly get along with Moy Wing, as the business is not too good. In order to avoid trouble, the newcomer is sent to help Shu-lung in another laundry. Moy Fo has then begun to learn the trade, an apprentice of Shu-lung.

"I have been here about two months. No, I don't like it here. In China, people were talking about going to the 'Flowery Flag' [America], and I was dreaming, too, about coming over. Now I am here. What I see in this country is just like this: working day and night.

"I had thought our people were doing a big business here. I thought my brother had a big store. But all of us Chinese are just laborers. I have to work so hard in order to earn a small sum of money. [He was a beginner at the time.] If I had only realized the hard work I must do, I would rather stay home. I would rather stay in the village, feeling content to be a farmer.

"I don't know how to iron well enough yet. I am not allowed to iron shirts, as Shu-lung is afraid that I will spoil the shirt. If a shirt is spoiled, he has to pay for it. I can help to iron rough things such as underwear, towels, and shorts. Some people can iron 18 shirts an hour, but I don't think I can do even four. The iron is too hot. You might burn the shirt, if you don't know how to handle it. If it is too cold, well, of course, the shirt would not be burned, but you can't do a good job with a cold iron. You must have it just right and do it quick. Ironing is by no means an easy thing.

"One thing is good in this country, so long as you are willing to work hard, you don't have to worry about eating and clothing. But in China, you have nothing to do. People don't know what to do in China.

"I? I was doing nothing in China. I wished I could get a good job but I didn't have the ability. People must be a school graduate in order to find a good job. In manual labor you earn almost nothing. All I thought of was coming over here.

"As far as a living is concerned, of course, it is better here. But one has to leave his family and perhaps is forced to stay here years. It is awful. Although one can earn little in China, he can see his wife and children in the morning and his parents in the evening.

"Now I am here. My brother has spent several thousands of dollars for my trip. I have to work for years in order to help him pay back the debt. I wonder when I can pay the debt."

One Sunday, Moy Fo's brother, Moy Ying, in Chinatown, said this about his brother, "That fellow is dead lazy. His mind is not quite on the job. He has been here almost two or three months and yet he doesn't know how to iron a shirt. I spent almost seven thousand dollars in Hong Kong money to get him over. If I had known he is so absent-minded, I wouldn't get him over. What worries me is the money which I owe for bringing him here."

Like others, Moy Fo is not at all at ease with the new life. He seems, however, to be re-orienting himself. He is disappointed, for he finds the Chinese here are "just laborers," and, being a sort of loafer in China, of course it is not so easy for him to stay home "working day and night." But since he realizes how hard it is to make a living in China, he concludes that "as far as making a living, of course, it is better here." This notion of his is very likely leading him to a decision to adjust to the situation. In making any adjustment to the situation, he is not exactly expressing an idea of an individual, but that of a person who is a member of the group—a personal adjustment which is expected by other members of his group, to be regarded as a well-behaved person.

Despite all disappointments and hardships, the newcomer is likely to make some sort of adjustment to the situation. He is brought into a situation surrounded by relatives and friends upon whom he has to depend. He can survive now only as a member of the group. In the course of time, the newcomer is gradually accommodated to the mode of living, sharing the idea and hope of the old-timer. In the following cases, the newcomer is beginning to adopt a sojourner's attitude.

> (4) A young loafer.
> I don't know how to iron shirts yet. They don't let me do it. They are afraid that I would spoil the shirt. What I am doing is to iron the underwear, shorts, and other rough things. I am an employee, but they pay me well. Sometimes I earn as much as twenty dollars a week. I save the money, of course. I have to pay off my debt for my trip. It is a big amount and will take a year or two to pay it off.

This newcomer is a young village boy who has never enjoyed sophisticated city life, who is not status-conscious, and may be able to make an easier adjustment to the laundryman's mode of living.

Another boy of sixteen, working as an apprentice in a laundry shop of his clansmen, says:

> I have just come—about six months ago.
> I like America better than China. Things are nice here. People [Chinese] eat much better food here in America. In the native village, we didn't eat chicken even once a month. But here we have chicken for dinner often— every Saturday.
> Soda water is a kind of rare treat in the native village. Here we drink it several times a day, like water. I remember that it was a dream to have a drink of soda water when I was a little boy in the native village. It costs fifteen cents a bottle back there, but fifteen cents was too much money in those days. And you could not buy it always. They did not have it on the market.
> I am beginning to learn how to iron shirts now. It is easy. . . .
> The only thing I don't like about laundry work is that we stay inside all day. I like to go out on the street and see something. We could not stay within a whole day in China. . . .
> In a few years, they [father and uncle] expect me to be able to go home and get married.
> My mother and two sisters are in China. They want my father to return to China now. How can he? Where can he get the money to make the trip? . . . My uncle does not pay any attention to him [father]. He gambles and cannot save enough.

The attitudes of these youths can be said to be shared by the majority. Being brought up in the Chinese village where economic security and material comfort are poor and scarce, and suddenly finding themselves in the superiority of plenty of everything here, they tend to express satisfaction.

As the newcomer appreciates the material convenience and comfort in America, he would gradually acquire a sojourner's attitude that his present life is only to be considered temporary. The boy has expressed his like and dislike of this country, to be sure, in only a limited sense; that is to say, in the social world and material environment that his elders and the immigrant group as a whole have created for him. He has very little to say about the general public, people who live next door to him and the people he sees in the city street. He does not live in America, in the sense that his immediate concern is to make money. Soon long working hours and lack of recreation are taken for granted, but his ultimate aim is to make a fortune.

3. Becoming a Laundryman

Laundry work is hard, but the newcomer stays on. He is no longer a shun-hsueng-lei. He is one of the many who come and stay on. Soon he can endure long hours just as well as his fellow countrymen. He has made the adjustments to fit himself into the mode of life. He may not be very happy about it, but he soon adopts a philosophy of life expressed by one laundryman as follows:

> You need a certain amount of money to establish a business. It is rather risky to start a new kind of business unless you are familiar with it. In my case, it is hard for me to work in a chop suey house. To play safe, I think laundry is much more gainful. People may not realize the money our people made during the last War. Income in those days was as much as fifty dollars a week. Some got more. . . .
>
> Do you know why so many Jews are in laundry business after the war? Because some of us Chinese told them. Now Jewish laundries are all over. They, too, find it a good enterprise.
>
> One loses nothing in this line of business and possibly makes a dollar out of ten cents. All you have to do is to put in your time and labor. The important thing is to do a good job.
>
> It is a very hard job, sure enough. But there is nothing else to do. This is the kind of life we have to take in America. I, as one of the many, do not

like to work in the laundry, but what else can I do? You've got to take it; that's all.

The happy moment comes every week-end, though, when the work is done and the profit is to be divided. Sometimes you thought it might be about forty to fifty dollars but when it turned out less than that, you felt disappointed. However, so long as you have some income, you feel a sort of satisfaction.

It is commonly known that the Chinese laundryman complains about his hard work, which is described as "dog's life" [*gouming*] and "slave labor" [*nuli gongzuo*] and so forth. He takes it in preference to being jobless and penniless, scorned and forsaken by friends and relatives. The preceding document, however, seems to sum up the whole situation as far as the chance of the Chinese immigrant goes in choosing his occupation. If he leaves the laundry, he can work in a chop suey house. The earning and the mode of life of the chop suey enterprise is no better than the laundry. People who have gone into the chop suey business have suffered more risk. To many Chinese immigrants, laundry and chop suey work are just the same, unless one has the special asset to operate a successful chop suey restaurant as its proprietor. Some try but fail. The laundry business, on the other hand, needs a much smaller capital investment, and is relatively safe from closing up. Among the Chinese immigrants, many have had experience in both chop suey and laundry work. It seems that there is no difference in the status or prestige values attached to the two lines of occupation. The values are attached only to success or failure of the person in the business adventure. This is essentially related to economic gain: "No matter what you do, make money and save more money, so that you can go back to China as soon as possible," is the motto in the mind of the immigrant.

Generally one does not attempt to go into a new line of work, particularly in the case of the Chinese laundryman. His choice is limited by the few occupations open to him. In recent years, Chinese are doing pretty well in the grocery store business in some of the southern states. Information gathered indicates that a portion of the Chinese population in the North, Northeast, and Northwest is moving to the South. However, I have seen Chinese laundrymen who had gone into the grocery business in the South but came back North again to re-establish their laundry.

On the whole, the Chinese have made no attempt to invade the labor market with the general public; they found the laundry and are willing to stay with it in spite of individual dissatisfactions which are largely of social rather than economic significance. We will take up this matter in later chapters.

CHAPTER IX

THE OLD-TIMER

THE NEWCOMER soon becomes fully employed or taken into partnership by someone of his clan or by a friend and neighbor. At length, he has adjusted like anybody else of his own group, not only in getting acquainted with the daily and weekly routine on the job, but also in the sentiments and attitudes that the group symbolizes. He has become, in other words, an old-timer who has gained economic security but lost his individuality and normal home life. He is a man of the frontier—the cultural frontier.

1. Laundry Work as a Job

The Chinese laundryman has an occupation but he is not prepared to settle permanently in America or remain as a laundryman all his life. Conversely, the laundry work is conceived as a job to do for the time being, and the sooner it can be terminated the happier he will be. He hopes to have a better life when he gets a chance to return to China. The laundry work, therefore, is a stepping stone toward a goal—to make a fortune and return home. No Chinese laundryman, so far as I know, has ever seriously attempted to organize his life around the laundry, saying, "I feel at home in this country and laundry work is my life, my career, and my ambition. I hope to be a prosperous laundryman." He tends, on the contrary, to be interested in the quickest way to save money and make a return trip to his home. That is why, perhaps, he is willing to work so hard. "If you don't work," says Sam Wong, "where do you get the money? What we Chinese come here for is the money, what else?" This utterance sounds simple, but it is very representative. It is something he speaks of himself, signifying a will and a hope. Attached to this hope, he has all sorts of reveries, as the hope is expected to materialize in the near future.

When the war is over, we overseas people will have a great chance if we have money and go back to China. You can imagine how poor the people will be. If one brings home a large sum of money, he may be financial lord of the poor masses.

We can invest our money in business later. All we have to do now is to work hard and save money.

Del-nea-ma! When the war is over, I don't think I should go back immediately. I'll wait until the general condition is pretty well in order. That will be the time. I will wait several years or longer.

I'll go to establish my home in Nanking. I don't want to go back to Kwongtung. If I have the chance, no one can possibly expect me to go back to the village—too primitive. Not even Canton. I would hate to reside in Hong Kong under the rule of the British.

I have nothing to think about in China except my old mother [not his wife and daughter]. She is the only person I have to worry about. . . .

I have no other hope but to get my money and get back to China. What is the use of staying here; you can't be an American here. We Chinese are not even allowed to become citizens. If we were allowed, that might be a different story. In that case, I think many of us Chinese would not think so much of going back to China. It is indeed comfortable to live in this country as far as material things are concerned. . . . Many would get a woman and settle down here. [At the time of the interview, the U.S. Congress was considering the repeal of the Chinese Exclusion Act.]

Yes, indeed, the problem is where you can get the woman. For me, I would never marry a white woman. It just won't match. You have every difficulty; people look at you when you go out on the street, making you very uncomfortable. They won't let you live in a decent place. Later, the woman herself disowns you, as you are getting old and she would be no longer depending upon your support. I have seen many cases like this, for example, the case of Y. S. . . .

I would rather marry a Chinese woman if I choose to stay in this country. . . .

These Chinese girls born in America are not trustworthy. They are good money spenders and yet not good wives. They might deceive you. As a matter of fact, they are not willing to marry a *wah-chao* (overseas Chinese). Very few of them are virtuous; that is the trouble. . . .

Well, if I know I can't get a thing, I won't even think of getting it. It is no use to try. There are two sisters [white] in this neighborhood, pretty and good natured. When they come to call for their laundry, they act very friendly. I know they are just working girls, employed in a downtown department store as saleswomen. Some people may get sentimental ideas about the girls, but I, no matter how friendly they are, just look upon them as customers. I chat with them but I don't have any other ambitious intention. Why should I make myself miserable. Once you have done something wrong, you have to lose your business and you have to get out of here. This is a Christian town. These people are nice and gentle to you, but at the bottom they are very prejudiced against us Chinese. If you have done something considered immoral, here is no place for you to stay. They won't give you any more business; you can't help but close it up.

Del-nea-ma, when I have a lot of money and go back to China, I shall get a sixteen-year-old concubine. I shall enjoy life. You know, this will be a compensation for my lonely life all these years in America. I don't mean to get a well-educated one. Well-educated girls won't marry us old overseas. But, anyhow, I must get a young and pretty one. I don't care whether she is educated or not so long as she is young and pretty. A slave-maid will do! [*laughter*].

Well, I think my wife will not object too much if I insist on getting what I want. Once when Chung Yip [a neighbor] brought his mixed-blood wife back to the native village, his wife wept and grumbled with great grief. My wife saw that and remarked, "What is the use of being so foolish as to cry about it. It doesn't help anything. The more you cry the more wives he will get; he will get two more and what can you do about it. For me, so long as I have something to eat, I'll be satisfied. . . ."

After the war, there will be many women without a husband. Well, you have to do your duty by looking after the widows of our soldiers [*laughter*]. You can't let them remain without husbands, especially some of those young and pretty ones. It will be, therefore, a duty of some of us who did not go to war to support the widows they have left [*laughter*].

Some of these prostitutes we see over here are just better than no women. They are just instruments to relieve sex tension. It is more or less like masturbation—you have to use mouth water to get it in and after it gets in, that thing of hers is too loose. That is the kind of stuff you have in 305 [a small hotel in the Loop]. That's equal to nothing—tasteless. I don't care for that kind of stuff. That's why I seldom go to see a prostitute. You spend your money and gain no satisfaction.

The wishes of the laundryman in relation to a normal life as indicated in the preceding cases, are blocked. He is self-conscious as a member of his race, and as an individual in his lowly occupation. He complains that Chinese are not permitted to become naturalized, saying that if he could become a citizen, he would not think of going back to China. He generalizes that some of his countrymen would have the same feeling. This utterance is significant because it was made at the time the United States Congress was debating the repeal of the Chinese Exclusion Act of 1882;

the utterance, therefore, is intended, it seems, not so much to mean what he says, but rather to show his concern about the matter. The fact is that even if he could be naturalized, his problem, it is clear, would not be solved. He would still be confronted with discrimination and race consciousness that "people look at him when he goes out to the street," if he ventures to marry a white woman. And he would not be able to live in a decent place and probably his hope of quitting the laundry would have to be given up.

To enjoy a better life, he projects a hope for his future with a plan of action when he gets back to China. The plan of action, in the preceding case, may not represent the majority, but it is interesting and significant in that it reflects the man's inner dilemma and the satisfaction he needs most—sex and family life.

Furthermore, the preceding case seems to represent those young and ambitious men who are quite prosperous, and who have a feeling of some certainty of their return trip to China sooner or later. In fact, they probably have already large savings and are least, in the eyes of his countrymen, a "good son" (*hao-joi* [*hauzai*]), in spite of his occasional patronizing of prostitutes. His thought of his mother, his self-consciousness in response to the friendly white girls, and his impression and prejudice about the American-born Chinese girls generally, may be ascribed as typical sentiments and attitudes of a well-adjusted Chinese immigrant.

The problem, then, is how to save money so that he can take his return trip sooner. The success or failure of this end, of course, depends upon how the laundryman orients himself toward this goal. There are, however, individual situations which different persons must face. Some want to quit laundry work to return to China and to live in style; but they seldom have any definite idea of what it is going to be. Usually the returned laundryman buys land and builds himself a fine house, but over-spending and the failure to find a suitable occupation may force him to seek re-entry to America.

To remain permanently in China, one must have a large fortune so that he can be self-sufficient and find a place in the business world in China. But very few returned overseas Chinese from America can fit themselves into the business world in the Chinese city. Few of them go home with a large fortune.

There are alternatives. Some progressive and ambitious young laundry-men take time out to attend trade school. They learn radio and automobile repairing, how to operate a photo studio, or tailor shop, some even learn to be aviation pilots. Some try hard but fail. The following case, for instance, is very discouraging:

> My life is all determined; I have no hope but to remain a laundryman. I used to be very ambitious. . . . Do you know I spent about four thousand dollars taking aviation courses? You heard about it, haven't you? Well, just this incident is good enough to discourage me—I shall never be able to go back to China.
>
> Right now my heart is gone. All I care is to take life as it is. When I have money I would buy something good to eat and there is a girl [prostitute] I can find, I go to see her. I am getting old too soon. I must enjoy myself before I am too old. So long as I have a place to sleep and something to eat and I can manage to send a few hundred dollars home—I take life as it is. I can't expect a life better than this and it is no use to try.
>
> Last year, my old temptation got back into my heart. I planned to go back to China to enlist in the National Air Force. After reconsideration I changed my mind. You see, I am forty years old now; I am not so sure whether I can be of any use to the government. To fight in a battle is not child's play. One needs training. There are many young able bodies in China. Although I had a little experience flying, what I learned is not enough. Besides, I have a family to support. If I should die, I don't care. I have not the slightest fear of dying. There are so many good able young men who have died already for China. I have no reason to fear. The trouble is that I have a family and I would not be useful. I am already too old. I would be more useful if I stay alive and support my family.
>
> If I had taken up the aviation courses consistently, I could have gone back to China long ago. I worked in Chicago for six years and it was a good business. I spent all the money I saved and a year of my time taking aviation lessons and I went broke—without good result. I needed more money but I had no more.
>
> I could save money before, but not now. I spend as much as I earn on gambling, prostitutes, and so on.
>
> We organized a club in Chicago under the Nationalist Party [*Guoming-dang*] in Chicago. I had my own plane. It was badly damaged and later I gave it to the club. Then I had to travel all over the country gathering subscriptions for the club.
>
> Some of the fellows went back to China and became "big shots." Wong Kong-shen is a former member of our club. I don't know where he is now. He could have been killed in an air battle in China.
>
> I have been in many cities in the Middle West and East. We were trying to get some contributions from Chinese people to support the club. I was quite enthusiastic at that time. "Aviation as National Salvation" [*Hangkong Jiuguo*] was the slogan. It got every penny out of me.

Now, I seldom take part in public affairs. I have enough of it already. If they ask me to contribute for war fund, all right, I pay my just share, too. But if they ask me to run around like I did before, no sir, not me. They blame you when you fail and you have no reward when you succeed.

Now most of my old gang in Chicago are all gone. People are not talking about training young aviators in this country any more. The students trained for commercial aviation are not good for air combat. When they get home they have to be retrained again by the government. If one wants to study aviation for war purposes, he must find out how to get in the American Aviation Academy.

His unsuccessful attempt to become an aviator makes him self-accused, indifferent, and perhaps a little embittered. Money and time are lost and yet his hope of returning to China is in a far distant future. The philosophy of taking things as they are is merely the negative behavior of a once ambitious man. He was once an important figure in a worthy cause; now, his friends and former associates have forgotten him. He is restless—a patron of prostitutes and gamblers. Hopeless, he sees no way to get away from the laundry. He is, in the sociological term, a disorganized person. The fact that he has been unable to save money means he will never be able to take his trip home. He may make desperate attempts to win money by gambling. But few Chinatown gamblers make enough money to get away from the laundry and return to China.

The document as it is presented here, however, is not to be used to forecast the life of the man in the future. It is significant here only to illustrate that in trying to quicken or assure a better livelihood in China, the laundryman has turned to a new approach—to invest money in a technical skill. I have seen people, among them some laundrymen, who returned to China with either skill or a trade. The latter would prove to be a good investment, for it helps the one who returns overseas to make a living with his training. It is, in a sense, an asset superior to money. Without a skill or a trade, others may have to seek for another entry into this country and return to the laundry again.

Some old-timers change their line of business; Mr. Laundryman quits the laundry and becomes Mr. Chop Suey Man. Others become storekeepers or Chinatown grocers. Some fail and return to the laundry. Going back to China is the vital concern of all. An unsuccessful business venture makes the person sensitive and disorganized. In the following case, the man likens his mode of life in America to serving a prison term:

I have been in this country over twenty years. It is easy to become a bum here.

No, I have never been back to China. In case one has had bad luck, how can he help but become a local bum. I have remained here long, much longer than I expected. . . .

We Chinese who are in this country are like convicts serving a term. Some serve longer while others serve only a few years. People say usually that gamblers are persons hopeless of going back to China. But some gamblers did go back to China. Yes, most of them cannot, that is right. Those who could go back were exceptions; they were just lucky. I do not gamble, but I cannot go back. I am worse than a gambler.

Why? Because I have had bad luck. Every business I touched was a failure. Yes, I made a lot of money during and after the last world war. I had over ten thousand dollars at the time. I did not decide to take my trip home because the exchange rate was not favorable. You had to give eighty to ninety dollars gold to exchange one hundred dollars Hong Kong money. You lost too much. But that was my only chance to return to China but I didn't go. Instead, I invested my money in business. I put some of my money in a chop suey house and afterwards the rest of my money opened a store in Chinatown. They are all lost. My partner was Chang Hong, you know him. That *kai doi** (son o' bitch) made me lose four to five thousand dollars in that store. [The store is still in Chinatown but suffers very poor business.]

I used to sell laundry supplies, too. But I lost money also. See, hard luck— what can I say.

I was so disappointed and disgusted, for a couple of years after that period I laid low and was aimless. I was doing nothing but eat and sleep, having not the heart of getting ahead. Finally, as some of my friends urged and encouraged me, I found this place. I have been here about three years. The business is all right. I can make a living, except the business is not so good this summer as it was last year.

I bought this place from a man by the surname of Wu. It was at the corner of 53rd and Ellis when I bought it. I moved over here afterward. This is a much better place; I don't have to sleep down here at the rear of the shop. I have a whole floor upstairs. I pay thirty-five dollars a month for rent. Two large rooms upstairs are included. It is a better location with the school building right across the street.

I had only seventy dollars in my hands when I bought this place. You don't have to invest too much money on this kind of business. The money I had was not mine either. I was penniless. It was borrowed from some of my friends. When I was doing nothing in Chinatown, I used to be around Ho Toy [one of the chop suey restaurants in Chinatown]. That was where I met this fellow [Fong, his employee]. After I fixed up this place I took him along. He had nothing to do also. He has been with me ever since.

All my clansmen are in New York—about one hundred of them. I am here in Chicago alone. Yes, there are two men here having the same surname with me. I heard about them. I have never gotten together with them, though. Most of my friends are from Chungshan. I am from Toyshan, you know.

Expressions of gloomy feeling about their mode of living are quite common among laundrymen. This man is so conscious of his long stay in America that he seems to suffer tremendous inner conflict between his hope of returning to China and his present difficulties in business ventures. Frustrated and disappointed, he labels himself as a prisoner of the situation. Prisoner indeed in the sense of social isolation, hard and monotonous, long working hours, loneliness without normal family life. He remains in the laundry as something imposed upon him, and he is restless, seeing no hope of returning to his family in China. Particularly, in this case as in many others, the laundryman has suffered from loss of life-long savings. Misfortunes of this and other kinds disorganize the individual, further preventing him from organizing his life around his occupation. He takes the laundry work merely as something to live by.

This man is maladjusted, but if he is not too old, he must not be considered a hopeless case. So long as he is still working, there is yet a chance. Some take their last trip home with very little money, provided the homeland tie is still maintained. We shall consider this situation in fuller detail in a later chapter.

The last night before his departure for America, one traveler told his wife that he would be home in three years. He reached America but found his sojourn here much longer than expected. He stayed abroad thirty years! Some Chinese immigrants cannot take an early return trip back to China because of the heavy burden of family support. They have to send hundreds of dollars home during the years in order to keep a large family comfortable. Others want their sons and daughters, nephews and nieces, brothers and sisters to be well educated. The youngsters are sent to schools in the cities; some of them getting college and post-graduate education from the support of Mr. Laundryman in America. Others are bombarded by letter-bullets from friends and relatives requesting help. To play the role of benefactor is morally sanctioned as a right and duty. Doing his duty efficiently, one finds himself with hardly enough saved for his return trip. He stays on with the laundry, working hard year after year, sick and tired. But he still projects a hope. The next cases are to illustrate well-adjusted types of persons who have more or less sacrificed their individual welfare for the sake of the well-being of the family group, especially the education of the children.

Being a laundryman is no life at all. I work fourteen hours a day and I have to send home almost all my wages. You see, I have a big family at home. My mother is still living and I have an unmarried sister who is going to school. My own children, five of them, all are in school too. My brother here—he is no help; he has a family here and what he earns is just enough to support his family. I figure I send home about fifteen hundred dollars a year, at least, sometimes more.

I seldom go down to Chinatown—not every Sunday, anyway. Unless I have some business matter, I usually go to Chinatown only once a month. I sleep and read here Sunday. I don't go to movies often. You don't understand a lot of the things they say in the show. Sometimes I get tired and fall asleep in the movie theater.

I buy lottery tickets but do not patronize any other Chinatown gambling. I used to play *ma-jong* [*majian*] when I was in Canton. I do not have the energy to enjoy playing it any more. . . . I have never had any luck.

People think I am a happy person. I am not. I worry very much. First, I don't like this kind of life; it is not human life. To be a laundryman is to be just a slave. I work because I have to. If I ever stop working, those at home must stop eating.

I am not healthy at all. I feel my backaches all the time. My health has improved however since my tonsils were removed. Then I have other troubles, like headaches. I am not an old man yet, but I feel old. How can a man feel good when he is forced into an occupation he doesn't like?

But I get used to it. After you are on it for so many years, you have no more feeling but stay on with it. After all, you can't get rich but you don't have to worry about money as long as you can work. If my father had let me stay in school, I could have graduated from middle school; then I might not have come. I could find something to do in China. It is better to be a poor teacher in China. You could have been happier.

In this country, one must know English enough to do something other than laundry work. I was not allowed to have a chance to study English when I first came here. My father and uncles had an idea that those who knew enough English were those who could become bad. He meant, to fool around with girls and so forth. I was foolish to listen to them though. Think of that sort of old ideas! How stupid!

I have a building in Canton. It cost my father about nine thousand dollars. My family is now living on one of the four floors; the other floors are rented. It is lucky we don't have to pay rent, otherwise my responsibility could be heavier. That was all my father left us.

This is a case of a second generation of Chinese laundryman. He had a modern education and lived a life of ease and comfort before coming to America. Since he has been here over ten years, he is now an old-timer. Although he finds his mode of life very unsatisfactory here, he plays the role of a family supporter, son, husband, father and older brother.

Ordinarily a man of his social position, especially in the case of the older generation, would feel content. But this man suffers from tremendous inner conflicts. Perhaps he acquired modern ideas when he was in school in China. In fact, this is the type of person who is most likely to take laundry work as a job.

In the course of time a man of this type may not grumble any more, taking the life and work for granted. His main interest is to make the money and he does his duty as best he can.

> It is too hard a job for me now—my hands and feet are not so alert as they used to be, getting old. Sometimes I have an awful headache. I am really thinking of going back to China. My doctor advises me that I need a good long rest. My family want me to return. Now the question is how can I have the money. I have hardly enough even if I sell this business. It is worth at most fifteen hundred dollars. Moreover, I shouldn't go home until my two younger children graduate from middle school [high school]. My older son is teaching school in Canton, but he cannot earn enough even to support himself. So I think I have to stay here for another year.
>
> Certainly I shall come back to this country again. I shall have to get a return permit. I can come back here after one year of staying in China.
>
> You see, really I am not too old yet. I am only too weak. After a year of rest I hope I can be strong again. Perhaps I shall get one of my children over here. But I can't say anything now. My older son wanted to come over. He wanted to go to college here. After learning that I am weak and that my financial condition is poor, he changed his mind. He mentioned nothing about his coming over anymore when he wrote recently. He wants me to go home instead.
>
> But I don't want to give up yet. I hope to be able to build a Western-style house somewhere in the city and enjoy my old age. . . .
>
> Well, I want all my children to be educated and independent. So long as they can make their own living, then I don't have to worry about them. Then all I need will be just enough for old age with my old wife.

This is a case of an old man who used to take laundry work as a job. But now his view has changed, partly on account of his economic situation and partly on account of his family responsibility. In his old age, sick and weak, he still must struggle along. He now has only enough money to take his return trip, but not enough money either to retire in his old age nor to do something else in the old country. Under his estimation of his own financial condition, he would have to return to this country again. He would like to "build a Western-style house" and "enjoy my old age" with his old wife. The man, it seems, not only has made adjustments to his situation, but also has modernized his view of life, particularly on this point of retirement and old age.

On the financial question, the situation seems to be typical. Many old-timers went back to China with very little money. A return entry to America very likely would be planned, and a return permit had to be obtained from the U.S. Immigration authorities.

They are, therefore, in America for the last trip. If one does come again, he may or may not be able to do as he wishes. He may not be able to take his last trip home at all. His fate, therefore, depends upon his luck.

2. Fate of the Old-Timer

Those who returned to China and found something else to do, and those who took the last trip and retired in old age, are considered fortunate. But some of the laundrymen have lost hope of making the last return trip. Some, worse still, have never been back to China even once. Now they are old and poor. The sojourner takes a life-long sojourn in America.

Many a laundryman has been working all his life and yet is destitute in his old age. He can neither take his return trip to China nor save enough for a rainy day. At last, as he is too feeble to continue to work, he retires to Chinatown, or joins a relative or friend as a dependent. He is what is known in the immigrant term as *lo-wah-chao* [*lao huachiao*] (old overseas Chinese), a term with a descriptive meaning of those who are either staying in America too long or with too small a chance of returning home for retirement—old overseas Chinese.

There are two types, on the basis of a return trip, among the lo-wah-chao: Those who have never returned to China, and those who have returned at least once before but failed to make the last time. The former type, no doubt, must be some sort of character. The following case reveals the causes of his fate:

I have been in this country over forty years already. No, no, I had no chance to go back—not even once. Yes, I was in Indianapolis most of the time and I had been always working, too, but the trouble was: I did not keep my money. Well, most of it went to the purses of some women, and some, well I gambled and lost.

Some people have no money because of bad luck. I did not have bad luck, I might say, but I have no money just the same. I had my own business and it was a pretty good business, too, all these years. After I sold my place, I was always employed.

Then my feet bothered me. I could no longer stand too long with my feet. [*Showed feet by lifting up trousers; might be a syphilis case.*] Both are black, see. It doesn't hurt so much lately. And my age—I can't endure long hours of work any more. I suppose I am finished.

I came to America at the age of thirty-three and now I am seventy-two. ... All I did was to make money and have a good time. I spent most of my money for women; that is why I got this "good" pair of feet now.

I had been a pretty free spender. As I must be entertained by women from time to time, I must also make the money. If one has no money, how can he be loved by those women. I always made good money to spend, but my gay time made me broke often. I didn't look upon money as money so long as I had a good time.

My people at home? I have nobody back in China; they are all dead. I never write them for thirteen years now. I don't bother even to think about people at home. Right now I am alone, just waiting to die.

I have a grandson in China. He is twenty-four years old now. He sent me a picture of his a few months ago [*shows picture*].

No, he is not married yet. I don't bother whether or not he is married. He is a farmer in the native village.

Why? I can't even get along myself. I am not hoping to get back to China. To die in America is all right.

Yes, I can still work. This old dog-life of mine, it seems I have to work until the day of my death.

I came to Chicago right after the Fourth of July this year. I have never borrowed any money, seldom, anyway. But I have borrowed from here and there since I came to Chicago. I owe people about fifty dollars now. I borrowed fifteen dollars from a niece a few days ago.

... As I am now without money, they don't look upon you as a human being. Del-nea-ma, those clansmen of mine are really very hard.

His hopelessness makes him speak indifferently and scornfully about the common goal: the return trip to China. He pretends that he has nobody in China but immediately produces a picture of his grandson and shows that he does have concern for people in China and cannot forget his people at home. In his old age, he may have thought about going back to China, but he has not written home for the last thirteen years. He probably would not speak so indifferently if he had sent money home.

Most of the men who become lo-wah-chao seem to have personality problems. They are demoralized either by sex or by gambling. The frank and somewhat indifferent tone in the case shown above is amazing. It is characteristically a temperamental sign of the easy-going, romantic type.

When a lo-wah-chao is too old to hold the strenuous job of the laundry, he may return to Chinatown. Sometimes he is so feeble, no one would call him to help at all; he then can be a hanger-on in the gambling house, depending on some "good-luck money" given him by the winners. If he still has financial resources, he may join the gambling house business and become a *lao-ka* [*laojia*], a person depending on the gambling world in Chinatown for a living.

> I used to work in the laundry at 65th and Cottage Grove. Do you know Lee Hong? I was thinking that I would be too old to endure a hard job in the laundry, so I sold it to him.
>
> At first a cousin of mine and I worked in that place; he and I could not get along so well. That was another reason why I thought I might as well sell it. I left that place six years already. Since then I have been living here in Chinatown.
>
> What else can I do, a man of my age? I have two shares in Fo Kai (a gambling house) and I work there two hours every day. What else can I do?
>
> You know one can't make much in this way. It is not a definite income, sometimes I receive more and sometimes less. It all depends on the luck of the house. I may lose money if the house goes broke.
>
> Sometimes I play *tze-fa* [*zihua*, one of the two kinds of lottery] almost every day—making pretty good, but sometimes losing every penny. As I gamble, income means nothing. You don't take account of the money that gets into your hand, you just get by and sometimes you have to go hungry. Take the last two weeks, for instance, I had about thirty dollars in my pocket all the time, and this week I have "no more nothing!" So you can say, gambling is bad business.
>
> Going back to China? How can I go back to China? Ah, it seems to be hopeless, you ask me. Unless I win on the lottery; if I catch three dollars eight spots, well, that is a different story. You can't possibly find me anymore. But how can I have such luck? It is difficult. It is mere hope, that is all.
>
> Yes, I have a son, grandsons, and a daughter-in-law in China, living in the native village. I haven't sent any money home for about two years. Now, I can't even make enough to support myself. Sometimes I plan to send them

some, but the only thing is I don't have it. If I don't gamble, I might save enough eventually. With a small amount on my hands, I tend to try my luck and that is the way it is.

Yes, my old wife is still living; she is living with my son, of course.

I have been here for a long time, about thirty-five years.

I returned to China twice. It has been nearly fifteen years since my last entry. Now, I am old and can't work any more. And I can't think of going back to China now. When I sold my laundry I had about four hundred dollars. I thought of going back then. Later, I spent some and gambled away some, and soon I found I had nothing. I thought of returning to the laundry business, but I couldn't get the financial help. I was forced to live in Chinatown.

Ah, as I get old and poor, even our cousins have no confidence in me. It is not easy to borrow money; I can hardly borrow a cent from them. Human sentiments become very thin.

He returned to China twice, but now he has to depend on his luck on the lottery if he is to take his last trip. The chance seems to be slight. Like others, he has tried luck, but luck won't come.

His misfortunre is clearly the gambling habit. This man is known as an opium addict. A lao-wah-chao tends to neglect his family in China.

To die in a foreign land, according to Chinese conventions, is a tragedy. Some old-timers would make a last attempt to escape such a fate. The next case is a man eighty-seven years old who still wants to take his return trip to China to join his family.

I have been in this country for almost sixty-five years. It is a long, long time, isn't it? I went back to China three times. This will be my fourth time if I can make it. It has been thirty-five years since I returned to this country the last time.

I came over when I was seventeen years old and now I am eighty-seven. I was a fool; I made a lot of money but did not know how to spend it. Right now, I still have twelve thousand dollars in the bank but it closed a few years ago [1929–1930]. I don't know whether I shall be able to get it back or not. I am waiting to see if I can get back my money so that I can go back to China. I could have already gone back if I didn't have to wait for it.

I was the one who established this laundry. At first it was not located here. I moved over here from the one block. I have been with this laundry ever since I returned here from China fifty-five years ago. When the business was getting better I asked two of my cousins to join partnership with me. He [his partner standing nearby] is one, and the other is dead. We used to make a lot of money here in this place, particularly during the war. I sent some home but saved most of it, because the exchange rate was too low. It took almost eighty dollars to eighty-five dollars to exchange one hundred dollars Chinese currency.

He [his partner] is not my close cousin; he is rather a clansman. I have two nephews and both of them are now working in the laundry on 57th Street.

I have only one son, but he is dead now. All I have in China now are some grandsons and a daughter-in-law. I think they are all right. I am going back to China. I didn't want to go back before. . . . That was why I wanted to keep this laundry even if I had to lose money from keeping it. The business became very poor; we couldn't make enough to cover the maintenance. I began to realize that I have been a fool. I have been a fool all my life. [Before he could make his trip back to China, this old man died, two weeks after this interview with him.]

For thirty-five years this old man remained in America after he had taken three trips back to China previously. Taking the advice of his relatives, finally he decided to take his last trip, in spite of the uncertainty about the twelve thousand dollars which he deposited in the bank that went bankrupt during the Depression. The case is interesting because it represents some of those who actually had personal property tied up which delayed their repatriation.

Often a lo-wah-chao is sent back to China by his clansmen. Some have no one in China; others prefer to remain rather than to take the trip. Actually, the life of the laundryman is not organized around his occupation here; it is organized around the possibility of the return trip, rather than the laundry itself. It seems only those who have their families with them in this country tend to have settlers' attitudes, which I shall describe in a later chapter.

CHAPTER X

THE LAUNDRYMAN'S
SOCIAL WORLD

IN THE American neighborhood, the Chinese laundry is a "China-town." Whatever contacts the laundryman has with the general public tend to be impersonal and commercial. His position is upon the symbiotic level of the community life. To his customers and other acquaintances, he is a thing and a stereotype. Only to his fellow Chinese is he a person. His relations with relatives and friends tend to be intimate and spontaneous. In company among themselves, laundrymen are free from lack of poise and race consciousness. The situation is similar, no doubt, in the cases of other minorities as well as the Jew, of whom Dr. Wirth writes:

> Within the inner circle of his own tribal group, he received that appre-ciation, sympathy, and understanding which the larger world could not offer. In his own community, which was based upon the solidarity of the families that composed it, he was a person with status, as over against his formal position in the world outside. His fellow-Jew and the members of his family to whom he was tied by tradition and common beliefs, strength-ened him in his respect for and appreciation of the values of his own group, which were strangely different from the alien society in which for the time being he lived.[1]

The social world of the Chinese laundryman is located between his quaint laundry shop and his racial Chinatown. Within this social world, people share common interests and conventional understandings; their relation is mutual and genuine, especially among members of the inner circle.

It is not that the laundryman is cut off from social contacts with non-Chinese, but rather a situation under which he can hardly unite "in his relations primary and secondary contacts."[2] The laundryman is not, to be sure, a marginal man. Rather, he is a sojourner, an individual who clings to the heritage of his own ethnic group and lives in isolation.

For the Chinese laundryman, to be able to speak English is something extra rather than necessary. It is not that he does not want to learn. He has, in fact, no time, no chance, and no facility for learning. He has not the incentive to learn English.

"In this sort of menial labor," one says, "I can get along speaking only 'yes' and 'no.'"

"If I knew how to speak and read English," says another, "I wouldn't have remained a washerman."

The majority of Chinese laundrymen speak pidgin English. Some talk so brokenly that their customers can only guess at what they are saying.

In leisure time and social events, the Chinese have a world of their own which is based upon the social solidarity of the families, the clans, and the kinship system. The American red-letter days sometimes are observed but with Chinese meanings converted to them.

1. Leisure-Time Activities

The problem of recreation for the Chinese laundryman is crucial. The world outside of his laundry is cold and strange. He strolls down the street with a lonely heart and a desire to get excitement after a week of strenuous labor. He seems to have no definite idea where to go for it. Going to a motion picture show is the most popular American recreation, but for a Chinese laundryman it is more of a way to kill time.

> INTERVIEWER: This cinema is so close by here, do you go to see a show often?
>
> C. M.: Once in a long time, seldom. On the week days, we have no time. Only Saturday afternoon and Sunday are free. But then people like to go to Chinatown and somewhere else.
>
> L. M.: You don't understand the talking—I seldom go. So far I have seen movies only twice.
>
> F. M.: I used to like movies very much. I went every day when I was not working, four years ago. A cousin of ours and I went to see a show every day because we had nothing else to do. Now, I don't care to see a picture unless I have nowhere to go.
>
> INTERVIEWER: C. L. goes to a show almost every Sunday.

c. l.: Well, that's because I don't care to go down to Chinatown, and I can't sleep all day long Sunday.

l. m.: Why don't you like to go to Chinatown?

c. l.: Just too lazy, that's all. We used to have a club there, but now, if I go down there, I have no place to hang around. What is the use to travel so far to go down there for nothing.

l. m.: Come! Let's go down to Chinatown after lunch.

Laundrymen from different laundries visit each other when they are free. A social gathering usually takes place in Mr. Laundryman's shop Saturday afternoon. But the party seldom lasts long. Unless they sit down and play ma-jong, as some of them do, the meeting would be adjourned after a big dinner. Then they want to go out for recreation. Where? To Chinatown probably.

Sept. 17, 1938; 5:30 p.m.:

moy: "Oh! You come just on time—a good dinner for you this evening."

I found Wai, the man who owns a laundry in the neighborhood, another middle-aged man, and a little boy about five years old there, besides Moy's partner and a helper. The man was introduced to me as a younger brother of Moy's partner. The boy is a son of their cousin who is a storekeeper in Chinatown. The brother used to be in partnership with them in this place. He sold his share to his brother and Moy and went to Detroit. Bringing the son of their cousin, he visited his brother and clansman and brought with him two big live lobsters.

Wai, a frequent visitor from the neighborhood was invited and he helped as a cook.

As soon as the dinner was ready, all sat down to plenty of food, fried lobsters, four other dishes of meat, several vegetables, beer, and Chinese liquor.

At the table, people were talking mostly about China's war with Japan.

After dinner, H. M., a young boy of seventeen, an apprentice in the laundry, was sent over to a store to buy several bottles of Coca-Cola.

Before the brother left, Moy was trying to make him take back the money he paid for the lobsters. The brother, playing sentiment, too, was reluctant to accept his cousin's offer.

"You are not making good these days," said Moy. "Take it. Come on! Take just two dollars, please! If you have caught eight or nine spots [in the lottery ticket], that's different. You can treat us then. . . ."

"It is worth less than two dollars," returned the brother. "Oh, don't do this."

"Oh, yes! You take this or I'll. . . . Please!" Moy insisted.

"No! I don't like to. . . ." The brother was rather stubborn too.

"Then I have to put it into your pocket. You. . . ."

"Oh! Would you keep quiet. . . ."

"You come to visit us from out of town, we ought to treat you. You need the money for carfare. . . ."

After a five-minute struggle, the brother finally accepted the money. He put the money into his pocket. Then he said he had to go to meet an appointment. Soon after the brother left. Moy took the boy home.

The other two members of the laundry had to remain in the laundry. They would not go any place until tomorrow—Sunday.

A social gathering of this sort represents a situation where a primary group relationships and control are observable. With father and son, uncle and nephew, brothers, and other relatives present, the Old World sentiments and taboos tend to be maintained. An essential characteristic of such a type of gathering is the absence of talk about sex. This is due to the presence of members of different generations of a primary group. A large percentage of Chinese laundries in the city consist of relationships of this type. Like the family, it comes to have a control function on the conduct of its individual members. Persons working in a laundry with this type of relationship are subjected to the influence of a set of Old World sentiments and taboos. When the members are by themselves, their conversations are not only under the control of the Old World moral sentiments and taboos, but also tend to be rigid and dull. Chinese elders maintain, in certain culturally defined way, personal distance from their junior members in order to keep their reverence. To respect the old, on the other hand, is a virtue of youth, and is still observed in this type of primary group relationship in the Chinese laundry.

In contrast, there is a second type of Chinese laundry where sex is the dominant subject of interest in the daily leisure-time conversation. The people involved in such a group tend not to be related to one another.

They may be cousins or clansmen, but are somewhat demoralized. Each member in such a group is more or less free; each minds his own business so far as his duty as a workingman in the laundry is concerned. The sex mores and taboos observed in the first type of laundry are out of the question here because of the absence of the venerable elder. The role of such a person in the group is due not so much to his age as to his status in the group. The absence of such a person may release the group from taboos, as shown in the following case:

Members of the laundry: Chan Ming-lung, 40.
                          Chan Ming-hong, 44 [partner of Ming-lung].
                          Chan Sai-kong, 55 [clansman—employed].
                          Fong Fook, 60 [unemployed friend of the partners].

MING-LUNG: Have you a girl for us? Introduce us to some of the girls. You must know many. [Ming-lung was operating the mangle while Ming-hong and Sai-kong ironed shirts, when the observer walked in. After ten minutes of exchange of greetings and about news of the war, Ming-lung suddenly changed to another subject.]
OBSERVER: I was thinking that you might get me a girl instead. I understand some prostitutes come to laundry shops, soliciting business. Any of them come to your place?
MING-HONG: Not in this neighborhood. I don't know why. [Admitted in a later interview girls did call.]
MING-LUNG: Sure, some girls [customers] come in here all the time, but they don't even talk to us.
MING-HONG: How about the office girl across the street? Does she like Chinese? [The girl was mentioned because they knew that the observer had business connections with the store across the street.]
OBSERVER: I don't know. Why don't you send old Mr. Fong Fook over to find out?
MING-LUNG: Yes, go ahead, Old Fook, go over. Ask if she likes Chinese. Go ahead.
FONG FOOK: Del-ka-ma! Go you to die.
MING-LUNG: Del-ka-ma! I told him to bring Sue, and he has never kept his promise. He said she is his daughter. Sue is his daughter, and she is pretty. Oh, I don't believe him [*laugh*].
FONG FOOK: Del-ka-ma! Go you to die. [*Qu si la*].

MING-LUNG: *Chot-chow!** [literally, "stupid as a pig"]. Is not it bad enough that she goes with black devils [Negroes]. Would you rather let the black devils have her. What about us Chinese?

MING-HONG: Del-ka-ma! She always goes to the dancing hall at Thirty-fourth Street, dancing with black devils. Both of the sisters do the same thing. This other one's name is Kitty, isn't it? You know them, don't you? [To observer, and observer happened to know who they were talking about. Sue and Kitty are two Chinese girls related to Fong Fook.]

OBSERVER: Yes, I know them. They are daughters of Fong Sun-yuin.

MING-LUNG: They are now living at. . . . Their father has a chop suey house in the neighborhood. Go and find them and bring them here, you, will you please [to Fong Fook]?

MING-HONG: Sue is better; I heard she is very hot. . . .

MING-LUNG: Always like to be fucked. Black devil's "big thing." Del-ka-ma! Hers must be broken already!

MING-HONG: Oh! No [*laugh*].

FONG FOOK: Del-ka-ma! She has gotten a job on the stage. She wants to think of you. She doesn't even know you.

MING-LUNG: I don't know her! What are you talking about? I have fucked her so many times that she likes me well and you dare to say I don't know her. . . . You go and ask her, chot-chow [*laugh*].

FONG FOOK: Del-ka-ma! Damn liar! This what the Americans say, "Damn liar."

MING-LUNG: If you don't believe me, go and ask her.

FONG FOOK: Go you to die.

MING-LUNG: Go you to die, Old Fook. She is your daughter. You must be crazy.

FONG FOOK: She is your daughter. How do you like it?

MING-LUNG: All I want is to get her and sleep with her—daughter or no daughter. Del-ka-ma, he says he has a wife, a white woman, and a young, beautiful daughter called Sue-hing.

OBSERVER: Is that true, Old Fook?

FONG FOOK: Del-ka-ma, no, no more daughter—they are married.

MING-HONG: He wants to keep his daughter for his own use—such a kind of kai doi! [*laughter*].

MING-LUNG: Gets his own daughter-in-law, too, such a kind of kai doi!

FONG FOOK: You, you go to die—all of you.

OBSERVER: I don't believe what they say, Old Fook, but can you get them girls really?

FONG FOOK: They have girls; they have both black and white girls.

MING-LUNG: Oh, I had a black one here the other day. Good, very good. She is half white and half black. Just hot and tight enough and good water, too. Gave her a couple of dollars and I had her the whole night long. Since I don't have Chinese girl and white girl, black one is better than nothing, see. The only difference is that of her skin, but I don't care. So long as she has a hole, it is all right.

OBSERVER: Are you telling me the truth?

MING-LUNG: Yes, that is the truth.

OBSERVER: Is that true, Ming-hong?

MING-HONG: That's true [*laughter*].

OBSERVER: What do you do Sunday, usually?

MING-HONG: Well, go down to the park and try to look around and see if there are any wild chickens.

MING-LUNG: Want to catch some and bring them home. Good? See, see this table here. We had entertained many girls right here with drinks. Make them drink first, see, until they get drunk, then begin to have affair with her. You come around Saturday or Sunday. If you have no girl to bring us, let us go out to look for some. It is easy if you have a car. You just drive around in the West Side. Just pick them up at the street corner. I have done this before when I had the car. They came in and took a ride [*pause*]—but I dared not do it though. Just gave them a ride for a while and brought them home. Some of those Polish girls in the West Side—it's easy.

OBSERVER: How long ago did you do that?

MING-LUNG: Oh, several years ago—soon after I came from Detroit. It was very romantic that time, looking for girls always. See, see here, I smoked a pipe too. Some of the girls prefer a pipe smoker for a sweetheart. So I began to smoke a pipe. I still keep some of my old tobacco. Here, do you want to try it? It is good tobacco, expensive.

OBSERVER: How many times did you pick up girls in the West Side? [*smoking*].

MING-LUNG: Several times. Dared not to do it that time. Some of them were too young. They were only fourteen or fifteen. Some were old enough. It is worse today; it's different. Make friends with them—buy them some gifts, see; that's what all women like. After you become well acquainted with her, she would be yours. Some may want to marry you, can't tell. But I don't know enough English—it is best to be able to talk to her well. . . . That's my trouble. Fong Fook, you bring Sue to me, I can at least speak Chinese to her.

FONG FOOK: Del-ka-ma! Again. You go to die.
SAI-KONG: She does not speak Chinese, though.
MING-HONG: Yes, they don't even speak Chinese; they speak English, even at home. These American-born girls.
MING-LUNG: Is that so? Well, they must be able to speak a little at least. They are Chinese, after all.

The Chinese laundryman, like other homeless beings, is especially fond of sex jokes and stories. This case is interesting not merely because of the unreserved sex utterances in their gossip, but the picture of their sex adjustment in an isolated situation. Jokes and gossip essentially are more or less the character of amusement between long working hours. It may or may not be related to actual experience. The language above is rather rough because of the presence of Fong Fook, an out-clan member, who volunteers his help in exchange for board and perhaps a few dollars for "carfare." The partners have no respect for Fong Fook, partly because of the latter's personality, and partly because of his dependency, his out-clan affiliation in spite of his old age. He had to be ridiculed and made fun of. There are many old men in different laundries who are not full-time workers; they are given room and board with the laundryman because they have no place to live; they are usually clansmen and kinsmen of the laundrymen. An aged uncle, for instance, may move to his nephew's laundry shop to spend his retirement years. The accommodation usually is mutual and expected. To help the uncle, or to get rid of him, the nephew may want to send the old man home to China at his own expense. Sometimes a group of friends and relatives may get together to contribute enough money for the old man's homeward trip.

The partners, if there is no discord among them, usually talk while they are working. They may make jokes about each other, or may tell stories and tales on various subjects. Sex and gambling are usually favorite subjects if there is no elder man present. Other subjects are war and politics, particularly politics in China.

In Chinatown, the laundrymen regularly visit each other in one or two places Sunday afternoon. They crowd around the room, some sitting down and some standing up, each of them contributing news and views on world politics, on personal occurrences during the week, on friends and relatives, and on their laundry business. In this way, most of them spend their Sunday afternoon. Every Sunday, the same group of people meet and discuss the same subjects. When one has talked enough in one place, he goes to another place. He stays for a while and makes a few more remarks then walks out to the street around Wentworth and Cermak Road. On the sidewalk he may meet a fellow laundryman and they chat for a few more minutes; one will probably ask the other: "How is the business this week?" The answer would be either, "The same as usual," or "Good, pretty good," or "Poor, very poor," or "Less business [or more business] than last week." If they have no important matter to discuss, they will soon separate. If it is dinner time, he may gather some of his relatives and friends for dinner in one of the eleven restaurants in Chinatown. In the restaurant, on every Sunday evening, the laundrymen dine together. There are the busiest hours of the week for the restaurant. At different tables in the dining room, the most interesting phenomenon can be observed in the grouping of the diners. Dining with him are very likely his clansmen. One can identify the surnames of the men at each of the tables, if one knows them; for instance, at this table are members of the Moy clan, and at another are members of the clan of Chan, and so on.

2. Social Events

The laundryman seldom goes to visit parks, museums, and other public and educational institutions in the community. Occasionally, he goes to a motion picture show and window shopping in the Loop. If he is young and ambitious, he may attend one of the eight Sunday Schools in which English and Bible lessons are taught. Wherever he may have been, he does not forget to pay a visit to Chinatown where he feels more at home, where he shops for daily necessities and attends to business matters, and, above all, where he is recognized as a person, enjoying a life of primary relations where sentiments and attitudes are warm, intimate, and spontaneous.

The social events the Chinese laundryman shares with fellow Chinese are festivals, rites, and ceremonies. The cultural life of China is rich in festivals, but only a few are sufficiently transplanted to the New World. Those which have been transplanted, moreover, are subjected to modification due to American circumstances. Perhaps the most persistently observed festivals are the New Year celebration (lunar year) and the so-called "Commencement of the Year"—the Spring Festival [*Chun Jie*].

For the Chinese immigrants, Spring Festival is a traditional annual social get-together for a banquet. It is usually planned for soon after the New Year. All members of the social circle are supposed to join for a hearty dinner of the most elaborate art of Chinese cookery. Due to the peculiarity of its secular function, and the elasticity of its time limit, it is possible for every family, every clan, every store, and every chop suey house and laundry shop to have a Spring Festival social get together. Perhaps most characteristic is the Spring Festival of the clan. Each clan chooses the date convenient to all, including the married daughters and their husbands and children. If it is a small clan, the banquet may be held in the clan house. The food is either prepared in the house or ordered to be brought in from the restaurant. Larger clans may have to make arrangements with a restaurant in Chinatown so that the whole dining room or a section of it may be occupied by the special party. When the participants arrive, they are all like a big family. The adult males and the family units all contribute a small sum of money as the so-called "oil and light fee" to the clan house. Sometimes, in case of conflict, one person may have to be present at two banquets in the same evening.

The banquet is usually followed by speeches and messages from elder men and celebrities of the clan, and of the community, too, on some occasions.

In the midst of this beautiful spring season, the Gee Tak Kung Saw [*Zhide Sande Gongsuo*] (a combined clan association) of Chicago, for the purpose of celebrating the birth of its ancestor, the ancient venerable Duke Ham Fo (a historical ancestor), held a social gathering in its clan house last Sunday.

At 5:00 P.M., a banquet was held in Wah Ying Restaurant and guests and brethren of the clan and their families came together with high satisfaction and delight. The party occupied twenty-odd tables.

Amidst the banquet, elderman Wu Chi-ten and Yong Hui-fong, held their cups up and drank to the health and luck of all, and people drank together, wishing each other the same. Then Chi-ten, the toastmaster of the meeting, began to announce the purpose of the evening. He went on telling the story of the origin of Wu, Chow, Tsui, Yang fraternity. He stated that the four clans were offspring of King of Tai [ancient Duke Ham Fo]. At the beginning, the surname was Ku and the different offspring of King of Tai were later awarded titles, and from then on the four names were used according to the titles. The history of the clan can be traced back for centuries. He urged his brethren to hold and to keep the old virtues of *yen* [*ren*] (kind) and *jen* [*ren*] (unselfish) for the good of all.

Following are the speeches and messages of the guests. They were intro-

duced as Mr. Lee Kong-lam, chairman of the National Consolidated Benevolent Association (C.C.B.A.); Mr. Chan Kong-fong, president, Oak
Chun Kung Saw [*Duqing Gongsuo*] (another combined clan association);
Mr. Yen Sai-jen, chairman, Yen Shee Kung Shaw [*Zhensi Gongsuo*] (a clan
association); and their messages were generally of greeting about the Spring
Festival and the necessity for co-operation between different organizations
in Chinatown. Each time after these good speeches, there was loud ap-
plause.

At last elderman Chow Yee-fen gave thanks to those who came to honor
the meeting. Both guests and members of the clan fully enjoyed the meeting
and it adjourned about 7:00 p.m. Later in the evening there was Chinese
music and opera melodies for entertainment in the clan house. The celebration lasted until 12:30 after midnight.[3]

The laundryman seldom closes his laundry shop to attend any social
function; to suit him best, any meeting has to be on Sunday. So the Sunday
crowd in Chinatown is largely a laundrymen's crowd; the chop suey
worker would not be free on Sunday, because that would be his busiest
day. To celebrate the Spring Festival as well as any other social get-together, the laundryman may join as member or as guest. He may be an
elder man of the clan and venerable guest of the family, store, and other
voluntary associations in Chinatown. His social activities, therefore, are
more or less tied up with his personality, his prestige, and above all, his
success.

I have been too busy lately; after one or two weeks I'll have more time
to attend this matter. You know, we Chinese have Spring Festival following
the New Year holiday. Once a year, they want to have something to do.

I was appointed secretary of our clan and manager of our clan woi [loan
committee]. This coming Sunday, there will be a banquet, Spring Festival.
They asked me to let you know, you be sure to come, too.

There will be two banquets for me this coming Sunday. Kung Wah Yuen*
is inviting me, too. They are conflicting with ours. They didn't know perhaps our clan would have our own Spring Festival this coming Sunday.

For the last two weeks, there were banquets, banquets, every Sunday.
Bing-lung had his last Saturday evening. His son called several times, asking
us to go to eat. We are far less busy here in America at this season. You
probably remember that in the native village, at this season, every family
has its own festival, taking turns for the whole month. With a grand-family
as big as ours, I used to attend one banquet every day for nearly a month,
getting sick and tired of eating meat, meat and fish, every day, every day—
too much of it.

But I like the way we have our Spring Festival here, though. Once a week, a big dinner is very nice. Last week was at Toy-wah's [a cousin]. He is the fellow who is fond of cooking. He cooked the best *doong qua chung* [*dong-guazhong*] (a special pot of wintermelon soup) that I have tasted for a long time.

Next week, we will have a banquet here in this place. There will be about ten coming. This place is limited in space; we cannot have more. Several years ago, we once had more than ten, though. Bing-lung brought his nephew and the nephew's six children. We had to put them all at one table, all the children, I mean, that small table in that corner.

Please come. We will have something you like. It will not be as good cooking as that from the restaurant, but Sing-yang [a partner] is a very good cook. Sing-yang has already called Chinatown, ordering a big capon. And we hope to have "doong qua duck" too. We got *yin wou* [bird nest] already sometime ago.

I am the secretary of our clan organization this year. I want to tender my resignation this Sunday when they are together. I have been on it for the last two years. It is quite a responsibility; keeping the accounts and taking the money is quite a little job. I would like to have some one else do it this year. I recommended Sing-yang last year, but they thought Sing-yang is gambling now and then. Cousin Chung-shih and Big Brother Chung-ying [the chairman] urged me to continue for another year. They said I have good handwriting and insisted I take it. You know, the trouble is that very few of us know how to write [Chinese].

The laundryman's leisure-time activities seem to take place between the laundry and Chinatown. Chinatown is the social center; the laundry shop is his home. He may like to entertain guests at his laundry. Guests, after all, are people of his social circle. If he wants to have a birthday party, for instance, he can either entertain friends and relatives in a restaurant or at his laundry. A feast in the restaurant is more formal and expensive. Such a celebration is likely to be given by a relative in his honor; particularly by a son, son-in-law, or nephew. Men over sixty may expect birthday celebrations given by junior members of their immediate family. Usually the laundryman prefers to cook in his laundry shop because getting dinner is something of a play activity, to say nothing about saving money. When he is not working, he must have something to do to occupy his time. The best time for a dinner with invited guests would be Saturday or Sunday. On his actual birthday he has to work without celebration. The dinner has to be postponed until Saturday or Sunday.

December 13, 1938: Chan Sang sent three dollars to Ann, daughter of his cousin, and a letter which read:

Dear Ann:

I am sending you three dollars; it is my Christmas present for you. I have not the time to look for something you may like. In fact, I don't know what you like. So I send the money, hoping you will use the money to get what you want.

This coming Saturday will be my birthday. I shall prepare a special dinner here in my laundry. I am expecting you and your brothers and sister. You can take a cab; I shall take care of the fare. Come earlier, for the dinner will probably be ready about six o'clock.

Uncle Sang

December 17, 1938: It was a busy day for Chan Sang. He got up at five-thirty in the morning and began to cook the dinner. . . .

Finally, about four-thirty, the young guests arrived. They didn't take a cab as Chan told them in the letter. They brought one dozen of oranges. It was a birthday gift. "You bring fruit, too! Your mother told you to bring this!"

The dinner was ready at six-thirty. Chan Sang sent Chan Ming over to the chop suey restaurant in the next block to get some of the people over to eat. Soon Chan Ming returned: "They are too busy at this hour; they can't come over."

Chan Sang then took over to the chop suey house one-fourth of the cooked capon and some roast pork himself. He soon returned to join the party. Besides the children, there were five adults. Eight of us finally sat down and began to eat. It lasted us three-quarters of an hour. There was the best kind of Chinese wine—*ng ka pe* [*wujiapi*].

After the dinner, Chan Sang took all the children home to Chinatown in a cab.

January 4, 1931: One of the relatives in Chinatown was going to give a birthday party. Aunt Sun-lan reminded Chan Ming to invite Chan Sang last Sunday. Chan Ming was telling Chan Sang that both of them were invited and Chan Sang would be the guest of honor.

"Are you sure that she wanted me to the dinner?"

"Most certainly," answered Chan Ming. "If you don't believe me, ask Ling-po."

"Yes, I heard that she asked him to invite you," said Chan Ling-po.

"All right."

The next day, Chan Sang went down to Chinatown. He walked into a Chinese grocery store. He ordered a six-pound live chicken and one dozen oranges. He told the clerk to wrap it up with red paper because it was for a birthday present.

He took the package over to his relative, Aunt Sun-lan's house, and the old lady met him at the door.

"Aunty, this is a little something from me, for this evening."

"Oh, Brother Sang!" exclaimed Aunt Sun-lan, "you shouldn't have done that. All I want is that you come to dinner. As you spend so much money, I dare not invite you the next time. Uncle Teh-hing left me five dollars and said a dinner should be prepared. So I thought I would ask some of our cousins together. I told Brother Ming to remind you, too. But you shouldn't have done this! I don't want to make you spend the money."

"That's all right."

"Thank you! Oh, thank you, Brother Sang! And you be sure to come back Sunday."

"If I am late or don't show up, don't wait for me," replied Chan Sang. "I don't feel good these few days."

Chan Sang can be regarded as a typical character in the social life of the Chinese laundryman in America. He is usually very generous in spending money for social purposes. His inner social circle are composed of members of his clan and kin. The clansmen and kinsmen are his guests and he is their guest. Some of the distant relatives with whom he may not have anything to do in China, in America become much closer to him. This is the case between Aunt Sun-lan and Chan Sang. In China, they are members of different villages, and, in celebrating a birthday of Aunt Sun-lan's husband, Chan Sang would never have participated. In America, Chan Sang's relation with Aunt Sun-lan becomes closer. It produces a new social solidarity. A person with such sentiments and attitudes is fighting for status in the inner social circle. If he is not recognized in the circle as expected, he may be very indignant. The feeling of T. C. in the following case is a good illustration.

A birth ceremony was held last Sunday for Moy Wing's second grandchild. . . . In another store, several relatives and neighbors of the family were talking about it.

K. L.: Moy Wing's second grandson's birthday ceremony is today. Are you invited, T. C.?

T. C.: No! I don't know anything about it.

C. C.: Why? Your partner is invited—both of you are related to them.

T. C.: How can I ask them to invite me! *Del* (fuck)! I don't care.

S. T.: You can't blame them. You have been in their place, haven't you? I heard only those who gave presents to the baby are invited. Many of us know them, but we haven't given the baby presents. So I, too, am not invited. They don't invite you because they are afraid you will spend money.

K. L.: I am glad I am not invited. I am different from you, T. C. If they invite me I would have to spend at least three dollars. If I have three dollars, I can have all I can eat in any of the restaurants, too. You shouldn't be mad.

T. C.: Who's mad? . . . I don't care if my partner is invited. We two are in the same laundry, but he is invited and not me.

S. T.: But Ah Chung [father of the baby] may be looking for you, T. C. He may not have a chance to find you at all.

C. C.: I tell you, since I know they have a baby, I wouldn't want to go to visit their place. I don't care to spend money for a present. If I visit the place, it is not nice not to give any present. So I avoid going to their place this two weeks. I would wait until it is over. If I happen to see the baby, I then can give it a dollar or so for candy money.

S. T.: I don't know a thing. I just won't go to their place. I don't feel bad not to be invited. When their first grandson had its birthday ceremony, I made a present of three dollars. There was no dinner the last time. Instead of a dinner gathering, a cooked chicken and roasted pork cutlets were distributed to each giver. I don't know why it is a dinner this time.

C. C.: Well, they are having quite a few guests. You can count who will be there this evening. The son-in-law, the son-in-law's brother's family, Moy Wing's cousins, Hsin-hing, Kwong-sun, and Moy Jak. With so many persons, it will take three tables.

T. C. left the place without saying anything more; he looked not pleased at all. And S. T. said: "T. C. is a strange fellow. He doesn't feel happy if he is not invited."

"That's funny," responded C. C., "He doesn't care if he has to spend ten dollars—he would feel better. Such a silly fellow."

In spite of the indifferent remarks in the conversation, the issue in this case seems to be clear: the expectation of being included in a given circle is defined by clan and kin relationship. As both belong to the same clan, T. C. thinks that since his partner is invited to the party, he should be invited also. Whether the incident is a misunderstanding between T. C. and the family is another question. The case is interesting to illustrate the character of the inner circle of the laundryman's social world. It is essentially based on the clan and kin system; it is a social world of relatives. The laundryman seldom establishes primary contacts with people other than his own clansmen. In his social world, individuals with the same surnames are by virtue of this his *hing doi* [*xiongdi*] (brethren); individuals related to him or to his immediate family by marriage are *chan-chieh* [*qingqi*] (relatives by marriage); and individuals from the same native district are *hiang-le* [*xiangli*] (neighbors). He is bound up with these people not only in social activities but also in business ventures.

3. New Social Activities

The Chinese laundryman, although having either vague or superficial ideas about American holidays and other social activities, often takes part in some of the American institutional activities as a chance to get some extra satisfaction. Christmas, for example: the Chinese laundryman, to a certain extent, observes it, but with a different meaning. So Christmas is called Winter Festival [Dong Jie], which is an annual affair of ancestor worship comparable to Christmas because it comes shortly before the New Year. He observes Christmas by sending presents to some of his relatives and friends. To his customers he usually gives Chinese tea, li-chi nuts, silk, and chinaware. The presents are handed to every customer as the latter calls for his laundry. Unlike the ordinary Christmas gifts, the laundryman seldom wraps the packages with Christmas paper; the packages are not even named for the receivers, because the giver does not even know the names of his customers. In case he does know the name, to wrap it properly and enclose a card in the proper form is sometimes beyond his ability. He may not have the time to bother about it, anyway.

Every year we spend at least forty dollars, buying tea and li-chi nuts for our customers. It is once a year and the Americans regard it as their biggest day of the year. We don't feel good if we have nothing to give them. In this way, we feel good and they feel good, too, see.

No, very few of our customers ask for it. It is always we pass it out and they take it.

Yes, we pay special attention to some of our best customers. We have one family that does about five to six dollars' business with us every week. So we buy some Chinese tea, some li-chi nuts, and a pair of vases for them. We have another good customer, a widow and a young daughter. Every time she brings laundry, it must be a big bundle. So we got something for her and something for her daughter, too. We have about a dozen of such good customers.

The present, it seems, is essentially given with an economic motive, but not entirely without a human touch. Christmas may not mean the same thing to him as it does to Christians, but it is a celebration; Chinese love festivals by heritage. He gets satisfaction thinking that his customer would appreciate the present. Under some special condition, in order to feel better, the present becomes almost necessary to the laundryman for his customer. The celebration of the Christmas holiday in this fashion is not at all uniform. In certain neighborhoods where customers usually are of a poorer type and the business relationship is more or less on an impersonal basis, the laundryman may not feel it necessary to give presents to his customers. This is the case in some of the Negro areas. It is by no means without exception; Chinese laundries in the so-called "Black Belt" do distribute tea and li-chi nuts at Christmas time. A laundryman with poor business in a white neighborhood may not feel it necessary to give, also. There are also laundries where only good customers receive gifts.

> Well, some places just pass it out to everybody. We found it is not necessary to do it. We buy something only for our good customers, those give us much more business. This is merely to express our thought of gratitude for their patronage.

Occasionally the laundryman's customers repay him with presents which he does not expect. It is also an interesting practice that laundrymen exchange greeting cards among themselves. On many occasions, gifts are bought for children of friends and relatives—once a year as an expression of human sentiment.

As an old Chinese proverb says: "Getting in the village, follow its customs; going down the river, follow its current," [*ruxiang suisu chushui suibo*] the Chinese laundryman observes Thanksgiving Day; he calls it *Fu-Qai-Chih* [*Huoji Jie*] (Turkey Festival).

> "Just eat it once a year," Chan Sing remarked while he held a big piece of turkey meat between his chop sticks. "It is a good thing—just like our Chinese festivals. Since we are in this country, we like to eat turkey, too, although it is not our own custom."
>
> I told him Thanksgiving was not merely eating turkey. "Well," he said, "if the American give thanks for their good life—but only Chinese Christians believe in God. . . ."
>
> "Whenever the Americans have a holiday, they can really enjoy it. They

have family and relatives and friends, men and women, boys and girls. They have lots of places to go. A holiday means something to them. That means to have a real good time. What can a Chinese immigrant do? Nothing. He can only go down to Chinatown. A holiday is just like any other day. That means some of the gamblers lose more money on the gambling tables.

"Americans are different. They have parties at home, with friends and relatives. They enjoy some good music and have some fun together. We can have the same thing in China, yes, but not here.

"Eat turkey does not mean anything, since everybody eats turkey today; we, too, eat it, that's all."

This is how some of these lonely men eat turkey at Thanksgiving. It is nothing more than something different to eat. The following case, however, shows that laundrymen, too, get their friends and relatives together and celebrate the holiday with social meaning:

In the Charlie Moy laundry a twenty-five-pound turkey is roasted besides preparing other Chinese dishes. Soon three men arrive, and two more are expected. Another half hour of waiting, the expected guests still did not show up. The sixteen-year-old boy got on his bicycle and rode away. About twenty minutes later the lad came back alone.

"Granduncle T. K. is still too busy," said the boy. "He did not think he could come."

"In that case," said his father, "you had better bring some turkey over to him. Here I cut a piece. It takes you only ten minutes. And on your way, you might as well drop in to see Lo Loh [Old Loh]. If he is still home in his laundry, ask him to come to eat turkey."

Hurriedly, the boy again went out on his bicycle. When he came home again, everybody sat down to eat and drink heartily.

"Eat! Eat as much as you can!" F. M. urged everybody. "After dinner, we will go down to Chinatown. Maybe there will be another turkey dinner." He was mentioning some places where he could be invited if he showed up in time.

"Really turkey is not as good as chicken," said H. M., "but if Americans eat it, we, too, can have some. It is only once a year for this festival, that's all. It is a big day, American big day. But Americans don't have so much to eat as Chinese do in our festivals."

An additional chance of a social get-together, the abundance of food in a feast, and the "once a year" attitude give one a feeling that the laundryman is celebrating a Chinese festival to one familiar with the folk life in the Chinese village. The psychology of it is that the laundryman misses his Old World Festivals. Eating turkey on Thanksgiving Day means to him something of a substitute. To be sure, both on Christmas and on Thanksgiving Day he can close his laundry shop for a holiday because his customers are celebrating and would not come for their laundry. On the days of Chinese festivals, however, he is too busy to celebrate or has actually forgotten all about them. He participates in some American institutional activities because he is just as human as the others. He is bound to have a different interpretation of the event.

NOTES

1. Louis Wirth, *The Ghetto* (Chicago: University of Chicago Press, 1928), p. 26.
2. R. E. Park and E. W. Burgess, *Introduction to the Science of Sociology,* 2d ed. (Chicago: University of Chicago Press, 1924), p. 286.
3. *San Ming Morning News,* March 17, 1937.

CHAPTER XI

THE LAUNDRYMAN'S FOLKS
IN CHINA

THE SOCIAL LIFE of the laundryman bears the imprint of village sentiments and attitudes. He has left in China his folks whom he may not have seen for many years, but his life and work are unmistakably bound up with them. Through letters and return trips he maintains his social status in his native village; he plays in it important roles in public welfare as well as in personal, business, and domestic affairs. As he occupies a superior economic position, he becomes a philanthropist, a benefactor, and a friend-in-need to the old folks at home. To his family he is the support and the head.

1. "Wanted—Either Money or Man"

The illiteracy of the village folks, especially the women, provides the greatest barrier to communication by letter writing. The Chinese women in the village usually cannot write. In most cases others write for them. A woman has to dictate her ideas and thoughts to a friend or a professional letter writer. Under such conditions, unless the letter writer is someone in whom she has confidence, her feelings and thoughts are likely to be reserved and constrained. Because a letter is written by a third person, most of the letters the laundryman receives from home are rather rigid and formal. Often the Chinese complains that he has heard nothing from home but two things: His people want "either money or man"; that is to say, whenever his folks write, it is either asking him for money or asking him to return home. To return to China, he must be sure to know, himself, when it will be. But he seems to be disgusted by reading letter after letter from home, all of them requesting money.

On the other hand, the laundryman himself may not be very literate.

Most of them can read Chinese fairly well, but the majority of them write with great difficulty. Those who cannot write have to get someone else to write for them. For this reason, among others, the laundryman may not write home very often. When he does, the letter is almost always accompanied by money. When he has not the money ready to send home, he may either not write any letter or postpone it.

When all brothers are married, a large family may break into smaller units and each brother then looks after his own family. His primary responsibility is, so to say, to support his own wife and children. The division may take place even when one of the parents is still living, particularly the mother. Among the brothers, however, help and assistance, financial as well as moral, are something righteous and virtuous. Since the laundryman is in good economic circumstances, he cannot let his poorer brother(s) remain destitute. He will help his brother or other relatives when they are in need. The mores of the Chinese people compare brothers to one's own arms and legs; one cannot do anything, obviously, without arms and legs. It becomes one's duty and moral obligation to help one's brother; otherwise the family loses face. If he refuses to fulfill his duty, his conscience bothers him, and he loses his status among his folks. He may be spoken of as "not virtuous" or even inhuman, in certain cases. Generally, when the Chinese immigrant sends money home for his wife and children, he also remembers his brother and sister, nephews and nieces. He sends them not only money, but also presents such as a watch, clothing, shoes, or a fountain pen. When he sends money for the new year (lunar year), which is almost a *must* (because to the Chinese folks, it is their Christmas), he provides each member of the greater family a certain amount as a gift.

The letters in the following series represent fairly well the "wanted—either money or man" pattern. They are arranged in chronological order. The six letters, covering a period from May, 1938 to January, 1939, were received by Mr. Han from his brother-in-law, his older brother, his wife, and his nephews. Each wrote his own letter, with the exception of his wife's letter which was written by his older brother on her behalf. The series, therefore, is considered typical of correspondence between the laundryman and his folks at home.

Ho-mou, Senior Brother-in-law, to you I write with respectful greetings:

I am now writing to you with a special purpose. You have been keeping your self silent so long and have not been sending money home and Second

Sister [wife of receiver] has begun to worry. How and what are you doing
now we know nothing about.

You have not written home a single letter for the last year. What has
happened? My Brother must be industrious and save his money. It is a bad
idea to spend money freely. You must realize, my Senior Brother, you are
getting old now but it is not too late yet to start again.

We are all well in the village. Please do not worry about us. We hope
that you are well and your business is good in America. As soon as you
receive this letter, please let us know how you are getting along.

Brother, Ming-leong
May 4, 1938

Ho-mou, like many other fellow laundrymen, for one reason or another,
neither writes nor sends money home for many months. He has to be
reminded by the folks at home. The letter was written by a man, Ming-
leong as we call him, who is the husband of Ho-mou's younger sister, and
who, himself, had been in America and was a laundryman. Ming-leong's
letter seems to bring results because it takes the form of good advice, or
more correctly, persuasion, as the next letter reveals.

Ho-mou, Senior Brother-in-law, to you I write with respectful greeting:

Your letter arrived January 12 with a check for three hundred and twenty
dollars Hong Kong currency. Of this amount you allotted fifty dollars to
Mother Wo [Ho-mou's mother], fifty dollars to Older Brother Ho-yin [Ho-
mou's brother], ten dollars to Cousin Wai-wah, ten dollars to Nephew
Kwong-pui, and the rest to Second Sister. I have divided it as you wished
and I take this opportunity to thank you for them.

You have said also, my Brother, that I should advise Second Sister to be
careful with her expenditures. I did mention this to her, my Brother. The
money you sent home last time was spent for the sake of your daughter.
There was no extravagance. You can understand that, please, so that there
is no cause to grumble.

My Brother has been abroad many years and you know how Mother
awaits your return. She wants you to be industrious and rich and return
home in the near future.

Our district, Kwang Hoi [Guanghai], is not distressed by Japanese invad-
ers. But prices for foodstuffs are getting very high. . . . [The writer writes
about his journey from the village to Hong Kong.]

Second Sister can hardly get anyone to write for her. She has asked me
to do so. I want you to know it is not necessary for me to write a separate

letter now. We are well at home and we hope you are the same.

Brother, Ming-leong
January 12, 1939

Whenever the laundryman sends money home, the largest amount generally goes to his own family unit, and proportionate amounts are given to those relatives he thinks need help. One receiving a gift responds with a thank-you letter. The following was one such letter from his older brother:

Ho-mou, my Younger Brother, I write as if I see you personally:

I have not seen you for years and hope always that you are well, and your business is successful, and your work is good, and you can come home in the near future, and we can enjoy the family reunion. It will not only be mother's joyous moment, but mine, too, my Brother. The whole family will be happy indeed.

In care of Brother Ming-leong, you have sent home three hundred and twenty dollars. You are so nice to give me fifty dollars and Mother fifty dollars. Your thoughtfulness is well appreciated and I thank you very much, my Brother.

I have stayed home so long and feel depressed. I think of going abroad, but there is no way. Not a single reliable way.

Due to the Japanese invasion, the business I established in the village is reduced to nothing. The transportation is completely dead, no goods can be shipped anywhere. My capital is small and the family expenditure is large. Foodstuffs are getting high priced and I find it difficult to maintain the family from starving.

Our *fong-shiu*[1] is not so bright for me and my wife to have children. So I arranged to get a concubine. September 13 last year another child was born to me. It is a son! I gave him a name—Wing-ling. This is an offspring of Teh-chang.

It is Mother's seventy-seventh birthday this year. She is still healthy.

November 16, last year, I gave a birthday ceremony for Wing-ling when we worshipped our ancestors. At the day of 17, suddenly, Mother fell down. Her right leg was hurt and she couldn't walk thereafter. Three months have passed and now she seems to be a little better.

Now my son Bah-chung [older son] is now seventeen, growing up to be a man. Owing to my financial difficulty, I cannot send him to school any more.

My Brother has sent home a letter, scolding Sister [wife], because she is extravagant. I don't think you are right, my Brother. I have been home all these years, and I feel that she is a dutiful woman at home. She is industrious and careful with her expenses. I remember once you sent home three hundred and once you sent five hundred. The money has been spent virtuously. She was not extravagant. Because my Niece [your daughter], Sunmei, was very weak, we had to send her out to Hong Kong for medical care. Over one hundred dollars was spent for the purpose. Then we arranged her marriage. We spent another hundred-odd dollars. After her marriage, on account of her illness, she couldn't have strength to carry on her household duties. Then we had to buy a slave-maid [indentured family servant] for her. That cost about ten dollars. And village activities and other necessary expenses needed a lot of money to carry on.

Unfortunately, my Niece (your daughter) died! And this required money, too. And there are numerous expenses during the year.

As an eyewitness, I don't think Sister is extravagant.

My Brother had not sent any money home for more than two years and you can imagine what the condition can be.

Sister has conferred with me and she wants to buy a son to be your heir. I presume you will agree with us.

You said she hasn't written to you for the last two years. But you can realize and understand the whole situation. She is sad and weary for the death of the daughter who was childless. What can you expect from a woman who does not know how to write even her own name? Please understand her and forgive her.

From Mother down we are all well at home. We hope you are well abroad.

Older Brother, Ho-yin

The letter shows that even after the daughter's marriage, the mother continuously has given her daughter financial as well as moral aid. Financial aid, in general, is given to those who cannot help themselves. In this case, the daughter evidently married into a very poor family. Her mother was the only person who could do anything for her. Her laundryman father, however, due to his physical distance from home, may not have understood the situation. He thought his wife was extravagant, but his older brother wrote to defend her, insisting that it was only virtuous to spend money for the sake of the sick girl.

If either the father or mother is still living, he or she becomes a symbol of the large family group. The children and grandchildren must think about his or her wishes and sentiments. They write about him or her, and if one wants his brother to help arrange his son's or daughter's marriage, it is the mother's or father's wish to become a grandparent which is given as the principal reason. Such a reason may be just a sentimental expression to cover up individual selfish wants, but it is very appealing and convincing.

Due to the absence of her husband, the woman was left at home without a son. This is the most disappointing matter in traditional Chinese family life, especially for women. To be without offspring is an unfilial deed. Under such a circumstance, in the native village, women can purchase a son from a poorer family. In this case, the wife conferred with the older brother, and the older brother suggested it to her husband.

The following letter was written by the older brother on the wife's behalf. We can see that it expresses the older brother's idea as well as the wife's.

Husband, my Good Man:

For we are poor and you have to leave home and go abroad to make a living. How time has gone by so quickly! You have been in America for ten years. I hope my good man abroad is well and his business is prosperous and he is coming home soon with wealth. I shall be the most happy woman on earth.

Through Brother-in-law, I have received two hundred dollars from you recently. The money has been already made over to me. Please do not worry about it.

My Good Man says this poor woman, I, am extravagant. Yes, you have sent home eight hundred dollars in the recent years. But within these several years, with all the necessary expense and our unfortunate daughter, we needed a large amount of money. I spent the money for the life of our daughter. I can face the Heaven and Earth that I am innocent. Both Mother and Older Brother know about it. It is not that this bad woman, I, like to be extravagant. My Good Man can investigate. Please do not be angry.

I heard that my Good Man is suffering from the old malady again, please be easy with your heart and not hurt yourself with anger.

You said I did not write to you for two years. For our short-lived daughter's unfortunate death and the money I have spent for her sake, I am bewildered. I just don't have the right mind to say anything. For several times I asked Brother-in-law, Ming-leong to write for me. Did he or did he not write? I don't know why you say I don't write at all.

Upon receiving this letter, please write to her Peaceful One [mother] and Older Brother. Why did you send him money without a letter? Her Peaceful One [mother] is old and she lives with your Older Brother. She is well taken care of. As one of her sons, you ought to do your own duty.

As Older Brother spent most of his money on his house, he is now hard up. Lately he often talks of going abroad. The reason he does not decide to go is that he worries about the Old Mother. He could have gone two years ago.

Nephew Bah-chung is now a young man, but Older Brother has no money to arrange his marriage for him. My Good Man can confer with Third Younger Brother and should think of some way to help Big Brother so that he may be able to arrange Bah-chung's marriage. It is to save the face of our family and let nobody talk about us.

Big Brother's Concubine gave birth to a baby son last year. The whole family was happy.

The whole family are well at home and I hope you are in good health, too, in America.

Your Concubine,[2]
Le Shee[3]
January 16, 1939

If a brother, a nephew, or an uncle needs money for a legitimate business, he may appeal directly to the laundryman in America for help, especially in the case of the marriage of children. When the young man is about seventeen or eighteen, he is about the age to be married. If his father is too poor to arrange it, his richer uncle may take the responsibility. One laundryman received a telegram from his brother in China; it read: "Ling marries. Eight hundred dollars." The laundryman had to make a loan to raise enough for his nephew to be married. Sometimes the brother may not have to ask for it. And there are those who refuse to accept responsibility. Sometimes the money is not a gift but a loan.

In the next letter by the nephew, the young man was too bashful to mention his marriage. He may have written just for courtesy, or on the order or suggestion of his father.

Second Uncle, I write to you with respectful greeting:

I have not written to you for a long time, although I think about you often. You have been abroad about twenty years. Your Nephew, I, read your letter to Father and learned that my Uncle had suffered from heart illness. Please take good care of it. As soon as you save enough, how I wish to see you come home. You will see Grandmother and all of us. Foreign country is not a place for you forever, my Uncle.

I, your Nephew, am seventeen this year. I have been in school for a few years but I have learned only a little about sciences yet. Now my father has no money to support me through school and I stay home, farming. I can't go to school any more.

Second Aunt went up to the mountain to gather some wood one day last August and she forgot to lock the door. Maybe she didn't forget but the robber broke in. Everything in the house was taken.

I want to tell you also that whenever Second Aunt does any worshipping during the year, she worships [ancestors] alone. It is too lonesome for her. She wishes to get a boy to do it for her. Please let her do it; let her get a boy.

I thank my Uncle most kindly for sending my Father the money early this year.

I hope you are well in America and you are making a lot of money, too.

Nephew,
Bah-chung
January 16, 1939

Sometimes nephews and nieces as well as sons and daughters might ask the laundryman to send them all sorts of personal things—from jewelry to playthings. Or the laundryman might do it of his own free will. In this case, the laundryman was a somewhat disorganized person. The family is always the social unit rather than the individual. Since the laundryman gave fifty dollars to his brother, the father of the young man, the nephew takes it as given to him. He writes, thanking his uncle and tells him his difficulty, namely, not being able to continue in school on account of his father's financial situation.

The next letter, which was from the son of the sister to whom the laundryman had given ten dollars as allowance, is brief and simple. It is merely an acknowledgment of the receipt of the gift. It, however, illustrates the relationship to different kinds of nephews. The brother's son is always closer than a sister's son. The sister's son belongs to the other clan, with a different surname. A maternal uncle, however, may or may not take equal responsibility toward his sister's son. The situation, of course, is always modified by the individual relation.

Uncle, Venerable One, I write to you with respectful greeting:

I received ten dollars Hong Kong money from you lately. I thank you very much. How I would like to see you come home and be with us in the near future, too.

Now Canton is captured by the Japs, our commodities here cannot be shipped to the village. For this reason, the prices of foodstuff in the village are high, very high. One bag of rice costs from eight to nine dollars. How can the poor families back home manage to live!

However, everybody at home is well. I hope you are well, too, in America.

Nephew,
Kown-pui
January 23, 1939

The gift of ten dollars from the uncle to the nephew, in this case, is merely to illustrate an existing social sentiment. The report of hardships may be considered implicitly a request for further help from the uncle. There are brothers-in-law who write urgently, requesting financial support from the laundrymen. Other relatives write for one thing or another to which the laundryman often remarks, "People back home seem to think we can pick up gold on the streets; when they write, they ask for either money or man."

2. Personal Business

The laundryman is the support and head of his family in spite of the fact that he lives thousands of miles away from home. Generally, the wife's conception of herself is that she is merely his housekeeper rather than his partner; that she is keeping the house and rearing the children merely on his behalf. This is at least the feeling the wife has when she is so bored by her husband's delay in writing and in sending sufficient money home. She will write and say, "It is an awful duty to manage this household of yours!" She has to consult him on every important matter before action is taken, and he alone can make the decision. In case his wife or anyone of his family disobeys his wishes, he may punish them by cutting his financial support to the family, or at least threatening to do so. If his wife is proved to be unfaithful to him, he can even disown her with or without legal procedure. There need be no divorce nor any other legal action, for he has the moral support of the relatives and he is away from China. What he has to do is simply cut off his relation with her by putting an announcement in the local magazine or newspapers.

> An Important Announcement of Leong Sing-wing: This is an announce-
> ment: In the 11th Year of the Republic [1922], my late wife Chan Shee
> died. This misfortune left my home without a mistress. In the 13th year of
> the Republic, I returned to China from America. In that year I married
> Chung Chang-wo's daughter, Fong-shiu, of Hing Village, as my second wife.
> I lived with her for several months and when the time limit of my return
> to America was near, I was forced to leave home and came to America
> again. My only hope was that Fong-shiu keeps my house dutifully and
> maintains her virtues as a woman and that would relieve my worry about
> the domestic affairs.

I have never thought that Fong-shiu would violate moral principles and neglect her duty as a woman. Good virtues are gone from her heart. Bad news has repeatedly reached me. In order to find out the truth, I entrusted my uncle, who was on his way back to China, to inquire into her case. He reported to me that Fong-shiu was really doing something immoral. I, therefore, cut the relation with Fong-shiu ten years ago. She and I are no longer husband and wife. I gave her freedom to remarry or do anything she chose to follow. I also had an announcement in the press to this effect. This case was known then.

Now I hear that Fong-shiu is still behaving disorderly. By presenting false facts, she tries to borrow money from here and there. I am afraid that some of our neighbors might fall for her tricks. For this reason I hereby take this opportunity to announce once again, hoping that no one can be cheated by her. This is sincerely announced by

Leong Sing-wing of Tan On Village,
at present in Chicago[4]

In the folk society of the Chinese village where social control is based on conventionalities, gossip, and greatly reinforced by moral codes, adultery is only occasional if not rare. The announcement is interesting as showing the authority of the man over his wife. The woman may enjoy higher status and prestige in this village community partly on account of the well-being of her husband, and partly on the basis that she is a good wife and a good mother. She is trained to love and obey. She is entirely dependent upon her husband. If her husband is in America, she is a *Gum-Shan-poo* [*Jinshanpo*] (Golden Mountain lady). This is a matter of pride for village women folks. It means economic comfort and social prestige. But, sometimes, it means also long separation. For one reason or another, her husband in the "Golden Mountain" neither wrote nor sent money for months. She wrote letter after letter but never got an answer. She wrote to relatives, asking for her husband's whereabouts. She heard rumor and gossip about her husband. If she is illiterate, she must ask a third person to write for her. But if she can write, as is the case in recent times, the letter may reveal further the culture of the group and the status of woman in relation to her laundryman husband in America.

Hup, My Husband:

In reporting the affairs of the family, I have written you previously and I think you must have received my letters. But you have never answered me; in fact, you have not written home for one whole year! Such an act of yours makes me most miserable and always worried. Why don't you write home?

Too busy? But we are tormented longing to hear from you. Because I have had such an anxiety about you, I have gone to fortune tellers, to the temples, to road-side deities of wood and clay, begging for blessings and for your safety. It was because of you I acted very stupid. I was upset and restless. I have done all sorts of silly things because I can't help it.

What crime have I, your unworthy Wife, committed, that you punish me by applying such a terrible torture—not writing me for one whole year? Even if I have done wrong, as my husband, you should teach and scold me. If I deserve it, I can take it gladly. But now you pay no heed to me; you ignore me. I ask, what is the reason for all this? If you don't tell me clearly why you don't write for so long, my heart will never be sweet even after my death.

My Husband, please be a man of virtue. It is well said: "One day's husband and wife, hundred day's sentiment" [*Yiye fugi bairi'en*]. You and I are not bound by a road-side accord but by legal marriage. As I tried so hard to help you get over to America, you have now gold and silver, but you have lost your sense of duty to the family. You make people laugh at us!

There is gossip around here about you that I overheard. I don't know where the news came from, but it is hard for me to bear. It comes into my ears with great pain and I can hardly stand it. I tried awfully hard in taking it. I am passing my days, thinking of you always. If you don't have money, why can't you write just a plain letter? Just tell me that you are well. What sort of husband are you not to write home for one whole year? If you don't think of me, you should have thought of your old Mother. Observing your recent conduct deserting your family like this, I don't understand. As you are a person who has studied the books of the sages, you must have learned the *li* (rites, a Confucian concept) and *yi* (righteousness) from them. Why is your conduct so contradictory to what you have learned? I never dreamed that you could treat me like this. You are very cruel. When I get emotional, I want to bite off my finger and write this letter with my own blood. I didn't do that because, I thought, when you see the letter, you might feel very badly. But all that I have said is from the blood of my vein. All I ask you is that you think clearly and carefully and that you can come to us, getting rid of your sin. It is not too late for you to do that.

Upon reading this letter, please think it over quietly. Cousin Ming-lei sent several hundred dollars home last June and now he sent another five hundred. He sent this money through my mother's place. Let's look at Ya-ying's husband; he writes every month. How happy others are to be "Golden Mountain women" and I, too, am a "Golden Mountain woman" [*Jin-shanpo*], but I have a lot of sorrow and sad days. It is because of your heartlessness.

Please, Husband, send me a letter every month. You are worrying us to death. In writing this letter, I hope, however, that you are well.

> Your wife,
> Teh-oi
> November 17, 1939

This sort of letter may or may not work. It will, of course, depend upon the individual. If her estranged laundryman husband still neglects and ignores her, she is helpless. There is no such thing as divorce suits or desertion charges against her husband. The very last recourse she has is to write to relatives who are also in America, seeking moral support. The relatives may give her husband a heart-to-heart talk, or even a scolding. Overseas Chinese in America know this situation full well; everybody minds his own private affairs. If one chooses to be a gambler, a prostitute patron, or patron of other vices, it is the individual's own business. No immigrant elderman can do anything. In America, morality is defined differently. Patronizing a prostitute, for instance, is an unthinkable thing in the Chinese village, but in America it becomes something considered unavoidable or inevitable. Thus Mr. Laundryman may keep a mistress or gamble, and the public will not condemn him. In some serious cases he may lose social status in his inner circle, but he is never an outcast. But if his wife commits adultery in the native village, she immediately becomes the butt of gossip in the whole community and is persecuted by the public.

A third person sometimes intervenes in one's family affairs. The laundryman may receive letters from his relatives in China, requesting him to be a *fo-hing* [*fuxiong*] (elderman). Sometimes a money matter is arranged between one person in the native village and another person in Chicago. One of the letters a laundryman received read, in part, as follows:

> Please give the statement enclosed to Teh-soon, I wish he would pay me back the money so that the interest would not increase to a great amount. Please advise him. I shall appreciate the trouble you take for me.

Instead of writing for mediation of loan and other financial matters, others seek consultation in domestic discord. Here is a letter written by a widow to her husband's third cousin.

Mei-yo, Second Lord:

About Sun-wah's schooling, the last term has just passed and I am afraid
that he cannot go back to school next term. I don't know whether or not
my Brother-in-law [Teh-him] can be responsible for Tse-li's education. Upon
reading this letter, please have a good heart; please talk to my Brother-in-
law and ask him to let Tse-li continue his schooling. If he consents, I wish
he would send the money through Cousin Lem-shee. Then I shall receive
the money and send Tse-li to school again. If he doesn't want to be responsible for it, ask him if I can sell some of our land. All I ask is our
share. I must send my little son to school to be educated.

Now Sun-wah is studying in Canton and my sister-in-law goes back to
the village. She gave all the spending money to Ah Lan [niece]. When Yu-
toy [the slave-maid] goes to market, she asks Ah Lan for the money. Ah
Lan said to Sun-wah angrily: "Get out of here if you choose to do so!" She
took Sun-wah's suitcase out to the hall. I can hardly believe that a twenty-
five-year-old woman like Ah Lan can say such a thing. After all, they are
cousins. How could she say that Sun-wah is not her uncle's own bone-and-
blood, that he is purchased with two or three hundred dollars, and all our
land and property are theirs and Sun-wah has no share.

You see, my sister-in-law and her daughter treat us like outsiders. My
sister-in-law also said to Sun-wah: "Well, if your uncle wants you to go to
school, you write to him and ask him for the money. Don't ask me." All
Sun-wah's school expense my sister-in-law refuses to pay for. I, therefore,
write to tell you, Second Lord. Please advise my Lord Brother-in-law. Please
ask him to give me his instruction, a way for me to follow. I hope to hear
from you soon. We are well and hope you are the same.

                                                    Sister—Chan Shee
                                                    April 26, 1926

The clansmen, especially close cousins, consult each other concerning
their family affairs. If one wants the moral support of his clansmen, he
must act according to the advice of the elder men and the mores of the
group. In the above case, after the death of his brother, the laundryman
is expected, according to the mores of the group, to take care of his
brother's family. In spite of the personal conflict between the two sisters-
in-law, which, by the way, is rather common in the old Chinese family
system, the fact remains that helpless relatives must be taken care of. The
woman, Chan Shee, is evidently seeking moral support from an older man
whom she thought might have some influence upon her brother-in-law. It
is quite common among the laundrymen, that elder men intervene in
personal affairs.

The laundryman, though living in America, is not only a mediator of personal and private affairs but also an elderman in village politics. The clan in America serves as a governing body for village affairs. In fact, the clan in America seems to be more authoritative than the elder men in the native village, because the immigrants here in America occupy a superior economic position. The following document shows that a villager appeals to his cousin for intervention in his case which may be brought up in the clansmen's assembly in America.

Brother Ta-poom:
Nephew Tze-won:
    I write to both of you with respectful greeting:
    I hope you are well and your business is successful.
    At the beginning of the year, your Younger Brother was chosen as the captain of the village guards. I have been faithful to my duty and nothing happened until recently. A Yu-Lum Festival [*Yulan Jie*] (a festival for women) was held in our village at the 19th Day, 7th Month, at seven o'clock. According to the custom, at the opening of the ceremony, the guards must fire a few shots to assist the spirit of the event. The head of the ceremony, Bim-lin, came to the guard's quarter and called: "This is the opening of the ceremony, why don't you fellows come out and fire a few shots?" Upon hearing this I took my gun and walked out with him. In front of the Temple of Five Gods, I fired two shots. Suddenly the barrel of my gun broke. Many people saw me at the time.
    At the twentieth of the Moon, the head of the village, Tak-mon called a meeting in regard to this matter. Many elders were there. But eventually there was no definite decision. If I have to pay the value of the gun, it is not fair. I fired it for the interest of the village. It was just an accident. Lately I overheard that the head of the village was going to write to the Lum Kung Shaw [*Lingsi Gongsuo*] (Ling Clan Association) in America, to let our brothers in Chicago be the judges of the case. Whether I should pay for the gun or not depends on you. If the case is brought up to the meeting in Chicago, please stand up for me. Why should I pay for it as I fired it merely for the good of the village. Moreover, I am a guard. According to the military laws, no soldier should pay for his gun. As I have thought it over again and again, I decided to write to you to help me and defend me. If you, Ling Brothers, should decide that I have to pay for the gun, who is going to be the village guard from now on? We, the guard, are on the service basis. As a poor person, how can I have money to pay? It is over two hundred dollars, you see.

So Brother, if the case is brought up in the meeting in Lum Ling [clan house], please be kind to me. I am closing this letter, wishing you all good luck.

Your poor Cousin,
Lin-teh
28th Day, 7th Moon, 24th Year [1935]

Elder men in the native village do not have final authority. A case may be appealed to their clansmen in this country for further consideration. In almost every clan in America, the laundrymen play an important part in their village affairs. They become elder men away from home. An assembly of clan brothers may be called on a Sunday afternoon in Chinatown in case of important business concerning their native village. In many instances, they are the supreme judges of the village public affairs.

3. Village Affairs

Hey! All members of our organization ought to know that this meeting is concerned with the renewal of the lease for the land in the Lo-Yuo-Valley in our village. It is important that this be attended to at once.

A special meeting is to be held on the 25th of February, Sunday evening, at seven o'clock in the Moy's Kung Shaw [*Meisi Gongsuo*] (Moy Clan Association). We must talk the matter over together and send some money home immediately. As this concerns every one of us you are, therefore, invited to be present at the meeting at the given time. We must fight and win.

Sam-Ser Society in America of Ton-Foin[5]
22/2/23 [February 22, 1923]

The laundryman, among his clansmen in America, is not only an elder man of his native village, but also a contributor and administrator of its public affairs. The preceding bulletin shows that an assembly of clansmen is called to discuss a question of official business in the native village. A meeting of this sort has two functions: (1) the clansmen here must contribute money and (2) they must decide upon a plan of action so that they can suggest or even instruct the elder men at home what to do.

The village affairs vary from one village to another. They are generally concerned with the public and social welfare of the village community. When certain public work needs to be done in the village, the elder men appeal to their clansmen in America for financial assistance. This type of affair may vary from education to a law suit. Often immigrants contribute enough money for their village to run a school for their children. One village may carry on a law suit with another village for years, and the laundrymen here back up their native village with moral as well as financial support. The village may need a recreational center, a reading room, repair of the ancestral hall or a building on the public square; and the laundryman who is in the American urban community plays an important role in native village affairs. What is most interesting is the following document in which the village elders appealed to their clansmen in America for assistance for one of the villages. In a joint letter, the elder men in the village proposed to their brothers in America:

> Our Brethren, we write this letter to you and send you respectful greetings:
>
> We are separated, yet we think of each other all the time. We have given much good advice for the betterment of our clan. We are ashamed even to mention this, due to our weakness and incapability to accomplish anything.
>
> Lum-su graduated from the Academy of Law in Canton and returned to our village. As principal of our village school he has done a great deal for our social welfare. We think his success will be great. We are waiting for some money from overseas so that we can do still more in the future. Our school should be registered in the Bureau of Education in Canton. It needs a library and some scientific apparatus. We hope, through the school, to train our youth to be useful persons.
>
> The world has changed a little. In the old days of the imperial examination we expected some great men by fong-shiu. Now one has to graduate from school. We cannot depend on fong-shiu any more. It is the time to depend on money. One has to have money in order to support a son, so that he may graduate from school. If there is not enough money, the genius is wasted.
>
> Lum-su studied in the Academy of Law for three years. He has spent thousands of dollars. His brothers supported him. In the early days of the 6th Moon this year, there will be an examination for lawyers in Peking. Lum-su is planning to take the examination. We know, in this day, one needs to worry not about lack of wisdom, but lack of money. If Lum-su should win, he must have about two or three hundred, would only be enough for traveling expenses.
>
> If Lum-su should lose this opportunity, it is not only the misfortune of himself but also of our whole clan. Who is going to be responsible for the public work in our village? The custom of sending funds has been abolished, but, anyhow, we should do something for Lum-su at this moment.

We, who live in the native village, have not strength [money] enough to help him. What we do now, our brethren, is to appeal to you people in the "Golden Mountain." We assume, our brethren, you are men who give your best. That is why we write to you. We, the undersigned, for the sake of our clan, know you will approve this matter and that each of you are glad to open your pocket and make your contribution. It is easier if all cooperate to this end.

If Lum-su is successful, it will be good news for us all. Upon his return, he will do something for our village to repay your kindness. Please don't disappoint us.

[twenty-eight names]   Signed [thirty-nine names]

During the old days of the imperial examination, this sort of grant-in-aid to competent scholars of their clan seems to have been very popular among the immigrant group. The mores of *kuang-chung-yueh-tsy* [*guang-zong yaozhu*] (enlighten clan and glorify your ancestors) still prevail in the minds of the people. In order to "enlighten" one's clan, a man of distinction is regarded as the hope of the mass. The whole clan is obligated to support the achievements of this scholar, for some day he may bring fame and glory back to the village. So their laundrymen brethren in America are called upon to do their duty. So they helped the scholars who took the examination for imperial degrees during the time of the monarchy. Therefore, it is proposed to render financial support so that a modern law student may take his trip to Peking to take the official examination. Thus a personal career becomes a public affair.[6]

Perhaps the sentiment of supporting a man to achieve distinction is not so popular now, by virtue of the fact that it always involves personal feeling; but if the village as a whole is endangered by external foes, then the issue becomes serious. A letter which one laundryman in Minneapolis wrote to another in Chicago shows the spirit of unity and responsibility, in spite of personal indifference or conflict among them.

Mei-yo, Virtuous Nephew:

The last time I saw you was two years ago. Now you are in America over a year and I trust you are doing well. I should have written to you long before now. The business is poor and I am in debt too much. I am living in distress all the time. That's why I have not a right mind to write. Please excuse me.

We have received a letter from Uncle Fen-yu. He told us that our village planned to build a village wall. He said that the overseas brethren had contributed one thousand dollars sent home for the organization of the village guards.

We also received a letter from Older Brother Sai-chen, saying that the provincial army was ordered back to Canton. The policemen sent by the magistrate also left their post and returned to the county seat. The elders of our village were in conference the first part of the Second Moon, resolving that we must recruit more village guards, twenty-two for the old village and sixteen for the new village, and that the guards' wages are four and a half dollars a month. In order to raise enough funds, it is decided also that each landowner contribute forty cents per hundred catties of rice, each male-head contribute sixty cents each year, and each household contribute twenty cents each month, and that a campaign should be started among our brethren in America.

You and your brethren in Chicago proposed that each person should contribute twenty dollars for a fund for organizing the village guards. Brethren in this city agreed with you. Immediately we sent word to our brethren in Duluth and other towns. We also wrote you of our consensus. We also wired Nephew Teh-hsin the same day, asking him to act. We told him to write back to the elders in the village, proposing the guardsmen should be increased in number.

Twice we wrote to Duluth but heard nothing. Seeing such a poor response, some of us here cooled off. Later I heard that Sai-lung arrived from China recently and he told our brethren in Duluth that Mo-ming was killed on duty, fighting with the robbers but his family received no benefit-money from the village. That is why folks over in Duluth are so indifferent to our proposal. [Most of the men in Duluth are Mo-ming's close cousins.]

If, for such a small matter, they become indifferent with the affairs of the village, it is indeed too bad. We cannot let our village become a second Fo-chow [a neighboring village, overrun by robber bands].

Now, as there are no soldiers staying in Fo-Chow, there is little hope to expect peace in our village. In case we lose our village, it will be the fault of our lack of co-operation. I am sorry to say that we might expect the worst.

When I wired back to Hong Kong, I should have let you know beforehand. But it was so urgent I had not thought of it. The money I spent for the telegram should be a responsibility of us all. So I hope you people in Chicago can help me out. I shall write again soon, and now close this letter with my best wishes that you all are well.

Uncle Sai-shun
May 1, 1922

Now as well as then, the sojourner is much concerned about the old folks at home. The letter above serves to indicate social unrest and political chaos before and after the Revolution in 1911. The countryside was overrun by robber bands. To safeguard their native village from danger, the clansmen in one city acted, and expected help from clansmen of another city. Some may have been here in this country for many years; but whenever a contribution is called upon for the welfare of the native village, the response is usually unanimous. Usually after a period of consultation and discussion, the clan members act collectively on all important matters concerning the public welfare, as well as the public safety, of their native village. There may be politics and conflict, but, if the cause is just and the leadership strong, as in the case shown above, disturbances are soon smoothed out.

The Chinese laundryman keeps in close touch with his family, his clansmen, and kinsmen, and his village community. He plays important roles and is often expected to be a benefactor and leader in promoting individual and public welfare. With his economic power, the old folks at home are more or less dependent upon him, and so he and members of his family may be recognized and may enjoy higher social status. We shall take up this point in a later chapter when we describe the laundryman's return trip home.

NOTES

1. *Fong-shiu* [*fengshui*]: Strictly translated, the term means wind and water. It is the belief that the location where ancestors are buried has a relation to the prosperity and health of the family, the clan. The spirit of the ancestor makes great men in the clan. The ancestors' spirits wouldn't be able to do it unless their bones were buried in a proper place. The location and its setting between the mountain and river make a good burying ground. The creator of this ground must be the fong-shiu man, an expert in this matter. If the wind and water fit together beautifully, the location becomes sacred. If one buries the bones of one of his ancestors there, he can expect a great success in the future.

2. Sometimes, in literary style, the wife humbly addresses herself to her husband as his concubine.

3. Le Shee means daughter from the Le clan. She seldom gives her own name, especially if the letter is written by a third person.

4. Appeared in *Hoi-Ying Min Po* [*Haiyin Mingpao*] (People's News of Hoi Yin), 13th Year, no. 3, March 1, 1940.

5. An announcement found in one store in Chinatown. Sam-ser is a subclan

of the Moy clan, which is the largest clan in Chicago. Ton-Foin is the name of the native district [*Lumei Duanfen Meisi Sanshe*].

6. Often students who are studying in America may get financial assistance from their laundryman cousins in the form of a loan or gift, depending upon the personal relationship between them.

CHAPTER XII

THE RETURN TRIP
TO CHINA

THE RETURN TRIP to China, for the laundryman, is something more than the happiness of rejoining the old folks, of family reunion, and of economic security; it is the human seeking for social status in the Chinese traditional sense. To glorify one's own village or primary group— *fu-quai-re-quai-ku-shiung* [*fuqai er gui guxiang*] (to return to the native village with wealth and distinction)—has been a motto of ambition and expectation among the people.

In America the Chinese laundryman is a nobody; loss of status and exclusion may encourage the sojourner attitudes, and therefore, may lead him to seek recognition only in his native land. Upon his return to China, he is commonly called *Gum-Shan-hog* [*Jinshanke*] (guest from Golden Mountain) and he becomes a man of deeds and influence among his folks.

1. Departure for China

Each and every laundryman looks forward to a chance to return to China, with the sense of *fu-quai-re-quai-ku-shiung*. His wealth (*fu*) required for the trip is usually obtained by saving, but there are other ways of gaining money, such as gambling, profits other than laundry, and the value of his laundry shop. In fact, if one wants to return to China, one usually just sells his laundry shop. If it is a good one, it may be worth thousands of dollars. The sum, for many, is enough for the return trip, especially in the case of aged laundrymen who have failed to save during the years.

After selling his laundry or quitting his job, he usually stays several days or weeks in Chinatown. During this time he visits his relatives and friends, and attends to business which must be done before his departure. He goes to one of the travel agents in Chinatown who takes care of his railway and steamship tickets. He pays his dues to clubs and associations with which he may be affiliated. And, most important, he makes arrangements with an agency or "fixer" who deals with the U.S. Immigration Service, to obtain for him a return permit in case he is eligible and desires to return to this country. It is safer to obtain a return permit anyway, in many cases, even if one plans to stay home for good.

His relatives and friends shower him with gifts and dinner parties. The gifts vary from money to toilet articles. The most popular of all is the giving of toilet soap. The would-be Gum-Shan-hog may receive dozens of boxes of expensive toilet soap, enough to pack half of his trunk full. Cousins and neighbors come bringing presents, presents, and presents. They come with something for him to take back for their families, too—shoes, clothing, jewelry, and money. In the old days, American gold pieces, five- and twenty-dollar gold coins, were the most popular gift.

The returning laundryman must have more than one trunk if the gifts and presents have accumulated. The more trunks he brings, the more he impresses his old folks. When he gets home, his folks hold their breath with excitement at the moment he opens his trunks. He, too, perhaps, has the greatest satisfaction in his life—that after all the years of hard work he is rewarded with the pleasure of a giver.

The return trip is essentially a business affair, however. No one can go back to China if he owes his friends and relatives too much money here. On the other hand, to make the trip more impressive, the larger the amount of money he brings with him the better. If friends and relatives are indebted to him, it is a good opportunity for him to collect what they owe him. In fact, the borrowers, for sentimental reasons, must make good. If anyone cannot do it, he explains his difficulties and makes other arrangements.

One of the relatives may have a personal message for his family. He confers with the returning man and entrusts him with plans and authority to act. He is, therefore, a representative not only in private affairs, but also, as we have seen in the preceding, in matters of public welfare and interest. When he arrives in the village, he automatically becomes an elder man. He may have tremendous influence and prestige concerning the public affairs of the village.

On the eve of his departure, some of the close friends and relatives accompany him to the station to say *shum-foon* [*shunfeng*] (smooth sailing, an equivalent of bon voyage).

The expenses of his trip are made as economical as possible. The steamship ticket for him is in the lowest category—steerage. The returning laundryman seldom goes even second class. It is not because he cannot afford it, but rather he wants to save money, or would feel too strange to be different from the rest of his fellow countrymen. On board a steamship he may feel just as uneasy and strange as in America. In the steerage most of the people are Chinese. Some of the social life is like that of Chinatown in American cities. The men participate in the same kinds of recreation—gambling and gossip. He feels the days and nights are exceptionally long. He feels he is still a stranger and a sojourner until he reaches Chinese soil.

When the steamer arrives in Hong Kong harbor, he begins to feel that he is home. On the wharf stand his friends and relatives who are waiting to welcome him and give assistance. He feels the warmth of sentiments exchanged in their greeting.

When the Canadian Pacific liner arrived at Hong Kong the twenty-seventh of October, hearing some of our cousins were on board, I took the ferry boat over to welcome them. I finally got aboard and met our cousins. They were Uncle Sai-ling, Brother Teh-hing, Brother Teh-fong, Brother Teh-gum, and Nephew Tou-kwong. All their luggage was well taken care of. I fixed it so that the luggage would not be subjected to customary searching. Then, accompanied by Cousins Teh-hing and Teh-gum, I took Seang, Woi, Yuo, and Yang [daughters and a niece] with us up to Canton. Seeing the new governmental atmosphere, the improved streets, the new parks, and the new buildings; everything seems to be grand. Even Shanghai can hardly be comparable with the city of Canton now. Cousin Teh-hing and Teh-gum admired the differences between the old days and the present. Then we all went to Shui Ma Street [*Xiaoma Jie*] where our Third Brother had established his factory [then talked about the house]. . . .

Cousins Teh-hing and Teh-gum like the business very much. Each of them takes two thousand dollars' worth of stock. The company selects me as its treasurer. It will be started pretty soon.

The cousins will soon go back to the village. As soon as they can distribute all the letters and money which are in their care for different families, they will move their families out to Canton. In Canton they can assist Third Brother in the spinning industry.

Immediately the returned native is greeted as the man from Golden Mountain. He tours the city for purposes of sightseeing, and for the first time he feels as if he is somebody, for he is a man with means. His poorer brethren are indeed very friendly and warm. He has all the satisfaction of giving and treating his folks in an I-don't-care-about-money atmosphere, and they are proud of their Gum-Shan-hog and forever ready to please him.

After touring a week or so in the city, the Gum-Shan-hog returns to the native village. Or he may go directly to the native village first, without seeing the city. The news of his arrival arouses the village folks. The close cousins come in person to greet him with warm welcome: "Ah! So happy to see you come home with wealth." The homecomer opens his trunk earnestly and proudly, while the relatives and friends wait to receive gifts. In the trunk, he digs out the toilet soap with the distinctive smell of perfume known as "Golden Mountain smell" *Gum-Shan-shee* [*Jinshan shi*]. People speak of it as "smell Gum-Shan-shee." And there are candies and cookies and dry raisins, and toys and utensils in variety, that please the friends and relatives so much. His wife and members of his family are kept busy, passing the gifts out to families in the village. Soon every family in the village receives at least a bar of soap or a few candies and cookies. Within a day or so the in-laws and other kinsmen come from the neighboring villages. All the close relatives, both clansmen and kinsmen, receive larger gifts, sometimes to the amount of hundreds of dollars. The homecomer walks out to the village square proudly, wearing a pair of western trousers with a Chinese coat. He even speaks English on the street corner with other returned laundrymen, amidst his humble brethren, young and old. He begins to tell them stories about America at the request of his admirers, especially boys. He usually tells them how hard he has worked in America and that his business has been yee-shing-kuon (a clothing house). He makes the boys dream of the Golden Mountain and that some day they, too, may have a chance to be there. For his wife he may have a special gift—several gold pieces, or gold earrings and bracelets, and a diamond ring. He may bring home a sewing machine, a camera, and a radio. These become a center of attraction for the folks to admire.

An interesting experience of the returned laundryman in the native village is the new adjustment he has to make. For the change of physical environment from American urban community to the Chinese folk society is indeed a great contrast. He is surprised to find within himself a sort of strange feeling about things in his native village. He has to get acquainted with them again before he feels himself at home.

> After living in America for years, seeing American women here—for the first few weeks of my return to the native village in China, the Chinese women looked like monkies to me. "Oh, oh, how utterly these women-folks of ours lack beauty," I used to say to myself. "Look at that woman of mine; she doesn't even walk right. And this house, this door—so strange. . . ."
> After several weeks I gradually got used to it. You see some charm in the women again. It was a peculiar experience.

This sort of experience, to some individuals, may be just a step in reorienting their habit of living in the village, but to other individuals it may be a starting point for other activities. Some, being dissatisfied with the backwardness of the village, move to the city. This trend is growing in recent years. As a result, colonies of returned overseas people are found segregated in certain areas in the city. Most outstanding of these colonies are Tung Shan of Canton [*Dongshan*] and Shom Shui Po of Hong Kong [Sheng-shuipu]. In Tung Shan, where the returned immigrants from America built Western-style houses, their next-door neighbors are Westernized Chinese, government officials, and Europeans. Here the laundryman lives like a "bourgeois."

In the old days when the laundryman brought his fortune back to China, he built a house or bought a piece of land in the native village. He was then a typical "home builder." This still is a pattern, or had been a pattern up to the time the Chinese Communists began to seize control of China. It then became a growing tendency to believe that purchasing property in the city is a wiser policy and gives a brighter outlook. Those moving out from the village to the city, however, seem to be still a small percent in comparison with those staying in the village. The returning immigrants are still villagers. On the whole, perhaps, only those comparatively well-to-do are able to move their families to the city.

Nevertheless, the city-going move has been a growing trend. The overseas Chinese from America own real estate in almost every section of the cities of Canton, Hong Kong, and Macao. The poorer city masses look up to them as rich men. The laundryman can build his Western-style house beside the house of a high government official, or at least in the neighborhood. And he may choose to erect a four-story building right in the midst of the city slum.

For those who cannot afford to go into a real estate enterprise in the city, and who have no other means of making a living, the village is the safer place to reside. As a matter of fact, a returned immigrant can rarely stay with his family more than one year, on account of American immigration regulations. He, therefore, does not leave his wife and children in the city, unless for other reasons, he is forced to do so. For example, bandits have endangered the safety of the villages in some areas and have forced some of the richer families to move to the city. In the village, otherwise, the family budget will be much lower and social life much more congenial among the old folks.

2. Life Work of the *Gum-Shan-Hog*

Whether the returned laundryman chooses to live in the village or in the city, his life-long career is working toward a certain object and goal, that is, a better livelihood or higher social status—in the colloquial expression of the village folks, *chuo-sai-kai* [zuoshijie] (accumulating wealth). In America he worked like a slave in order to save enough to take a return trip to China. When he gets back to the village, his plan of action seems to be defined by the community. He has to give several so-called "big affairs." These are usually his son's and daughter's marriages, erection of a house, and purchases of lands and rice fields. In the old days, the more rice fields a family possessed, the richer it was recognized to be. The laundryman may send money home so that his folks can do these "big affairs" on his behalf, but most likely he prefers to attend to the business personally, as in the following case:

> I came to this country when I was a young boy. My father was here before me and I worked with him and my older brother in a laundry in New York. Right after the First World War, we made over four hundred dollars a week.
>
> We worked about seven years, and the money earned by the three of us was quite a sum. My father took it back to China. He retired when he was less than fifty. In the village, he built a house and got two or three concubines, enjoying life. He had money to live on until his death several years ago.

I have been back to China five times. The first time I got married.

. . . Ah! Family and houses—everything is gone now! I built a house in Fung Wong Kong [*Fenghuanggang,* a suburb of Canton, near Lingnan University] and it cost me eighty thousand dollars. It was just completed before the war broke out in 1937. Lee Cho-min once lived on my third floor. Do you know him? He rented it from us. It is gone now since the Japs occupied the territory. I have another house in Tungshan which I built the second time I returned to China. It is gone, too.

Before the Japs occupied the city, my family moved to Hong Kong. Now even Hong Kong has fallen to the Japs. I don't know where my family is— my wife, and three sons and a daughter. My oldest son is now seventeen, but the youngest one is only eight. Even if they were not killed by the Japs, they would be starved to death. They have no financial resource unless they receive money from me. About ten days before Pearl Harbor, I sent them $750.00 [*showed duplicate check*]. I wonder whether they received this money. I sent it air mail but it may be lost. I should have received a return card by now. It worries me sick.

With my two buildings in Canton, the rent collected would be enough to support the family. The rent for the new house is eighty dollars a month, and for the old house, sixty dollars. A hundred and forty dollars is enough for a family of five to live on, isn't it? Quite enough, for the standard of living before the war in China.

But now everything is gone—both property and family. No news from them. I am down-hearted facing this kind of situation. Now, I don't know when I can go back to China.

I may be drafted, too. I hold a citizen-son certificate. They may want me. I don't know. Even if they don't let me go to the front, they may draft me to work in production front.

The case presents a general picture of how the laundryman runs his life work. It is a movement back and forth between his homeland and the United States. The ideal life work is a scheme of saving money and a trip home every few years. While in China, the returned laundryman tends to show his wealth in all sorts of activities, defined by the social expectation and current interest, from marriage to investment in real estate and other business enterprises.

The case shown above, too, represents nearly a perfect cycle of the laundryman's career. He has been back and forth across the ocean several times. The first time he went back to China he got married. He probably stayed with his bride a year or so and then came back to America to work in the laundry again. After several years of saving he had enough for another trip to China. This time he built a big house for his wife and child, with some floors to let. After a period he again came to this country. For the third time and the fourth time he did not indicate what activities he had taken, but we could see that each time he returned to China, he and his wife had a new child. Since he is a man financially well established, his trips are relatively easy to make, especially with his right as an American citizen to travel. His returns on the third and fourth trips were probably merely reunion visits. On his fifth return trip, he built another house. Here with his wealth, he has achieved, perhaps, a higher social status—people of a higher social group live in his house. He singles this point out as an item of pride. Only the Japanese invasion in China has brought him misfortune; otherwise, he would probably make another trip in a few years and would choose to stay in China for good.

But economic and social chaos, and personal reasons, seem to force the returned native to seek for another chance to go abroad. The man in the next case stayed in China for six years, but finally returned to his laundry work in America.

I came to this country when I was a young man of twenty-one and first started to work in the laundry continuously for sixteen years. When I had money, I went back to China.

How much? Oh, I brought home about forty thousand dollars—American money. With that much I thought I would not have to come back here anymore. Finally I spent it all. I stayed in China for about six years until I was forced to get a paper for me to come back here.

Business is quite good. I make about twenty to twenty-five dollars a week [partner with cousin].

Nothing, I got nothing to do in China. I spent about nine thousand dollars for a building in Hong Kong. At first I estimated that six to seven thousand would be enough, but when the building was completed, it cost me pretty nearly nine thousand.

At first I planned to have the building built in Canton. As a matter of fact, I spent a year in Canton. I had my family in Canton and started looking for a suitable place for my building. Later the woman did not like Canton. We knew nobody in Canton and my wife got too lonesome. Finally we moved to Hong Kong.

See, for the six long years I had no income but outgo and with a family of five mouths to be fed I could find nothing suitable for me to do in Hong Kong. I have a cousin who spent about thirty thousand dollars on a brick factory. You know how he is doing now? He is penniless—lost everything. One must not try to do anything unless he knows the business. He had to depend on strangers and they sold him out. His products were sold on credit and his men double-crossed him. They collected the money and disappeared.

I, too, was thinking of starting a towel factory, but I realized I had no one on whom I could depend; I didn't start it.

Del-nea-ma! The best way was to enjoy life. I had a concubine and took life easy. Then I spent several hundred dollars a month. We patronized tea houses almost every day for a time, sometimes with friends and sometimes with my whole family.

I have rent from the building. It is a three-story building and my family occupies the third floor. I have eighty dollars income each month. What I have to send home now is about two to three hundred dollars a year; that will be enough. I sent only two hundred last year. The rent is high now in Hong Kong, with all those refugees in the island.

If I had about five or six thousand American money now, I would like to go back right now.

No, I do not worry about them [the family]. They have enough to live on and I should not worry too much. I just get homesick.

From both of the preceding cases we see that the Gum-Shan-hog tends to own houses which can be used both for profit and for residence. This is a new trend as compared with the old days when the Gum-Shan-hog bought rice fields. In any case an attempt, in general, is made to create a new type of livelihood so that he does not have to go abroad again. But in the case of a real estate enterprise rent alone is not enough to support a growing family. Sometimes the man is left idle; sometimes he is victimized by smart city chiselers.

A similar situation faces the Gum-Shan-hog in the village. He may arrange for his son and daughter to get married, and manage to build a house and to buy several pieces and rice fields, but he could not stay home except in the case of old age. The man chooses to reside in the village but, like the man who builds his home in the city, he may find his money is exhausted in the course of time. If he is, or thinks he is, still able-bodied, he will try to find a way to come back to America again. The following case is that of a middle-aged man who was unable to establish himself in China, was forced to seek re-entry to this country, and again got back into laundry work.

Finally I decided to sell my store and go back to China. I planned to stay in China for good. When I reached Hong Kong, in the Fall of 1935, there was a big strike [the May 30th Movement] and transportation was standing still between Hong Kong and Canton. Everything was in a mess. I stayed in Hong Kong for a long time, getting sick with worry, but I finally got back to the native village. I got married and remained in the village most of the time. I went out to Hong Kong only twice. I was home for about a year and my money was almost gone. I could not establish any business opportunity in China. The conditions were in such a mess, I had to come abroad again.

Finally I came to the United States [he was in Canada previously]. After I reached Chicago, I bought this place from a relative of mine. I paid over four thousand dollars for it. The business here used to be good. But ever since the depression, all the well-to-do people in this section moved away. Now only the poor remain. My business dropped down and today, this place is worth less than one thousand dollars.

I have never charged less than twelve cents for a shirt. Well, as long as I can keep it going, I am quite satisfied. What good is it to work so hard? This is no life.

He could not find anything to do in his native village. Perhaps he could be a farmer again like his ancestors. But once one becomes Gum-Shan-hog he probably refuses to be a farmer again for the sake of his social status. As he owns lands and rice fields, he becomes a landlord. He may have hired men to do the farming for his family, but he, himself, prefers to take another trip back to America. Then he thinks of some way for his son and nephew to come to America, too. Eventually the male population of the family is here in America, while the women remain in China. He is not forced to stay in China until he is in his old age.

The old-timer, as we have described him previously, plans for his last return trip back home if he can. He can make it with very little money, in some cases. Even if it is his final trip, he cannot fail to make some showing of a home-builder.

These words are to you, my Son Jo-Mei:

Ever since I said farewell to you and returned to China, I stayed in Hong Kong for one month. Seeing the expenses are so great, I came back to the village at the 20th of the First Moon.

As I am home, I begin to choose a date and have our house remodeled. I have it now raised up two and a half feet higher. Beside this I plan to build a barn house, rebuild the well at the corner and so forth. I have the contract already signed and it costs us altogether one thousand seven hundred and sixty dollars. Together with other expenses such as furniture, it is estimated to cost as much as two thousand and two hundred dollars.

The building will be started the 14th of the Second Moon. On the 12th of the Third Moon, we shall move in.

I am sorry to inform you that Chi-jon was arrested in Hong Kong and he was put into jail for one year. He can't come home until the Fourth Moon. His wife is now living in Hong Kong also. She is there waiting for Chi-jon, the bad son.

We have reburied your late wife, Lee Shee, at Ching Ming Festival [*Qingming Jie*] (a spring festival in which the graves of ancestors are visited). Your Fourth Brother brought her remains back to our native village for reburial.

When I was in Hong Kong, I learned about a pretty girl twenty-four years of age, a dress maker. She and her mother live in Shom Shui Po. The mother came to me, asking about your return. She said her daughter can wait for you for three years. If you like to marry this girl, you had better write and let me know quickly.

I spent so much money to repair the house, I thought only for your future. I hope you have had good luck this year. As you have money, send some home.

Our district is in peace now. If you send money, send it through Mr. Le Lui-fong. Don't send it through Chu Ke-chung. Give attention to this matter.

Father, Fung-lung
2/15/33 [February 15, 1933]

The old man did what he could for his family, and now he has retired. He is now in a dependent position in relation to his son who is still in America. The son, from now on, is solely responsible for the support of the family, and as soon as he has saved enough money he can take his own return trip and become a Gum-Shan-hog.

Many a laundryman, however, cannot take the return trip when he pleases even though he may have enough money and desire to do so, for the reasons described elsewhere in this study. He may, therefore, send money home so that his wife, his father, his brother, or other trusted persons may do the so-called "big-affairs" for him. He is keenly interested in investments in all sorts of business enterprises in the Old Country. There has been one company after another organized by Chinese in America in the interest of starting various industries in China, from a few thousand dollars in an ice-cream store to a movie studio, and what not. In China it has been known as "overseas capital" [*haiwai ziben*]. The overseas people have substantial influence in the economic life of China, particularly overseas Chinese from Dutch East India. To what extent Chinese from America help shape the economic order of modern China would need a full and intensive inquiry. It is obvious that what I have covered here in this study is limited by the materials gathered for this work. The impression, on the whole, is that the returned native from America has not been successful in his business ventures in China. The safest and usual way is real estate purchased in the native village or in the city. This seems to be the fundamental outlook. Social changes in China, particularly at this time under the Communist regime, have forced the laundryman to change his outlook on life. It seems, however, he still projects a hope that he can make his return trips as he used to.

3. Back and Forth Across the Pacific

The laundryman never takes a vacation in the American sense of the word. He works continuously, year after year, stopping occasionally on account of sickness or unemployment. If he is a well-organized person, he finally saves enough. He decides to go back to the Old Country to a reunion with his family. Back to China means that, on the one hand, he is away from his monotonous laundry work, away from cold and impersonal social relationships, and away from race consciousness and a feeling of inferiority, and on the other hand, with money and the prestige of Gum-Shan-hog, he can enjoy leisure time, be himself, and feel free. In short, he can have a real vacation.

If we consider his trip back to China as a sort of vacation, it is indeed unique—a nine-month vacation after working hard for a number of years. The successful one takes his return trip to China not necessarily to build a house or to arrange the marriage of a son or daughter; he may be driven merely by the desire to visit his old folks and have a family reunion. He goes at an opportune time. As the following letters show, a man took his first trip in 1922, the second in 1929, and the third in 1931. Here is the first letter he wrote to his cousin.

Teh-seng, Second Older Brother:

I am hardly aware that it has been several months since I left America. I should have written you sooner if I did not suffer from the loss of my son. Not long after I arrived home, my son died. It is indeed what is said, "Sorrow comes after joy." After what had happened, I had not the mind to do anything. It has been sad all the time.

I was living in Canton for several months. I have not been back to the village yet. The danger from banditry is still the same in our district. Fo-Chow Fort is still in construction; Ho-Mook Fort is just being completed,

and Yong-Shee Joy Fort is being constructed soon. There are no soldiers on
guard in the district yet. Because of lack of funds, the village guards unit
has been disbanded. Anything could happen any day. Now all the villages
in our district are in fear. Night-watching in every village has doubled its
personnel. And so it is in our village. I heard a robber band of several
hundred is in Ta-Lung Cave [*Talongdong*]. . . .

Younger Brother, Teh-gun
April 24, 1922

This letter is insufficient to show the character of his social activities
when he is back in China. It is used here merely to illustrate what concerns
the returned laundryman and his cousin the most—their families and their
native village. Again, it reveals the social and political chaos which brings
banditry to the countryside, which may be considered as one of the reasons why it is impossible for him to stay for good.

After nine months of "vacation" in China, the man came back to America again. Again he works in the laundry, and in 1929 he took his second
trip back to China, and again he wrote to the same man.

Teh-seng, Second Older Brother:

It has been two months since I said goodbye to you and left for China.

Things which you put into my care to bring home were distributed to
your folks according to your instruction. I also handed over to Nephew
King-wu [son] one hundred and ten dollars and to Older Brother Teh-sin
[brother] ten dollars. I trust they have written you about it.

You have asked me to talk to Second Sister [wife] about Niece Jean-yong's
marriage. You said you would not consent to be related to that Sha-lam
[neighboring village] family. Second Sister said that it was not the boy's
father who was robber, but his uncle. The outlaw had nothing to do with
the boy's father. What is more, they have requested to be our relatives, most
sincerely. After a little investigation by myself, I found Joy-yin [father of the
son-in-law-to-be] has a house and land and the boy is a good boy. Also the
boy can go to America. According to Second Sister, there is no other unfavorable aspect. Niece Jean-yong, however, has not quite decided yet. She
doesn't like it so much. That is why it is not yet an engagement. We must
rush word to you now to confer with you. Whatever decision you make,
please let us know as soon as possible. Then Sister can act.

I wanted to go back to the village very much and see everything. Our
village must pay the government about one hundred dollars in taxes. Several
elders were arrested. Uncle Sai-ba is one of them. Uncle Sai-sing and Cousin
Teh-yang luckily escaped. It is a mess now. So I must go back and see what
I can do. The fact is that we couldn't have owed so much. I heard it was

because Fen-goon and Sen-chang spent several hundred dollars for their private affairs and that was how it happened. Now the elders are in jail. These two persons are indeed useless. . . .

The district is now at peace, for self-government is established in every village. You must pursue our brothers in America to pay what they promised to contribute for the welfare of our village. I think we need money for public work greatly.

Some of the people do not like to stay in Hong Kong anymore. They all wish to move back to the village. If we can only insure the safety by building up village defenses, they would all move back. The expenses are too much in the city.

Your family and mine also are well. Please be eased with your heart. If Jean-yong's engagement were to be arranged, Second Sister must return to the village in October. And the next spring Jean-yong will be married. Please write and tell us your decision. We are waiting for your reply. Best luck to your health and business.

Brother Teh-gun

P.S.—Wife of Teh-mou [third brother] passed away the fourth day of the Seventh Moon. Two hundred dollars were spent for the funeral and I contributed fifty dollars and Second Sister-in-law contributed some ten dollars also. Notice this.

July 5, 1929

Uncle Sai-han came to Hong Kong recently. Talking to him I learned that our district is all right now. The farmers had a big harvest this season. Only the fishery is not in good shape yet. I think I will have to go back to the village and observe myself. I shall not move my family back until it is safe to do so. My health is not yet recovered completely. I still have stomach trouble from time to time. After I saw a doctor some time ago, it seems to be better now.

I am now living in ———. If you write me, please write to this address. Big Brother's family, your family, and my family are now living on the same floor together. The monthly rent is $17.50. . . .

Brother Teh-gun
July 11, 1931

"It is not suitable for us to stay in Hong Kong forever," Teh-gun said elsewhere, in view of their economic condition. The Chinese seldom considers his present livelihood alone, but the future of his son and other members of his family. He is aware of the fact that the money he has brought home cannot last forever. But in the village the family budget will be much lower. Economic conditions for the folks in the village are more or less self-sufficient, in contrast with the high dependency and greater needs in the city. As one sees no prospect of gaining a steady income beside the money he already has, in the long run he is inclined to believe that a retreat to the native village is a superior tactic. His whole life work seems to be focused on the safety and welfare of his family.

Notice that the man was in China for the second time in 1929, and he returned again for the third time in 1931. Probably, the last time he came to America was the latter part of 1929 or the early part of 1930, and he may have planned to stay here longer than one year. His letter reveals that his health was not so good. In order to recover one's health, the immigrants seek the best remedy; that is, to go back to China and take a rest, thinking the climate back there is more suitable. Further, when one is sick and doubtful about his own health, he wants to be with his family, for with them he may be taken care of. The man stayed in Chicago one year and went back to China for a "vacation."[1]

This letter illustrates the position of the Gum-Shan-hog among his old folks. He is a sort of mediator, benefactor, and elder man. He is concerned about the marriage of his cousin's daughter. In time of need, he gives money so that his cousin's wife may be buried. "So I must go back and see what I can do"; he seems to be willing to take responsibility as an elder man and to protect his native village. The next letter, which he wrote two years later, the third time he was in China, reveals the general situation of families in the overseas China.

Teh-seng, Second Older Brother:

It has been more than a month since I said goodbye to you and left for China. I have written you on my way home. I trust you have had the news. I am now safely arrived in Hong Kong.

The money you put into my care I have already handed to Second Sister [wife]. As both Jean-luo and King-wu are in school, the expenses are greatly increased. There are a great many other miscellaneous expenses as a family resides in the city. Furthermore, prices for almost everything are up. According to my view, it is not suitable for us to stay in Hong Kong forever. Maybe I shall move my family back to the village in a few months.

A person may make his return trip to China with little money. After a few months, he finds he has not even enough money left for him to pay his way back to America. Under such conditions, he may either raise enough at home from friends and relatives, or he may write to his cousins here in America for assistance.

Teh-seng, Virtuous Younger Brother:

Your letter reached me, suggesting that I should stay home for a few months. But all I had was three or four hundred dollars and it was quickly spent. Now, food, clothing, and rent, all these expenses are tremendous and there are too many social activities in the city. What is more, there is no way to borrow. I find it hard to stay home any longer. I want to come back to America now, but I have no money for the trip. Upon reading this letter, Brother, please confer with Uncle Sai-quen and send me about two hundred dollars immediately so that I can get ready for my return journey.

When I was going back to China, I carried for you fifty dollars gold for your family. Now the foreign exchange rate is fifty-nineteen per hundred Hong Kong money. With the amount I had a check of ninety-six dollars with me. When I got home, I gave the check to Teh-sin. But he charged for his service six dollars per hundred. So he took off six dollars. He gave to your wife only ninety dollars. I trust your family has written to you about it. . . .

I asked Teh-sin for money to make my return trip. He told me he had not a cent. I also wrote to Teh-kung and Teh-kin [in America—both are the writer's own younger brothers]. But both of them had been out of a job. They cannot help me at all. I am therefore forced to ask you for help. Please confer with Uncle Sai-quen and help me out.

Your family and the Teh-sin Family are not happy together. I trust you must have known that. . . .

Brother Teh-wei
August 10, 1924

This man, who holds a return certificate, can come to America again within the time limit. He will be back here as soon as he has the money to buy the steamship ticket.

There is still another type of situation, that is the man who has neither money nor return certificate. The desperate attempt is made to be smuggled in, but smuggling is quite costly. Where can he get the financial assistance? He writes to his clansmen and friends. There are all sorts of ways and means of getting into America that can be arranged in Hong Kong and other places all over the world; the only difficulty is whether one has trustworthy friends and relatives here who are willing to give a helping hand. The next case is that of a man who has already made the connection in Hong Kong and expects to reach San Francisco from Singapore. In order to have enough money to pay the smuggler,[2] who usually demands a large sum, he writes to many of his clansmen and friends begging for help.

Teh-seng, Younger Brother:

I shall start my journey from Singapore at the latter part of this month and shall arrive at the Big City [San Francisco] about the middle of June. I have written to Lu Wei-chang, Wong Kung-ling, Granduncle Fen-jack, Uncle Sai-shun, Cousins Teh-hing and Teh-chung, asking them to help me. If they can each raise some money for me, I shall be grateful. I ask them to send the money to your place or Brother Teh-jen's place. In case you receive money from any one of them, please keep it for me. When I arrive, I shall wire you. I expect to use the money for urgent need.

I hope, too, that you and Brother Teh-jen will help me also. Please do what you can for me. Without your help, I shall not be able to get up. I shall be grateful to you all. Best wishes and regards,

Teh-hing
May 21, 1927

Some people return to China with a large sum of money, and, thinking that they will not have to come to America again, they do not apply to the U.S. Immigration Service for a return permit. In some cases they are not eligible for it, anyway. After the laundryman gets back to China, he either spends too much for his personal vanity or loses too much in business ventures. Finally he is penniless, and then he begins to think of America again. So he may have to take the risk of smuggling himself into this country. And there are ways and means by which he can gain entrance across the border from Canada, Mexico, Cuba, and from any other port of debarkation.[3]

This sort of back and forth movement ends usually only with old age. Some return to China only once, and it is in their old age. Others who have hardly enough even for personal expenses may be sent back to China by relatives, often through a contribution by a group of friends and relatives. Still another person has been back and forth across the Pacific many times, but fails to make the last trip. He is old and poor, facing destitution if he gets back to China, and there is one close relative such as wife, son, or daughter-in-law to support him. In such a situation, many choose to stay here and reside in Chinatown. Some are indeed lucky enough to go back to join their son and daughter with wealth and comfort in retirement age. But many in Chinatown do not have that chance.

NOTES

1. Other letters reveal that this man died soon afterward. He left several thousand dollars to his family. Information from other sources indicate that his adopted son gambled with the money and that the family was left destitute.

2. *New York Times,* April 9, 1916: "Federal Authorities capture C. Baker, thought to be F. Hawkins, smuggler, in act of bringing Chinese into U.S. from Canada."

3. See Lawrence Guy Brown, *Immigration* (New York: Longmans, Green and Co., 1933), pp. 275–81.

CHAPTER XIII

IMMIGRATION PROBLEMS

FOR THE LAST three generations the Chinese have been legally excluded from naturalization, and they have not been permitted to enter the United States as immigrants.[1] The Chinese Exclusion Act of 1882[2] was made on the basis of race in a political climate that did not represent the best American traditions and ideals. It was repealed only in 1943 as a matter of political expediency.[3] Chinese are now eligible for citizenship only under certain provisions,[4] and an immigration quota is established for "the Chinese person"[5] to migrate here as an "immigrant alien." Under the old laws, even a Chinese-American citizen could not bring his alien wife from China. The new law, as amended,[6] gives wives the right to come to this country non-quota, but not their minor children born prior to the father's naturalization. The Chinese quota[7] is so small that it is merely a gesture of good will from Uncle Sam.

Legal exclusion, no doubt, has played a part in producing Chinese isolation in this country. It is convenient, at this time, to give some consideration to the matter, so as to see to what extent, and in what way, the laws have affected the mode of life of the Chinese minority in this country. It is an attempt, however, to describe only those factors that are peculiar to the laundryman, since this study concerns the laundryman and not the whole Chinese population. We are interested in how the laundryman accepts exclusion and adapts himself to the situation, and how he responds to the new immigration law which makes him eligible for naturalization and immigration.

1. Under the Chinese Exclusion Laws

Under the Exclusion Acts, Chinese were among those ethnic groups ineligible for naturalization, and they could not come to this country as regular immigrants. Those who came as non-immigrants could only remain aliens, no matter how many years of residence they had in this country. The exclusion laws reduced the Chinese in this country in number, but the "Golden Mountain" was ever more attractive to them, and there were still ways and means by which the Chinese sought entry here, legally and illegally. In the Chinese laundry nowadays there are individuals who came as merchants, students, travelers, government officials, sons of American citizens and what not. Of course, many more were smuggled in: the seaman, the blockade runner, and the stowaway. There are several factors which may be considered as contributing to the social isolation of the Chinese laundryman.

Abnormality of the Sex Ratio

In the previous chapter I described sex maladjustment related to sex ratio among the Chinese in this country. The restriction of alien Chinese women to join their husbands obviously cannot be minimized as an important factor that causes sojourner attitudes in the Chinese laundryman. Chinese wives who are here now are either women admitted as the wife of a treaty merchant, native-born Chinese-American girls, or daughters of American citizens. As we understand it, most of the laundrymen have wives and children in China. Restricted by the American immigration law, it has been impossible for them to bring their wives to America, even in the case of an American citizen.

If the laundryman cannot bring his wife, naturally he has to send money to China to support her. When he has saved enough money for a trip back home, he goes without hesitation. But this privilege of traveling back and forth across the ocean, under the immigration provisions, is only for a few; they are the ones who are either American citizens or lawfully admitted aliens. It is safe to say that the majority of the Chinese laundrymen in the Chicago area are men without their families, and the sex ratio of male over female can be four or five men to one woman among the age groups from twenty to forty. The recent migration of war brides and citizens' wives may have eased the situation a little. But the normal curve for the Chinese population in the city will not be achieved for generations.

Since the Chinese laundrymen are unable to bring their wives, they have tried to get their sons here. Therefore, those who are citizens brought their sons in their own right, but there are those who have claimed the right of others. An American birth record, or even information about it, becomes a high-priced commodity. Some are willing to pay as much as four to five thousand dollars for the "fixing" of an entry as a son of an American citizen. It is reported that Chinese-American citizens tend to state to the immigration authorities the birth of sons rather than of daughters. Young boys are often seen in some of the laundries with fathers and uncles. Indeed, only boys keep coming, and very few girls; mothers and sisters remain in China. When the boys grow up, they are sent back to China to get married. Like their fathers, the young laundrymen keep their wives in China. After a year or so in China, one might come back to this country and report to the consular service or the Immigration Service that a son was born to him and his alien wife in China, even though there might not have been such a birth. Later he could sell the right to a fellow countryman or his own cousin by giving the latter all the information concerning the birth to enable an entry of the latter's son.

Another way to get into this country for permanent residence was to claim American citizenship by repatriation; young American-born children were taken back to China by their parents and grew up in China. Some of these people, like the so-called "citizen son," came by their own right, but again, the right could be sold for profit in many instances. In this category under the U.S. immigration law, one could come at any time himself, but not his alien wife.

There are laundrymen who have married in this country. However, in general, laundrymen seem to have less chance for matrimony with the exception of some of the younger and more progressive ones. Marriages among younger laundrymen tend to be arranged by their elders. Some brides were born in this country and have been in China for various lengths of time. Others could have come from China, like the boys, admitted as children of "American citizens."

Under the old immigration law, only a few laundrymen have a family in this metropolitan area. Home life and family living, for the Chinese laundryman, is out of the question. To remedy such misfortune, one's ambition and pride would be to get his son or nephew to this country to join him. The coming of the son is an attempt to re-create some sort of family life as well as economic asset. Those who could not get their sons here admired those who could by saying that the latter had achieved *ho-sai-gai* [*haushijie*] (good livelihood) or had "several pairs of hands" in America, which is an asset to accomplish economic well-being.

This peculiar feature of the husbands in America and the wives in China led the laundryman to feel that his stay here could be only temporary, and he tended to think of his home as in China regardless of his years of residence here. His hope and aim, therefore, is to make a fortune and to return home.

The "Paper" and the Role of the Fixer

"Paper" is a word the Chinese generally use referring to different kinds of instruments for immigration purposes. All Chinese lawfully admitted under the Exclusion Acts were issued a certificate which Chinese immigrants usually spoke of as *tze-mai* [*ziwei*], meaning the remainder of the paper or the end part of the paper. The certificate of identity was issued to both citizens and aliens alike. It was, and still is, regarded as a protection. Some people even have it kept in a safety box or in trusted hands; it is among one's valuables—in fact, for some people it is the most important paper in his life. It means freedom from fear and freedom of movement for taking trips to China.

The Chinese laundryman speaks about kinds of immigration paper. The most commonly known ones are: *kung-tze* [*gong zi*] (laborer paper), *sang-yee-tze* [*shengyi zi*] (merchant paper), and *hu-tze-joy-tze* [*tushengzai zi*] (native grandson's paper). A kung-tze has less value than a sang-yee-tze, for with the former one can only take a trip to China himself and be re-admitted to the United States; the latter, on the other hand, enables one to bring his wife and minor children. With a hu-tze-joy-tze one can establish his own citizenship in the United States and claim the right to bring his son and his son's son to this country.

There was no way for one to legalize his immigration status under the old Exclusion Acts. One had to seek for ways and means to do it by fixing. It was usually done by a fixer who had a connection with the interested party and a story called *hoo kung* [*kougong*] (testimony) was arranged. The fixer is a go-between for those who want to be "fixed" to turn to for help and information. There are several Chinese fixers in Chinatown who usually have connections with individuals with authority. A successful fixer would eventually become prosperous. Often he is a *chot-fen* [*chufan*] of an association in Chinatown; the Chinese term "chot-fen" is invented by the immigrants here in America, meaning interpreter or diplomat.

There is no such term in the Chinese dictionary. This and other usages are not understood by a person newly arrived from China; as one Chinese student puts it: "This is overseas Chinese language!" The chot-fen is usually a person who can speak English and has a fairly good status among his fellow countrymen. He is very likely an American citizen, too.

"Paper Name" and the Psychology of Fear

Connected with the immigration paper, there are a large number of Chinese laundrymen who have what is called a "paper name" [*ziming*]. It is simply not his own name, but one assumed on account of immigration implications; in other words, it is the name he claimed to have at the time he was admitted by the immigration authorities or consular service. It became a personal secret, and it must be used in all American dealings. It is not at all rare for close relatives such as father and son, brothers, and cousins to work together in one laundry shop, and they are not supposed to disclose they are so related to the Americans, particularly the immigration authorities. A father and his two sons are in town, but each has a "paper name" in the immigrants' language. So the father is under the surname of Chan, while the older son is Wong, and the younger son is Chang. Among the Chinese, however, they are known by their real name—no alias, or paper name. Chinese are generally aware that some people have an alias and they try to be quiet about it.

There are cases, too, where a Mr. Chan came to the United States as "Mr. Wong." Later he had a family here, but his wife became Mrs. Wong instead of Mrs. Chan to the Americans and all their children went to school and registered with the Selective Service and so on as Wongs. But they remain Chan in the Chinese community.

In China, it would be regarded as a disgrace to change one's surname. But to change or to assume an "immigration name" in America is justified as a necessity and protection. Obviously, a psychology of fear has developed among the Chinese in this country—fear of the exposure of fixed immigration status, and, in fact, a sentiment has developed that the disclosure of another's immigration matter is an evil act, and morally condemned as *Hai-chun-tse-ma* [*Haiqun Zima*] (Trojan horse). To illustrate this sentiment in view of group security, one laundryman said:

If I were an American citizen, I would certainly vote for Roosevelt for the third term. I would vote for him not because he is pro-China. It is rather because ever since he became president, there have been no arrests made on Chinese immigration authorities.

When Hoover was president, several raids occurred during one single year. It was terrible.

This, I suppose, is not merely a personal opinion, but also a collective sentiment of the group. The expression reflects the psychology of fear of the people who do not feel at home under conditions of exclusion and race prejudice.

False Relatives

As there are "paper names" there are, consequently, also paper relatives— individuals supposedly related to one another on the basis of implication in immigration fixings. One may have a real father and also a false-father in the city or another part of the country. Often the false-father may be one's own close relative, such as uncle, cousin, or father-in-law; others may be clansmen, friends, or kinsmen. Their immigration claims are kept a personal secret and their real relationship maintained as they are. There are many cases, however, where the false-father or false-brother is a total stranger. In many instances, of course, personal relationship would not be established and they would have nothing to do with one another as long as the financial matter was taken care of after the newcomer's arrival and he was admitted by the immigration authorities.

It is interesting, though, that some people are brought together by their immigration matters and try to maintain some sort of social relationship. The term *gaa-lo-doo* [*jia laodo*] (false-father) is frequently used in conversations, and such utterances as "according to the paper, I am supposed to be his brother" and "I share the same paper with him" are often heard. The false-father or false-brother is often needed to serve as witness or to sign affidavits in case a further immigration matter comes up. Some become very good friends while others maintain communication not so much for friendship's sake as for a safeguard or protection of each other's immigration status.

An old laundryman, for example, is supposed to have three sons in this country, but it is surprising that he cannot remember names or their whereabouts. It is also strange, according to the Chinese mores, that the father-son relationship can deteriorate to such an extent, even though there are cases of discord among fathers and sons. The real fact, in this instance, is that all the old man's three sons are just paper-sons or false-sons. They communicated with each other at first, but in the course of time, as there were no common interests or need of each other, they gradually forgot each other. A young laundryman stated that he had a brother in town, and his brother worked in another laundry on the North Side. He called his brother one day over the telephone and asked his brother a favor. The latter promised. In their real identity, these two young men belong to two separate clans, with different surnames. An old retired laundryman reported that he has no son and no other close relatives in this country. He did that because, according to his immigration status, he is supposed to have no one here. In reality, however, he does have one son and two brothers in town. A father goes to visit his hospitalized son once every week, but it is indicated in the hospital's records that the visitor is just a friend and not the father.

Connected with the paper-name and the false-relative is another item which should be mentioned here, the *hoo-kung* [*kougong*], or copy of false identity notes for the admission testimony before the Foreign Service or the Immigration Service. Each one of the individuals admitted into the United States through fixing probably would have in his possession such a document. It usually contains several pages of information covering detailed description of one's relation to the false-father and other relatives, sometimes going back three generations, the birth dates and places, physical and social surroundings of the people involved in the case. The hoo-kung is usually in Chinese, but not always. I have seen some in English. It is, to be sure, a personal, secret document. One often has to consult his hoo-kung in order to answer some of the questions he is asked. Others try to memorize it. But if the information is not needed for a long time, it is likely to be forgotten. Hoo-kung is, therefore, a record of valuable personal information. To keep it may bring profit in later years.

"Cho-Quon" or "Ku-Quon" and "Bou-Sze-Wei"

A large number of Chinese laundrymen in the Chicago area, no doubt, have no paper and hoo-kung and false relatives. Indeed, some of them got "fixed up" after their *cho-quon* [*chongquon*] or *ku-quon* [*guoquon*], or *bou-sze-wei* [*bao siwei*]; the terms mean "run across the pass," "crossed the pass," and "protected secret running"; all indicate ways and means of illegal entry into this country. Blockade runnings of the most dangerous sort are revealed in the following stories.

> Perhaps you have heard of the four Chinese who left El Paso cramped in the recess over the vestibule of the baggage car? They were bound for Chicago. The man who was to release them was mortally wounded by a railway watchman who caught him prowling about the yards. The man died before he could tell the car number or road. The four were never found.
>
> Later, in November 1911, the smugglers took fright at Federal operations, and it was then feared that some fifty Chinese might meet a similar fate. On another occasion, Guey Lum, Ju Fook-ngin, Moy Got, and Lee Ben-ine, when dragged from inside a car roof, had been four days without food and almost as long without water. Only last February, Howard D. Ekey, Chinese inspector, received an anonymous message: "Meet Michigan Central No. 57895—two Chinamen in car." The two were nearly frozen.
>
> Seven men were arrested on November 24, 1911, for smuggling Chinese into the U.S. at Niagara Falls in cars of furniture and household goods shipped back and forth. The Chinese were paying, it was said, $1,500 each to the smugglers. Moy Sun-yung might have lived in Chicago, happy and free to pile up American dollars, had it not been for his mother's love. Tenderly she wrote him from the old home, "I send this letter in honor of the first anniversary of my son's leaving China." That one sentence was Moy's sentence, arrested on suspicion of not having been in the U.S. three years, the letter he had been too good as a son to throw away convicted him and he was deported.[8]

It is clear that Chinese usually did not run across the border themselves; this was arranged by agencies and individuals who profited by the deal. The individuals and groups who were interested in the deal, to be sure, were not only furniture truck drivers but also men with authority and power, under cover.

The man who has come in illegally constantly lives in fear. He is willing to pay a high price for protection, if it can be arranged. Any paper to show that he has the right to live in this country becomes of value to him. It is better still to claim American birth, and if he is successful he can bring his son and daughter as American citizens. He may even bring another man's son as his own and make a few thousand dollars. But very few laundrymen have such luck, and few can afford to pay the price. Consequently, there are those who live here illegally, their only hope being to make a fortune and return home as quickly as possible. In case one has piled up enough money to start a new life in China, he may decide to leave this country for good. It has been, however, a well-known fact that few could accumulate a large enough sum of money to enable them to be so brave. With a few thousand dollars saved, but without a return permit, one might have thought of taking the trip home, but by the lessons that others have learned, he would not dare. If he takes a chance, he may be poor in a year or so, and there may not be another opportunity to get back to America again. So he decides to wait and to save more money. Case material in our study revealed strong evidence that accumulating a large sum of money seems to be very difficult, particularly in the case of one who has been a gambler. He tends to send his money home rather than to save it. He does that, not because he has planned to do so, but rather because he is forced to follow the demands and wishes of his relatives, both in China and in America. There are cases where men were all set to go but changed their minds at the last minute. For instance, one lost all his money at the gambling table the night before his departure. He went right back to the laundry again as soon as he got over his disappointment.

Under the Chinese Exclusion Law, there were, therefore, two types of people: (1) those who could go back and forth between America and China, (2) those who were not eligible to return here once they departed for China. The former might visit their families in China as long as they were financially able to do so; the latter, on the other hand, could not take the trip home without some sort of assurance of economic well-being in China. In other words, the latter might be financially comparable to the former, but he would be forced to remain ten, twenty, thirty, forty years or more without a single chance of family reunion. Also, he was constantly in fear of being apprehended and deported by the immigration authorities. Under the provisions of the Chinese Exclusion Acts, there was no way to adjust one's immigration status. An illegal entry case had to be fixed by fraud and perjury in order to gain the privilege of movement back and forth and protection from deportation.

2. After Repeal of the Chinese Exclusion Acts

On December 17, 1943, The Chinese Exclusion Acts were repealed by the U.S. Seventy-eighth Congress. The Chinese were then put on the quota system for immigration, and they were made racially eligible for citizenship. Under an amendment of the new law, the Chinese wives of American citizens were placed on a non-quota basis. The act of July 22, 1947, removed the racial restrictions from the "War Brides Act" of December 28, 1945, so that Chinese who served in the U.S. Armed Forces might bring their wives and children to the United States once they themselves became American citizens.

All these immigration privileges are the outcome of the war situation. This resulted in an improved situation. Progress often means some improvement but is not always altogether satisfactory. "Since the passage of legislation permitting Chinese to acquire citizenship, they have done so at the rate of 700 a year."[9] This number would be much higher if there were no limitation on eligibility for naturalization. That only those who entered before July 1, 1924, or those who are admitted for permanent residence under the new law are eligible for citizenship barred many laundrymen among the Chinese immigrant group from the chance to apply for citizenship. On the other hand, a number of them who had been illegally residing in this country had their immigration status adjusted through registry procedure.[10] Eventually this leads to citizenship. How many Chinese laundrymen in the Chicago area are eligible to adjust their immigration status? Perhaps it will remain unknown, for there is no way to find out. Personal contacts through social service agencies have given us a bird's eye view of the various situations under this category.

Mr. Gee Fong was admitted as a "transient alien" from Mexico in 1920. He was supposedly on his way home to China. On the date of his sailing, he showed up to be inspected and then went aboard the ship. But soon he was smuggled ashore again by someone who had made the arrangement with his relative in San Francisco.

After a few weeks of staying in San Francisco, he came to join his other relatives in the laundry business. He has been here ever since. He is quite prosperous but not enough so to leave this country for good. He could not take a trip to China because he knew once he departed, he would hardly have any chance to get back here again. Nor could he find someone "to fix him up."

In China he left his wife and a son whom he has not seen for more than thirty years. He has been supporting his family. Now he is a citizen and could get his wife over here to join him. Alas! The poor woman died a few years ago. His son, being born before his naturalization and over age, can only come under the Chinese racial quota. But it would be several years before he could see his son, for the Chinese racial quota is now very heavily over-subscribed.

There is very little chance for him to get married again unless he decides to go back to China.

Sam Wong was smuggled in from Cuba when he was a boy of fourteen, and now he is fifty-two. At first he worked for his uncle in a small laundry shop uptown. About ten years ago, he established his own laundry nearby.

He has been in this country ever since and has remained single because no woman wants to marry him here in this country. He has, however, financed a nephew to come to this country and helped some of his relatives both here and in China financially. He is proud to tell people what he has done to help people and that is why he has not much money in savings. Now Sam is trying to apply for naturalization. "It is good to be an American citizen," says Sam. "Some day I shall go back to China for a visit."

Bow Lung was admitted as a son of an American citizen in 1921, under an assumed name of Wong Ling-ching.

Some years ago he applied for a return permit with the United States Immigration Service when he was investigated and was found double-dealing with another case. He was denied a return permit. His expected trip to China was, therefore, canceled. He has been in this country ever since.

Since from his record in the Immigration Office and other documents he could collect to prove that he had been here since July 1, 1924, he was advised to adjust his immigration status through registry. He admitted his true identity and soon his certificate of lawful entry was issued to him. Consequently, he got his first paper and his petition for naturalization was submitted to the local immigration service for approval. He will get his citizenship in due time.

Chin Ming-yuen has been in this country since July 6, 1921, and should be eligible for registry. We believe that he tells the truth, but we cannot help him unless we can get hold of some documentary proof to show that he has been here ever since that time.

Chin has been moving from place to place every few years. Because he has been in fear of being arrested by the immigration authorities, he tended to destroy some of the papers which contained his name. All people who knew him in the first several years have gone away or passed on. He could not even get a witness to make an affidavit for him. No police lists had his name, and so the United States census did not have his name. After a period of seeking, Mr. Chin got discouraged. He gave up. Told the social worker who was trying to help him that he was "going to buy a paper" rather than apply for registry.

Joe Hom was smuggled in from Canada when he was sixteen or seventeen; accompanying him were some of his clansmen who were many years his senior. Joe had gone to Sunday School where he learned English.

In 1925, he married an American-born Chinese girl. He had gone into the laundry business first, then turned to chop suey business. The new venture was a failure and he returned to the laundry business some ten years ago.

Several children were born and Joe's laundry business became prosperous. The family live in the house which Joe bought four years ago, a few blocks from the laundry shop. The children now are all grown up and two of them are in college. He and his wife work together all day and the children help, too, in the afternoon.

People take it for granted that Joe is an American citizen. Before the repeal of the Chinese Exclusion Act, Joe would have been deportable. Now he can adjust his immigration status by registry. He once decided to get it straightened out, only to become discouraged by the difficulties of getting proof of residence that he had been here since July 1, 1924.

Joe was talking about taking a trip to China. That was at least one of the reasons he wanted the American citizenship. But it did not seem to be worth the trouble, for he had to go out of town in order to get people he knew to sign affidavits for him. The only person who could testify to his early residence was his Sunday School teacher, but he had lost contact with her in recent years. The old lady could have passed away.

Finally, Joe gave up. "Too much trouble," he said. Since July 1, 1948, he became eligible for application for suspension of deportation also, under section 19(c) of the Immigration Act of 1917. No action has been taken.

It seems that ever since the repeal of the Chinese Exclusion Acts, the Chinese laundrymen, among others, are anxious to take the opportunity of applying for American citizenship. To acquire American citizenship, however, is tied up with expediency; for example, the greater freedom of movement between this country and China seems to be primarily important. This greater freedom of movement, of course, includes the right to bring into the United States members of the immediate family, which is an instrumentality of social and economic security, from the point of view of the Chinese laundryman.

Table 13.1 is a comparison of number of Chinese persons naturalized and number of Chinese-Americans departed from the United States to take up permanent residence in China during the ten-year interval between 1939 and 1948. It shows the greatest mobility was before and after Pearl Harbor. It is not clear why so many native-born Chinese-Americans went to China in 1940. It is obvious, however, why such a large number of them took their trips in 1946. It was right after the end of the war and the sojourners took their return trips home. Many of these native-born citizens, it seems, hoped for prosperity and a good life in postwar China. In the years immediately following this homeward rush the number of

TABLE 13.1
Naturalized Chinese and Chinese-Americans
Departed to Reside Permanently in China
(1939–1948)

Year	Number of Persons Naturalized	Number of Persons Departed		
		Total	Native-Born	Naturalized
1939	30	921	894	27
1940	20	1,447	1,378	69
1941	57	660	630	30
1942	45	62	50	12
1943	497	3	2	1
1944	731	16	16	0
1945	739	33	29	4
1946	599	1,144	971	173
1947	831	557	478	79
1948	763	373	337	36
Total	4,312	5,216	4,785	431

SOURCE: Immigration and Naturalization Service. Compiled from *Annual Report, 1948*; S. Rept. 1515, 81st Cong.

departures was reduced sharply. Evidently it was due to the political situation in China; hope turned into disillusion. The traffic at the present is at a standstill while the "cold war" hangs on.

On the other hand, migration of people from China to America has increased tremendously. Among others, the coming of "wives of citizens" and "war brides" seem to be most significant. During the fiscal year of 1948, it is reported that of 3,987 Chinese admitted, 3,193 were wives of citizens.[11] From April, 1946, when the first ship arrived bringing wives and children of soldiers to the United States, to June 30, 1949, 5,099 Chinese war brides and 583 of their children were admitted.[12]

Now many Chinese-American citizens can claim the right, under the new immigration law, to bring in their wives. As a participant observer in Chinatown, in Chicago as anywhere else, one hears people speak about the increasing number of women and children. A visitor to Chinatown may see some of these young newcomers who still wear Chinese dress.

The dawn of a new era of Chinese immigration is the coming of many "war brides" and citizens' wives, instead of the few merchants' wives under the old Chinese Exclusion Law. Many of these women, no doubt, are wives of laundrymen. Usually the laundryman's family lives not in Chinatown but in the neighborhood where his shop is located. If the local housing situation cannot accommodate his family, for economic reasons room may be made in the rear part of the laundry shop as living quarters. If both of these conditions are out of the question, the alternative would be to rent a place in Chinatown. Living in Chinatown, however, is very inconvenient for the laundryman and his family. Living in the rear of the laundry shop with children, of course, is not according to the American standard of living. It seems that in many instances the laundryman had no choice. Some of the more prosperous laundrymen tend to buy a house in the neighborhood, in the areas where toleration is observed. A house is preferred which is right next door, or in the same building in which the laundry shop occupies the ground floor. Those who have less means may look for a laundry shop where there is sufficient space to accommodate the family.

Chinese laundrymen who have wives and children with them tend to live the same mode of life as the others. The wives may work side by side with the husbands, and if there are any children it becomes necessary to have the home and the shop conveniently located. The wife has child care problems while helping her husband.

The birth rate among these young laundrymen's families seems to be high in the Boston area. The situation in Chicago may be expected to be the same. It is, however, only a personal impression based on some social service contacts; exactly how the situation stands quantitatively is, I believe, obtainable, but beyond my capacity at the present time.

It is also an impression that these war brides and wives of citizens are young, although not without exception. An old woman is less of an asset to the laundryman; he is, therefore, rather inclined to bring a young wife. There are those who reported the death of their wives or bachelor marital status to the immigration authorities, but, in fact, they have wives in China. I have seen cases where the men support two families, one in China and another one here in America. The wife in America, in the Chinese sense, is a concubine.

The most interesting thing is the educational and social background of these young women. In case one is a village girl with very little education and modern influences, the adjustment to the American environment may be easier and she will be more content. In the case of a woman who has received her education in the city and has become a so-called "modern young," indoctrinated with modern ideology, her adjustment to the laundryman's mode of life may be most unsatisfactory. How many of them are village girls and how many of them are modern girls? It seems most of them, as far as the laundryman's group is concerned, are village girls. Certainly the correlation between personal background and present social adjustment is significant. The statement made above, to be sure, may only be regarded as a hypothesis; materials to substantiate it are needed. Inquiry into the total situation of the adjustments made by these new arrivals is indeed an interesting project. The situation should be substantially alike in every metropolitan area.

Some of the newcomers express their interest in becoming American citizens, while others have not given it a thought. Again there seems to be a difference between the village girl and the city girl. The village girl declines to apply for American citizenship and the reason mainly given is that she is unable to pass the citizenship examination because of household duties which prevent her having enough time to study English. The city girl, on the other hand, considers citizenship as a personal asset and she tends to set her mind to obtain it. This matter, of course, is tied up with the personal influences and social contacts in each individual case. What are the typical urges for applying for American citizenship? In what way does the naturalized citizen exercise his rights as a citizen? These seem to be interesting questions that need fuller inquiry.

Connected with these questions, we may ask how the Chinese-American citizens vote in elections. An answer to this question is based on daily experience for several years rather than on systematic inquiry. In the laundrymen's group very few register and vote; most of them do not even give it a thought. The difference between a voter and a non-voter seems to be related to personal interest, influences by others, and the capability to speak and read English. A large number of the China-born citizens, particularly among the laundrymen's group, cannot even speak English. Even if they intend to vote, they need someone to help them register for voting, and provide leadership in their civic education. There is no demand for such service, from their standpoint, and consequently leadership along these lines is not supported by popular interest. In other words, the Chinese laundryman is rather inclined to be interested in politics in China and about China. Like the non-citizen, he reads the Chinese immigrant newspaper and is very much more interested in the political situation in China than in America.

After the repeal of the Chinese Exclusion Acts, there still remained some social problems. The new legislation has given some relief to sex and family problems, reduced illegal entries, lessened fear and suspicion, and increased chances for better adjustment.

Conversely there exist cases of minor children separated from their parents, and family reunions prevented by some legal technicalities of the United States immigration laws. There are also a large number of individuals who, under various legal technicalities or procedural requirements, cannot be naturalized or adjust their immigration status. They still buy and sell American birth rights; others are still being fixed. A laundryman, for instance, who became a citizen recently turned to a fixer for help to get one of his sons into this country. An alien laundryman may pay a citizen laundryman for bringing his son or nephew to America as the latter's own. People still use assumed names and other deceptions. A large number of aged men in the laundry as well as in Chinatown are poor, homeless, and in ill health; at least a portion of this group are prevented from taking their return trip to China, and their fate is more or less, directly or indirectly, related to immigration technicalities. The Immigration and Nationality Act of 1952[13] may bring further developments to the situation, but these are still unknown.

3. Conclusion

Three generations of exclusion had given the Chinese in America a feeling of insecurity and inferiority, and the consciousness of being discriminated against. He had developed all sorts of ways and means of protecting his interests and immigration status. The sudden removal of exclusion and permission for him to apply for citizenship and migration caught him unprepared. The application for naturalization is more a social and economic expedient than a full realization of the meaning of citizenry.

Sons of the younger and more progressive element in the laundrymen's group have reacted to the repeal of the Chinese Exclusion Acts with a new outlook. This element, if it increases, may lead to a period of transition.

NOTES

1. According to the Immigration Act of 1924, no Chinese could be admitted as an immigrant alien on the basis that he was ineligible to apply for citizenship.

However, certain classes of Chinese had been admitted as non-immigrants, and among these are included: (1) Chinese persons shown to have been born in the United States, and their children; (2) ministers, professors, and students; (3) visitors traveling for pleasure and visiting; (4) government officials, their families, attendants, and employees; (5) bona fide seamen; or (6) transient aliens on their way back to their homeland. The Act technically did not apply to those who previously were permanently admitted and were returning from temporary visits abroad.

2. Kenneth Colegrove, "Chinese Exclusion Acts," *Dictionary of American History,* ed. James T. Adams and R. V. Coleman (New York: Charles Scribner and Son, 1940), I, 325–26.

3. U.S. Congress, House of Representatives, *Repeal of the Chinese Exclusion Acts,* Hearings before the Committee on Immigration and Naturalization, U.S. House of Representatives, 78th Cong., 1st sess., on H.R. 87558 (Washington: Government Printing Office, 1943).

4. Only those who came before July 1, 1924, or those who came under the new Chinese racial quota are eligible for citizenship.

5. A Chinese person is defined as "a person who is of as much as one-half Chinese blood, and is not of as much as one-half blood of a race ineligible to citizenship. . . . If the father were Chinese and the mother were part white and part Japanese, let us say, such a person would be regarded as a Chinese person; if his father were Chinese, and his mother were Japanese or belonged to some other race ineligible under our law, that person would be regarded as inadmissible and would not be entitled to the benefits of this new law." See *Federal Register,* IX, No. 32 (Tuesday, February 15, 1944), 1691–92.

6. Bills were introduced and passed in the 79th Congress to amend section 2 of the Chinese Act of December 17, 1932, so as to give non-quota status to alien wives of American citizens.

7. The "Chinese racial quota" is 105 per year, and is not to be confused with the "Chinese Quota," which is 100 per year for the migration of white persons residing in China. The Chinese racial quota, under the existing laws, must cover all Chinese persons no matter where they were born. "This situation regarding other quota aliens under existing laws is definitely different in that the question of nativity, and not of race, is largely the determining factor. As a specific example, a person of European ancestry, born in a non-quota country . . . is not charged to any quota, being a non-quota alien. Also, a quota-alien whose ancestry springs from a small quota country, who is born in a large country, such as Great Britain, is charged to the quota of Great Britain. But in the case of the Chinese, the person of Chinese race, regardless of where he was born, is charged to the quota for Chinese. Thus, a person of Chinese parents, if born in Brazil or another independent country in the Western Hemisphere is not regarded as having non-quota status but is charged to the quota of 105 for Chinese persons." See *Interpreter Release,* XXI (1944), 86.

8. Stanley R. Osborn, "Stories of Blockade Runnings," *Chicago Herald Ex-*

aminer, April 2, 1913. See also a recent report by David McConnell, "Millions Slipped into U.S.—Alien Smuggling Big-Time Racket," *Boston Globe,* May 25, 1952, a report of the world-wide situation.

9. U.S. Congress, *Report of the Committee on the Judiciary, Immigration, and Naturalization Systems of the United States,* S. Rept. 1515, 81st Cong. (Washington: Government Printing Office), p. 141.

10. Application for registry of an alien under the Nationality Act of 1940. The applicant must submit documental proof that he has been in this country continuously since July 1, 1924. Sec. 346 of the Nationality Act of 1940.

11. *Report of the Committee on the Judiciary, op. cit.,* p. 140.

12. Helen F. Eckerson and Gertrude D. Krichefsky, "A Quarter Century of Quota Restriction," *Immigration and Naturalization Service Monthly Review,* VII, No. 7 (January, 1950), 93. See also "War Brides," *ibid.,* VI, No. 12 (June, 1949). It is reported that as of December 31, 1948, 5,062 Chinese war brides and 567 of their children were admitted.

13. Public Law 414, 82d Congress of the United States.

CHAPTER XIV

PERSONAL CONFLICT AND
THE MODE OF LIFE

THE CHINESE LAUNDRYMAN has immigration problems and
other problems. For instance, how he gets along with his partner and
fellow worker, how he treats the non-conformist, what adjustments he
makes in the light of cultural differences, and what he thinks of Americans. We shall consider these questions and the concept of personal and
cultural conflicts.

Personal conflict occurs when two or more persons hold different opin-
ions and attitudes toward certain things, and instead of rational discussion, the individual reacts to it with temper. In the laundryman's situation,
this seems to be aggravated. Several factors involved in this problem reveal
that it is related to the nature of the laundryman's mode of life on the
one hand, and the life organization of the individual on the other hand.
Personal conflicts among Chinese laundrymen derive, in other words,
from the strain of long working hours, congestion in a small space, the
monotony of the work, and the weariness of other personal problems. So
he becomes unreasonable and irritable, and this sometimes results in
breaking up a partnership, quitting, or dismissal.

1. Irritable Temperament

Like the marriages of Hollywood movie stars, there is hardly any laundry
where all is well and happy. The Chinese laundrymen tend to get on each
other's nerves, so to speak. The following cases reveal the irritability as
purely a clash of tempers:

The other day [Monday] when I was ironing, the drying room door was open and the steam from within was let out and it made me so hot. I opened the front door a little to get some relief.

Him-sun was operating the mangle machine in the rear. Somehow he knew the door was open and he called, "Is the front door open?"

I didn't answer him. A few minutes later he rushed out and slammed the front door closed. I was so mad and angrily shouted at him, "Why did you close it?"

"If you are hot, go back to the rear and iron!"

"If you are cold, have a blanket around you!" I retorted. You know he should not rush out like that; he got on my nerves. What he should do was to call to my attention that he felt cold and not to slam the door so hard. I was mad, of course. When I angrily protested, I could see his face was red.

Then he calmed down. He realized later that he shouldn't fuss any more about the incident. He forgave me just as though nothing had happened. That is the good nature of Him-sun.

After the outburst of temper, his nephew, Kock-ying, whispered to me, "That's good, I am for you. He is too bossy in this place."

He is an elderly man, you see, and he thinks we younger fellows must respect and obey him all the time.

Having heard the story, Chan-shui, the chop suey house friend reminded Chan-ming, "I don't think you are right, Chan-ming, you just have 'the temper of the cattle.' He is your elder man. Why, slamming the door is nothing. Why must you shout at him? Is respecting the old a virtue to you? Your outburst of temper for such a small thing—that is bad."

Chan-ming walked out, not at all pleased.

Pui-ying and Hsin-lum have not been able to get along with each other for some time, and each complains to me that the other is lazy, untrustworthy, and incompatible. Oh, too much trouble. I tried to mediate, but without any real tolerance and understanding among themselves, no one can do any good. You see, they are really fussing for no good reason at all. Pui-ying told me that Hsin-lum almost had another outburst of temper last week. It started when Pui-ying was cooking. He was attending the other things and forgot to watch the fire. The rice got burned a little. It was not too burned, according to Pui-ying. Hsin smelled the burn and he took the whole pot of rice and dumped it into the backyard. They started to quarrel. Later Pui-ying cooked another pot of rice and other dishes, but Hsin-lum refused to eat with him. He had to cook his own meal.

Later Hsin came to me and I asked him about their dispute. Hsin-lum complained that Pui-ying was too selfish. He cooked only what he liked to eat. He said Pui-ying purposely burned the rice so that it would do some harm to his health. And that Pui-ying doesn't know how to cook and yet Pui-ying insists that he cook most of the time.

How can they get along as partners if they can't even sit down at one table to eat? I scolded Hsin-lum for his shortcoming of outburst of temper in this incident. I hope he listens to my advice this time. I told him that if he uses his temper too much, nobody will like to be his partner or employ him any more. But that man Pui-ying—his shortcoming is that he is too stingy and indeed a little selfish sometimes.

They were talking of breaking up the partnership. I told them if they sell that place, both of them will be out of a job for a long time. That place makes money only if they try to get along.

Del-ka-ma! To tell about him will make you laugh! Just the other day, he came back with a face of a mourner. It was quite late. I sensed that it must be a losing battle with "Uncle Four" [*Sisu*] (*fan-tan*, a gambling game). I didn't want to ask him or his temper would burst out again.

The next morning, he didn't say a word to me also. About noontime, Toy Shing, the grocery store man came. Among the other items, I asked Toy Shing if he carried some *sei quar.* "Sei quar!" he shouted, "you don't know even how to call the name of the melon!"

I was surprised and so was Toy Shing. Realizing it was the gambler's superstition, Toy Shing turned and said to him, "Brother Tuck-leong, how was the luck yesterday?"

"Del-ka-ma! Don't you talk about it again. All you people's fault! You should say it 'sing quar' [*sungua*] instead of 'sei quar!' [*xigua*] [Ed. note: This passage relates to the gambling superstitions with lucky and unlucky words. The Cantonese *sei* for watermelon sounds the same as the word for death.] Don't you bring any of such thing in again! It brings me bad luck."

I listened to all these and got excited. I was on the verge of giving him a piece of my mind, but after a thought I controlled myself. I told Toy Shing to bring in some mustard greens, instead.

Two days later he told me without asking him. He lost about a hundred fifty dollars last Sunday. To work with such a gambling devil is very difficult. When loses, he can't even work—everything seems to get on his nerves. You can't even talk to him. Asked him to hang up the clothes in the drying room, he was mad about the stove and complained that it was too old or small. Scolded the stove, murmuring and fussing on unimportant matters. Oh, it is annoying, driving me crazy sometimes.

Once, he gave me two hundred dollars and asked me to send it back to China to his family for him. I was delayed by other matters that day when I went downtown. I didn't have the chance to go to the bank before it closed. I told him the situation and he said he wanted the money back. Of course I gave it back to him. The next week, I learned he lost the money on gambling the Sunday before. He went to Cousin Kong-sun and complained about me, that I made him lose the money and so and so on. Then Kong-sun questioned me about this matter. Then I came back and scolded him. He knew that it was his own fault. He didn't dare to say a word. But he was resentful and picked on the cat. He happened to walk toward the inside and the cat was in his way. He kicked it so hard that I thought it was killed.

This was not the first time. If it was the first time, I wouldn't get so mad. He always comes back as late as one and sometimes two or three o'clock after midnight. Every time he got home, he woke me up. I am a person who can hardly get sleep again after being awakened. He doesn't realize that a hard-working man needs sleep, particularly in this type of work. We work from morning until nighttime. As for myself, I need at least eight hours sleep.

I talked to him many times; he can either come back earlier or stay out and come back to work in the morning. But he won't take my advice. Last Sunday night, he returned as late as 2:00 A.M., and he was inconsiderate—closing the door so loud that it woke me up and at first I thought a thief had broken in. But it was him. I looked at the clock and it was two. I was so mad I "helloed" him.

I thought he was a good partner, for he could work quickly. But I found out that he cared only for the laundry work. He seldom touched other work that needed to be shared with me, such as keeping this place clean. I do all the shopping for food as well as for supplies. As soon as the shirts are ironed, he leaves for a good time.

I don't know where he goes. He has a group of those good-for-nothing fellows somewhere in town. They have some sort of club—gang together to play ma-jong and fool around with women. I never ask him. If I do he won't tell me anyway.

After a fight last Monday, he declared that he would like to have me take over his share or get someone else to join me. I am planning to buy his share.

A few days later, the partner who planned to drop out was talking to his friends, complaining about the partner who stayed:

He is just like a house-mother in that place. Too particular. You can't even smoke. Naturally a smoker is bound to drop some ash on the floor sometimes. On many occasions he got mad just because of that. He had to clean this and that all the time and left the laundry work undone.

He likes string beans cooked with beef. Almost every meal we eat that; I get so sick and tired of it. Then he said, "If you don't like this, why don't you go out and buy something you prefer." Sometimes I bought something but he fussed. I remember, it was near Chinese New Year, I bought one pound of dried oysters and some sea weeds and other imported things from China. It cost about fifteen dollars. He said it was too expensive. Once when I cooked a pot of oyster, pork, and sea weed soup he ate a little but said it was too "cool" [a comment related to folk beliefs in a balance of *ying* and *yang* or "cold" and "hot" elements in nature]. Later he got a little cough and blamed me, for I cooked the soup which was not fit for his health.

As a working man, naturally one wants some recreation on Sunday. He wanted me to return to the shop to sleep about nine. I certainly cannot sleep so early. When I returned a little late, he said I woke him up and he couldn't sleep and so on and so on. Life should not be so hard and monotonous, you can agree with me. It is hard enough, as a matter of fact.

He is just like a fussy old maid, picking on everything you do. I am going to give my share to him. Let him do it alone or he may like to get someone else to join him. I can't stay any longer with him.

Emotional ups and downs are likely everybody's personal experience, but the fact that an individual is unusually irritable seems to indicate that in some area of his life he is under stress and strain. The individual is dissatisfied in various degrees with his social and emotional outlets. In the case of the Chinese laundryman, as the preceding materials reveal, his mode of life has something to do with it. However, the crucial point in this problem is the fact that, in similar situations, some people can tolerate each other better, while some tend to get into personal conflicts with each other irrationally.

It seems the laundryman tends to be more irritable on Monday, Wednesday, and Friday, for these are washing days, and the work is harder and perhaps the work itself can hardly be evenly shared. Outbursts of temper, irritations, and disputes over a small matter sometimes provoke serious consequences. It may not only result in breaking up the partnership but also in disowning of close relatives. As described in the preceding chapter, partnership and employment in the Chinese laundry usually involve peoples of one's own kinship group. Father and son, uncle and nephew, and other close relatives are found working side by side in the Chinese laundry. This leads us to consider the nature of the next item.

2. Conformity Versus Individuality

Certain conventional ways of conduct are expected to be observed in the presence of the elder man. For example, there must be no talk about sex, no talk about gambling, and to a certain extent, no swearing and joking. But the congestion in a small shop and the long hours with monotonous work, make the close-relative relationship in the Chinese laundry harder to adjust to, because one has no relaxation nor any place to escape from conventionalities. Under such a psychological complex, it seems to be evident that close relatives find it expedient to work separately. In many instances, some people began to work together in one laundry shop, but the result became a break-up either peacefully or bitterly.

My son? I don't know where he is now, to tell you the truth. I heard he is now in New York, working as a waiter. I don't have his address, for he has not written to me for a long time. I wrote to him and I didn't get any answer. He does not look upon me as father any more I suppose.

Nowadays, you can't control the young people. You just say a few words to them and they revolt against you. That was how mine walked out.

I brought him over here to this country when he was eighteen years old. He was not a very bright boy. If he had a good mind, I would let him stay in China. Like his older brother, he would be in college. Since he did not want to go to college, he himself asked me to get him over here. So I decided to do as he wished.

Well, he began to work with me. In the first two years he behaved. Then he began to join some of these young chaps down here in Chinatown. You know what they do; they either gamble or hunt for some of those women here who smell blocks away. Then, where can you get enough money for him to spend once he mixes up with them? At the beginning, he wouldn't dare to take money out from the cash drawer. Soon, without my consent, he took money. Once he took all the money I had—two hundred seventy dollars. I scolded him and he talked back, saying that I was despotic. Another time he took nearly one hundred dollars from the drawer just one day after I gave him fifty dollars for expenses. He said he needed the money to send to his wife. I couldn't believe it. Later I learned from home that he had never sent that money to his wife. I was so mad I asked him to go. I gave him only fifteen dollars a week. I thought that was enough for him to spend.

Last summer, listening to the advice of his gang, he left me. He took a suitcase and left when I was visiting Chinatown on Sunday. Then three weeks later, one of my cousins saw him and gave him some good advice. He came back the following morning. Cousin Sun-ming scolded him for being unfilial, leaving me alone here, saying that I was so disappointed I might drop dead sometime, and that I am too old to live alone. He came back but acted all right just a week or two. He started to join bad company again. He was arrested by the police on a charge of disorderly conduct. It cost me about a hundred fifty dollars.

What else? Such a restless fellow is bound to get into trouble with women.

As soon as I got down to Chinatown, I had my ears full of complaints about him. People say who is who's son! How unfortunate I am!

After that I didn't pay any attention to him. Later I heard he went to New York. I haven't seen him for over a year, now. I asked some of our clansmen in New York to look for him. He hasn't supported his wife and child in China ever since. I am the one who does it.

This, it seems, is one of the extreme cases of conflict between close relatives in the Chinese laundry situation. The Chinese laundryman had tried to observe the Old World tradition and conventionalities, but he often found it hard to keep up with the social condition here in the American urban community. All sorts of new values attract the attention of the younger generation. Again, the mode of life in the Chinese laundry perhaps tends to make the younger person more restless. He seeks relaxation and pleasure in his leisure time. Since he is away from home and from normal sex life, he tends to get it clandestinely or by other substitutes.

The old man is more content with the mode of life. He is interested in accumulating money, in the return trip, and in his retirement to a good life in China. He tends to supervise the younger generation according to his ideas, and it is all for the good of the younger generation as well as his own. As it is traditionally observed, a good father thinks always of the welfare of his offspring rather than his own. In America, he is disappointed with the bad behavior of the younger generation.

On the other hand, there are some fathers and elders who become habitual gamblers. They lose their hard-earned wages, year in and year out on account of gambling debts, and come to dispute with the youth. It makes the younger generation feel indifferent and disgusted. As one young Chinese puts it, "In this United States, one can hardly follow the virtue of filial son and grandson."

Such a kind of man. I have nothing to do with him. No matter how much money he makes, he throws it away within the same day. He has been here longer than I have. I have been back to China three times while he hasn't taken the trip at all.

When he was in Ironwood, he made a lot of money. Well, when he had money, he did not recognize me as his brother. He spent it on gambling and prostitution. I couldn't even get a cent from him.

Now he is old and can't work very well. He was just here the other day. Penniless. Has not been working for some time. Asked me for money. I gave him hell. I told him two weeks ago that I didn't want to see him any more. He asks me for money all the time now.

He confessed that he has not sent any money home for more than two years. He couldn't help it. He wanted to save money but he hasn't earned much in recent years. His only hope is to win some money from the lottery.

These are types of conflicts between close relatives in the Chinese laundry. The maladjustments indicate symptoms of social disorganization. To what extent conflicts of close relatives create disorganization, personal as well as social, we do not know. The fact is that there are laundries in which close relatives work together in spite of the urban circumstances and influences.

According to propriety, the elder, particularly a father or uncle, must be respected. On the other hand, his venerable prestige has to be maintained by himself. It is taboo for a father to swear in front of his son. It is undignified to talk about sex matters to the younger men. For the son, of course, it is sinful to say "del-nea-ma" against the father, and to tell a sex joke in front of him is an insult and a direct challenge to his venerable prestige. A tolerant father, in some instances, would walk away in order to let the youngsters have some fun sometimes.

In the Chinese laundry, the work is so monotonous, people usually amuse themselves with jokes and sex stories as a sort of recreation. If an elder man is in the group, the gossipers have to be careful not to offend him. It often creates a situation that makes people reticent. Perhaps under such a situation, people seek emotional outlet from this kind of personal relationship more fervently.

3. Wage and Hour Disputes

Another matter which may create a conflict situation in the Chinese laundry is the wage and hours dispute. In the Chinese laundry, the individual skill is measured by the number of shirts one can iron per hour. According to information gathered, the average skill is about ten shirts per hour. Obviously there is a variation among different individuals, and it becomes a personal asset for an individual to iron more shirts quickly and nicely. Then there is a difference between the kinds of iron used and the difference between age groups; young and able-bodied men probably iron faster than old and weak men. Notice in the description in Chapter 6, that wage distribution in the Chinese laundry tends to be evenly divided. What happens if two persons of two extremes in skill work together in one place? Of course, if the two are close relatives and friends, perhaps sentiments of loyalty, duty, obligation, and affection may overcome the idea of fair play. Often, however, people are less sentimental and more money-minded. There we find some area of dispute in the Chinese laundry. Individuals may work in the same laundry, the same number of hours, but one works much faster than the other and yet they are paid the same amount of wages by the employer. The following case illustrates that the fast worker quits his job:

> After I worked there for several months, I decided to quit. Del-ka-ma! Both he and his cousin [employee] are slow, especially Tuck-lin [employee]. He can iron only seven or eight shirts an hour. Oh, what a clumsy fellow. Sometimes I became impatient and showed him. He tried but soon he forgot all about it and went back to his own clumsy way.
>
> The iron must be hot enough and the shirt must be adjusted in a proper way. I showed him to start with the collar but he didn't follow.
>
> Del-ka-ma! I did almost twice as much work and yet I got the same amount of wages. The business has been slowly reduced during the last two or three weeks. I got only twenty dollars a week last Sunday. What is the use of working so hard and making the money for another. I told Chung-yih that I wanted to take a rest—told him I had not been feeling well.
>
> Del-ka-ma! Let the two of them toil themselves to death without my help. They have to work deep in the nighttime now, I am sure.

It seems the difference in skill is not too great, on the whole, among the Chinese laundrymen. So the disputes about wages and hours are not serious. The fact of the matter is that skill related to wage disputes gets mixed up with other personality differences between the individuals, as the preceding pages have indicated. In the following case, a young laundryman planned to visit friends in Detroit. In order to leave his duty in the laundry, he must get the consent of his partners. The partners are relatives many years his senior. The excerpt reveals emotional disturbance in the laundry.

> "You know he is working much faster today," said Jemmie's partner in a mocking tone. "It is only noon, and he has all the dried clothes moistened

already. When he wants to go to Detroit, he is fast indeed! He is restless. I think he couldn't even sleep last night.

"There are a lot more things to do after we finish our regular work. He is supposed to chop the wood and to have the stove ready for next Monday. He won't be able to go after lunch [Saturday].

"You know what he says to me?" Jemmie's partner continued. "He says, 'Brother Chan-shiu, suppose you take care of the odd jobs for me this Saturday, all right? Let me buy you a can of tobacco.'"

"Ha! Who wants your tobacco?" I retorted. "Have I not the money to buy my tobacco? I let him have it. It is really nothing important about paying a visit to Detroit; he is just restless."

Jemmie could not leave for Detroit until late in the afternoon after he had done his duty as usual. His three partners, of course, let him go, but did not give him any encouragement.

Any non-conformity seems to disturb the equilibrium of the partnership. Leaving the job on a busy day, particularly causes hardship on the other fellow worker. Men therefore stay on with the job even though suffering from minor illness. A catastrophe developed when a man got a complication from a bad cold, for instance, and died with pneumonia because he insisted on keeping on working when he needed the rest.

In order to be a good partner and a good worker, the working hours should not be counted. The number of hours depends upon the volume of work which, in turn, determines the amount of income. According to the established routine, the work must be done before retiring. Under this condition, the laundryman has developed a pattern of work which may be called a slow-steady working pattern. The slow-steady tendency, of course, is conditioned by the long working hours. He simply has to learn to endure the working hours, which are nearly twice as long as the standardized pattern of American workingmen. It creates conflicts if one starts to fuss about wages per hour. As indicated in a previous chapter, the laundryman does pay his Negro-woman helper wages by the hour, in some instances.

4. Cultural Conflicts

Conflicts from the standpoint of cultural differences do not affect the organization of the laundry, at least not substantially enough to upset the human relations among its members. Culturally speaking, the laundryman has conflicts confronting him because he is a stranger in the community. In a preceding chapter[1] the description of the laundryman celebrating Thanksgiving and Christmas reveal, to a certain extent, evidence of acculturation. These activities, however, also reveal cultural conflicts. He takes over the cultural form of celebration but not the cultural content. Christmas and Thanksgiving mean nothing more to him than the mangle, the electric fan, and other machinery he has adopted in his laundry shop in recent years. In other words, he is bound to have different conceptions of the American mores and folkways. Further, he tends to see things American from his own cultural standpoint. One of the outstanding customs which the Chinese laundryman cannot understand is the parent-child relationship in America. To him, it is unbelievable that children would leave their parents in old age without support.

An elderly man was in Old Chung's laundry shop; he came in for his laundry. Mr. Chung seemed to be very friendly to the customer, asking after his health and letting him take the bundle with not enough money to pay.

"That's all right," said Chung sincerely. "No make no difference—only fourteen cents. You pay next time. No pay all right. I not care."

The old man was so old that he could hardly walk. As the old man left, Mr. Chung began, "This old man? He is really tormented by his old age. Both he and his wife are just as old. They have lived in this neighborhood for a long time. He used to have plenty of money, I know. Now they are old and poor and no one takes care of them.

"He has many children—four or five sons and three daughters, too. It is strange, as soon as the children grew up and got married, one by one they have all gone away and left this old couple alone.

"In China, this old couple would be the most proud and venerable grand-parents, but things are different in this country. 'To have sons for old age; to have rice for hunger,' is an old saying, but to have sons in this country equals having none. When I see this man, I talk to him, and to my surprise, he doesn't seem bothered about it. He doesn't take it badly even if his children treat him and his old wife badly like this.

"To me it is a very bad custom the Americans have. Some children, after their marriage, come back to visit the old parents, and may give the old parents some money in case of need. But in this case, only one of the girls comes back once in a long while. She is the only who gives the old couple some money to spend.

"Yes, they told me they are on relief and that is why they can live. I have pity on him. I often let him have the laundry without paying for it. When he had money, he would pay it the next time. He is a good old man.

"He had two shirts and six collars in his bundle; how could it be enough as he brought only thirty cents?"

This case is an example of Chinese filial piety versus American individualism; Chinese familism versus American urbanism. The old laundryman thinks the American way of life strange and bad because "as soon as the children grow up and they are married, one by one they all go away, leaving the old parents helpless." And he was surprised to find that the deserted old father for whom he had so much sympathy was not at all resentful of the treatment of the children.

From the laundryman's cultural background, he cannot understand the American way of life, and is almost certain to misunderstand it. When he sees American women on the beach and on the street, half nude and wearing sport clothes, it seems to him indecent; when he sees men and women embrace and kiss openly in public places, he thinks of it as "animal behavior." On the basis of his impersonal contacts and hearsay, the Chinese laundryman gets a stereotyped conception of the moral conduct of American women.

American women are more coquettish, and Chinese women are very reserved. Our Chinese women really devote themselves to their husbands. . . .

American woman would say she loves you so long as you have the money. When she marries you what she cares is to get hold of your money. If she can't do what she pleases, she would leave you sooner or later.

After all, Chinese women are more virtuous. Once she is married to you, that means a life-long wife. She would not leave you even if she is treated wrongly. For sure the American woman would demand a divorce as soon as her husband paid no heed to her. Some even sue the husband for divorce because of sexual incompatibility [*laughs*].

This sort of comment, of course, is naive and one-sided. But the Chinese laundryman sincerely believes that his culture is on a higher moral level in regard to sex and marriage.

The Chinese laundryman seldom comes into personal contact with his customers and neighbors. One, for one reason or another, may claim the local policeman, local banker, or any other local personality as a friend, but his claim, in some instances, is more or less boasting of his social connections in front of his countrymen. His claim of the friendship of the local policemen is indeed very interesting. One reason seems to stand out clearly—that he needs the protection of the officer of the law. The officer,

obviously, is only doing his duty, and sometimes he may be a little friend-
lier. In general, the laundryman feels that he is being discriminated
against, and any friendly gesture his neighbor makes may be very touching
to him.

> A lady came in for her laundry a while ago. She was nice and talked to me
> about the war in China. "I just hate to see them [the Japanese] go over to
> China and kill so many peace-loving Chinese. That just isn't right." She
> said that.
>
> She is very nice to us. She was in China for fifteen years. Her daughter
> was born in China. The daughter is now seventeen, a nice girl indeed. She
> comes to call for their laundry sometimes. Once she said, "I am Chinese,
> too; I was born in Shantung [Shandong]."
>
> As a matter of fact, all those who have been in China are nice to us here.
> Do you know why? I'll tell you the reason. See, they were treated nicely in
> China. In China they were highly respected and appreciated. The Chinese
> did not discriminate against them. Probably most of those who have con-
> nections with whites in China are Chinese Christians.
>
> Well, the whites in China have no chance to meet bad Chinese, the lawless
> and unscrupulous people. So white residents in China have a good impres-
> sion of China and our Chinese way of life. When they come back to this
> country, they still have good feelings toward us. That is the reason, for
> instance, that this family is so nice.
>
> Those Americans who have not been in China are not so friendly. Some
> of them hate the Chinese, and some don't look upon Chinese as human
> beings. These types of people generally are the lower class of Americans.
> They are the ignorant type.

The Chinese laundryman is rather inclined to think that discrimination
and prejudice against him originate from some segment of the American
population, as stated in the excerpt, and that it is "the lower class of
Americans," and "the ignorant type." The cold, impersonal, and hostile
world around the Chinese laundryman tends to exacerbate his sojourner
attitude. The sentiment of patriotism is developed in relation to his desire
that China be strong and prosperous so that he does not have to stay here
much longer. The Chinese overseas produce great patriots. "Overseas
Chinese are the mother of the revolution," said Dr. Sun Yat-sen, to whom
Chinese immigrants in America gave great moral and financial support.
The recent war against the Japanese invasion, for example, cost every
Chinese laundryman in the Chicago area from $12.50 to $18.50 bi-

monthly for several years, besides many other special contributions. His moral support of the war effort is shown in the following excerpt:

> Reading *San Ming Morning News* today, I learned that some of our brave men killed one more traitor in Shanghai yesterday. Del-ka-ma! Chan Lo is the name. He had been China's delegate to the League of Nations and yet turned out to be the enemy of the nation. I just don't understand the psychology of such evil men. I am so delighted that he is killed. The best thing was to kill them—all the traitors! Del-nea-ma! Who can be so heartless as to be a traitor!
>
> A man like Wang Ching-wei. He dares to speak openly for compromise with the Japs! I wish Chiang Kai-shek had caught him right in Chungking [Chongqing] and had his head removed. He is worse than a traitor. He tried to destroy our united front. At this period of national salvation, what good is it just to be interested in political power. All we have to do and must do is to unite and to fight the Japs. Kick them out of China first.
>
> Those who refuse to contribute to the war fund ought to be punished. I have just paid my bi-monthly dues last week. I paid eighteen-fifty. According to my business, I would not have to pay so much. What of it? If we should lose to the Japs, what good is the money? So I decided to do my best. Some are beaten for refusal to pay the war fund. I think they deserve it.
>
> The students in this country are very busy for our war effort, too. We should do our best in every walk of life. How much money did you students raise from the bazaar two months ago?

While the sentiment expressed represents the majority, indifferent reactions occur, only to be subdued by strong public opinion which sanctions a measure of punishment. The non-conformist has to follow the current consensus.

> C. T. Moy, native of Wen Wah Village, Toyshan, operates a laundry shop at 703 Washington Steet, Evanston. His business is very good. He loves to give big talks. Because his National Salvation Fund contribution is past due for some time, inspectors have been to his place, urging him to pay. Instead of following good advice, he was very indifferent, refusing to talk.
>
> He came to the headquarters of the National Salvation Association [*Jiuguo Hui*] on Sunday, June ninth. The officials of the committee thought that he has repeatedly violated the rules and spoken insolently, so they gave him some last advice, that he might yet fulfill his duty to the cause of national salvation. But he was so irrational that he spoke without sense of responsibility and reason. The officials of the committee saw that in order to teach him a lesson, it had become necessary to punish him. The committee, there-

fore, ordered that his picture be taken to be printed in the newspaper as
an unpatriotic violator.

The committee further ordered him to pay the overdue fees right away.
Surrounded by a large, angry crowd of our countrymen, he realized he was
wrong and apologized.

This interest in the homeland is a trait of the sojourner. He has no
difficulty in rallying support from members of his ethnic group. The
supporters of any cause of public interest are likely not to be circumscribed
by legal technicalities. Further, "when you are a Chinese, you are treated
the same as any other Chinese, whether or not you are an American
citizen." Many Chinese laundrymen are American citizens, but they regard themselves as Chinese. One may buy U.S. War Bonds at his own
free will, but he may be compelled to contribute to the "cause of freedom
in China."

Whatever understanding and opinion about American ways of life the
Chinese laundryman has, he is not free from values and attitudes as con-
ditioning factors of the radical situation in this country. There is very little
personal contact, and he never has a chance to share the American way
of life, except superficially on a few occasions. The evidences of cultural
conflict are most frequently seen between the first and second generations,
but the laundryman is alone in this country, he has no family here, and
the conflict is reduced to the minimum.

In conclusion, it seems that the Chinese laundrymen have more conflict
among themselves than with the general public, because they live in a
world of isolation. They fight prejudice and discrimination with sojourner
attitudes, and with patriotism.

NOTES

1. See Chapter 10, section 3, *supra*.

CHAPTER XV

THE CHINESE LAUNDRYMAN
AS A GAMBLER

IN PRIMITIVE SOCIETIES without money, people may gamble with any commodity. In the civilized world, there is the stock market as a legitimate business enterprise, and the state lottery as a means of raising money for worthy causes.[1] Gambling, if not an inherent, is at least a universal human trait.[2] "The gambling impulse, in and of itself, is nonmoral and not immoral. There are, however, a small number of cases where gambling becomes immoral because it becomes excessive and goes beyond the limits of control by the person, or because it brings misery and suffering to the person or to his family."[3] But why do some individuals of certain social groups over-indulge in gambling?

> We Chinese people in America—there is no gambling if one person is alone, but as soon as two persons get together, there is gambling.[4]

This may be an exaggeration, but is descriptive, in one of the laundrymen's own words, of his conception of Chinese gambling in America. In a small Michigan city, for example, there are only two chop suey houses and several laundry shops. One of the laundries was visited one Saturday afternoon. There was a crowd of about fifteen persons playing ma-jong and *pai-gow* [*paijiu*] (a gambling game played with cards) in the rear part of the house. In cities such as Richmond, Virginia and Indianapolis, Indiana, a Chinese gambling center is found near the central business district. In metropolitan Chicago, the gambling enterprise in Chinatown (as of 1940) consisted of about 350 men who depended upon it for a living. According to reliable information, during the period of prosperity in the twenties, there were from 80 to 140 fan-tan tables and more than 30 lottery units, besides other kinds of gambling, in operation in from 10 to

15 gambling houses. In 1938, eight regular gambling houses had survived
the depression with a decreased business. After the Japanese attacked Pearl
Harbor, gambling in Chicago Chinatown seemed to rise to a new height.
Two new gambling houses were established and "people now have more
money to gamble," according to an informant who was once a Chinatown
gambling house boss and now is a laundryman, still holding some gambling interests in Chinatown. And another informant had this to add:

> Now, people are earning better, but they cannot send money home. They
> don't want to put it in the bank either—afraid it will be frozen. So many
> carry their money with them.
> You should see some of those young fellows gambling each Sunday. Some
> of them have always one or two thousand dollars with them, and when they
> play, they play heavily.
> How foolish these people are. I have been in this, and I am sure they will
> be victimized at last. People can never get smart, I don't know why.
> The gambling business in Chinatown is the best now for the last fifteen
> years. People now have money to gamble.

In recent months, some of the fifteen or more gambling houses in Boston Chinatown have suffered a losing business. Why? According to several
informants, many of the young men have brought their wives and children
from China, under the provisions of the new U.S. immigration laws, and
because of family relations, they no longer frequent the gambling houses.
The situation is very likely the same in Chicago or any other Chinatown.
On the other hand, some of those who have no family here would have
more money to gamble, because they cannot send any more money to
Communist China. It has become illegal to do so under a U.S. Department
of Commerce order.

For the Chinese laundryman, gambling is a means of recreation; it is
also an expression of the human aleatory impulse of taking a risk and
gaining something for nothing. But to understand gambling in Chinatown,
it is necessary to understand its background in China.

1. An Old World Trait Transplanted

Outdoor games and sports for adults have never developed in China.
Instead, there are all sorts of indoor games for thrills and excitement,
originating in ancient times. During the Han (206 B.C.–220 A.D.) and

Tong [*Tang*] (618–907 A.D.) dynasties, gambling served as entertainment in social gatherings and was sanctioned as non-moral. Chess was an ancient pastime and "thought to be a game for scholars, nor is it confined to that class, as the street chair-coolies may be seen playing while waiting for hire."[5] Betting on quail-cock fights and cricket fights are also games seen in modern China.

Lin Yutang observes that there is a peculiar characteristic of Chinese gamings. "Teamwork is unknown. In Chinese card games, each man plays for himself. The Chinese like poker and do not like bridge. They have always played ma-jong which is nearer to poker than bridge."[6] Gamble states: "those who sought to introduce new games devoid of gambling have met with success for a time only to find that, before long, the old games with the thrill and excitement of money stakes are taken up again."[7] These fragments of fact introduce the question of Chinese gambling in America. The socially isolated Chinese transplanted some of the Chinese games, which in America, as in China, are means of seeking thrills and excitement. The popular gambling game the Chinese transplanted is fan-tan, which is humorously nicknamed "Uncle Fan" in America. It is equivalent to roulette in the Western world. In China, as in Chinatown, fan-tan gambling is monopolized by some syndicate. Some of those opulent fan-tan houses in Macao, the Monte Carlo of the Orient, attracted the attention of some journalists.

> The Portuguese colony at Macao, located opposite Hong Kong on the South China coast, yesterday awarded in open competition the fan-tan gambling monopoly to a Chinese syndicate for a period of five years. The Chinese syndicate agreed to pay $700,000 annually to the Macao treasury for the gambling monopoly. The monopoly is considered immensely profitable since its clientele is drawn from both the British colony at Hong Kong and the Chinese metropolis, Canton.[8]

> In the gambling hall stands a long table with a heap, at one end, of the usual currency of China, a nickel coin with a square hole in the middle, called cash. When the moment comes, an absent-minded Chinaman seated at the table scoops away the smaller heap from the larger one, and immediately covers it with a metal bowl. When the stakes are placed, he lifts up the bowl and begins to count out the cash, four at a time, with a long pointer. There may be a complete number of sets of four in the pile, or there may be one, two, or three cash left over. This is the chance that gamblers put their stakes on. [Ed. note: Either one, two, three, or four coins will remain. Whoever guesses the right number wins.]

Gamblers of recognized social existence assemble on the first floor, in a balcony which overlooks the gambling table. They are served with tea and cigarettes, and suck pumpkin seeds while they make their wagers. When their choice is made, a little basket on a string is let down with their money in it, and a shrill voice announces the number that it is to be staked on. You see a good many women in these places, fat women for the most part, unbecomingly attired in their usual jumpers and black silk trousers. A thin, bent old man beside me with drooping eyelids had that false air of good breeding which distinguishes habitual suitors of fortune in our casinos.

Down below, the working people stood around the table in a crowd. They come in and watch the play a few minutes, clutching the few hard-earned coins that they hope to multiply exceedingly by grace of an unknown power. Suddenly they make up their minds, stretch out their arms and place their stakes. The croupier at the end of the table has the sore look of perpetual boredom that European croupiers have. Finally he uncovers the heap of "cash" that he has put on one side, and begins to count them out deliberately, four at a time. There is a dead silence. When the end draws near so that the result can be foreseen, a thin murmur runs through the crowd. When the result is announced, they receive it in silence.[9]

A picture of the gambling public in the Chinese village cannot be seen more vividly than in the description by Lu Hsun in his immortal novella, *Life Story of Ah Q.*

After conquering his enemies by such ingenious means, Ah Q would run off to the tavern with a light heart, drink a few cups of wine, jest and quarrel a bit with the drinkers, and after scoring more victories, return to the Tuku temple with a light and would soon fall asleep. It he had any money, he would join the noisy and sweaty street gamblers, distinguishing himself both in noise and sweat.

"Four hundred farthings on the Black Dragon!"

"Hi! There it goes!" the dealer shouts, sweat streaming down his face. "There goes Heaven's Gate ... and Human Harmony with a vengeance! Pay up now, Ah Q!"

"A hundred on the vengeance, no! hundred and fifty!"

Gradually his money would find its way into the pockets of other perspiring gamblers. Obliged to withdraw from the inner circle, he would watch from the fringe, shouting and perspiring for the active participants. He could not tear himself away until the party broke up, when he would return to the temple with reluctant steps. The next day he would go to work with swollen eyes.

But who knows that it is not a blessing for the Tartar to have to lose his horse? Unluckily Ah Q once won at gambling which almost proved a defeat, a blot on his unbroken record of victories.

This happened on the day of the village festival. There were open air theatricals according to tradition, and near the stage there were, according to tradition, several gambling stalls. The guns and drums sounded very faint in Ah Q's ears, as though miles away; he could only hear the barking of the dealer. He won and won, his coppers turning to dimes, dimes into silver dollars, silver dollars growing into a big pile. He was excited and happy.

"Two dollars on Heaven Gate!" he shouted.

Suddenly a fight broke out, no one knew who against whom or why. When the commotion had subsided and Ah Q had crawled to his feet, the gambling stall and gamblers were no longer there. He felt aches here and there on his body, indicating that he might have received a few blows and kicks. People stared at him wonderingly. He went back to the temple with an air of preoccupation and after recovering his wits realized that he no longer had his pile of silver dollars. As the gamblers were mostly from other villages, there was nothing that he could do.[10]

In the Chinese villages, fan-tan sometimes is not tolerated by public opinion, but it always finds its patrons in the marketplace. The country gentlemen play ma-jong in their studies, while farm hands and laborers play *neu-pai [niupai]* and *tin-kau [tienjiu]* in the village bachelor's house. Poker is quite popular, but bridge is unknown.

In any American city where there is a Chinatown, fan-tan is probably in operation. In the Chinatown of a metropolis like Chicago, there are lotteries and other gamblings called *jop-do [yadu]* (sideline gambling). It includes ma-jong, neu-pai, and tin-kau. Today, ma-jong is played everywhere—in gambling houses, in stores, clubhouses, clan houses, and even in the laundry. Neu-pai and tin-kau are patronized, like ma-jong, in gambling houses as well as in private retreats, but fan-tan and lotteries are strictly monopolized by Chinatown gambling houses under direct control of the "tong." [Ed. note: Literally meaning "hall," used referring to various Chinatown organizations, in English the word often connotes an illegal mafia-like organized crime.]

Fan-tan may be considered as gambling proper in Chinatown, but lotteries lead all other gambling in patrons. Many people, including women and children, who do not bet on fan-tan or play other games, are patrons of lottery tickets. There are two kinds of lotteries in Chinatown: *bai-ku-peie [baikepiao]* (white pigeon) and *tze-fa [zihua]* (word puzzle). The maximum winning paid off on the former is three thousand dollars, and on the latter, three hundred dollars. At the present time, there are eight houses in Chinatown, as shown in Table 15.1.

We have no way of telling accurately to what extent laundrymen participate in Chinatown gambling. Quite a few laundrymen who go to Chinatown each Sunday seldom take part in any gambling. This group, however, may bet on white-pigeon lottery occasionally. Every Sunday afternoon laundrymen come from all parts of the metropolis to Chinatown, and all evening and night all the gambling houses are crowded with chance-taking fortune seekers, pursuing excitement. Some, as a matter of fact, just stay on with the gambling to kill time or get stimulation for the sake of stimulation, and they create the busiest time of the week for the places, as shown in Table 15.2.

With the laundrymen's participation in gambling on Sunday, the numbers increase approximately two-thirds. Table 15.2 does not fully reflect the most intense gambling hour of the day, for 9:00 P.M. to 10:00 P.M. is not the busiest hour. By this time, some of the gamblers have probably gone back to their laundries, for they have to start working early Monday morning.

There are a number of lottery agents who visit laundries and chop suey houses daily, earning their living by the 5 percent commission from the gambling houses and 10 percent from the winners, catching six spots or more. These agents visit only their friends and relatives. The lottery ticket buyer would not purchase from a stranger. This is a matter of trust and confidence. One may make his bet by telephone to a store which has

TABLE 15.1
Gambling Houses in Chinatown, Chicago (1939)

Gambling House	Number of Fan-Tan Tables	Number of Units White Pigeon Lottery	Number of Units Tze-Fa Lottery
Money Make Money	4	4	1
Strange Strange	4	8	1
Wealthy and Noble	2	0	0
Singapore	2	0	0
Coming of Luck	2	0	0
Cave of West Lake	4	0	0
Source of Wealth	2	0	0
Source of Progress*	2	0	0
Total	22	12	2

NOTE: All, except one place, are in the new Chinatown, between Cermak Road and Wentworth Avenue. The gambling house in the old Chinatown is indicated by an asterisk. Names are translated literally.

TABLE 15.2
Distribution of the Number of Fan-Tan Gamblers in
All the Gambling Houses in Chinatown

Gambling House	Sun.	Mon.	Tues.	Wed.	Thurs.	Fri.	Sat.
Money Make Money	28	13	29	50	67	38	50
Strange Strange	56	27	46	64	56	29	44
Wealthy and Noble	50	0	0	0	0	0	0
Singapore	63	0	0	0	0	0	0
Coming of Luck	23	0	0	0	0	0	0
Cave of West Lake	106	32	0	32	0	0	0
Source of Wealth	12	0	0	0	0	0	0
Total	338	72	75	146	123	67	94

NOTE: This sample is a weekly enumeration from November 19 to November 26, 1935, during the sample hour of 9:00 P.M. to 10:00 P.M.

assigned someone to take care of lottery buyers, and the store gets a commission from the gambling houses. Practically every store in China-town serves as a lottery agent. The store is responsible for bringing the ballot to the lottery office, and for paying the gambling house the amount bet on behalf of the buyer. In case the buyer wins, the agent is responsible for informing the buyer as soon as possible and asking the winner for advice on how to handle the pay-off. Of course, the agent would receive 10 percent of the total pay-off.

2. The Gambling Complex

The gambling situation created in Chinatown for the laundryman is a complex of elements. It involves all sorts of psychological urges, conflicting interests, and social pressures, so that an individual is more or less trapped into the situation. The laundryman has been working hard all week, and on Sunday he wants a thrill and relief from dullness and routine. Hong-ping may sometimes speak indignantly against gambling, but since he has nothing else to do he joins the gambling party.

Last time I lost forty dollars in the Lime House party. That was a party sponsored by the National Salvation Committee, you know. Since it was a special occasion, I went just to take a look but eventually I lost forty dollars.

This time I brought only forty dollars with me. I was trying to get back my money. But if I lose, I wouldn't lose much, see?

Someone asked me to play ma-jong. "No!" I refused. "It takes too much time. I want to go home early." After a while I stood by the neu-pai table and watched.

"Del-ka-ma! I'll put my money down all on one hand," I thought, "and if I lose, I'll go home." Then I stuck one dollar into my other pocket—that was for carfare to go home, in case I lose. Then I put all the money I had down.

"Well! I won! Next I put out the same amount. Again I won. Then it was my turn to be the banker. Kung-po saw it, he put seventy dollars against me and Yang-chui had about one hundred dollars. Then I threw down the dice. I was the victor, but my number was not big enough to win over my biggest opponents. If I had had six more points, I could have cleaned up the whole table. Well, anyhow I won about three hundred dollars within a short time.

Then I quit. If I were to stay longer, I would lose it back to them.

The loser wants revenge. If he is not a habitual gambler, he is able to control himself and stop gambling as soon as he makes some gain. Both the preceding and following cases represent a type of gambler who bets occasionally; gambling to him is more or less a pastime. In this particular situation the party was organized to raise money for war funds, and attending such a party has a patriotic motive and, of course, is a social event that everybody is invited to attend.

I had no intention of gambling. I was up there looking here and there, trying to amuse myself. Finally I stood beside Kai-chung and he said, "Look at that table there. All of them gambling are clansmen of yours. You had better go over to join them, too. That will make it a family affair."

I walked over and took a look. It was Shui-lung, Tunk-li, Chang-wai, and Shui-hing. "Hey, why do you have to get together at one table?" I said to them. "It does not look nice at all."

"What of it?" answered Shui-lung. "Who knows who we are. Come on, you want to put down your bet?"

I put down one dollar. Ah! Lost. Then I put down two dollars. Ah! Lost again. Ah, wah! [comparable to "wow"] Del-ka-ma! This was excitement. Then I put down five dollars. It brought no luck, either! Next I put only two dollars. I won this time. Next I put down seven dollars. Lost. Then I put on two. No luck.

Within a short time I lost fourteen dollars. Del-ka-ma! I was not going to play it anymore. I quit and turned over to bet on fan-tan.

First I put down five dollars. I won. Then I doubled it. I won also. Soon I had fifteen dollars. Then I put it all down. Won again!

So I won forty dollars. By this time Tung-wei saw me. He urged me to keep on. But I was ready to quit.

"No! That is all," I responded and left.

But unless one leaves Chinatown immediately, he may get back to gambling again, for the winner tends to think of winning some more, as for example in the next case.

At first I won about sixty dollars. If I had known when to stop, I would be a winner. Del-ka-ma! It was too early to go home. It was only seven o'clock, so I want to eat. After supper, I went back there again.

Then I began to bet again. Finally I lost fifty dollars.

No, I lost what I had in my pocket in addition to twenty-five dollars I got from Sing-chang [a cousin]. It was seventy-five dollars altogether.

In order to avoid losing money by gambling, some gamblers try to keep away from Chinatown, at least for a time. Others have tried to reform.

Wong has changed recently; he doesn't go down to Chinatown every Sunday. He used to be quite a gambler, but now he seems very much a *ho-joy* [*hauzai*] (good son). Hom-shih, his boss, told me that Wong sent one thousand dollars back to Hong Kong a few months ago, paying off an old debt. He seems now to be aiming to save money.

Wong was asked why he did not want to visit Chinatown. "I don't like to go down to Chinatown unless I have something to do. It is too far—it takes about two hours. It is tiresome. I would rather stay home and get some sleep.

"My second son's marriage? Del-ka-ma! Even I, myself, merely hold my penis with my hand when I go to sleep [meaning his wife is in China and he has no woman to sleep with]. Let him wait. I have no money just now. I am not living better than he is. He is only a boy as yet.

"No! No! I am not going to gamble anymore. I simply don't go down to Chinatown. How can I gamble? You are sure to lose in the long-run. A person like Yow-tom, for example, has won about twenty-five dollars every week for the last several weeks. But bad luck came last Sunday. I think he was cleaned out. When he came home he was so gloomy. I did not want to irritate him. He went to bed without washing his feet. His cheerful eyes disappeared. When he wins, he is cheerful and talkative. But he was too quiet last Sunday night.

"Well, he even denied that he lost in gambling. He said he went to a hotel and slept until five o'clock and then went to Chinatown and had something to eat and then came home. I don't believe this story.

"He can't fool me. As a gambler myself, I know when a gambler stops gambling. When he is winning, he won't stop. He only stops when he loses to the last cent. Then he may stop until he has money for the next time. It is said, 'The fucking penis and the gambling hands.' The gambler won't stop until his money runs out."

The reformed gambler may persist in saving his money, but it takes strong will-power. Staying away from Chinatown by remaining in the laundry shop is very dull and very lonely, indeed. No one can completely hold out for a long time. He may go down there once in a while and make a bet for some extra money. In case he loses a little, it does not matter. He may get it back some other time.

Other people purposely avoid going to Chinatown for several weeks in order to accumulate a larger amount of money for a stronger attack upon the gambling houses.

> I lost a couple of hundred dollars recently. As a matter of fact, I didn't gamble for almost three weeks. My luck is gone lately. I just throw away my money if I keep on gambling. So, I'll wait until my luck comes back.
>
> Last month, I pretty nearly cleaned up the Sing Ka Po [Singapore, a gambling house] treasury. The difference was decided on the last couple of hands. I won over eight hundred. I would have broken their bank if I had won the last two hands.
>
> I started with about two hundred. But if I had won, I would have had two thousand and six hundred dollars in my hand now. I wanted to clean them up and get my money back. With it I could go back to China for a visit. Del-ka-ma! They got me instead.
>
> I have not gambled since then [April 28, 1938].
>
> It is the way gambling life is. I only gamble with my spare money. It is nothing too serious. If I have luck, I win a couple hundred, and the same thing when I have no luck, I lose. Take tonight for example, in case I could get a couple of *ma-po* [*yabao*] (jack-pots), I would have a couple of thousand in my pocket now.
>
> I was thinking of playing another hand. I finally decided not to do it. When luck comes, it stays. I have about thirty dollars left. I keep it for the next time.
>
> You must be wise when you gamble, but most of the time it depends wholly on luck. In case I lose, I call it "hard luck," and hope to get it back next time.
>
> It depends mostly on luck. The last two Sundays, I won about fifteen hundred dollars. I thought if this luck should keep on for another two or three weeks, I could go back to China.
>
> It is indeed strange, sometimes. When luck comes, you are never disap-

pointed. Time after time, from table to table they have to pay you. As I won enough money I bet heavier and the boss became afraid of me.

I was winning until Keng-po [relative] asked me to lend him one hundred dollars. He was gambling and was losing. He came over, "Give me one hundred dollars." I gave it to him. After this, my luck had a bad turn.

There is another incident which I know caused my bad luck. I had a dog here. It had white fur with two yellow spots on its back. It was a "dog king" [*gouwang*]. As soon as I had it, my luck came along with it. It was very unfortunate for me to lose that dog. It went out of the door and disappeared. I looked all over, but I could not find it any more. . . .

Oh! Since I lost that dog, I have had hard luck in everything. When I came home on this Sunday evening, I found my place was robbed. The burglar came in from the back door and took all my small change and several bundles of laundry. I found two bundles out on the corner the next morning. I had to pay those customers whose laundry was stolen.

Ever since Keng-Po borrowed that one hundred dollars from me and the loss of my "dog king", I have had bad luck. I am hard up now. I have lost about six hundred dollars in two weeks [June 17, 1938].

It seems the gambling Chinese laundryman is aware of the fact that, in the long run, he will be victimized by the game of chance, yet, once he is in it, he is tempted to seek revenge. In the course of time, the gambler tends to lose his personal life orientation; his outlook on life becomes more or less oriented to seeking pleasure and pain sensations so as to offset his dull and monotonous daily routine in the laundry, and his impulse, after all, is to win in order to achieve a certain purpose. Gambling, therefore, is often related to the hope of taking a return trip to China. It becomes the only means to that end for laundrymen who have been victimized by gambling.

As usual, the gambler tends to be superstitious, believing in luck and in hunches. Any superstitious object, move, utterance, or symbol may mean "bad luck." But any sign considered as lucky would make him take a chance of gaining something for nothing.

Once I saved about fifteen hundred dollars with which I planned to open a chop suey house. My partner-to-be didn't agree with me on some matter of the planning. I was disappointed. Seeing I had not enough to do it alone, I brought the money down to Chinatown and gambled with it. I thought if I could win about three more thousand, I would go back to China instead of opening any restaurant.

But I didn't really mean to gamble away all my money. It was a strange dream I had that made me do so. The night before I gambled with the money, I joked with Ho Lung, a fellow worker of mine, saying, "Ho Lung, give me a dream so that I can win something on the lottery." I said this to him regarding him as a ghost. Then I fell asleep soon afterward. That night I was really dreaming about Ho Lung's ghost. He came and said, "You have no luck on lottery; you better be on fan-tan. . . ."

Del-ka-ma! I believed this hunch. Then I said to myself, "Well, I have not enough money to open a restaurant, why not try my luck? This may be my chance. Then I brought about one hundred dollars down to Chinatown. I began to bet on fan-tan. Bad luck! I lost all I had in my pocket.

The very next day, I went down to Chinatown again. An English fellow wanted to challenge me. He had been betting heavily. He took a great big bunch of bills out of his pocket and showed them to me. I was then playing tin-kau, you see. Del-ka-ma! Finally I lost again.

From that time on, I lost my head. I kept on gambling until I lost everything, within two weeks. Think of my misery!

I seldom gamble in recent years. Only occasionally I walk into the gambling house. Sometimes I put out a small bet. I quit without getting too serious about either winning or losing.

It is evident that luck and hunches seem to be merely elements of the psychological complex of the disorganized personal adjustment. There are cases that show efforts at reorientation which fail time and again and eventually an individual may spend every dollar he earns to get revenge. But hunches and dreams keep on playing an important role in the world of Chinatown gambling, in spite of the fact that some dreams are not answered favorably.

Hunches and dreams are believed to bring luck not only in fan-tan and other kinds of gambling, but also in betting on lottery. In some instances, the bettors are extremely lucky, as in the following case:

Him-wah is not a gambler; he has never bet on fan-tan or any other kind of gambling. He seldom bets even on the lottery. Two weeks ago he needed some money badly to send home. He had been thinking how to raise the money and did buy a lottery ticket, hoping to win some money to meet the economic pressure of the moment. But after two weeks of trying, he only lost money. Then this happened, according to his own story:

My relative, Old Mr. Goon Shih sent me three dollars from Minnesota; he asked me to buy a lottery ticket for him. He had already marked out the characters on three different tickets. As soon as I received his letter, I walked to the drug store to call up Chung Lim [an agent]. I gave him the order exactly according to Old Mr. Goon Shih's letter. Immediately after I repeated the characters and the message, I recalled the dream I had last night.

I dreamed I was walking on the street in the rain. The next morning, I found the motor of my wash machine out of order. I had to get a man in to fix it. While I was out, it was really raining. At that moment, I thought of betting on the lottery. But after I got back to my shop, I forgot all about it. Then I received the letter from Old Mr. Goon Shih. He wanted to take a chance and sent three dollars. Since I had to go out to call up the agent on his behalf, I might as well take a chance, too.

If it had not been for him, I might have forgotten it entirely. I have lost so much on the lottery, I dared not buy big. I bet only fifty cents.

"Wait a minute," I called Chung Lim's attention, "I want to buy a ticket, too!" I thought about it for a moment, then decided to take "Hang-Lo-Yee," meaning "walking in the rain," according to my dream and what I did that morning.

Late that night, after my shop was closed, I was getting ready to go to bed. Suddenly someone knocked at the door. When I opened it, Cousin Shui-pui came in.

"You caught NINE spots!"

At first I thought it was Old Mr. Goon Shih who had won. But Cousin Shui-pui assured me that it was my fifty cents on "Hang-Lo-Yee" which caught nine spots.

It happens very, very rarely that one catches nine spots. I won one thousand dollars. But I have spent all the money now. I sent five hundred dollars home and some for paying an old debt. I spent fifty dollars on the lottery the following day, and have given away some sixty dollars to different persons.

I should have bought a dollar and a half ticket instead of a fifty cent one. I could have won three thousand dollars instead of one thousand.

The winner gets excitement and satisfaction just from being able to have his winnings in his possession, and he has the urge to win some more. He is restless. He has the money but still has a disorganized personality. He cannot sleep or eat, and thinks only of winning some more, according to the following story:

Del-ka-ma! It is the strangest thing in all the world. Several years ago I won four thousand dollars within one week and a half. I won more than two thousand dollars in one single afternoon. After I got so much money all at once, I just didn't know what to do with it. You didn't feel like seeing a girl either, nor even like getting something to eat. You are so happy that you can't even sleep. Very funny. Then you think all the time of going back to win more.

I thought of going home. As a matter of fact I had already sent two thousand back to Hong Kong and I kept about three thousand with me. At that time I had to fix a return permit. I went to Moy Lum, but he informed me that I had to wait two or three months.

What is the use? In the long run money goes back to them [gambling houses]. I waste every penny I earn. Now I can never expect to get back to China unless I win three thousands on the lottery.

Del-ka-ma! Finally I lost all of it.

The interesting point in this case, and to be sure in many other cases, is whether or not he can successfully make his return trip to China. In this situation he can seldom control his gambling impulse of taking more and more risks, and, motivated also by revenge, he has become a habitual gambler. He may be heavily in debt and may deprive himself of daily and personal needs. When he wants money for something, he has to depend upon his gambling luck, as in the following case:

I want to build a porch so that we can keep cool during the summer months. It would cost about seventy or more. Well, that is just the trouble. I have not the money for it.

I thought I might as well try the luck. At first I won about thirty dollars. I should have quit then. But I did not. As if there was a devil in my mind, I thought I could win one hundred, for thirty was not enough to have the porch built. And I had not paid the rent yet.

I walked out already. Later I was asked to play ma-jong. Then I played a round but made only five hundred points, on the basis of five dollars per thousand points. I won just two and a half dollars.

Then we went to eat in a restaurant. After supper, I should have come right home, to save my money. Instead, I went into the gambling house again. I was still winning. At one time I had about sixty dollars in my hand. Then I started losing and eventually I lost every penny, including fifteen dollars of my own.

What a low-down one I am!

If a man loses, he thinks his luck will be better next time, so as soon as he has money he takes another chance, each and every week. If he wins, he wants to win more, having all sorts of things to do with the money. If the amount won is large enough, he plans to take a return trip to China and pay off his debts, buy land, and build a house; if it is a small amount, he may buy something which may or may not be necessary and useful. He seems to realize that the money would go back to the gambling house anyway, if he does not buy something which he would not, under the present condition, use as a commodity for gambling.

That's the trouble. No matter how much I earn, I gamble it away. Every month, I pay the rent and pay for other utilities and I have no money left. All gambled away. Well, you hope to win something, you see. But, in the long run, you are really the loser.

When I win, I take the money and go downtown. You know what I do? I buy a watch, a radio, a fountain pen, a camera, or an overcoat. I have bought a lot of such unnecessary things. It is good policy to buy something, you see, useful or not, because you have something, anyhow. The money goes back to the gambling house if you don't get something for yourself. See this radio [*pointing to the radio on the table*]. It cost thirty-five dollars. I bought it when I won a hundred dollars last year. See, to have something is better than nothing.

Sing Ka Po [a gambling house] lost over six hundred dollars last Sunday. It had to be closed in order to prevent further loss. The house, too, has bad luck sometimes. I won just fifteen dollars. To gamble, either win or lose, for me doesn't matter much. I feel just the same when I lose. Some people are different. When they lose, they get very depressed and mad. They would lose their temper easily and are irritable at everything. Don't go near to Siu-wai when he loses. I am not that kind of person. I don't feel so upset at all when I lose. One cannot expect to win all the time, anyway.

About two years ago when I was loafing in Chinatown, I lost over eight hundred dollars within a month. That was the period when Chan-po was the treasurer and he asked me to be the pay-off man. About a hundred or so at a time, within a short period, I lost all the money I had in the bank. I took part in all kinds of gambling. I bought heavily on tse-fa [a lottery]. Gee-goon and Gow-kee, who operated the lottery units were afraid of me. I could possibly clean up their business. I bet eight or nine dollars a character. Sometimes I won over a hundred dollars on one betting.

As soon as I reached Chicago, I was offered a job in the gambling enterprise here in Chinatown. . . . I didn't like to take it—what is the wisdom of working for nothing; I mean, of the money I earn I can keep nothing. The money would not be mine. However, I did stay for two weeks. I worked as a pay-off man on the fan-tan table. I gambled myself, but I couldn't save a cent in my pocket. I realized that, and I thought I had better keep away from Chinatown. So I went back to work in my father's laundry.

Once I won one thousand four hundred forty dollars for Lee-chung. At that time, he caught three thousand dollars in the lottery. Then he brought all that money to the fan-tan house. He gambled with it and within an hour or so he lost almost half of the money. I stood beside him, betting myself. Then Fook-sun suggested to Lee-chung, "Let Yick-kung play for you, change luck, go ahead."

Then Lee-chung handed over to me his money. Within half an hour, I won back for him one thousand four hundred and forty dollars. I kept the 2, 2, 4, 4 strategy and won. Then I handed the money back to him. It was my biggest gambling. . . .

You wait and see, some day I am going to clean up Gee Gun's tze-fa house. I bet one dollar on *pon-qai* the other day but it turned out to be *han-wen* [ed. note: phrases bet upon in tze-fa]. I shall watch him carefully and then hit him with eight or nine dollars on one bet. He can't get away with my money. I don't lose in betting tze-fa, on the whole.

One Sunday evening last month, I lost eighty dollars because I wanted to win a couple of free tickets to a show. When one gambles he expects to win. If he loses, it is his hard luck.

The most dangerous time for a gambling laundryman is when he is unemployed and has a large sum of money on hand. He is bound to visit Chinatown, and perhaps a game of ma-jong is usually his way of taking a vacation. His recreation is likely to be in and out of the gambling houses in Chinatown. And the bigger the chance he takes, the heavier he loses. Yet he knows the gambling house is the eventual winner. His gambling impulse becomes routine, and what he gets from year to year is the pleasure and pain sensation.

3. The Gambler's Chance

Few are the persons who win their return trip to China by gambling. One experienced laundryman and professional gambler stated that only 40 percent of the Chinese immigrants returned to China, while 60 percent remained and died in America. To what extent is this statement accurate? No exact quantitative data are available to substantiate it. There are other factors correlated with the sojourner's failure to return to his homeland, but excessive gambling seems to be the most tragic one. The following case is a typical example:

I have been here in this country thirty-five years. How old do you think I am? Well, if I am not yet sixty, I am within one or two years of it.

I have never been back to China. I am a bad gambler—can't save enough money to take the trip.

. . . I have been working in this place for over thirteen years. I should have a lot of money by this time. But, alas! Every penny I earn, I gamble away.

I have a son here. He is working in a laundry on Sixty-third Street. He came about three years ago. He is married and has a son. His wife and son are in China.

I earn about eleven dollars to twelve dollars a week. Business is poor this year. Usually it would be much better around the Fourth of July. We had over seventy-dollar business to do this time last year. Look at this year's business; it is not encouraging at all.

We have a Negro girl to help iron. Yes, spend a little more money. What of it? No matter how much I earn, I cannot keep the money anyway. Why should I work so hard and bring all my money to Chinatown and lose it. I might as well take it easy. No matter how much I earn, the money is not mine. Sometimes I lose my last penny. I have to borrow money from people I know in order to have carfare to come back here. . . .

Del-ka-ma! I am poor already and yet there are so many ways they can squeeze money out of you. We have to contribute to the war fund and the air force fund. According to my idea, as long as China continues to fight, she will win.

July 8, 1938.—I lost until I was penniless last Sunday. I did not even have enough money to pay my carfare home. Finally one of my cousins saw me and said, "Do you want to go back now? Come with me. I will take care of your carfare." Then I took the same street car with him and he paid my fare. If I had not met him, I might have had to borrow seven cents from some one. Ah! Being a gambler! So useless!

I have been losing for the last three months continually. My cousin teased me. "Sing Ka Po [a gambling house] lost at least one thousand dollars this afternoon. Why didn't you go and receive your dividend?" Del-ka-ma! Some one else was lucky but not I.

July 14, 1938.—I have not had even fifty dollars in my hand during the last five years. See, what a break I had. We earn just "several dollars" each week but I can't save it. A loser in gambling every Sunday.

So long as one is a gambler, he is in a mess always. No matter how much you win once, eventually the houses are the winners. You can't get away with it. If the gamblers were always winning, how then can those people in Chinatown live? Sing Ka Po lost one thousand dollars last Sunday. Well, it has gained more than it has lost this Sunday.

If one had to win, he must have big money to gamble with. A poor fellow like I am, I only bet with quarters and half dollars, that wouldn't do any good. You have to bet heavily in order to win much. I have not enough money to gamble; that is why I lose all the time.

This Sunday I won about six dollars at first. I should have gone downtown or come back here to Sixty-third Street to see a show. But I had no company to go to the show with. I hang around in Chinatown. Finally I got back to the gambling table again. I lost all, including my own eight dollars.

I usually sleep until three o'clock every Sunday. Then I get up and go down to Chinatown. I don't come home until midnight. I hang around in different gambling houses the whole afternoon and the whole evening. . . .

I am an awful lottery buyer, too. When I bet I put at least two dollars

TheChineseLaundryman

---

on a ticket. I usually telephone Kee Chung Lung or Sun Hong Sing [stores] to bet on the lottery during the week days, too. Last week I lost eight dollars on the lottery, telephoned to Chinatown twice, it cost me four dollars and when I was in Chinatown, I bought two times at two dollars each; it cost me another four dollars.

Ha! A gambler is indeed a useless person. He is hopeless.

December 15, 1938—Two of us can finish the work and can make a few more dollars. But what difference does it make? The more I earn, the more I lose in gambling. I don't want to work too hard for the gambling house! I would rather keep her [Negro girl] and take it easy. . . .

I missed a seven spot luck on the lottery last Sunday. I would have had at least three hundred dollars in my pocket by this time if I had bought it. See, I earned only eleven dollars last week. The first thing I did that afternoon was to go to the drug store and buy a carton of cigarettes for one dollar. About one-thirty I went down to Chinatown. As a rule, I spend two dollars every Sunday on the lottery. I bet on the same words week after week. I had it in mind when I was riding in the street car that I would do that the first thing when I reached Chinatown. I had a little dream, a dream about the lottery.

When I reached Chinatown, instead of going to buy a lottery ticket, I went into Sai Woo [a coffee shop]. Sipping my coffee, an idea came into my mind. I thought I might as well take a chance on fan-tan first. I thought if I could only win two dollars, I could buy more than one ticket on the lottery. So I walked through the door which linked the coffee shop and the gambling house. I put on two dollars first. Lost! Another two dollars. Lost also! Then I put on my third two dollars. Ha! I lost three hands. So six out of my ten dollars were gone. How could I buy any lottery with only four dollars? I thought then it was no use of buying any lottery, for I was having bad luck anyway.

Del-ka-ma! I almost stepped into the lottery house. It seemed as if there was a ghost making me change my mind. I thought I had better keep the four dollars and bet fan-tan later. I might yet have a chance to win my money back and then buy lottery tickets later.

So I walked over the street to Wo Tai Chow [a gambling house] and I stood by and watched the betting first. I was afraid that I might lose the rest of my money quickly. I just stood there, watching other people play for hours. Del-ka-ma! I was almost tempted to put on my money but I tried hard to control myself.

Finally one of my neighbors asked if I wanted a cup of coffee. "Come on," he said. "All right," I responded, "I had a cup not so long ago but I can take another. Let's go."

Then I walked over to Sai Woo with him.

Del-ka-ma! I saw your clansman winning the other day. Oh! He made it big. He put on about fifty dollars in one hand. I think he won at least four or five hundred dollars. You know, that one at North Kedzie Avenue. He must have a lot of money. Is his business good? He wins all the time.

Then I walked over to Kee Kee [another gambling house] and saw Hom Po [a partner]. I stood by and watched a little while. I then put on one dollar. The numbers turned out to be 4, 5, 2 at the moment; it tempted me. I caught two dollars. It was 4; I bet for 4. On the next hand I put two dollars. I kept on playing until almost eight o'clock. I was winning. After I exchanged my checks into money, I got twenty-one dollars. I paid loans of ten dollars, right there to different persons. It was the right thing to do. I have to pay back the money, otherwise they won't have anything to do with me.

Then I walked out to take a look at the lottery result. Ha! Ah! Ya! Del-ka-ma! I found I could have caught seven spots on the lottery if I had bought it during the daytime! How very unfortunate! I would have at least three hundred dollars now. See, two dollars on the seven spot would win about four hundred dollars. I could very likely buy back about fifty dollars and the other fifty would be commission for the agent and other for gifts and dinner party.

I am sure I have no luck. Something acts like a ghost within me to make me lose all the time. Almost got rich, at least for three hundred but it turned away from me! How happy I could be now, if I won the money. Week after week, my pocket is rather empty. The best chance is to win on the lottery. That's why I buy lottery tickets every Sunday. Sometimes I telephone to Chinatown and buy a ticket during week days. One who has not much money to gamble can't win much on fan-tan. so I think my only hope is on the lottery.

Look at Keng-po; he won three thousand dollars on the lottery last week. It was last Saturday; Fong Ming-shih went to his store and dictated the ten characters. Keng-po made a mistake. He marked five characters that Fong didn't intend; Fong's ticket was corrected. Then Keng-po said to Fong, "If you don't want this set, I will take it myself. See who has the luck." Fong didn't mind, of course. What was the result? Keng-po caught eight spots on the mistaken ticket while Fong caught only four spots on his. It was Fong who brought Keng-po the luck. Things are strange sometimes.

The mind of the gambling laundryman seems to exist primarily in the world of gambling in Chinatown. His trip back to his homeland becomes hopeless on account of his gambling habit. And yet he seems to cling to only one thing—the luck of winning on the lottery. While it is in itself a dubious proposition, this hope, however, is shared by many others, especially those so-called "old overseas Chinese" whose economic condition is not promising.

The habitual gambler is restless whenever he has money in his pocket, and immediately he thinks of taking a chance in an effort to gain back what he has lost. When he has no money, his time is extremely dull and purposeless. He may have to borrow money to gamble, or use an unscrupulous means to obtain money in order to satisfy the drive to get revenge. An extreme gambling impulse often brings the individual misery and suffering.

July 12, 1938.—I went down to Chinatown about one o'clock last Sunday. I stayed until three and then I went downtown, window shopping. Oh, I walked more than twenty blocks, passing by the door of some of the movie houses, looking at the pictures on display. I didn't like any of them. I didn't go in.

Finally at six o'clock, I returned to Chinatown as I was pretty hungry. I went in a restaurant and had something to eat. After the supper I came right home.

I could have stayed longer, yes, if I had had the money. I had no money to gamble with, so what was the purpose of staying? So I came home earlier than usual.

What? I lost about seven dollars before I went downtown. I had only one dollar and some small change when I left for downtown. I thought I had better leave before I lose to the last penny. When I returned to Chinatown I still thought of taking a chance with fifty cents. But I was not so sure. I hesitated to get into the gambling house again. Finally I decided to come home.

You can never win anything if you are too anxious and nervous about it. To win, one must have a lot of money and deal with it boldly. You must not be afraid. Put down the money on a big stake—don't care whether you win or lose. You always win this way.

I have not much money to play with and that is why I am the victim all the time. Sometimes I have made up my mind that I must not go to Chinatown or gamble again. But what shall I do? I can't sleep all the time every Sunday. I can't stay here the whole day long. Eventually I can't resist the temptation. As soon as it is about one o'clock, automatically I would put on my shoes and my coat and soon I would be in Chinatown.

August 31, 1931.—Sure, where else is there to go besides Chinatown? It is only once a week. I have nothing to do in Chinatown, but as soon as it is one o'clock every Sunday I can't help thinking about going there. Sometimes I am almost sure that going to Chinatown means losing money. Just the same, when the time comes, what you are likely to do is put on your shoes and coat and there you go.

As I lost so much a week before last, I decided not to go down there last Sunday. But I couldn't resist the temptation. First I stayed home to read the book you brought me until five o'clock. I felt so lonely that I put on my coat and went out to take a walk along the Midway. Then a thought came into my mind that it was all right for me to go to Chinatown for supper. It seemed as if I had something to buy there, too. As I walked up to the street corner the street car ran along. Other people got on the car and so did I. I was in Chinatown anyhow.

I did not gamble, however. Yes, I was in a gambling house, watching other people betting. I had no money otherwise I might not have been able to resist the temptation.

After supper I went to buy some food for Monday. Then I went to Chung Wah Association [C.C.B.A.] to hear the speaking, public lectures against the Japanese invasions in China, you know.

After the speech it was nine. I came right home.

September 22, 1938.—I was in Chinatown the whole day last Sunday. No, I didn't bet much on fan-tan. I lost about two dollars and I quit.

When I was in another gambling house, I was asked to play tin-kau. I accepted and sat down. I didn't get up until half past seven. I won at first, about ten dollars. Soon a man won continuously, six or seven hands, when I was a banker. I was broke. Finally I lost about six dollars.

Then I got up and went to get something to eat. After supper it was about eight. I came right home.

October 20, 1938.—No, I did not gamble last Sunday. I had no money. For the coming three or four weeks I had better stay home. I lost too heavily week before last, more than fifty dollars. The most miserable thing was that the money was not mine. Someone else entrusted me to keep it and I gambled with it.

I had better not think of going down to Chinatown for the coming three or four Sundays, that's all. I have to save the amount to pay back to my cousin.

The business is getting poorer and poorer. I make about ten dollars a week. It will take at least four more weeks to accumulate fifty dollars.

Think of it! What good is a gambler? A gambler is just a hopeless person, that's all. A man comes over to this country with great hope. But gradually he realizes he is in a helpless situation. If he is a gambler, he might as well consider that he is a goner.

A person like me can't be expected to have a chance of going back to China anymore. . . . How can one go back to China if he loses every penny he earns?

October 27, 1938.—Yes, I was in Chinatown for a while. But I did not stay long. I did not plan to go down; I just passed through after Sunday School.

Yes, the Sunday School reopened. I did not want to go but the church sent me letter after letter, urging me to attend the class. I was so lonely that day, I finally went back to Sunday School.

Everything was as usual—nothing special. My teacher, a man, the same man, was teaching me to read the Bible, the Christian Bible. I have no heart to learn to read it. I am getting too old to learn English anymore.

After Sunday School, I could have come home directly. But I thought about going to Chinatown. I thought I could at least spare one dollar to buy a lottery ticket. If I win, all my problems are solved.

Caught nothing! One more dollar is gone, that's all. But I didn't even get into the gambling house. I came right home after I learned I lost the dollar. Sure, I waited for it. I waited about an hour before the result was out. I caught only three spots.

Then I came right home around five-thirty.

March 22, 1939.—I got up about one o'clock Sunday. I went over to Sixty-third Street and had a cup of coffee and a cake. I then walked back and forth on the streets, looking for a good movie show. But I didn't like any of them. About three o'clock I took a street car to Chinatown instead.

I had about thirty-five dollars in my pocket. No, I didn't earn that much that week. I had only fifteen dollars as my wages. I won some money the week before last, see. I won about forty dollars that day. I paid back a man five dollars I owed him. During the week I telephoned to Chinatown to bid eight dollars on the lottery and spent about ten or fifteen on something else.

This week, del-ka-ma! I lost all. As soon as I got down there I walked into the gambling house. I put five dollars on and then another five dollars until I lost fifteen in ten to fifteen minutes. Then instead of putting on five dollars, I put on only one dollar. I stayed about an hour and a half and all my money was gone.

When you saw me at the street corner I was already cleaned up. The man who was talking to me was a cousin of mine. He wanted to borrow some money from me. He had bad luck! I had only enough carfare to get home. And he came to ask me to let him have five dollars. I told him my fate.

He lost also. He gambled in another house. He thought I had luck. I could not help myself that time.

Del-ka-ma! I hadn't even money for my supper. Later I met a fellow by the name of Moy. He invited me for dinner. After dinner I came right home to sleep.

I thought of going downtown instead. I wish I had gone downtown, window shopping. Or up to a hotel and see a girl. It would be far better than going to Chinatown and gambling with the money.

But it is very strange. As soon as I am in Chinatown, I can't help but go to the gambling house.

This case, perhaps, presents a clearer picture of the man and his environment which molds the social isolation of the Chinese laundryman and also his disorganized personal life. Gambling at first is just a recreation, but becomes pathological because it kills the man's self-control and his hope of making a return trip to China. He failed to save enough for the trip because of his gambling activities. Gambling seems to be something imposed upon him. Once he is in it, he cannot free himself from it. He almost hates gambling, and yet he is irresistibly attracted to the gambling house. He has suffered from losing his money and from abandoning the hope of returning to China. But his life would be extremely dull without gambling in Chinatown. At least it provides his lonely life with some pleasure and pain sensation from the gambling. And he hopes to win on the lottery in order to gain his return trip to China.

As a member of a one-sex group, there is absent the normal restraints of home and family. Besides, he has surplus money in his pocket above his daily needs. The world of the gambler becomes his world. There is a great probability that he may drop into a gambling house to look around. Soon he is likely to take a chance, for there is "nothing else to do," and "nowhere else to go." "If you don't gamble, what are you going to Chinatown for?" is often an utterance of some significance, as far as Chinatown gambling goes.

NOTES

1. Other examples are the Irish Sweepstakes and the Mexican Lottery.

2. W. I. Thomas, "The Gaming Instinct," *American Journal of Sociology,* VI (1901), 750–63.

3. E. W. Burgess, *Report to Governor Horner,* June 24, 1935.

4. Private interview document.

5. J. D. Ball, *The Chinese at Home* (London: The Religious Tract Society, 1912), p. 314.

6. Lin Yutang, *My Country and My People* (New York: Reynal and Hitchcock, 1935), p. 173.

7. S. D. Gamble, *Peking: A Social Survey* (New York: George H. Doran Company, 1921), p. 230.

8. *Chicago Tribune,* November 12, 1930.

9. A. Bonnard, *In China* (London: G. Routledge and Sons, 1926), pp. 312–13.

10. Lu Hsun, "Life Story of Ah Q," trans. Chan Wong, *China Today,* II, No. 2 (November, 1935), 37–39.

CHAPTER XVI

SEX AND
PERSONAL DISORGANIZATION

SEX AND PERSONAL disorganization, under certain situations, may be correlated. The Chinese laundryman represents a minority, having a sex ratio of male far over female since its first migration to the shores of California in the gold rush period. A majority are married, but their wives remain in China and they can visit their wives only when they are able to take the return trip home. In many cases, it means years of waiting and long separation. Barred, in this way, from normal married life and legitimate sex relations, and emancipated from primary-group control in the mobility of city life, the laundryman is inevitably led to seek sex satisfaction with prostitutes. It is obvious that sex tends to become a social problem when the ratio in a given population is predominantly male over

TABLE 16.1
Sex Ratio of Chinese in the
United States (1860–1940)

Year	Male	Female	Per Cent		Males per 100 Females
			Male	*Female*	
1940	57,389	20,115	74.1	25.9	282.5
1930	59,802	15,152	79.8	20.2	394.7
1920	53,891	7,748	87.4	12.6	695.5
1910	66,856	4,675	93.5	6.5	1,430.1
1900	89,341	4,522	95.0	5.0	1,887.2
1890	103,620	3,868	69.4	3.6	2,678.9
1880	100,686	4,779	95.5	4.5	2,106.8
1870	58,633	4,566	92.8	7.2	1,284.1
1860	33,149	1,784	94.9	4.1	1,858.1

NOTE: Data compiled from the U.S. Census, 1860–1940.

female as in the case of the frontier. But the problem that the Chinese minority faces is not so much the numerical abnormality of so many men to one woman; it is rather the social situation under which one either has to stand long separation from his wife or remain single as a bachelor.

1. The Laundryman Defines His Own Situation

In the Chinese village where the immigrants come from, young men marry around the age of seventeen or eighteen. Male bachelors of thirty and female "old maids" of twenty-five are rarely seen. While the youngsters are growing, their parents arrange their betrothal through a match-maker, and as soon as they are in their teens, the marriage takes place as a family affair. The married son and his bride live with his parents, and with his brother and his brother's wife and children, too, in case the family has more than one son. All in the village are of one surname and everyone is, under the clan system, related to each other.[1] Each person is born into a lineage-rank which must be socially observed. One's conduct conforms to the mores of the clan. Village community life is static, with human behavior under primary-group control.

In the American urban community, the laundryman lives in a situation of a transitory character. He is only a sojourner, and being a foreigner of a distinct cultural background he can hardly make primary-group contacts with non-Chinese, particularly with individuals of the fair sex. Under such conditions maladjustments become inevitable. The mobility of city life readily leads the laundryman to seek sex satisfaction in vice and promiscuity.[2]

The Chinese laundryman seldom or never participates in the American types of night life such as the tavern, the cabaret, the roadhouse, and the dance hall. The immigrant term *cheeh-gai* [*cejie*] (soliciting or dragging on street), which is different from the ordinary Chinese term for prostitution, becomes a popular word used by the Chinese immigrants. It seems that the common type of women the Chinese laundryman had first come into contact with for sex satisfaction was the "street walker." One way or the other, the laundryman met the woman of loose character on the street corner. Moved by her charm and bewildered with sexual hunger and loneliness, the temptation is too strong to resist. He gets the address of the woman and passes it out to some member of his immediate circle.

In some cases, the girls and pimps visit the laundry shop and leave names and addresses on business cards or in handwriting. So, within a social circle, a number of addresses are circulated among its members. Individuals may visit the places alone or go in company.

Recognizing food and sex as essential needs of life in the face of absence from normal married life, the Chinese laundryman comes to justify his behavior in terms of his situation. It becomes "all right" and "nothing wrong" as everybody knows that everybody is having the common experience.

> Mr. Chang is an industrious person; as he works hard and quick, people talk of him as a worthy partner, for he irons eighteen to twenty shirts an hour. But people also speak of him as a stingy person. Some of his clansmen think that he must have saved thousands of dollars. "Oh, he has a lot of money," one said once. "He has a good business and he does not gamble. All his money is either in the bank or sent home to China. He is one of the rich men of our clan."
>
> He does not gamble, but goes to see a prostitute once in a while. "That fellow!" Hsin-ming was relating a story about Mr. Chang with a prostitute, "he used some of that 'love water' on his thing. It took him about half an hour from making the girl. Oh, that head of his thing was nearly skinned. The girl knew that he used a drug; she was mad." Hsin-ming went with Mr. Chang in the adventure and joked about Mr. Chang's stinginess even with sexual experience.
>
> "Oh! You shut up!" retorted Mr. Chang. "How about you? It was you who began to use that sort of thing. . . . I didn't feel it any different but it was all right though. And her, she didn't please me at all. Give her two dollars and had to get out of the place quickly. Among us in this country, who does not go to see girls at all? That is all right, isn't it?"
>
> "Really it is nothing," Mr. Chang continued, "but the only worry is getting venereal disease. Lucky I never caught it. I use those so-called "merry widows" [*fengliu guafu*] (a highly colloquial term for condoms). You don't feel it so good, but it is the only thing that can keep you away from the danger of getting disease. But I don't have any of them now. I forgot to buy them."
>
> "What am I going to do in case I have it? You have to spend a lot of money and suffer from pain before you can get rid of it. That's why I say better not go to prostitutes too often. One makes a mistake if he patronizes them too frequently. No, I go only once in a while."

"Among us in this country, who does not go to see girls at all?" he asks. It represents the conception that patronizing prostitution is justified by the exceptional condition. Unless there is excessive indulgence which causes misery and suffering, the personal status of the individual remains unchanged among his fellow men. In their adventure, the old-timer seems to lead the way. Once the newcomer tries it, he comes to share the common conception of the group and begins to think it a natural thing to do. Mencius, the Chinese sage, was often quoted as saying that "food and sex are instincts" as an alibi among the group.

> It is nothing. I see it now. I did see a girl when I was in Detroit. Well, I went with one of my cousins. No, he is not my real cousin. We just belong to the same village, you know.
>
> I don't see it is anything wrong. To see a girl is a common thing to do, especially in a foreign country. That does no harm so long as you don't get sick from it.
>
> Oh, oh, yes . . . I go. I go to see girls here, too. Where? Well, in a hotel. The hotel right across from the big post office, downtown. There are some girls and pretty ones, too.
>
> Have you ever seen the leg show at R. Theater? Many Chinese were there one Sunday afternoon. There is nothing exciting if one sees it a few times. But the first time I saw the leg show was in Detroit a year ago. Oh, it was worse than this in Chicago. I made me terribly excited. Terrible thing.
>
> I don't care to see such a kind of show any more. I prefer stage shows. That's why I like the State and Lake Theater best in Chicago.

It is interesting to notice, under certain circumstances, that the patronizing of prostitutes may be related to other forms of sexual stimulation, such as burlesque, movies, and picture books. In some Chinese laundries, picture magazines such as *Life, Look,* and screen periodicals are seen. Evidently the laundrymen do not read the words, but they can look at the pictures and respond to the sex appeal of the female figures. In the movie he can at least get some sort of satisfaction. Because of the dramatic actions and the 'close-ups" in the movie, it is more stimulating. But the sexual demonstration in the burlesque show, as the laundryman in the preceding case puts it, is a terrible thing. When passions are aroused by the "leg show" seeking relief with prostitutes is the consequence. In this situation, any moral scruples are overcome. Individuals come to understand each other because they have a common interest, namely, the desire for new experience and the relief of sexual tension. Once rapport is established on the basis of mutual understanding, they may exchange addresses of women and go together for an "expedition."

Barbara S. is my movie sweetheart. She is so pretty and has a lot of sex appeal to me. . . .

Oh! I go to see a movie show every Sunday evening; I have nothing else to do otherwise. I don't go to Chinatown. [He is a reformed gambler, trying to avoid Chinatown gambling.]

I go to Jackie's [American friend] only Saturday. So I have to spend my Sunday evening in the cinema.

Del-ka-ma! This Barbara S. sometimes acts very licentiously. Do you remember the last time I went to cousin [his clansman, a young man who keeps a white girl], that was the time after I saw Barbara act. I was just too aroused after I saw the picture. I went over to ask Him-kin [a neighborhood laundryman] to go to my cousin's place with me.

Then I spent two dollars.

This case represents a type of individual who, different from most of the others, instead of participating in the social world in Chinatown, makes social contacts with neighborhood non-Chinese. In some cases personal relationships may be developed. The Chinese may be welcomed to the non-Chinese's home. In this case Jackie is of Italian descent. However, a laundryman, although unattached to Chinatown's social world, is still a member of a small circle of Chinese in the neighborhood. He kills his time in the cinema and he may patronize prostitution alone or with company. But often he would prefer to go with company; in company he has more fun and is less self-conscious, perhaps.

Early in the afternoon, I dropped in to see Kwok Sang and Bing Lung. Before I could sit down, Bing Lung started to tease him.

"Got some new address?" he began to ask me; that was his usual inquiry whenever he had a chance to see me. "You want to go? Let's go tonight. How about it?"

"Are you sure?" I responded. "All right. Let's go. Maybe Kwok Sang wants to go with us, too, don't you Kwok Sang?"

"If you go—sure," said Kwok Sang, smiling.

"Oh! No! You go too?" Bing Lung said to Kwok Sang mockingly. "You are too young yet."

"What do you mean by too young? Del-ka-ma!" lamented Kwok Sang.

"No! You shouldn't go!" Bing Lung didn't seem to agree, but he turned to me and asked, "All right? Let him go?"

I said Kwok Sang could go and then we went over to Ching Lum, trying to get him to drive us.

In the evening we were together at Ching Lum's place. We started out at nine o'clock. First he headed for the place on the Near North Side, you know where there are Filipinos. In this place there are two girls. One of them has been an inmate of a big brothel on —— Cottage Grove Avenue. Now she and her friend are doing a private business. When we reached there, we rang the doorbell three times, but there was no answer. An old woman from next door peeked out and said to us, "I think they are out for the evening and they probably won't be back until eleven o'clock."

"Let's go to another place," suggested Bing Lung. "Go to that place at —— Cottage Grove Avenue. . . ."

"Go to that Black-Devil-Nest?" Kwok Sang interrupted.

"What's the matter? Are you afraid? I said you are too young!" Bing Lung was teasing Kwok Sang again.

Soon we were at our destination, but nobody seemed to know the exact number of the apartment. We rang, but no answer. We walked right up. Ching Lum insisted that it was apartment number six. We went by the door of number six; there was the noise of a crowd within, singing, laughing, and talking loudly.

"What is this! Oh, let's get out of here. I won't go in there even if there are girls. . . ." Bing Lung was afraid himself.

"Where shall we go then?" Ching Lum asked us. "Ah, let's go to look for the big brothel. Let's see . . . I know, just a few more blocks the other way."

A few blocks away Ching Lum stopped the car. Bing Lung and Ching Lum went out to look for it and we sat in the car waiting. About ten minutes later they came back; they could not find the big brothel either.

"Del-ka-ma! You don't even know the name of the party, how can you ring everybody's doorbell?"

"Where shall we go next?"

"Oh! Let's go to —— South Park."

"Del-ka-ma! But there are only old hens. . . ."

However, we soon reached the place. I was there once before. When we got in, the mistress told us that no girl lived there, but she could call a girl for us quickly. Soon a girl by the name of Jean came. She was tall and about twenty-five years old. Nobody seemed to like to take her. We were trying to be evasive. Finally Ching Lum took the girl first. Not more than ten minutes, he was through! The girl came out and took Kwok Sang by the arm. She dragged him into the room.

"You got to let the poor girl make a little bit more," the mistress said to us. "She can't come from such a far distance to make only one dollar."

When Kwok Sang was through we left the place. The mistress appeared to be very friendly. She has had a few girls, one of them a pretty mulatto, Elizabeth, who is a college student. She promised to make arrangements so that she might be with us next time.

On our way home Kwok Sang said, "I don't feel anything at all, del-ka-ma! She is too old and her body is too hard—not soft like other young chickens."

"Del-ka-ma! Bing Lung, you made me come with you," began Ching
Lung, "and tried to make a fool out of me. I won't come with you next
time."

"Look here! Jean is your girl, isn't she? You recommended her, didn't
you?"

"Let's go back to the Hill Street place."

"No! Go home."

A group adventure, in itself, can be considered as a means to relieve
sexual tension, particularly in this incident. When they had such a hard
time finding the place and the girl, going from one address to another,
the desire for sex satisfaction was dissipated and the "expedition" became
just a way to kill time. Often a laundryman takes part in an adventure to
the brothels or call-flats without feeling passionate or even desirous of
sexual satisfaction. He goes along because he has nothing else to do. On
the other hand, he would not take the trouble if he had to go alone. But,
in the company of a few persons the adventure becomes a sort of leisure-
time activity. He is, so to speak, seeking stimulation for the sake of stimulation.

The Chinese laundryman would hesitate to go alone to the brothel, the
call-flat, or apartment, which are generally located on the Near North
Side, the Near West Side, or in the Black Belt, unless he has been in the
place before in company with others, or he is quite sure about the character of the place. It seems he would rather patronize the "hotel room"
than take the risk of visiting other places, for he has heard of being
arrested and being robbed in such adventures. On Saturday and Sunday
evening he may sneak into a hotel where he can rest and stretch himself
after a week of hard labor, and he can also make an arrangement with
the bell boy to get a girl. The hotels which the Chinese patronize are
usually small ones in or around the Loop.

About 11:30 P.M., I walked upstairs and told the clerk that I was waiting
for a friend and that unless he showed up I wouldn't want to sign for a
room. I chose a chair in a dark corner to sit down and smoke.

As soon as I was on the second floor, I saw three Chinese who apparently
didn't know each other. I could see the embarrassment and uneasiness
among them. One tall man, about fifty, was standing in front of the elevator,
waiting for the bell boy to take him up. One young man who was about
thirty, standing in front of the counter, paid for a room. Another man,
about fifty, was sitting on a chair close to the stairway. Within a few minutes

two more of them came up, very shy and uneasy. They looked at the man who sat on the chair but ignored him. Playing his nose with his fingers, the other man didn't even look at them. One of the men asked the clerk if there were one-dollar rooms. The clerk replied that the cheapest one would be a dollar and twenty-five cents. Soon they signed up for two rooms. The clerk rang the bell, but the bell boy [Negro] didn't come down right away. They had to wait about five minutes. When the bell boy came down with the elevator, he brought one Chinaman down. Meanwhile one white man came upstairs followed by another Chinese. This fellow was quite young. He walked to the counter and said something to the clerk that I couldn't hear. Soon I saw him go right down without signing for a room. The next time the elevator came down, there were one middle-aged American couple and one Chinaman. He went straight to the other man who was sitting there waiting.

There is a term *tsu-ga* [*zhujia*] (hometown), referring to a certain hotel which an individual steadily patronizes. The busiest time, of course, is Saturday evening. The laundrymen sometimes tell each other their own experiences in the hotel and become its client. The experiences sometimes are pleasant, but sometimes they are rather disappointing, as in the following case.

(S. W.—age 45.) They had nothing to do for the whole afternoon; the work was done before noon. One of the partners had gone. S. W. and two other partners remained to look after the business.

He remained until 10:30 in the evening, the closing hour for the shop. Here is the story of the remainder of the night.

Del-ka-ma! I went over all the city's hotels but couldn't get a "meal" the whole night, last night. Not a girl could be found. It is really prohibited during this election time. I was in at least six different hotels and all disappointed me. Del-ka-ma! she was a little bit too old or. . . .

I thought I could get one later, see. It was then the third place I went. First I was back to my "tsu-ga" [the hotel he always rooms in] at —— Street and Michigan Avenue. I know the bell boy, see. After I signed up for the room, the boy took me up. I asked him to get me a girl. He said he couldn't do that. "I don't care for this room, then," I told the bell boy. I gave him twenty-five cents. I went downstairs and asked the clerk to refund my deposit. Then I walked over to that place between Michigan and Cermak Road. The clerk told me all the rooms were taken. Then I went over to that one at State and Cermak, and I had a "no," too. Then I walked down and got a bus driving south. I didn't care where it took me. The bus went straight down to Fifty-fifth Street. I got off there and took a walk around the neighborhood. I saw many Negro women on the street. I was kind of afraid to talk to them. I had over one hundred dollars in my pocket. Finally I found a hotel in that neighborhood. I walked in and asked for a room. I was exhausted. "No. Sorry, we have no single room left to-night." Had a "no" again! And no girl, too, of course.

Del-ka-ma! What could I do? I took the same bus line back downtown again. I got off at Michigan and Van Buren and walked West. It was about two-thirty at that time. I saw a couple of girls at the street corner but they didn't even look at me.

Finally I arrived at 305 [a hotel]. "No room, sorry," again. Del-ka-ma! I turned around the corner to another hotel. Well, they had a room but it cost me one dollar and seventy-five cents. I was so bewildered by that time, even five dollars, or ten dollars, didn't matter much. I took the room. I had a bath. I slept until ten o'clock. . . .

Del-ka-ma! Let us go to Charlie Yick [in Joliet]. There is a red-light district. I heard there are plenty of pretty girls. How far is it?

Occasionally, the hotels as well as other resorts for prostitutes may be raided by the police and remain for a period under strict law enforcement. When passion finds no relief, the laundryman goes to some of the *tanyuo* [*zhanyou*] (comrades) for addresses of resorts. Some laundrymen keep a list of addresses which may be passed out among close acquaintances. Some are too timid and shy to look for other places, but one can always, under ordinary conditions, find prostitutes in the hotel.

(S. Y.—age 50.) . . . I lived in that hotel for almost a month after I sold my laundry.

Yes, the hotel rent was twenty dollars a month, but could not I see any girl as I stayed right there? I had one almost every night and sometimes four or five times a night. In this way I spent almost one hundred dollars a week.

I simply couldn't resist the temptation. You stay awake until four or five o'clock, thinking about it. You couldn't go to sleep until you had a girl. Del-ka-ma! The bell boy wanted to make money too. He came and knocked at my door every night and asked if I cared for a girl. He said, "Nice girl," and I said, "Yes." There were two really pretty ones. I had both of them over one night two or three times. Del-ka-ma, twenty dollars a night. The bell boy fixed it up for me. I tipped him one dollar.

Money was spent like sand. I thought, sometimes, I better have some good times before I couldn't have it any more. What matter is money anyway? A person like me does not have much of a future. . . . I see very little chance for me to accumulate money to go back to China.

Without hope for the future, lonesome and discouraged, at vacation time, some people, like S. Y., room in a hotel where they can spend their money like water.

Often laundrymen bring their clandestine sweethearts to dine in Chinatown restaurants. Facing his fellow men in the community, it seems he is hardly himself. He is shy and lacks poise. But he has no other place to entertain his fair lady. He probably would feel much more self-conscious if he took her to an American place.

Most of the laundrymen, however, are not quite so romantic. They want to keep the affair secret. It is "all right" to patronize prostitution, but it is "not nice" to make it obvious and notorious. The vice of prostitution is not immoral but non-moral, for in America he is forced to live the life of a married bachelor.

2. The Married Bachelor

The Chinese laundryman is a married bachelor in the sense of his long separation from his wife and his abnormal sex life in America. He must choose to repress his impulses or to accept any temptation which comes to his doorstep. Many get used to sex repression and divert their interest to something else. The majority, however, take chances with any woman of loose character. In certain areas of the city, street walkers and over-sexed women call upon him at his shop and try to flirt with him. In the following case, the woman approaches the laundryman for work. When she is told that he has not enough business to employ her, she offers her own body to the laundryman.

(Y. S.—age 60.) A white girl came in the other day, begging for a job. She said she came from Cleveland and used to work for a Chinese laundry there. Well, I just told her frankly that I couldn't hire her. First, I had not enough business, and secondly, the prejudice was against me. I could not give her a job. Then she began to tell me that she hadn't anything to eat since last evening. She knew no one in this city. And she began to cry when she was ready to leave. Well, she had my sympathy. I called her back and gave her fifty cents. "Take it and buy yourself a meal," I told her.

Then she asked if I wanted a good time with her so that she could get a few dollars for her room rent. I told her I couldn't do that. I had no bed ready for that and I was not in the mood. Then I got the impression that she might be a prostitute. But, since she talked as if she knew how to do laundry work well, she must be an experienced hand, too. But in a desperate situation no one can stand against evil thought.

She told me she was twenty-one years old. She came to Chicago to look for a job. She has already been here for three weeks and yet couldn't find anything to do.

In many Chinese laundries where there are fathers and sons, uncles and nephews, brothers, or other relatives such as in-laws working together, sex is taboo, and the fair visitor is likely to be disappointed. The best prospects for her are single-man places, but for one reason or another he may not be a good customer, either. In this case, Y. S. is an old man. He gives big reasons for not accepting her proposal. If she visits the right place, she may make more than room rent. Women of doubtful character may be seen in different laundries; they are *lao-kai* [*laugi*] (sweethearts). A girl comes for some money or a dinner in the laundryman's shop. The next case, for example, is good evidence that, under certain conditions, the laundryman can hardly resist the temptation because he is lonesome and sex hungry.

(T. M.—age 40, West Van Buren Street.) There was a Filipino fellow who used to meet a white girl in our place. Standing outside our counter, they talked sometimes very long, and sometimes just a few minutes, and they then usually went out together. They had been doing so for several months. It might be that the Filipino fellow got tired of her. Finally he brought her into our place and let her get acquainted with us. We talked about prostitutes, about sexual intercourse, and about marriage. Then she began to approach me. I could hardly refuse. And so I took her out to a show.

After the show, she bought a set of cards and went back to my place again with me. My partner understood. He walked out and went to a show himself. Then the girl and I sat down and played cards. As soon as she and I were alone, I became sentimental. I couldn't control myself. She gave me the same reaction. When I put my hand on her breast, she asked me to kiss her. "You darling, come and kiss your baby!" she said. I kissed her. Then I had her on the bed with me.

I asked if she was married. She told me she was single. I believed her because she had been around with the Filipino. She said she liked me better than the Filipino. From then on, whenever she came she brought something to eat—fruit, candy, cake, and cookies. She ate it with us and talked for hours.

She was fat, with two breasts. She said she was nineteen. When I had intercourse with her, she was very active. After it, I offered her some money, but she refused to take it, saying that she was working and had enough to support herself.

She was one of our customers. Sometimes she brought a bundle of soiled clothes with a man's belongings in it. I asked to whom the man's clothes belonged. She told me that it belonged to an old man in the apartment. Once she told me that the clothes belonged to her brother.

One day she came in and talked to us as usual. Leaving for home, she said she would call again tomorrow with some ginger ale. The same night the Filipino came in. He knew I was pretty good to the girl. He advised me that I better quit her, saying the girl was a married woman. In spite of her married life, she went out with different men and made them a lot of trouble. The Filipino said that he was one of her last victims. He warned me that I should get rid of her. I was much upset that night, but I began to realize I must not let her fool me any more.

The next day, as I knew the girl was coming, I went out to a show alone, and left a message with my partner that in case she came, he should tell her my uncle was dying in the hospital and I had to break our date.

In the afternoon she brought with her four bottles of ginger ale. My cousin gave her the message. "I don't believe that," she said to my partner. "He is not home, because he wants to avoid me!"

A few days afterward she came again. I apologized and said that I was sorry to break the date. I told her myself that my uncle was dying in the hospital and the hospital phoned for me. She said the same thing to me; she didn't believe me.

From that time on, I decided not to talk to her, "Why, don't you love your baby any more?".... Oh, I understand...." But I did not care for whatever she said. Maybe she realized that. Then she did not come so often. She didn't bring anything to eat anymore. After several weeks I did not see her at all.

It was last Friday, at about ten o'clock at night, when we were still working, she came in unexpectedly. She talked to us as usual. Finally she told us that she had been to a doctor's office. She had to spend at least twenty-five dollars. My partner asked her what was the matter. "I don't know," she said, "but anyway something is wrong with me."

"That I know," I interrupted, "you must have a baby." She just stared at me with a silly look. Upon leaving she walked near me and whispered, "If I have a baby, you are the one who has got to take care of it."

I was so upset after she left. I wondered if she could make any trouble. Can my name be spoiled? What I want now is not whether she can sue me, I want to get it over with so that nobody knows anything about it. She can't put the thing on me! She had been the mistress of the Filipino. What is more, she is a married woman. Now if she has a baby, how can she blame me?

The Filipino has moved away and she moved away, too. I don't know where she lives now. She lived only three blocks away from our place last time. I had never seen her with any other man except that Filipino.

The trouble was that she didn't take my money after I had relations with her. If she had taken my money, why, then she was just a regular prostitute. . . .

I hope she will not come back again. Oh, yes, I told her I could not do anything more with her because my wife didn't like it. She said, I might have a wife in China, but not here. You see, she seems to know something about our Chinese people here.

From now on, "C.O.D." method is the safest. Doing something like this with that girl is too troublesome.

This is not a case of barter but of promiscuity. The motive of the woman, however, is unknown. For T. M., he seems profoundly moved by the woman's romantic gesture. Without the Filipino's warning, he might have become a victim of exploitation, as have others according to tales current among the immigrants. Ordinarily, the laundryman, ever longing for a sweetheart, is only too glad to have any personal contact with the fair sex. He is interested in sex experience and satisfaction, but not in marriage. But he is apprehensive of getting into trouble, especially with a married woman. Above all, the laundryman would try to avoid a law suit.

The love life idealized by the married bachelor is not with the call-flat girl, in the "hotel room," or with the street walker. He dreams of real romance with a housewife.

If I wanted sex, I have had many chances. Some women come in here once in a while, but I didn't care for it. I sent them away. There was only one woman who played a good trick on me. She came in and gave me her address and told me to go to call for her laundry.

"You must come about twelve," she said. "don't you come earlier than that, for I may still be sleeping."

I believed her and went to her place at twelve. When she opened the door, I found she wore only a nightgown.

"Are you a Chinese?" she asked.

"Why, yes," I answered. "You know I have my shop there."

"Oh, I like you," she said and opened her gown. "See how big my breast is?"

She made me sit down and she sat right close to me. And her hands and feet began to act. I was excited but also fearful. I got up to leave.

"Don't go! You must do it," she said and began to undress and asked me to do the same. She even helped me.

After the act, she gave me two or three dollars of work to bring home and she paid for it, too. See, it is not necessary to spend money on women.

Sometimes she gave me a bath before or afterwards. She put some chemical in the water. After I was through, she came and helped me get dressed and said, "Now, you go back to work." She was really a *kai ka po* [qijiapo] (mistress).

Sometimes she prepared a good lunch for me. I remember on one occasion eating two big juicy pork chops with her.

Her husband went to work at eleven o'clock. That was why she wanted me to come later. She told me not to be afraid and that she did not like her husband. "Even if my husband comes home and sees us, it doesn't matter. I can handle him," she said.

I went to her house many times. Whenever she moved she gave me her new address. She even sent her husband over to give me the address.

It was three years ago. I don't know where she is now. She may be out of town. She told me she used to own a house. I guess she lost it. She once lived in an apartment about six blocks away.

Occasionally a woman comes in, looking for business. Once a woman who knew some woman down in Chinatown asked if she could come inside. I told her no. I told her I had no time except on Sunday.

"Let me have a drink of water," she requested.

One teacher in the Sunday School was good to me. She told me all her personal affairs. If I wanted to, she would give herself to me.

To what extent this story is true is another question. But it represents the ideal type of romantic love about which the Chinaman dreams. The story may be perfectly true, it may be wishful thinking, or partly or wholly invented. The fact remains that tales of this sort are heard from time to time and even appear in the immigrant press.

A "steady woman" is indeed hard to find. But the employment of mulatto girls in the Chinese laundry is a new development of like nature. In some laundries, the mulatto woman works steadily for years as a helper. Many of these girls are very accommodating. They learn to eat Chinese food and some of them are treated nicely. Rumor circulates that so-and-so has lived with his Negro helper, and so-and-so keeps the girl as a mistress as well as worker. Some of these affairs end in trouble.

This is not the one; she is the cousin. I am sick to think that I treated her so well and she tried to deceive me. Her whole family is not good except this one. She stood up for me when the other one wanted to fight me in court.

She got a lawyer and sued for her back wages. Del-ka-ma! I paid her too

much for her work. This girl here knew all about it. At that time both of
them were working here. Only she [the one who sued him] worked steadily
and this one worked part-time. I paid her rent for her every month besides
her daily expenses. I went to see her only when I had time. Once when I
went to see her I found a man with her. He was unemployed. She let him
live with her. That was all right. That was her own business. But I couldn't
support her and her sweetheart.

I let her come back to work just the same but gave her fair wages, two
dollars a day. I told her that was her wages and that I could not be responsible for anything else. Del-ka-ma! She bought food and drink for that fellow
and the money was quickly spent. At the end of the month she couldn't pay
her rent. She dared to ask me for it. I told her to "go to hell." I told her to
ask that fellow for it.

Then she was mad and went home. She wouldn't come back to work the
next day. I felt relieved. But a couple of days later her mother came and
begged that I must help her just once more. I gave her five dollars and told
her mother that was all I could do. I told her that she should never come
back again.

Then I heard she was sick in bed. I guess that was an idea of that guy.
They asked a lawyer to send me a threatening letter, stating that I owed her
thirty-five dollars back wages. Del-ka-ma! A black-mailing method! No one
but a "ka-doi" [Chinese name for male prostitute] could stand such a thing.
I got a loan of fifty dollars and a lawyer to defend me.

They learned about this. At the day of the hearing, she didn't even dare
appear. The case was finally dismissed by the judge. Del-ka-ma! She wanted
to threaten me! They thought a Chinese could be easily fooled.

Some of these females have no conscience at all. After that, her mother
came and apologized. She told me that the guy had gone and asked me to
go to see her again. Del-ka-ma! I won't touch such a bad smelling thing
again.

The most interesting and significant point about this case is that the
laundryman is anxious to find a solution for his unsatisfactory love life.
Perhaps he justifies keeping a mistress by the custom of concubinage in
China.

He comes in contact with the mulatto girl through employment, and
sex relations are a natural consequence. Sex crosses the racial border in
spite of race prejudice.

Because of his social position in the urban community in America, the
laundryman seldom comes into personal contact with white women. In
case he does, he tends to give anything to please her. But conflicts arise
easily, due to difference in cultural backgrounds.

3. Maladjustment

Patronizing prostitutes and keeping mistresses are frequently manifestations not merely of sexual isolation but also personal maladjustment. Some laundrymen, preoccupied with sex, neglect the duty of supporting their family, lose interest in the return trip to China, and eventually lose their social status among their fellow countrymen. When a man gets deeply involved with women, his friends and relatives worry about him and he may become the butt of ridicule.

> c. m.—Ling-boom has gone to see his mistress. Every Saturday he leaves without eating his dinner. He is now living with Jill. Do you know that street walker down in Chinatown? She used to live in Ho Bak-chung's apartment. Since Ling-boom is interested in her, she has moved to a place outside of Chinatown.
> c. l.—I wonder where they live.
> l. m.—I don't know exactly, but I can guess. It is somewhere on North Clark Street.
> c. m.—Ling-boom used to be a good son. He didn't gamble. Every weekend he spent only fourteen cents to go to Chinatown. Sometimes he even came home for dinner. He saved all he earned. But look at him now! Ever since he got mixed up with that bad smelling female, he has become an extravagant spender. I saw her once in Chinatown, wearing a splendid fur coat. Later I learned that it cost Ling-boom about three hundred dollars.

His partners, cousins, and friends can only talk—feel sorry for, or indifferent to, him. Gossiping controls some individuals, but a maladjusted person does not seem to care what others may say. Sometimes he will even talk boastfully about his sexual adventure.

> (h. m.—age 50.) Employed by a clansman in a laundry shop, he earns only twenty to twenty-five dollars a week. He used to be a gambler and spent every Sunday in Chinatown. Now, he spends his weekends with a woman [white] he met in the neighborhood which is populated by poor white and Negro families. The woman, Jean, is well known among Chinese groups as a street walker. Jean had been married but was divorced. She is now living with a teen-age daughter. Her affair with H. M. is of the clandestine type.
> "Well, sure, I shall go to see my 'family.' Sure, I go there to see them every week now. I have a family here in America and another one in China.

"No, I haven't sent any money to that family in China for two years. All I have to take care of is this family here. With this family here I have a white woman to sleep with. The heaven makes man and woman for the purpose of sex, I cannot do without it.

"How much do I give her? As much as I can afford. Sometimes I give her all I have in my pocket. It all depends on how she pleases me, see? If she is sweet to me, I would give her even my bones. So if I win thirty dollars this evening [gambling in Chinatown], I shall give her at least twenty-nine.

"What? Sure! Sleep with her and have her as many times as possible [*laugh*]. Ha, she likes it. She is a hot one."

H. M. was roasting a chicken which he was preparing to take with him to Jean's place. It was cooked in Chinese style. Soon he packed the chicken and a pot of rice. He left the laundry late Saturday afternoon. He does the same thing almost every weekend.

"Sure, I saw Jean the other day.

"How much? I gave her more than she expected. I gave her twenty-five dollars. Del-ka-ma! She was so pleased that she pressed many kisses upon me.

"Sometimes I give her only four or five dollars. She isn't so sweet, of course. But it's all the same. I can stay with her anyway.

"Usually I give her about ten dollars for a night. It is good to have a steady woman like this, isn't it? Her daughter is growing up, now. She is almost fifteen.

"Oh, no! Jean would never let me touch her daughter. She sends her daughter away when I go to see her. . . ."

He has not sent money home to China to support his family for two years and shamelessly refers to his clandestine vice as "another family." He gambles to win more in order to please his mistress. The similarity between this and the next case seems to be that both neglect to play expected roles in their primary group and that both are gamblers. Their differences are in the character of their relationships with the women. The former established a sort of "kept mistress" relationship. He belongs to an older generation and would be satisfied if he could maintain the relationship with the same woman, perhaps with a family touch. The latter keeps up a sort of barter relationship with women. He is restless and would take up with any woman. He spends for a good time, but not for family living and home life. In general, however, they are both demoralized.

I used to go to dance halls almost every weekend. There I spent all my money. When I worked in the other laundry, I earned from fifty to nearly one hundred dollars a week. When I had money, I had a real good time. Then I went to night clubs every Saturday evening, spending a whole night there. In the morning, I took a girl to a hotel.

There are some night clubs in the "Black-Devil's Nest" [Negro area] at Fifty-fifth and State Streets. There are two around the neighborhood. One is better than the other. I have been in both of them many times. Sometimes I just pick up black girls on the street corner. They are walking back and forth on the street, looking for a man.

I would rather starve than not see a girl and have a good time.

Go down to Chinatown? Yes, sometimes I go down there to try my luck [gambling]. I lose sometimes. Then I spend less for the girl, that's all.

But I earn only about ten-odd a week now. I do not have much money for a good time now. That is why I have to get along with this female. Dotty is her name. She is quite expensive, too. She wants at least three dollars or she won't let me. . . .

Last New Year's Eve I went to a night club with her and spent twenty-five dollars. Del-ka-ma, it cost me three weeks' wages. You see, the business has not been so good near the end of the year. I make only about ten dollars a week.

Oph! How bad a man I am!

My wife in China? Oh, she can go out and look for a lover, too. I can't blame her. Of all the things I am doing here, I have no right to blame her if she does the same. She is also human, see. So I don't care if she has a lover in China.

I have not sent any money for a long time. Well, my family does not need my support, see. We have property in Canton. So I can spend what I earn for a good time.

When did I begin to see prostitutes? Oh, the first two or three years I didn't dare go. Once I saw a leg show downtown. My sexual impulse was so overwhelmingly aroused that I went to see a Chinese prostitute in the Old Chinatown at Clark and Van Buren streets. That was the first time. Then I went back to see the same girl afterward, several times. Then people took me to see white girls—you know, in some of those hotels in the Loop. Then, when I had money, I went to those places alone. Later I went to dance halls and night clubs, becoming an old hand.

One day the investigator visited the laundry when Dotty came in. Dotty, a mulatto girl about twenty-five, arrived about four o'clock. The following scene took place:

LUM: Here she comes—lo-kai [sweetheart]!

DOTTY: Hello, honey. Hello [to others in the house].

PARTNER: Hello, honey. What do you want? Come to sleep with me?

[*Dotty ignored partner but turned to Lum.*]

DOTTY: Lum, give me five dollars, dear.

LUM: What? No money. I haven't got it. No money.

DOTTY: Come on! Before the store closes. I want to buy some stockings and a handbag. Come on, give me the money.

LUM: Del-nea-ma! You don't let me *del-hoy** [literally "fuck you"] and just come to get money. I haven't got it.

DOTTY: Come on, before the stores close. Hurry up. Give me the money.

LUM: No, no money. You kiss my *lin joy** [penis] and I will give you three dollars.

DOTTY: Oh! You bad boy! What do you think I am. I'm not that kind of a girl. I'm no street walker. Kiss your . . . nothing! Come on, Lum.

LUM: No money. You search my pocket if you don't believe me. [*Dotty put one hand into one of his pockets and he embraced her. He hugs her closer while she flirts with a look and says*]:

DOTTY: Will you give your baby some money to buy something to wear? I got to buy some stockings. I have nothing to wear.

LUM: No. You ask the man who lives with you for it. You give him del-hoy all the time.

DOTTY: Don't you say anything bad about my brother! Can't I let my own brother stay with me?

LUM: Is he your brother? I don't believe you.

DOTTY: Believe it or not. But give me the money, please, honey. The store closes soon. It is almost five.

LUM: You searched my pocket; I have no money in it.

DOTTY: But it isn't in your pocket. Come in here [*She leads him toward his sleeping compartment.*] Now go in there and get some.

LUM: Del-nea-ma! You don't let me del-hoy. You haven't even given me a kiss yet.

DOTTY: Well, kiss me and give me the money.

LUM: Your mouth smells bad [*while he kisses her*].

DOTTY: Come on now, you bad man.

LUM: How much did you want?

DOTTY: Five dollars.

LUM: No, I don't have five. Here, here is three. Three is enough.

DOTTY: No, five! I have to buy a handbag, too.

LUM: All I have is five dollars. Want three?

DOTTY: Give it to me! [*She takes the money and begins to leave.*]

LUM: You come back here again.

DOTTY: Yes, I'll be back.

PARTNER: Well, another three dollars. This is the second time she is paid this week. What a girl. All she wants is money. Whenever she comes, she asks for money.

Finally Dotty came back with her stockings. She put down the box on the table, and Lum, taking her hand, led her inside. They were alone about half an hour.

January 8, 1939.—Haven't seen Lum for about a month. Saw him in

Wah Ying Restaurant this evening with a girl. She was introduced as Edith. Lum was asked where he met her.

"She lives here in Chinatown. She is good. She does everything I ask her. She spent one whole night with me last night. I got a bottle of those 'little sweethearts,' see? Del-ka-ma! I made her four or five times. She cried while I was working on her. So pleasant.

"I happened to win on ma-jong yesterday. I gave her twenty dollars. I have known her about two weeks. She got almost one hundred dollars from me already. I bought her a dress that cost me thirty-five dollars."

March 24, 1939.—Visited the laundry in the afternoon. Lum said he had been downtown today. He had his watch repaired. He was going to China-town for supper.

"Are you going to Chinatown tonight?" asked his partner. "Come back for lunch. Come back to fix up the account."

"Sure, I'll be back," said Lum, "but don't wait lunch for me. I may sleep until one o'clock [in the hotel]. Anyway, I'll be back tomorrow afternoon.

Later Lum told the following story: "I lost three hundred and fifty dollars New Year Sunday [Chinese lunar new year]. Del-nea-ma! Just threw two hands of dice, I lost two one hundred dollar bills. I dare not tell it to anyone else. I went over to Toy Fa Toy [a gambling house] and gambled fan-tan. Fifty dollars a hand, and within a few minutes, my other one hundred dollar bill went over to 'Uncle Fourth' [fan-tan]! Then I walked away and bought four dollars on the lottery. Then I walked back and forth with only forty-odd dollars in my pocket. Finally, I decided to go to see 'Beautiful Girl' [Dotty]. I stayed overnight with her.

"Del-ka-ma! Ever since the New Years Day, I have lost a lot of money—fifteen hundred dollars in Feng Ming Hin [another gambling house]. I borrowed three hundred dollars, and another three hundred was left in my care, and all the wages for these months are gone.

"I sent only one hundred dollars [about thirty dollars in American currency] home for the kid [his son] to go to school. I'll stop supporting him after he reaches thirteen. He is now ten. I have to take care of the girls here first; that is the most important business.

"That one at home? Oh, she can live all right. . . . I would rather starve than not see a girl and have a good time."

This is the cry of the "playboy," Chinese style. The type represents the worst character among the Chinese minority, certainly not the majority of the laundrymen. Lum is a type among those younger men who are either obsessed with sex or influenced by bad companions. The strenuous, monotonous, and routine work of the laundry, plus lack of marriage and home life, tend to make him either shy and retiring, or bold and aggressive, in sexual adventures. Individual differences in social environment and life organization lead some persons to excessive indulgence, finally resulting in complete personal disorganization.

The story of Lum represents the natural history of the immigrant's sexual maladjustment. At first there is sex isolation, the attendance of a State Street leg show, followed by the visit to a Chinese prostitute in Chinatown, then later, trips to Loop hotels with white prostitutes, first with others then alone. Later he has romantic affairs. Finally, he patronizes dance halls and night clubs, which very few laundrymen would have the audacity to attend.

> In Chicago, at least a fourth of the patrons of taxi-dance halls are Orientals who are elsewhere ostracized because of color. Of these Orientals, nine-tenths are Filipinos, and the Chinese contribute virtually the remainder.[3]

Chinese laundrymen, however, have very little to do with the taxi-dance halls. Their Chinese patrons, it seems, are much more likely to be chop suey house waiters. Plaza Dance Hall, 1210 North Clark Street, ran an advertisement in the local Chinese daily paper, announcing:

> This dance hall has invited some fifty beautiful young girls who can be chosen freely by our patrons as dancing partners. Our dear Chinese friends are also welcome to bring their own lady friends. The hall is open from 9:00 P.M. until the morning. Come and have a good time.

An invitation of this sort may attract some of the younger laundrymen. On the whole, the dance hall is not popular among Chinese laundrymen. They tend rather to patronize "the hotel room," the "call-flat girl," and the street walker.

In conclusion, the Chinese community condones and excuses prostitution as natural and inevitable for the sojourners separated for long years from home and family. What it frowns upon and condemns are sex affairs which are demoralizing; that is, which interfere with the purpose of life in America, namely, the support of the Chinese family and the accumulation of money for the return trip to China. In spite of this community attitude, there are a large number of individuals who are completely disorganized on account of sexual maladjustment. Obviously sex is always associated with other vices—gambling, opium addiction, and more recently, betting on the horses. Sex, therefore, becomes a social problem; it breeds diseases of all kinds. Information gathered reveals that the rate of venereal diseases, and mental disorders related to venereal diseases, seem to be quite high among the Chinese minority in this country. To what extent this health problem is related to sexual maladjustment is certainly an interesting question. Prostitution is the oldest vice of the human race, but its best remedy is no doubt happier marriage and family life. The Chinese minority is still predominantly male. As on the frontier, sex is a social problem. The sex ratio of the Chinese population in the United States, however, seems to show trends toward equalization, particularly since the recent war. This tendency is shown in Table 16.1.

NOTES

1. One-clan villages are found particularly in South China, but not without exception. Several clans reside in some villages.

2. E. W. Burgess, *The City* (Chicago: University of Chicago Press, 1925), p. 151, defines promiscuity as "primary and intimate behavior upon the basis of secondary contacts." [Ed. note: "secondary contacts" meaning relations with people one barely knows.]

3. Paul G. Cressey, *The Taxi-Dance Hall* (Chicago: University of Chicago Press, 1932), p. 109.

CHAPTER XVII

OUT-GROUP CONTACTS AND DEVIANT TYPES

SOCIAL BARRIERS may prevent personal contacts between Chinese and Americans, but there are always exceptions. Some Chinese laundrymen find friends and companions in the outer world through Sunday School attendance, inter-racial marriage, and neighborhood acquaintance. These contacts, to be sure, are deviant types—deviant in the sense of unusual and not representative since the majority of the laundrymen do not experience such contacts. Feeling content in the laundry-Chinatown world, the latter are timid, indifferent, and reluctant to seek social contacts in the broad cosmopolitan community.

The question considered in this chapter concerns the nature and vitality of these deviant contacts. Are those who make personal contacts with non-Chinese thereby removed from the stream of the laundry-Chinatown world?

1. Sunday School Attendance

At present eight churches[1] in Chicago offer English and Bible lessons to Chinese on Sunday afternoons. This meeting of the Occident and the Orient once a week has a unique character and a history of its own. Interestingly, teachers and pupils of the Sunday School for Chinese meet with different aims. The teacher's purpose is thus expressed by a churchman:

> The chief aim of the Chinese Sunday School has always been to win the pupils to Christ, at the same time it is necessary and of great importance that the Sunday School give them personal help in every way possible. The

efforts of the Sunday School have resulted in a large measure of success. While only a small minority of the pupils have accepted Christ as their personal Savior, with but a few exceptions, they have given a splendid response to the efforts of their teachers.[2]

The following observation by a teacher illustrates the actual relation between the teacher and the pupil:

> I have been in this school for twenty years. I have met some nice boys. I come to help them and know what they need. We get something from each other. I am not paid here. It is pure service. However, I like this work for I want my Chinese friends to believe in the Lord Jesus Christ.
>
> Then she looked out of the window and suddenly exclaimed, "Oh! Here comes Jimmy. He hasn't been here for so long."
>
> A few minutes later a young Chinese man came up and the greeting began, "How are you Mrs. D.?" "Oh! How do you do, Jimmy! I haven't seen you for so long. How have you been?"
>
> "Well, I have been working hard. Every Sunday I help my uncle in his restaurant. His business is poor. Sunday is his best day, but he can't hire a man to help him. I have to help him."
>
> "Well, that's a good boy, Jimmy. But when you find time, come back to see us, will you? How long have you been away from here?"
>
> "Oh, about two years."
>
> "Well, how have you been?"
>
> "I pass by this way and I thought I might as well drop in to see you."
>
> "Well, it is nice to see you, indeed. Do you know my husband died, and my son and daughter are all married and I am living alone in that eight-room house? Jack [another of Mrs. D.'s pupils] was sick and I had him with me for a week. He is all right now. Some day I am going to have some of the boys in to my place and have a nice tea party, Chinese tea. . . ."
>
> "Sorry to hear Mr. D. die."
>
> Finally Mrs. D. turned and introduced Jimmy to me and the other boys. Jimmy was smartly dressed, clean shirt, shining shoes, blue-green new suit of clothes, looking like a playboy.[3]

Mrs. D., in this case, represents those teachers who are exceptionally devoted to the work. To win pupils to Christ, what counts is not Bible lessons, not English teaching, but sincere friendliness and personal help. An interview with Mrs. Blachley, superintendent of the Chinese Sunday School of the North Shore Baptist Church, further reveals the picture of teacher-pupil relations.

> She spoke of one Chinese boy who had attended the school. She said

most Chinese rearrange their names in a curious Chinese-American combination. "This young fellow," she said, "we call Peter, since that is the
American name he combined with his own."

Eight years ago Peter came to the school. There was a mother and her
daughter teaching in the school. Peter first had the daughter as his individual
teacher. Later he was given to the mother. This woman became most attached to the boy. He, himself, called her mother, and she gave him something of the affection and attention she would have given a son. Later he
became very ill. Dr. Blachley was called and said that the boy must be
operated upon for appendicitis. The Chinese have a horror of all operations.
It was only when the woman whom he called mother came, telling him that
she would go with him to the hospital, that he became reconciled.

Mrs. Blachley spoke of an old Chinaman named Mook connected with
the Sunday School. One day he went to her house to tell her that his nephew
was about to arrive from China, and would she teach him English. She
agreed.

A short time later, the old man appeared with a gawky awkward boy
who seemed almost paralyzed by the strangeness of the situation. She said
that the old man loves to treat any situation with formality. On this occasion, Mr. Mook made a speech, commending the youth to Mrs. Blachley's
care. He then went away.

The boy, left alone with a strange American lady, seemed to turn numb.
He was too afraid to learn anything at all. Hoping to win him, Mrs. Blachley
brought some fresh doughnuts, offering him one. He took it, turning it over
and over in curiosity. After holding it in his hand a while, he put it in his
pocket and carried it away with him.

Mr. Mook had said that he was taking the boy to the public school on
the following day, but right after school he would come again to Mrs.
Blachley. He never appeared.

Mr. Mook did, however, inquire how the boy was progressing. When he
found the boy was not there he went in search of him. He soon returned,
dragging the reluctant fellow along. Now he made another speech, this time
in Chinese. He said his nephew would be grateful to this lady and that she
was willing to become his American mother.

After that day, the boy was no longer afraid. Together with his study
with Mrs. Blachley he continued at the public school, reaching the seventh
grade after three years. He still calls Mrs. Blachley mother and her husband
he calls Dad. He calls them upon the phone quite often.

There was a delicate jade figure with a teakwood base upon the table.
Mrs. Blachley said that this was a gift from her students. Upon the wall,
too, hung an excellent Chinese print. She went into another room to bring
back a curious picture made from cork beautifully colored.[4]

Chinese immigrant boys are often sent to the Sunday School by their elders to escape bad influences in Chinatown. Every Sunday the young Chinaman goes to Sunday School from his father's or uncle's shop. In a few years, he can speak the language of the customers better than his father. He probably is the only person in the laundry shop who has out-group contacts. To his teacher and friends in the Sunday School he has no Chinese name. He is Peter Wong, or just Peter. If the *sen-sang-poo* [*xianshengpo*] (woman teacher)[5] is kind to him, he can't wait until Christmas to give her a present of Chinese art. By her personal influence and persuasion, the "heathen" Chinese may even "take Jesus as his savior." Naturally, only some teachers are successful, depending upon the individual situations of both the teacher and the pupil. A sen-sang-poo writes triumphantly to one of her pupils, commending his choice of "the Christian way."

Dear friend John:
    Your Easter letter came yesterday, and made me so glad. It was a beautiful letter, for I could see it was written from an enlightened heart. I think you must have written it as soon as you got home from church on Easter Day. I have sent your letter to Paul, for I know he will be glad to read it. Now my heart is full of thanksgiving, for all my students have chosen the Christian way. I talked with Mr. Carr by telephone last night and he was pleased to hear about you, for he remembers you very kindly, and is sorry you cannot be with us. Next Sunday, I will show him your letter.
    Our Chinese church service in the sanctuary was lovely, indeed. After the communion, Dr. Jones gave a good talk. After the meeting closed our picture was taken in the church.
    We have not had time for our English class for the past two Sundays, but now I hope we shall do some real studying and thinking together.
    I thank God for your Christian choice, John, and I pray that your faith will continue to grow into a richer and more beautiful spirit-life.
                                                                Sincerely,
                                                                Mary Watson[6]

The Chinese Sunday School becomes a social world. Social activities such as church and house parties, Chinatown dinner meetings, sight-seeing trips, picnics, and personal visits are observed between teachers and pupils occasionally. Through their weekly contacts with the Sunday School teachers, the young laundrymen observe and learn to accommodate themselves to the American way of life, including dressing, mannerisms, etiquette, habits, and sentiments. For instance, they participate in the

Fourth of July picnic and send Christmas presents and greeting cards, not only to the teachers and American friends, but also among themselves, too. In case the teacher is considered very kind and helpful, she would receive a very expensive present every Christmas. In return, the teacher, too, gives the pupil a present which is usually a personal need, such as necktie, shirt, pocketbook, a Bible, or whatnot. In some instances the pupils compete in presenting their sen-sang-poo expensive Christmas gifts. This may become scandalous, especially gifts to a young sen-sang-poo whose sex is more fascinating than her Bible and English lessons.

Fundamentally, in contrast with the aim of the church, young laundrymen come to Sunday School for either of both of two things: to learn to speak English, and to get a touch of the fair sex. They accept religious teachings as a necessary accompaniment. Their primary motive, however, is a desire to learn enough English to be an asset in making a living. Most of them quit Sunday School as soon as they think they have learned enough or feel they are too old to learn any more. There are very few middle-aged pupils in the Sunday School, to say nothing of old men. The faithful middle-aged pupil, if there is one, would be made head-student. Anyway, the Sunday School for Chinese is characteristically a world of young, ambitious laundrymen who are not as yet deeply involved in the China-town world and are restless for contacts with the fair sex after a week of toiling in the laundry shop. So the popularity of the Sunday School depends not only upon good facilities for learning, but upon the number of young, pretty teachers also. The nature of this attraction is similar, perhaps, to the case of the hobo as described by Nels Anderson:

> He is often profoundly touched by the women of the mission who stand on the street corner and plead with him for his soul's sake. Young and attractive women invited more attention because of their sex than their message. Though he may have little or no interest in the religious appeal, his feeling for those women is generally idealized and wholesome. The missions have learned the value of young and attractive women and employ them extensively as evangelists.[7]

In the Sunday School, the pupil tends to select his teacher, negatively speaking. If he does not like the teacher assigned to him, he may drop out of school or be absent too many times. In other words, he is not a regular attendant. The young laundryman in the following case came from out of town where he had a very devoted teacher whom he appreciated and admired very much. When he attended this new place in town, he was assigned to an old lady to teach him. Then repeated absences occurred. This may be a selective reaction, although he says that she is "all right, too." He is self-conscious with young women in the church. He would like to know the name and occupation of his teacher's daughter but he is afraid that people may think ill of him. His story throws more light on the reason for this attitude.

My present teacher, Mrs. Franklin, is all right, too. She is an old woman. Several weeks ago, I didn't feel good and I was absent for two successive weeks. Mrs. Franklin refused to teach any other pupil but me. The third week, when I was there, she was absent because she thought I might not be coming any more. Then the fourth week she went there again but she could not find me; that was a rainy day—I didn't go. She missed me again.

She has a daughter who is also a teacher in the Sunday School. Whenever she goes, her daughter accompanies her. The mother and daughter always go together. Mrs. Franklin does not want her daughter to go alone. Her daughter is about twenty-five years old. I don't know her name, and I don't know her occupation. I don't like to ask her. I am afraid that they may have a wrong conception of me, see. People may think that I want to make love. So I must be very reserved.

Several years ago, in this same Sunday School, a teacher was in love with her pupil and they were going to get married. The parents of the girl refused to consent to this marriage and the case was brought up to the church and quite a scandal resulted. All the young teachers were dismissed; those we have now are old ladies. Oh, yes, there are young ones in the school but they teach only those shun-hseung-lei [newcomers]. As soon as you pick up a few words or dress up nicely, you would not have the young lady as your teacher any more. They did the same thing to me. When I first went there, my teacher was young. And now I have Mrs. Franklin, an old lady of sixty. Well, I don't mind that. I only go to the school because I want to learn English. I don't care whether my teacher is old or young so long as she has patience to teach me. I am not going to the church to look for a girl. That is why I hesitated to talk to Mrs. Franklin's daughter.

Mrs. Franklin is a type of woman who wants recognition. She used to teach me how to sing. She brought some song books from home and taught me. She wanted me to learn so that I could sing in the meeting. If I sing, her daughter can show her skill on the piano, too, by accompanying me. Once I promised to sing and she let her daughter practice with me. But it was only once. Later I told her I wouldn't care to sing any more.

We did not have to study the Bible before. During the individual tutoring period, only a reader was used. There was no Bible lesson except in the

meeting period. Now we have to read and recite the Bible as well as the
textbook. Most Chinese don't like to read the Bible.

This school used to have sixty to eighty Chinese pupils, but since the
scandal and the Bible lessons, many come no more. Mrs. Jones, the superintendent, is very concerned about it. She usually stands behind and watches
our every move.[8]

It seems that self-consciousness and group consciousness, in various
degree, can be observed among these young Sunday School attendants
when they meet their teachers and other people of the church. To make a
good impression, they try to act nice and polite, and sometimes they are
over-sensitive. One may even decide to become a Christian to make a
good impression and gain friendship with the church people. For him, to
become a Christian is a method of accommodation.

Mrs. Jones asked me whether I wanted to become a Christian. I replied
I was baptized in the Presbyterian church in New York. She said I must be
baptized again, for the Baptist church is a different denomination. According to its creed, I must be baptized again if I want to become a member of
this church. So I had nothing to say but "yes." She was pleased.

Well, finally I was baptized in front of an audience of more than two
hundred men and women. Six other Chinese boys were baptized with me
the same day. The pastor gave a special message to us. He said something
in favor of us. I sat with my teacher. In front of us was our piano player,
the youngest teacher in our Sunday School. She turned frequently and
glanced at me, smiling. We did not speak to each other, though.

Gee! After I was baptized I felt the people were more friendly. The superintendent held my hand, without letting it go for a long while. Others
came, shook hands, and offered congratulations. That piano player had
seldom spoken to me before but now she not only says hello; she asked how
I am getting along and calls my name, John.

As you are baptized they then think you are a good man. That is the way
I feel about it. I am sure the other boys feel so, too. If you are not a Christian
they would think, "Well, these Chinese boys are a bad sort. They have no
interest in our religion. All they want is to learn English. What is the use
of teaching them?"

They seem to appreciate our becoming church members. They would say,
"Well, this is a good boy, this John Chan. He has a good character, otherwise he would not be a Christian and a member of our church."

See, in order to have their confidence, I chose to be a Christian.

I met my teacher's daughter last Sunday by the stairway of the church. I
talked with her while people were rushing out. She told me that her mother
was sick at home with a cold. This girl is not a teacher. They would not

let young girls be teachers any more. She came only to accompany her mother. But this time she came alone. I wonder why.

Before I joined, I learned that I would not have to pay much as a member of the church. Chan Sun, a kinsman of mine, who is a head-student of our Sunday School, is a member of the church for seven years. His laundry shop is only a few blocks from the church. He suggested that I should let them baptize me. His idea is that it is not so much a matter of believing a religion; it is a closer association with the church people—it is much nicer to follow their creeds.

No, I had not been asked why I wanted to become a Christian. I guess for Chinese boys, they make it easier. If I was asked, I wouldn't know how to answer in English, anyway.[9]

This strong desire for recognition, to the degree of converting himself a Christian, may be an individual trait. Most of the Chinese who attend Sunday School do not become Christian, even though they may attend it for years. Actually, the laundryman learns very little English. Most of them drop out before they can speak intelligibly. For some of them, particularly those of a younger and more progressive type, the Sunday School is a source of out-group contacts from which he may get personal help and social recognition and a touch of feminine attention which is in great paucity in the laundry-Chinatown world.

This matter of learning English seems to create some sort of dilemma, particularly among the laundrymen's group. Stories are told to indicate that to be able to speak English is not so much of a personal asset as a cause of personal disorganization. Elders, therefore, strongly object to young laundrymen attending Sunday School or taking up English lessons elsewhere. The reason is simply this: "Once he learns how to speak English, he goes to fool around with American girls." The worry of the elders may be over-anxious, but the matter seems to be deeply rooted in the isolationist attitude to keep the young folks from becoming too Americanized. On the other hand, we have elders like Mr. Mook (see p. 274) who insists that his nephew must learn the language. The latter may represent the change of attitude in recent years.

2. Interracial Marriage

There are only a few interracial marriages among Chinese laundrymen. They are interesting because, in spite of primary relationship with his non-Chinese wife and children, the laundryman still shares the attitudes and values of his own ethnic group. Husband and wife in a mixed marriage feel more at home residing either in the laundry or in Chinatown than elsewhere. The husband can only be a laundryman, and in case he must make a living by other than washing and ironing, he can do so only within his own ethnic group. He can be an agent of a tailor, a jewelry store, a loan bank, a coal dealer, a laundry-chop suey supply company, doing business with the Chinese. He can run a traveling market with a truck, selling meat and vegetables and all sorts of imported Chinese goods and other miscellaneous things to laundries and chop suey houses. He may also become a *lo-kar* [*lao-ka*]—a Chinatown gambler.

Gou-yen-gkai-poo [*jiaoyin guipo*] (married to devil woman) or *gou-yen-gkai-neu* [*jiaoyin guinu*] (married to devil girl) is often uttered to denote deviation from the ethnic group's social norm. It means giving up hope of returning to the old country, and other social connections of the individual with his friends and relatives. But the Chinese immigrants do not discriminate, in general, against interracial marriage. I heard some of them remark that half-breed children are better looking, particularly the girls. It is, therefore, the cultural differences and the racial situation which create disapproval. However, approval and disapproval are becoming more and more an individual matter. Often it is mixed with envy of the "doomed man's" good fortune. The same person may hold contradictory conceptions of the same marriage at different times. The mixed marriage seems to occupy an anomalous position between two social worlds: the world in Chinatown, and the world at large. As soon as a white or Negro woman has married a Chinese laundryman, she has probably had to relinquish her former social contacts; meanwhile, she seldom takes part with her husband in the social world in Chinatown, and, as a result, the family is at the margin between two social worlds, and it may involve tremendous inner and cultural conflicts among members of the mixed marriage.

The laundryman of the mixed marriage is essentially still a sojourner, it seems. In youth and middle age, while the family is still dependent upon his financial support, it remains intact, even when, as is sometimes the case, it suffers from economic and personal discord. But as soon as the children grow up, they are independent, and soon they cross the racial border to marry outside the group. By that time, the old Chinaman is too old, and he may not be able to support the old wife any more. Instead, he is now in a dependent position. In contrast to the Chinese mores, his children are reluctant to support him. Even his old wife does not want him any more. Thus the career of the man has moved in a circle and eventually ends somewhere not far from its starting point. The following case is an illustration:

I have been in this country sixty-two years already; I came at the age of twenty, and now I am eighty-two. At first I was in San Francisco for two months. Later I went to Portland when I met many of our cousins and Hoy Yin [Haiyen] neighbors. About three years later I went down to South California and then returned to San Francisco for a while. From that city I came eastward to Kansas City. I finally reached Chicago about forty years ago. The first time I stopped in Chicago some five or six weeks but found nothing to do. At that time I had two cousins who owned a laundry shop in K., a small town in southern Illinois. They wrote and asked me to go to their place. I then went there. Later I joined their laundry as a partner. I was, at that time, in charge of call-and-delivery work. There was no automobile; we used horse and wagon. Later in that very town I married that Flat-nosed Female. And here I am. If you count backward from now, it must be forty-odd years. This is all my life and the end of it is just as you can see.

One day in K., as I delivered a bundle of laundry to an old customer's house, I met my future wife visiting her aunt. The very next day the little cousin of hers named Mabel came to our laundry shop and said, "Charles, my cousin who talked to you yesterday liked you very much. She wants to see you again. Won't you come over sometime?"

"No fooling?" I responded.

"No. It is true!" answered Mabel. "I think she is crazy about you. That's what she said. She said you are a nice man."

I did go over to the house and spent the rest of the day with her. We soon became pals. I sometimes took her to eat ice cream or have a drink of beer. I had saved some five hundred dollars.

After I met her I spent quite a bit of money on her, but I had no intention of marrying her. I just fooled around with her. I wanted to go back to China. If I should get married in America, I would like to marry a Chinese Christian girl. I wrote to Mr. K. Y. Lee, a friend of mine in San Francisco, asking him to find me a Chinese Christian girl. Lee answered me later, advising me that I had better marry a slave-maid. He said he could get me one at any time but, in order to do that, he needed at least six hundred dollars to cover all the expense. I thought it over and was undecided. Finally I was forced to change my mind. This girl was really good and sweet to me. She asked me many times when could we get married. "Do you surely want to marry me?" I responded at last.

"Why, I do," she said.

"We are going to get married then," I proposed.

"If you want me," she suggested, "let us be engaged first. Get me a ring

with both of our names on, then it will be mutual." A few days afterward
I bought her the ring. It was what they call an engagement ring, you know.
Then about two weeks later we were married.

I have three sons and one daughter. The daughter, the youngest child of
the family, married an American fellow who later went to war and was
killed in Europe [First World War]. She had a child about six months old
which she left to my wife to care for. My daughter became a chorus girl.
She went with the troupe from place to place. At length she was in California
where she finally died after a long illness. Before she became a show girl,
both my female and I suggested that she look for a Chinese fellow and
remarry. Del-ka-ma! She never listened to you. We didn't hear from her for
almost four years. I guess she must be gone. She was a very pretty girl, you
know, otherwise she wouldn't be able to get into show business. But just
so things go, without a good ending.

Two of my sons are making a good living. Only my second son has been
unemployed for three years. The first and third ones have good jobs and
have married white girls. The first one is working in the post office, and
the third one is a radio operator in N.P. Of the three, the third one is the
smartest. He makes at least two hundred dollars a month at this time. He
is very healthy and has powerful arms.

As soon as they married white girls, that meant they were not my sons
anymore. I have never been invited to any of their houses. In fact, I tell you
the truth, I don't want to go. They would not expect me. My sons may be
all right, but their wives are different. They might complain if I went to see
them. As long as I have a place to stay in Chinatown, I shall get along. I
don't want to bother them. If my sons want to see me they can come here.
Only the Flat-nosed Female comes to see me often. After all, I think, she
has been a very good wife. She wouldn't stick with me if she had not been
all right. She is now over sixty. As I am now separated from her, she depends
upon my sons, particularly the first and third ones. Each of them probably
gives her twenty dollars each month. She probably has enough for food with
that.

That piece of land on which the little house was built is my property. I
bought the land about ten years ago. My wife, my second son, and the
grandchild are living there. That land cost me three thousand dollars.

I am sorry that I bought it now. If I hadn't spent the money on that, I
could have it saved in the bank, and now, if I wanted to go back to China,
I could make use of the money. But it is done; no hope any more.

It was three weeks ago when I met my first son and his wife and children.
My son called me "Pa," and the young woman followed suit. She shook
hands with me, too. Although she may not like me, yet she must act nice,
you know.

My old wife wrote me a few days ago, asking me to come home. She
said she is sick. I know she has been ill for some time. You know that

American women are too serious, even over a little unimportant illness. I do not have a penny now. How can I go? I need at least three or four dollars to buy my railroad ticket. I shall go to W. J. M. [a gambling house boss]; maybe he can give me a few dollars. I own a few shares of fan-tan in his house. He still owes me some money. When I worked under him I could get a few dollars from him any time. Ever since that house changed hands, I have had nothing to do with him. In fact, I haven't gone over to his place for a long time. I wonder if he can give me something this time. I heard that he is also broke. He lives with an actress [Chinese]; he spends thousands of dollars on her. . . .

I have also a few shares of fan-tan in the house right across the street, but I haven't received any profit from it recently. All the chop suey and laundries have no business; how can you expect to share profits from the gambling house?

S. P. owes me two hundred dollars, but what can I say now! I am now living in his store and eat here, that's all. Sometimes I don't feel right to ask him for money. Once I asked his wife for five dollars. She gave me only three; she did not have five. I took that anyhow and used it to buy myself a new pair of trousers.

I can't go back to live with the old female. It will be troublesome, for I have no money. The sons wouldn't support me. What they give to my old female would be just enough to buy food. They don't have to pay rent and the electric bill is small. Every winter they burn at least five or six tons of coal for heat. Before the real cold days, while the coal costs less, the old female bought enough for all winter. It will cost fifteen dollars a ton in the winter, but the same thing only costs twelve dollars at this time.

We built the house ourselves. Wah-yen [second son's Chinese name] bought all the materials and started to build it. Later it was impossible for him to do it alone, so he hired a man to assist him. It is a very nice little house. They painted the outside and made it fireproof within. While the house was being built, Wah-yen had some money. He paid about one thousand dollars to have the paving done. All the rest was my responsibility. At that time the first and third sons were already married.

I finished paying for the land only a few years ago. We finished it by borrowing some money from the post office. It was my first son who read the contract and found out that that was the last month in which we could clear our property. But the balance was still more than four hundred dollars. My son told me that if we couldn't pay off the balance the last month, the company would take over our property. "But what can I do at this time?" I asked him. "If you have it, you had better pay it. I have really done my best."

"I don't have money, either, Pa," said my son, "but we can borrow some money from the post office. Because I am an employee, we can make a loan from the post office, and the interest will be only one per cent. Suppose we borrow three hundred dollars and try our best to collect the rest. We must pay it or our property will not be ours." I agreed, and finally we raised enough to pay off the mortgage.

The company finally sent us the paper. It was first kept by the old female. Now, the first son was afraid that his mother might misplace it or lose [it], so he is keeping it.

I had better stay here in Chinatown where some people talk to me. I pass my time more easily here. If I go back to the farm, it will be too lonesome, you know. Besides, I have no money. It is not so good, as I have to depend on them. Here in Chinatown I might expect a few dollars from time to time. If the fan-tan house makes a profit, I would get a dividend from it. A few dollars is better than nothing.

Wah-yen was here the other day, telling me that he has no job yet. He just can't get one; that's all. My grandchild is growing up now. He will be graduated from public school next term. He will be fifteen this December. We hope my third son can get him a job as an office boy in the telephone company. But the most important thing is whether he is a smart boy or not. Like my third son, my grandchild may get his first job at the age of sixteen. I hope he can get a job.

It is nothing but hope, though. I hope to go back to China, too. If I had fifteen hundred dollars now, I would certainly like to go right now.

I am the second son of a family of four brothers. My father was a farmer. My oldest brother came to this country about six years earlier than I. After thirty-odd years of sojourn here, he returned to China a blind man of sixty, and died afterward in China. The other two brothers have never been in America. My third brother has a son whose name is called Jo-shun. I wonder what he is doing now. My youngest brother is still living, I guess. He has a son called Fook-yeih. A few years ago Fook-yeih was going to be married, my brother wrote to me, asking for financial help. I had no money on hand at that time. I asked Pui-sang to help me out. He replied that I could write a letter first and give it to him and he would take care of it; he would send a check to my brother on my behalf. I thought that what he promised was just fooling me. I didn't want to write unless he could give me the money I asked for.

So I could write to my brother, but what good was it without sending him any money? I was ashamed, but what could I do? Since then I haven't heard from my brother any more. Later I heard indirectly that Fook-yeih did get married. Ah! What can I say?

I had nothing to do in San Francisco. In Portland [Oregon] I learned to be a cook. I got a job afterward on a plantation about fifteen miles away. I was told later, after I quit the job, that the boss, a Frenchman, was one of the richest men in the country. I worked on the plantation as a cook for three years. I had no good reason for not staying right there. Ah! I was young and restless. As I look back on the bygone days, I was just a fool. If

I had stayed in that place long, I might have made a good fortune and returned to China long ago. I remember the boss was very kind to me. I ate as much as I could. But I was lonesome and I did not know enough English to speak to the people there. Finally I decided to quit. Was I not a fool?

Then I went back to Portland and became a loafer while staying in my cousin's place. My cousin urged me to go back to the plantation, but I did not feel like it. Then I received a letter from my brother. He was in Bakersfield and asked me to go there. I worked in his laundry. I was too young and restless, and I quarreled several times with my brother. I left his place and went to Los Angeles. I expected to find something to do there. But how could a stranger find anything without help from friend or relative? Well, I stayed in Los Angeles for a few weeks. One day I met a countryman from Kansas City. He told me that Cousin Feng-sing and Cousin Sai-kee were in Kansas City. I got their address and wrote to them. A few weeks passed and finally I received their reply; they urged me to go to their place. But, poor me, I didn't have enough money for my railroad ticket. I wrote to them again. When I received the money they sent me, I started for Kansas City.

My cousins in Kansas City treated me kindly. They paid me fair wages. And I was there for three years. During that time I went to Sunday School and desired to learn English. Neither Feng-sing nor Sai-kee were sympathetic to that. They thought I was too restless. In Sunday School, however, I was the best pupil in the class. Among the pupils, the principal, Mrs. Bell, liked me best. My teacher, Miss Miller, told Mrs. Bell that I should be promoted and sent back to China as a missionary worker. Rev. and Mrs. Bell told me if I were baptized, they would most certainly recommend me. They wanted me to make up my mind. I was quite pleased and excited, but I finally decided not to accept the offer. From that time, it seemed to me, they were cool toward me. Oh, if I had only accepted their invitation, I could have been an entirely different person. Instead of ending my life in despair, I should have had a pastorate in one of the churches in the city of Canton, like Foo-yun, a cousin of mine. I would enjoy my old age with respect and honor. Oh, but what a fool I was.

Because of my attending Sunday School and other matters, I did not get along too well with my cousins Feng-sing and Sai-kee. They teased me and mocked me. I decided to leave. The next stop was Chicago. At that time Chinatown was not here, but was located along South Clark Street. There were a few stores already there, and there were all sorts of gambling. I was expecting to meet some of our Hoy-Yin neighbors there.

At that time, in K., I had two cousins doing quite a prosperous laundry business. They probably heard that I could speak a little English, and they wrote and asked me to join them. Here, in this town, I met that Flat-nosed Female whom I later married. She is not bad, after all, otherwise she wouldn't stick with me all these years. But if I had married a Chinese woman instead, I would have a better life in my old age. I am so lonely. I have three sons but they are equal to none. I made a great mistake in buying that land. If, instead of using my money that way, I had saved my three thousand dollars in the bank, I could go back to China now [1938]. I was a fool. . . .

At last my business in K. was very slow. We could hardly make a living. Hence I thought of coming to Chicago to find something else to do. Before the whole family moved here, I came first and looked around to see if I could find any better job. Because I had learned how to print in K., I accepted a job that a countryman offered me to paint a sign for his shop. I decided to do a good job, for the first time, as an advertisement. I printed the letters in gold, and it certainly was an excellent job. But, alas! Imagine how much I was paid for it. That man gave me only seventy-five cents! Although there was no agreement as to how much he would pay for the work, I had never thought that my reward would be so small. I was disappointed. Meanwhile, someone advised me to find a place in Chicago and do laundry work again. I took this advice. Finally I found a place on Lake Street. I started to arrange an office in the front part and the residence in the rear. As soon as everything was fixed, I went back to K. to bring the family, my female, my oldest son, and myself—there were only three of us at that time.

My first laundry business was successful for about three or four years. Business began to go down at the beginning of the third year. My earnings were not enough to maintain our living. In order to support the family I searched for more sign-painting jobs. I did that only on weekends, of course; sometimes I had three or four signs to work on during one weekend, but most of the time I had nothing to do for four or five weeks at a time. Anyway, that was not the best way to solve my needs. I decided to move. Later I found a shop on D. Street. My family lived in the same neighborhood, about one and a half blocks away. I paid only fifteen dollars a month for the flat—cheap rent in those days. At first things ran along all right. My female came to the laundry shop and helped, too, when I was too busy. We had our suppers right in the shop. Business was all right in this place until the end of the fourth year. Then it dropped from one hundred and seventy-two dollars to only about eighty dollars a month. Again my difficulty came back. I began to realize that the laundry business was unfavorable. I was sick and tired of it.

What then should I do? I continued to do sign-painting jobs whenever I could find one. Besides this odd job I had a new way of making a living. That was selling fish. I went to the fish market and bought some thirty pounds of butter fish. Carrying my fish in a big basket, and riding the street car, I sold it to different Chinese shops all over the city. I paid the market a wholesale price of about fifteen cents a pound, but I sold it at retail in different Chinese restaurants and laundry shops for thirty-five cents a pound. Sometimes I had bass and trout. Fish at that time was not sold by the pound, but by the piece or head, for these kinds of fish. I could usually charge twenty-five cents a head, but my wholesale price from the market was about ten to fifteen cents. I did well in the fish business. Sometimes I made as much as five dollars a day.

Well, I had been selling fish for at least three years. Oh, you can imagine how toilsome it was to make a living that way. It was indeed not an easy job, but if you were poor, you had to do something to support the family.

Impatient with my fish-selling job, I went to Chinatown and tried my luck at gambling. At first I was not serious about it, but I was tempted. Every now and then you stand by the table and watch how people play and you want to take a chance, too. One just spends a few evenings in Chinatown and he learns the games. At first I bought lottery tickets. I had never won eight or nine spots, but I caught seven spots several times.

Anyway, for many years, I was partly a sign-painter, a fish-seller, and a gambler. I did not stop selling fish until my two older boys worked in a shoe factory. After they began to work, my responsibilities were not so heavy. I thought I could take life easier for myself, and so I turned professional gambler in the later years. Then I did not sell fish anymore. I became a shareholder in some of the gambling houses in Chinatown. At that time I was around S.W.C. mostly. Then this place was established; I have been around here ever since. Time flies so swiftly, that twenty-five years have gone by like a blink of the eyes.

At that period I owned ten shares of fan-tan in different houses. Once, near Chinese New Year's Eve, each gambling house distributed its dividends to its stockholders. In the time of prosperity, some people made a fortune from gambling house profits. One day I went in to see Big-headed Shun and he just handed over to me a new fifty-dollar bill. I was certainly delighted to see the handsome profit. I put the bill into my pocket and walked away happily.

During the war, gambling in Chinatown was prosperous. I remember I could make at least a couple of hundred dollars a month. At the same time my sons each earned about fifty dollars a week. One evening the older boy was reading the newspaper and he saw an advertisement about a piece of land for sale. "Hey, Pa," he said, "why don't we buy this piece of land? It is cheap. Let's find out about it. What do you say?" He made us all excited. Finally I agreed to be responsible for the down payment and the boys would help on the installments. And we bought the land. Later we built a house on it. It took a long time to pay for it, and the boys did not help me very much either. I was the only one who paid for it until the very last. I was making good at that time. If there had been hard times like there are today, the land would not be ours any longer.

The case may not reveal the whole situation of the interracial marriage

of the Chinese laundryman. It serves the purpose, however, as an example
that the inter-racial marriage did prevent the man from having a chance
to make his return trip to China. Three things in this case stand out
clearly: (1) it shows the marriage in itself is a marginal type in the conflict
of values and attitudes, at least from the standpoint of the laundryman;
(2) the man finally retires for his old age, not with his family, but in
Chinatown, and it is, perhaps, a result of the conflicts of values and
attitudes; (3) though he retires in Chinatown, his relations with his family,
at least with some of its members, is not completely broken off, yet his
status within his family circle has been lost and he experiences inner
conflict facing the situation with his cultural background. In China, the
old father with married sons would be the most respected and revered
person in the family circle. The sons, in order to be filial, provide the old
father with all means of comfort and enjoyment. The return to Chinatown
for old age is not merely for economic reasons; his race consciousness is
an important factor. He is still talking about a return trip to China.

I have seen a Caucasian wife of a Chinese laundryman remain to keep
his failing laundry shop going, with the children living in the rear part of
the shop, while he works somewhere else in a more prosperous place.
There are also cases of desertion and divorce among the Chinese laundryman's inter-racial marriages. There are also cases of Negro women
who either cohabit clandestinely with Chinese laundrymen or decide to
go through with a wedding by a justice of the peace.

3. Neighborhood Acquaintances

Who are the laundryman's neighbors? The church people and interested
women in the neighborhood, as previously described, may be considered
as individuals, among others, who have more or less personal contact with
the Chinese laundryman. In contrast to his customers, these people are
interested in the laundryman as a person, although some of the customers
may be friendly, too. Without claiming to be exhaustive, it is necessary
to extend further our description of the laundryman's social contacts with
other than the people of his own ethnic group.

The out-group contacts of the Chinese laundryman may be considered under three types of situation. In the Sunday School situation, he
meets Christian gentlemen and ladies who primarily want to convert him,

while the laundryman, on the other hand, wishes to take the opportunity to learn some English as a personal asset in business and social events. The Sunday School contact, however, may or may not be a neighborhood contact. It is voluntary, and in case the laundry shop is in the same neighborhood with the church, the laundryman may receive special attention. While helpful and friendly, this sort of contact tends to be maintained on the secondary level, with only a few exceptions.

Like his Sunday School attendance, the laundryman's contacts with the fair sex are often away from the neighborhood. His prostitution patronage positively may not be considered as a personal contact at all, but it may lead to personal relations; for instance, the prostitute eventually marries the laundryman. Under other circumstances, within the neighborhood in some poorer areas of the city, women of adventurous character sometimes exploit the laundryman's loneliness and offend him with her coquetry.

She lives in the next block and her brother and sister play around the backyard. We knew the children first. She often comes over to take the youngsters home. One day she came over, dressed up nicely. I asked her where she was going.

"Going to a show," she responded. "Do you want to take me?"

It was Saturday afternoon, see? Good, I had no reason to disappoint her. Then we decided to go downtown. She preferred to take a Yellow Cab. Well, all right, a Yellow Cab. I gave her a nickel and she went out to call a Yellow Cab.

I spent about four dollars that evening. She was very coquettish, but she kept herself away from me. In the cab I wanted to embrace her and kiss her, but I dared not, del-ka-ma!

She is a very pretty girl. Last Sunday she came over and said that her mother wanted to invite me for a picnic in Riverview Park.

I spent about ten dollars that day. Well, all they did was to prepare some sandwiches and some fruit. I was the one who paid for the tickets, both for entrance and amusements.

It was only up on the merry-go-round that I embraced her shoulder. She wanted to try everything. I didn't even have a chance to touch her. She made me mad—I had no satisfaction.

Then she came in to ask me to buy her a dress. I told her I had no more money.

"Oh, you are too mean!" she said.

She comes whenever she wants something. She wants me to iron her dresses and do her laundry.

She tries to make friends with my partner, flirting! And she asked him to take her to a show, too. She made me jealous. That girl is certainly making a fool out of me. She makes me spend all my earnings on her.

Personal interaction may cultivate a more intimate relationship, as shown previously in the case of mixed marriage, or it may be broken off due to the failure of establishing satisfaction to one or both persons involved.

But the out-group contacts of the Chinese laundryman in the neighborhood are rarely sexual. The laundryman, lacking family life, may have a tendency to make friends with neighborhood children. Some of the neighborhood children are kindly treated by the Chinese laundryman who gives them things to eat and small tips to a child who may like to run an errand. Boys are seen working for the laundryman as part-time helpers, and some of them share the laundryman's supper of typical Chinese food. From the children, the laundryman may get to know other members of the family or vice versa.

> When I was about fifteen years of age I made the acquaintance of a Jewish boy who was very much liked by a Chinaman who operated a prosperous laundry shop on the Far North Side of Chicago. This Chinaman, who was very influential among his own people, would take my Jewish friend to Chinatown almost every Sunday and allow him to sit in on various council meetings as well as participate in some of their play activities. I would anxiously await my friend's return home from Chinatown in the evening in order to listen to him tell me about his experiences. He promised me many times that he would ask his Chinese friend to take me along on one of their Sunday trips to Chinatown. I was overtaken by curiosity but at the same time I was afraid. Finally, my friend and I went to the Chinaman's shop and I was introduced to him. It happened to be lunch time so we were invited to join him in the rear part of the house. As one might expect, we had chicken and boiled rice. The rice was served in a wooden bowl and was to be eaten with chopsticks. My attempts to use the chopsticks were futile, and I was finally given a fork. After we finished eating, my friend asked the Chinaman to show me his apartment in the basement. The table was pushed aside and the carpet was removed, revealing a "trap-door" in the floor. We went down some stairs, and to my surprise I saw a most luxuriously furnished and intriguing apartment. There were rich rugs, carved chairs, curious tapestries, handmade incense burners and various other "knick-knacks" of a Chinese nature, including an opium pipe which he claimed he did not use and which claim I could not help but doubt. I had gone to this shop not only to meet the Chinese friend of my friend, but to make arrangements for the following Sunday to go to Chinatown with them. We

made the arrangements, but the "pipe" was always in my mind and I became skeptical about going. Frankly, I was afraid. That Sunday I excused myself by telling my friend that my mother had found out about my plans for that Sunday and that she refused to let me go with him.

Although the story is told by a third person, it reveals, nevertheless, the characteristic friendship between the Chinese laundryman and a neighborhood boy. The narrator of this story, as we can see, can hardly shake off his stereotyped conception of the Chinese laundryman as described in Chapter 2. The stereotype is a barrier to the boy's desired adventure in Chinatown; the opium pipe is a symbol of the stereotype. Americans in the neighborhood seldom have any personal interest in the laundryman beyond an impersonal exchange of greetings. Occasionally there are individuals, who, being more or less unattached to any neighborhood group, strangers in themselves, so to speak, tend to be more cosmopolitan and not too particular to accept the local Chinese laundryman as a "friend." It seems the most characteristic out-group, neighborhood contact of the laundryman is where he is taken into a neighbor's home to participate in leisure-time activities, sharing the sentiments and attitudes of the neighbor and his friends in social interaction.

I was in Jim's house playing cards last Saturday. I lost about ten dollars. That son o' gun came to get me. I was thinking of going to a show after supper. Before I left, I had to fix the washing basin. Then Jim came in and declared that they needed partners. I couldn't very well say no to him. So he took me over in his car. The game was on until two o'clock in the morning.

At the beginning, I wanted to stay only a couple of hours and they agreed. As a matter of fact, Jim was the one who moved that we stop early. Son o' gun, he was losing. Forget what he said. And we played on until I lost—and he lost, too. The fellow, Tom, won.

Del-ka-ma! I had to walk twenty blocks home in the rain and cold. There was no more bus service after one, see? They asked me to stay all night. Jim said it would be all right for me to sleep on one side of his wife, and he would sleep on the other side of the bed. But I didn't feel like it. I didn't know it was raining until I got down to the street, and what a long walk.

His wife sometimes stands behind me, touching my shoulder with her big breast. Oh, I feel its warmth pleasantly. And she sits right close to me with her arms around my neck, helping me out. They don't care, these Americans. A Chinese woman wouldn't be so coquettish.

Yes, I have known them many years. He is the fellow who operates a vegetable store around the corner. I am the only Chinese they are friendly with. I have been in his house almost every weekend and sometimes twice a week.

I have just returned from Jim's place. I lost one dollar. At first I met Charles in the street and he said he was going over to Jim's. So I got into his car and we were there in a few minutes.

You know, Jim's wife gave birth to a baby. She said I had been trying to avoid them. "Since I came back from the hospital, you never come. Jim was looking for you last Saturday, but he couldn't find you."

So I had to go over or she would be mad at me. Soon after we were in, Maria, Jim's sister, brought a chest out and passed it around. That was the way they were trying to raise money to buy the baby a carriage.

Well, Charles took out his pocketbook and put in one dollar. Seeing what Charles did, I took a dollar bill and put it in, also. And it was June's turn. June is a relative of the family. She reached for her purse and she put in fifty cents.

I, too, had some change in my pocket. I put one dollar in, to follow Charles. In case he put in a coin, I would have done the same. But I don't want them to think that we Chinese are stingy.

They have about fifteen dollars together. The chest was opened and they counted the money. Maria said she was going to buy it tomorrow.

Ah, how funny these Americans manage their business.

Jim asked me to go to their farm this weekend. They have a farm in a small town about thirty miles from here. I was there last year. I didn't have much fun, though.

I couldn't sleep the first night. The next morning I got up early and took the boat and rowed and rowed it across the lake. When they got up they couldn't find me. Finally, they found I was sleeping in the boat.

Del-ka-ma! He sure had a good time. He had a woman to sleep with, but I had to sleep alone. It was not just that, but I couldn't sleep. I just can't appreciate such a kind of vacation.

I think I am not going tomorrow. Del-ka-ma, not going—no fun. I better stay home. Perhaps I better go to a show instead. If I go, I will have to prepare some food. Last year I cooked three roasted chickens. Boy! They were certainly delicious. We ate them all up the first evening at the farm. All had a good meal. Jim and his wife and their two kids liked the chicken so well I'll have to cook the same again this time if I go.

It is interesting to note that many a Chinese laundryman claims the neighborhood policeman as his acquaintance and personal friend. As a stranger, perhaps, he is psychologically in fear of being robbed or being a victim of vandalism by local boys' gangs. The officer of the law, of course, is a needed friend. It is obvious that the laundryman may make a special effort to establish contacts with the local policeman, trying to make friends with him in one way or another. In the same psychological feeling of insecurity, and the desire to do business peacefully, the laundryman might try to tolerate the neighborhood gang. He may succeed in making friends with the gang leader, and so "Charlie, the laundryman, is O.K."

It is obvious that any out-group contact of the Chinese laundryman is more or less dependent upon whether he can speak English well enough so that others may understand him. This medium of communication many Chinese laundrymen lack, and that is why out-group contacts are apt to be the privilege of only a small percentage among them.

With the recent migration of more people of younger age, and the change in the political situation in China, attitudes and facilities to learn English have been improved. The young newcomers go to public schools to learn English in greater number, and the Sunday School attendance tends to decrease. There are also people taking private lessons. One of the reasons for this change of attitude is related to the desire to apply for American citizenship. The new immigration law requires applicants to demonstrate ability to read and write, as well as to speak, English.

NOTES

1. Church of the Brethren, Englewood Baptist Church, Larimer Baptist Church, North Shore Baptist Church, Second Presbyterian Church, Chinese Church (in Chinatown), and others whose names are unobtainable.

2. Rev. Elgin S. Moyer, "China at Our Door, a Brief History of Our Chinese Mission Work" (unpublished treatise).

3. Private interview and observation.

4. Interview by M. C. Kells, under the direction of Professor E. W. Burgess.

5. A term developed in America for women teachers in Sunday Schools for Chinese. No special term is used for men, for there are only a few. There is no such usage in China. Nor do they refer to women teachers in public schools as sen-seng-poo, which seems to be used only for Sunday School teachers.

6. Private collected document.

7. Nels Anderson, *The Hobo* (Chicago: University of Chicago Press, 1923), p. 138.

8. Private interview. The same person later was baptized and became a member of the church, as set forth in the next interview.

9. Private document.

CHAPTER XVIII

THE CHINESE LAUNDRYMAN AS A SOJOURNER

THE CHINESE LAUNDRYMAN, so to speak, is a sojourner, as the preceding chapters indicated. What then are the essential characteristics of the type, and by what peculiarities can the Chinese laundryman be explained as a deviant type on the basis of the particular situation he is in?

Theoretically, the premise of this study is essentially an attempt to isolate an element within the framework of systematic knowledge of problems in human migration in the so-called great society. It is an interest, particularly in the personal adjustment of the individual, rather than in the grosser effects of race and culture contacts in the changes in custom and in the mores; it is what the late Professor Park called the subjective aspect of human migration.[1] It is, therefore, a study of the attitudes of the sojourner; in other words, a study of the mind of the Chinese laundryman in the United States of America, as far as one may conceive that "mind is not so much the cause as it is the result of activities."[2]

The sojourner is comparable to the marginal man. They are both deviants. It seems the essential difference between the marginal man and the sojourner is the fact that the former tends to seek status in the society of the dominant group while the latter does not. In the case of the Chinese laundryman, this phenomenon is more obvious. To compare him with the foreign missionary in China, for example, the similarities and differences should be a matter of degree as far as the point of status is concerned. If one does seek for status, he is likely to be a case of the marginal man.

The concept of sojourner, like any other scientific concept, is adopted here as an instrument to enable a research worker to observe along a proper channel and "to catch and hold some content of experience and make common property of it."[3] The process of socialization, in the case of the sojourner, seems to be: contact, conflict, accommodation, and isolation. This study has taken the Chinese laundryman as a specimen, viewing him as one of the species in the variety, and trying to analyze his behavior as a type in the light of the process of socialization. Our focus of attention is how he is a sojourner, or what is his nature as a sojourner, and not why he is a sojourner. In fact, a full understanding of why he is a sojourner, or the cause of his sojourner's attitudes, cannot be scientifically verified unless we take up a fuller study of the "white man" in the situation; otherwise, what is said about the Chinese being unassimilated is exactly what Professor and Mrs. Hughes call a very lopsided view of racial contact in America when they say:

> Many books are written about the Negro problem in the United States; few, if any, about the white problem. In Canada, if one announces that he is about to study ethnic relations in Quebec, people assume that he means to study the French, not the English Canadians. Likewise, books and articles are written about the Japanese and Chinese in America, the Flemings in France and Belgium, and the Boers in South Africa. In all of these instances, although two or more groups are in contact, one is studied rather than the other, that one which people would ordinarily call, nowadays, the minority—the immigrant, the underdog, the self-conscious group. In current studies of anti-Semitic prejudice, it is not the Jewish minority, but the Goyim, the majority, who are studied. Emphasis is still on one, rather than both, of the groups in contact.
>
> Now there may be a certain practical logic in studying only one rather than both of a pair of peoples who live in contact with each other. The two groups generally do not know one another equally well. One may think that it is misunderstood; that it has grievances which the other group and the world outside should be made to hear. When ethnic attitudes are being studied, it is only natural that more attention should be given to the group whose opinions have more weight in the body social, economic, and politic. These practical considerations should not, however, be allowed to obscure the fact that the true unit of race and ethnic relations is not the single ethnic group, but the situation embracing all of the diverse groups who live in the community or region.[4]

Perhaps the Chinese laundryman behaves like a sojourner because this conduct represents a solution to a race problem, and his isolation may be considered as a form of accommodation. It seems clear in our study that the laundry as an occupation is related to the laundryman being isolated; the laundry is an instrumentality for isolation. The case of the Chinese laundryman seems to represent the nearest ideal type construction of the sojourner, because he exhibits the essential characteristics of the type. In summarizing the essential features of this study, the description of how the sojourner behaves may be tentatively interpreted as the following:

1. The Temporal Disposition of the Job

The Chinese laundryman does not organize himself to select the laundry work as his life-long career, and his sojourn in America is for one single purpose—to make a fortune or to make enough money to improve his economic well-being at home. In fact, he does not pick the laundry as his job; it is taken for granted because he is brought into a situation where he is expected to be one, like his relatives and friends. The newcomer may complain at first, but he would soon find out that the non-conformist gets nowhere. Then he makes adjustments to the situation and shares the common interest, the hope and dream of his relatives and friends—make a fortune by hard work and thrifty saving.

The "job" therefore is expected to be finished in the quickest possible time. Ideally, the job can be finished within a certain length of time, but in actuality, the ship of life is not all sailing in safe water as expected. Because of the situation under which new values confront the stranger, attitudes regarding the job may have to change. The newcomer then becomes an old-timer. He has developed habits of living like anybody else of his ethnic group; collectively, it is the mode of life of the group.

The "job" as a means of livelihood tends to be a product of Old World traits transplanted and urban circumstances in the country of the sojourn. It is a new social invention, to use Professor Ogburn's term. The Chinese became laundrymen at first to escape labor agitation against them; the technique is American, but the structure is Chinese.

2. Ethnocentricism and the In-Group Tendency

The sojourner clings to the cultural heritage of his own ethnic group; he is proud of it and thinks of it as the best, and therefore he tries to maintain it by all sorts of means. In order to do so he has to keep up his association with people of his own ethnic group, and therefore, an in-group tendency is created. Hence, ethnocentricism and an in-group tendency seem to be two aspects of the proposition, yet they are two aspects of the same thing, namely, isolation.

The forming of a racial colony, and the striving to keep the cultural heritage, tend naturally to achieve a psychological satisfaction or expression of "we" and "they" concepts. A mode of life is gradually developed out of such a psychological complex, together with the actual living apart from the general public. Only in the instance when it concerns the "job" may an out-group member be included as "we." But, of course, on such an occasion, the "we" may have a different meaning; it is very likely tied up with the "job." The sojourner seldom, if ever, organizes himself beyond the expectation of the job. And so we say he is non-assimilable. This aspect of the situation is clearly shown in this study; the Chinese laundryman is merely identified with the laundry in the symbiotic level in the community life; he is a person only with people of his own ethnic group. His occasional contacts with neighbors and customers are seldom personal. His social life is with Chinatown and his native land. In this social world he has roles to play and he is expected to play them. If he fails, he will be blamed. In the society of his sojourn, if there is any role that he plays at all, it must be related to his job, directly or indirectly.

The sojourner has never tried seriously to understand the society of his sojourn; he tends to look at it from the standpoint of his own cultural heritage. He is, therefore, biased in most instances. This does not stop the sojourner from an appreciation of some aspects of the native culture. In the case of the Chinese laundryman, he admires very much the American material environment; otherwise, he has very few ideas about America, for the reason that he is in extreme isolation. He does not read and write English, and may be able to make his customers understand him in English just intelligible enough to guess the meaning. As he cannot speak English well enough, it is hard to communicate with him. Without the proper means of communication, he is more isolated than sojourners in other situations.

3. The Trip and the Movement Back and Forth

Another interesting feature of the sojourner is his desire to go home, but when he gets home he finds it hard to stay and wants to go abroad again. This back and forth movement means that the man has gotten into an anomalous position between his homeland and the country of his sojourn.

In the beginning he ventured to take up residence in a foreign country with a definite aim. Soon he found that the job was taking a much longer time than he had expected. His original plan, as a matter of fact, has been complicated by new values and attitudes. As a means to an end, a new orientation has been adopted; he stays several years, and, when opportunity permits, he takes a trip home for a visit. The trip is an accomplishment, but the job can never be finished. Again he has to go abroad. In his lifetime several trips are made back and forth, and in some cases the career [job] is terminated only by retirement or death.[5]

In this study I described how the newcomer got into the Chinatown world, and his attitudes about the laundry at the beginning of his experience as a laundryman. Then he took laundry work as a job and became an old-timer. The social world in Chinatown is a home away from home, where old-timers seek personal satisfaction in warm, spontaneous, and intimate relations with fellow-Chinese. But the sojourner lives his mental life in China; his purpose is to make a fortune as soon as possible so that he can join his folks at home. While staying in this country, the Chinese laundryman plays a number of roles in China through letters and other means of communication. The ultimate goal, however, is his return trip home. Even if he cannot go home to stay for good, he should go back for a visit anyway. The return trip, at any rate, is like an urgently needed vacation that his fellow countrymen admire. Those who cannot take the return trip home are like Americans who never have had a vacation, feeling self-pity and without personal pride.

So the sojourner strives for the trip home. But as I have said previously, the ship of life may not sail in safe water, particularly in the case of the Chinese laundryman. He is a stranger in a strange land, where he finds himself excluded from the rights and opportunities of a normal social being—the underdog of the race problem in America. This situation has created some personal problems for the laundryman; the lack of emotional and social outlets seems to lead the man to personal disorganization, namely, gambling and prostitution. I have shown that gambling has been regarded as a means of achieving a trip home by winning at the gambling table or winning a lottery. But there are men who lose their chance to return home forever because of their gambling habit. Others could not go home because of immigration problems and sex maladjustments.

The ideal pattern of the sojourner's trips is at intervals of once every few years. This, some of the Chinese laundrymen do. Others take it once or twice in their lifetime. Still others have never taken a trip at all. Whether he takes a trip or not, the sojourner spends most of his lifetime in America.

Those who take fewer trips, or those who take no trip, may not necessarily lose their homeland ties and Chinatown association. They live in isolation just as much as those who take the trips. In their old age, if there is no chance for them to make the final trip for retirement, they retreat to Chinatown, where Americans are the foreigners. The mentality and the mode of life of the Chinese laundryman remain immutable in the characteristics just mentioned. To say this, of course, is not to insist that he has made no advancement in other aspects of life. He has made obvious adjustments in accommodation to his daily life as time goes on in his years of sojourn as a foreign resident. This change is gradual and unconscious—in clothing and other personal habits. But the job, the in-group tendency, and the meaning of his return trip home seem to be something immutable.

We are content, therefore, that these are the essential characteristics of the sojourner. Under different situations, the variation of the type may be found along the channel of these characteristics. Tentatively, these are some things we may employ for further research.

> The sojourner, to be sure, is characteristically not a marginal man; he is different from the marginal man in many aspects. The essential characteristic of the sojourner is that he clings to the culture of his own ethnic group as in contrast to the bicultural complex of the marginal man. Psychologically he is unwilling to organize himself as a permanent resident in the country of his sojourn. When he does, he becomes a marginal man.
>
> Both the marginal man and the sojourner are types of strangers—in Simmel's sense, products of the cultural frontier. No doubt, in many instances, the sojourner has something in common with the marginal man. It is convenient, therefore, to define the "sojourner" as a stranger who spends many years of his lifetime in a foreign country without being assimilated by it. The sojourner is par excellence an ethnocentrist. This is the case of a large number of immigrants in America and also of Americans who live abroad. The Chinese laundryman, for example, is a typical sojourner, and so is the American missionary in China. The concept may be applied to a whole range of foreign residents in any country to the extent that they maintain sojourner attitudes. The colonist, the foreign trader, the diplomat, the foreign student, the international journalist, the foreign missionary, the research anthropologist abroad, and all sorts of migrant groups in different areas of the globe, in various degree, may be considered sojourners in the sociological sense.[6]

There could be other types found through further systematic classification. Connected with this problem, a study of the second-generation Chinese in America with this conceptual scheme would be helpful in getting increased knowledge of the type. It is a proposition of a comparative study of the marginal man and the sojourner. The two groups are to be studied as two extreme poles, and eventually we will have types of adjustments by classifying and reclassifying individual groups of cases according to the conceptual scheme. Further studies have to be done on different ethnic groups in a given country, and one ethnic group in different countries. What are the characteristic adjustments of the Chinese and Japanese in Brazil and other South American countries? The mode of life of the Chinese in Canada is similar to America, but it is different in Cuba and Mexico.

Essentially the situations that create types in the area of race and culture contact should provide some clue of similarities. "Whether it be the treatment of the Czechs in the Austrian Empire of the Hapsburgs, of Fiume in the Italian Irredenta, or the British in India, or the whites in the cities of China, or the Chinese in San Francisco," says Dr. Wirth, "fundamentally the problem is the same, because the human nature aspects of the situations are akin to those of the ghetto."[7] It seems that the Jews in the ghetto as well as the Chinese in Chinatown are sojourners. The interesting contrast in these two ethnic groups, as we can see, is that the ghetto is the colony and also the "homeland"; the Jew takes no trips in the sense that the Chinese laundryman does, except that some of the Zionists cling to the belief that the State of Israel is their homeland. Perhaps the ghetto inhabitants are more of the borderline cases between the sojourner and the marginal man.

Foreign residents, in most of the cases, have no intention of acquiring the memories, sentiments, and attitudes of other persons or groups and tend to cling to the cultural heritage of their own. An interesting comparison should be made between the Chinese immigrants in this country and the American abroad. The missionary to China, for instance, is characteristically a sojourner like the Chinese laundryman. "Comparable with the case of the laundryman (Mr. C.) is that of an American couple who went to China soon after their marriage, took furloughs every few years, lived in a segregated compound among fellow-missionaries, sent their children back to America for education, and then, finally, came back themselves for retirement after fifty years."[8] The difference between these two obviously is in the situation and the function of the job performed. The degree of influence of the functional roles of the job in the social order of the respective countries of sojourn seems to be in two extremes. The work of the mission has virtually upset every institution of the folk society, while the laundryman serves only in the purely symbiotic level of the urban community in the struggle for survival.

NOTES

1. Robert E. Park, "Human Migration and the Marginal Man," *American Journal of Sociology,* XXXIII (May, 1928), 881–93.

2. Louis Wirth, *The Ghetto* (Chicago: University of Chicago Press, 1928), p. 75.

3. Herbert Blumer, "Science without Concepts," *American Journal of Sociology,* XXXVI (January, 1931), 520.

4. Everett C. Hughes and Helen M. Hughes, *Where Peoples Meet* (Glencoe, Ill.: The Free Press, 1952), pp. 18–19.

5. Paul C. P. Siu, "The Sojourner," *American Journal of Sociology,* LIII (July, 1952), 39.

6. *Ibid.,* p. 34.

7. Wirth, *op. cit.,* p. 282.

8. Siu, *op. cit.,* p. 41.

INDEX

(Names without family names are not included.)

Chinatown barber, preference for, 106
Chinatown: compared to Jewish ghetto, 137; Sunday social activities in, 144–45
Chinese-American, *see* Chinese in America or Chinese women in America
Chinese Consolidated Benevolent Association (C.C.B.A.), 38, 86, 87, 247
Chinese dating notation, symbolic use of, 88
Chinese doctor, preference for, 106
Chinese Exclusion Act (1882), 209–10n2: repeal of, 194, 202–9; denied right to naturalization, 194–95; and "paper" slots, 195–200; and blockade running, 200–202
Chinese grocery business in South, 120
Chinese immigrants: compared to Chinese students, 2; rural origins, 3; factors for leaving China, 3
Chinese in America: miners, 47–48; farmers, 48–49; railroad workers, 48, 52–53; fishermen, 49, 53
Chinese in Hawaii, compared to Chinese in U.S. (mainland), 3–4
Chinese labor, recruitment of, 44
Chinese laundryman, outside views of: forgotten by community, 13; distinct from other local businessmen, 14; as a public utility, 15; acceptable if he stays in his place, 20–22; a non-stereotypic view, 17. *See also* laundryman and laundrymen
Chinese person, immigration definition of, 210n5
Chinese racial quota (1943), 210n7
Chinese sons: immigration of, 195–97; citizen, status of, 196; paper slots for, 196, 197–200; different perspective of, 209
Chinese students in America, 2; compared to Chinese immigrants, 2–3
Chinese women: illiteracy of, 156; need to rely on letter writer, 156; stilted nature of letters, 156; viewed by returning husbands as less attractive, 180; American laws prohibiting immigration of, 194–97; types of currently in America, 195; and War Brides Act, 203, 206–8
Chinese women, stories of: Le Shee, 157–64; dependent role of, 164; male right to

disown, 164; Chung Fong-shiu, 164–65; social control of, 165; Teh-oi, 165–67; Chan Shee, 168
Chinese women in America: first in California, 44–45; attitude toward, 123, 143–44; types of, 195; post-WWII immigration of, 206–8; from village background, 207–8; from city background, 207–8
Ching Ming Festival, 186
Cho-quon, 200
Chop suey house, 120, 128
Chop suey worker, 147, 270
Chot-chow, 142
Chow Yee-fen, 147
Christmas, *see* Winter Festival
Chu Ke-chung, 186
Chung Chang-wo, father of Fong-shiu, 164–65
Chung Fong-shiu, divorced by Leong Sing-wing, 164–65
Chung Lim, 238
Chungking, 225
Chungshan District, 84
Chuo-sai-kai, 181
Citizenship, *see* Naturalization
Clothing store myth, 113, 179
Concentric zone theory, 34, 37–39
Conceptual framework, 1, 7; personality types, 1; assimilation, 2; natural history, 3; stranger, 3; symbiosis without communication, 3; marginal man, 4; deviant type, 7, 272; ideal type, 7, 296; urban ecology, 23; concentric zone theory, 34, 37–39; cultural frontier, 122; disorganized personality, 127, 238, 239; social disorganization, 219; personal disorganization, 250, 271; contact, 295; accommodation, 295; isolation, 295; conflict, 296. *See also* sojourner
Conflicting cultural values: filial piety v. individualism, 223; familism v. urbanism, 223; proper behavior of women, 223
Conflicts, *see* personal conflicts or work-related conflicts or cultural conflicts
Crocker, Charles, 48
Cultural conflicts, stories of: elderly customer, 222–23; American women's coquettishness, 223; sympathetic customer,